BATTLE CRY
COMPENDIUM

...a compilation of bulletin for prayer warriors and intercessor

Dr. D. K. Olukoya

...the Key to waking up your
prayer fire

BATTLE CRY COMPEDIUM
Vol: 6, No. 1-52
Dr. D.K. Olukoya

© 2013

The Battle Cry Ministries

322, Herbert Macaulay Way, Yaba P.O. Box 12272, Ikeja, Lagos
Website: www.battlecrystore.com
E-mail:
info@battlecrystore.com
customercare@battlecrystore.com
sales@battlecrystore.com
Phone: 2348033044239, 01-8044415

I salute my wonderful wife, Pastor Shade, for her invaluable support in the ministry.

I appreciate her unquantifiable support in the book ministry as the cover designer, art editor and art adviser.

All Scripture quotation is from the King James Version of the Bible.

All rights reserved.

We prohibit reproduction in whole or part without written permission.

Table Of Contents

Vol. 6.

Quenching The Strife Of Tongues	7
Catching The Horn Of The Altar	11
The Serpent In The Family Line	15
The Raging Altars Of Your Father's House	21
Dealing With Poverty Magnets	25
Release From Evil Covenants	31
When The Enemy Is Too Strong	36
When Your Battle Is From Home	40
Holy Rebellion	47
The Wind Of The Holy Spirit	53
The Eternal Destiny	58
The Fresh Fire	66
Paralysing Progress Arresters (1)	72
Paralysing Progress Arresters (2)	78
The Way Of Wholeness	85
The Tongue Of Power	91
The Evil Manipulators	96
The Destroyers Of Potentials (1)	102
The Destroyers Of Potentials (2)	108
Bad Link, Label And Mark	114
When The Winds Go Contrary	120
Deep Secrets, Deep Deliverance	125
10 Truths The Devil Does Not Want You To Know (1)	130
10 Truths The Devil Does Not Want You To Know (2)	136
The Mighty Hand Of God (1)	143
The Mighty Hand Of God (2)	149
The Battle Against Wasting Serpents	154
Problem That Are Not From The Enemy	159
The Final Separation (1)	166
The Final Separation (2)	171
The Goat & The Sheep	177
The Power Of The Sheep	182
The Dead Garden	188
The Old Pathway (1)	194
The Old Pathway (2)	200
Spiritual Patching	206
The School Of Stagnancy	214
Student In The School Of Confusion (1)	221
Student In The School Of Confusion (2)	227
The Last Warning	233
Your Time Of Visitation	240
Provoking The Finger Of God	244
Lessons From The School Of Tribulation (1)	249
Lessons From The School Of Tribulation (2)	252
The God Of Daniel	256
Personal Pentecost	261
The Mystery Of Terror	266
The Negative Dedication	271
The Negative Anointing	276
The Evil Conversion (1)	283
The Evil Conversion (2)	288
Fighting Using The Blood Of Jesus	293
Books By Dr. D. K. Olukoya	300

Foreword

This compendium is a compilation of messages that have changed the lives of many for good. Situations that seem hopeless to science and man were converted to testimonies.

The power of prayer is least exercised by believers. The art of warfare prayer is very important in the life of every believer.

"O thou that hearest prayer unto thee shall all flesh come" Ps 65:2

If you have not had a personal encounter with God, you may not appreciate some of the miracles and changes which have resulted in this compilation.

As you read these messages, I pray that God will meet you at the point of your need in the name of Jesus.

Stay blessed.

Dr. D. K. Olukoya

Quenching The Strife Of Tongues

Vol. 6. No. 1

Psalm 31:20: *"Thou shalt hide them in the secret of thy presence from the pride of man: thou shalt keep them secretly in a pavilion from the strife of tongues."*

There is a dangerous thing that has caused more destruction in this world, than any other one. It has no lock and life would have been a lot better for many people, if they did not possess that door. The Almighty pre-designed the human head to have four openings and made three of them come in pairs, but restricted the last to just one. The first pair of opening is the ears, then the nostrils, the eyes and the last one, the mouth. This last opening has caused more problems for human beings than the others put together. The Bible talks about the strife of tongues. Let us examine a few examples.

1 Kings 18:17-18; *"And it came to pass, when Ahab saw Elijah, that Ahab said unto him, Art thou he that troubleth Israel? And he answered, I have not troubled Israel; but thou, and thy father's house, in that ye have forsaken the commandments of the Lord, and thou hast followed Baalim."*

Note that the reply of Elijah was sharp and direct; it was fire for fire. He took the statement serious although the fellow talking to him was a king. He refused to accept what the King was trying to put on him.

1 Samuel 17:42-47; *"And when the Philistine looked about, and saw David, he disdained him: for he was but a youth, and ruddy, and of a fair countenance. And the Philistine said unto David, Am I a dog, that thou comest to me with staves? And the Philistine said to David, Come to me, and I will give thy flesh unto the fowls of the air, and to the beasts of the field. Then said David to the Philistine, Thou comest to me with a sword, and with a spear, and with a shield: but I come to thee in the name of the Lord of hosts, the God of the armies of Israel, whom thou hast defied. This day will the Lord deliver thee into mine hand; and I will smite thee, and take thine head from thee; and I will give the carcases of the host of the Philistines this day unto the fowls of the air, and to the wild beasts of the earth; that all the earth may know that there is a God in Israel. And all this assembly shall know that the Lord saveth not with sword and spear: for the battle is the Lord's, and he will give you into our hands."*

David replied the strife of tongues that were fighting against him. The Bible says: *"Death and life are in the power of the tongue."* Words are very powerful and many people have failed to recognise this fact and put it to use.

Words are backed up by beings or spirit personalities.

The words we utter do not come out in isolation they carry power.

Words are more than mere arrangements of letters or alphabets. They are like containers and may be filled with destruction - cursing or blessing. Even your own personal words can determine your destiny. When the devil came to tempt Eve, he did not simply shake his hands and feet. He simply spoke words; he projected his lying nature into the words and this made Adam and Eve to fall.

The enemies of our souls have learnt the secret of words; they chant incantations, curse people and use terrible weapons against people. Balaam came against the children of Israel; he was hired to use words of curses against the children of Israel.

God took this assignment seriously because He knew that if Balaam succeeded in issuing the curses, many terrible things would happen to Israel. I pray that any power that has been hired to curse you shall fall after the order of Balaam, in the name of Jesus.

Goliath cursed David by his gods. If such curses are being fired against you, you must be

able to speak words that will neutralised them. Also, you must not side the devil against God by speaking the devil's words.

If you are a serious prayer warrior, you should not speak words of discouragement, or fear, or doubt, condemnation, lies, confusion, disorder, disobedience or of bad health. If you do, you are supporting those who are already issuing curses on you.

You can overcome the wicked situation of evil words by speaking the words of life against their evil words. When a person is speaking the words of death, you will speak the words of life to overcome him. You will speak the words of deliverance to overcome demons; the words of healing to overcome sickness; the words of love to overcome hatred; the words of prosperity to overcome poverty. When you speak words that can cancel the strife of tongues, you will make progress.

The devil came to Jesus and told Him to bow down to him; to convert stones to bread; to jump down. Jesus had a response to all the things that the devil said. This is the strife of tongues.

The most serious war that can ever take place amongst men is the war of words. Even if they bomb each other, the starting point is the strife of tongues. The Bible says in the book of James 3:2-8; *"For in many things we offend all. If any man offend not in word, the same is a perfect man, and able also to bridle the whole body. Behold, we put bits in the horses' mouths, that they may obey us; and we turn about their whole body. Behold also the ships, which though they be so great, and are driven of fierce winds, yet are they turned about with a very small helm, whithersoever the governor listeth. Even so the tongue is a little member, and boasteth great things. Behold, how great a matter a little fire kindleth! And the tongue is afire, a world of iniquity: so is the tongue among our members, that if defileth the whole body, and setteth on fire the course of nature; and it is set on fire of hell. For every kind of beasts, and of birds, and of serpents, and of things in the sea, is tamed, and hath been tamed of mankind: But the tongue can no man tame; it is an unruly evil, full of deadly poison."*

Strife of Tongues In A Local Life:

1. **Curses issued by people or satanic agents.**

Unfortunately, this is rampant in our environment and people have turned curses into a play thing. Satan and his agents are always ready to curse people and one thing about a curse is that, it travels to the roots. When there is a quarrel between two people and they start to exchange words, one of them might have a satanic anointing which will cause a lot of havoc in the life of the other person. You must get ready to revoke any witchcraft curse working against your life.

2. **Angry Exchange of Words In Arguments.**

Some people are dangerous and the words they utter in hot arguments could act negatively in the spirit realm. It is better to avoid arguments of any kind. If you want to be filled with the Holy Ghost, you must avoid arguments.

3. **Incantations.**

A series of words used as a magical spell or charm. Satanists use this to subvert people's destinies. They are words used as evil diversions to control the mind and actions of a person in a negative way.

4. **Evil Reports.**

When a person tells other people about what the other person has done, it could engender all sorts of negative things in the heart of the listener. If the listeners happen to be occultic or wicked, something bad could come out as a result of the report; they will put it in their case file and act upon it. Such reports are made before herbalists, evil prophets, etc.

5. **Careless Abuses.**

Some people joke with abuses that can carry weight in the spirit realm.

Whether jokingly or seriously, negative words should be rejected instantly in the name of Jesus, so that they will not make an impact on your life. In the Yoruba dialect, some would say they are playing and utter terrible abusive curses like: ori e o da- (your head is not correct); were ni e- (you are mad); oloshi ni e- (you are wretched) and so on, reject such words immediately.

6. **Demonic chants by demonic people.**

7. **Swearing.**

8. **Evil prophesies etc.**

WHAT TO DO

1. Reject every strife of tongues.

2. Reverse them and pronounce the positive on yourself.

3. Return it to the sender

The strife of tongues has been used in creating problems in the lives of many people. It is so terrible that, God Himself has to do special things to protect them. Words that people speak to confuse other people's lives, are words incubated by satanic anointing and many people are labouring under the effect of such curses and incantations now. Most of those who issued these curses are unknown to the people suffering under their effect.

There was a sister whose uncle is a herbalist. One day, the uncle came with a wrapper and asked her whose it was. She recognised it as being a wrapper she had washed one day and put out to dry but could not find again. She had looked for it and assumed that it had been stolen. The uncle told her that someone brought the wrapper to the village to him for medicine against the sister. The person gave him her name and he knew she was the one, so he came to tell her. If the sister was not a Christian and if she was not the man's niece, the enemy would have triumphed over her.

I pray that any power, holding demonic night vigil against you shall be destroyed, in the name of Jesus. Beloved, I would like you to pray the following prayer points with the whole of your being, especially if you know that you have stubborn agitators who have made themselves your full time enemies and are issuing curses against you everyday.

However, if you are reading this bulletin and have not yet surrendered your life to Christ, you may not be able to return any arrow or darkness. I want you to examine your life and realise that you are a sinner. Acknowledge the fact that you cannot approach God in your present state. Confess your sins to Him, name them one by one and ask Him to forgive you. Claim the sacrifice that the Lord Jesus made for you on the Cross at Calvary. Appropriate it for the redemption of your soul; tell Him that you will never go back to the world or sin any more. Say bye-bye to the devil and the world.

I congratulate you on this decision you have just taken. My prayer for you is that the Lord will uphold you with His right hand of righteousness. He will keep you by His power and glory and will make His light to shine upon you. You will not depart from His path and every obstacle on your way shall be removed, in the name of Jesus.

Take these prayer points aggressively:

1. Every strife of tongues against my marriage, perish by fire! in the name of Jesus.

2. Every strife of tongues against my career, perish by fire, in the name of Jesus.

3. Every strife of tongues against my children, perish by fire! in the name of Jesus.

4. Every strife of tongues against my finances, perish by fire! in the name of Jesus.

5. You arrow of witchcraft curses, I reject you. I renounce, reverse you and send you back to the sender, in the name of Jesus.

Pray the following also aggressively:

1. Every arrow of hidden sickness, go back to your sender in the name of Jesus.

2. Every arrow of poverty, go back to your sender! in the name of Jesus.

3. Every arrow of dream pollution, go back to your sender! in the name of Jesus.

4. Every arrow of marriage destruction, go back to your sender! in the name of Jesus.

5. Every arrow of failure, go back to your sender! in the name of Jesus.

6. Every arrow of backwardness, go back to your sender! in the name of Jesus.

7. Every arrow of

affliction, go back to your sender! in the name of Jesus.

8. Every evil word spoken against my destiny, die! in the name of Jesus.

9. Every power that has refused to let me go, die the death of Goliath! in the name of Jesus.

10. Every arrow from the dark world, fired into my destiny, come out now! in the name of Jesus.

11. Every stubborn witchcraft, that has become my full time enemy, die the death of sorrow! in the name of Jesus.

12. Every satanic agent hired to curse my destiny die the death of Balaam, in the name of Jesus.

13. As the Lord lives, my testimony shall manifest, in the name of Jesus.

14. God arise! and let my stubborn enemies scatter, in the name of Jesus.

15. Let my miracles manifest and let my failures disappear! in Jesus name.

Catching The Horn Of The Altar.

In 1kings 1:49; *And all the guest that were with Adonijah were afraid and rose up and went every men on their ways. And Adonijah feared because of Solomon and arose and went and caught hold on the horn of the altar. And it was told to Solomon saying behold Adonijah feareth king Solomon for lo he hath caught hold on the horns of the altar saying let king Solomon swear unto me today that he will not slay his servant with the sword. And Solomon said if he will shew himself a worthy man, there shall not an hair of him fall to the earth but if wickedness shall be found in him, he shall die. So King Solomon sent and they brought him from the altar and he came and bowed himself to King Solomon, and Solomon said unto him, go to thine house.*

Situation that looks desperate, that look hopeless they are the fact of life and all the ages right from the beginning of the world the needs of men down to ages had always been the same there are countless examples of those who had been driven to despair, driven to hopelessness and their thought of giving up and such people think they have reached the point of no return situation, had become actively hopeless. The bible describe that kind of situation in Psalm 107:26, *they mount up to the heaven, they go down again to the depths their soul is melted because of trouble they reel to and fro and stagger like a drunken man and are at their wit end, then they cry unto the Lord in their trouble and he bringeth them out of their distress, he maketh the storm calm so that the waves thereof are still.*

When men throw up their hands and say this is a hopeless case, this is the end of it all, and it seems as if all ways are blocked. It is at that level God begins to warm up the trouble with many of us, we are becoming over familiar with God, over familiar with prayer, over familiar with sermons, over familiar with singing and so many come to meetings not expecting too much to happen than the usual that has been happening. They just come to prayer meeting like those people who were praying that Peter should be released from the prison. Here, we have men gathered for a night vigil, who didn't sleep at home and they gather together to pray. Here we have men and women gathered together who are praying but they are not expecting very much to happen. They raise up their voices in hot prayer, O God arise and release Peter and Peter came and was knocking at the door. The first person went and Peter said it is me open the door. The person said, no, you can't be Peter. How can you be released. They continued their prayer, "Oh God arise and release Peter". Somebody said, Peter is still at the door. Then they said, no it can't be him. It is his spirit and they didn't open the door, for the spirit to come in too. Some were praying and were expecting Peter to have died. They were expecting his ghost to show up. Somebody still came to say it is Peter at the vigil. They turned to the man who said it is Peter. Eventually, the door was opened and Peter came in. So it is possible to come to a meeting like that and you don't expect very much to happen. Unfortunately we don't know that God in his own mathematics is God of emergency, a God of suddenly, a God that would just appear when you least expect him to appear. Sometimes hopeless situation can be an incurable disease, it can be a failed marriage, it can be a failed examination, it can be failure to achieve ones ambition and aspiration. God is still in the business of doing the impossible. I remember one case which we had to pray about many years ago. This person was already dead. They put the person on life support machine. The machine was aiding his breathing. After sometime, the machine was switched off. They said there was no hope for him. But somebody cried unto the Lord. The Lord said, next week, your son shall be healed. As they were about to take him away to the mortuary, the nurse said, I can feel his body warm. The doctor then said okay, leave him there. All of a sudden they heard someone asking loudly for water. They rushed there and found that the person they presumed dead has opened his eyes asking for water. In many problems, men think that it is beyond solution. They are now pushed to men and women to look for destructive assistance. It is later that they discover that it is a minor thing in the hands of the Almighty. I know some people who have so much problem and they have committed suicide. I have seen people who have so much problem they began to punch themselves with drugs, I have seen people with so much problems that they ran into medical home and became insane, I have seen people who have problems and they went to diviners and star gazers, all this are destructive, they would only cause more problems for you.

I remember a brother we prayed with in 1994 he wanted to travel abroad by all means to go and study. Anytime he goes to the embassy, they refuse him a visa and say he should not go, then somebody told him that there is somebody somewhere who can help him and they took him to the man's place and when he got there they asked him what is your problem? he said I want to travel abroad and do my Phd. He had already had his masters, the man now said you need to swallow this things I brought, the brother didn't mind swallowing anything but the problem was that what they asked him to swallow was twenty one needles. He now said excuse me sir these are needles. The man said I know. He said but if I swallow it, it would perforate the intestine. The man said I know. While he was busy asking the man questions there was a lady behind him. The girl said Mr. man if you are not ready get out of the way. The girl had already brought 'Eba' she was putting the needle inside to swallow. When this brother saw a lady swallowing the needle with 'eba' he swallowed his own too, he got a ticket and passport he had no visa he wanted to travel. The man told him that when you get to the airport nobody will see you, you are invisible. By the time he got to the immigration officer, he was walking fast and they now called him and said you come here where do you think you are going? He now turned to the immigration officer and said you mean you can see me? That immigration officer now got angry. Are you saying that am blind? They dealt with him that day five years after he had swallowed the pins, problem started. The pin was now working on his intestine it was at mountain of fire that he vomited those swallowed pins he swallowed five years back. But if he didn't have a place where he could vomit them or after swallowing the pins he sat in the wrong place where they cannot help him, he would die and the same people would bury him. That is what happens when you use destructive assistance. Perhaps as a child of God, you are going through a very tough time, you are now feeling the heat, you even think that God didn't even care for you again. Am here to disclose to you that you shouldn't despair because God specializes in impossibilities. He is the great provider, he brings the honey out of the rock and bring out oil out of a filthy place. He will make a way where men say there is no way, he is the last minutes provider. I want you to understand this in your spirit. One of the most outstanding miracles in some of our branches abroad, was a white woman who brought in her husband, a white man, in one of our crusade and the woman said man of God I brought my husband here. You see man of God, his great great grandfather committed suicide, his great grandfather committed suicide, his father committed suicide. I don't see how he will not commit suicide because he has been trying to kill himself with knives and forks. I have been keeping them away in the house. I looked at the man I said do you want to die? He said certainly, but why did you bring him here? The lady said maybe you will do something to him. There were so many people for us to see that day so I said the man should sit there. I gave him some prayers to be praying he said he didn't know how to pray them that he is a catholic. I said no problem I will teach you, so we started praying. All of a sudden about ten minutes he stopped praying. I didn't hear anything from his side again. He kept quiet for a long time by the time I went there I asked any problem? Because I found out his face has changed he said sir as I was praying I saw Jesus and he stood by my side and he opened my head and put his hand inside the head and brought out a rope people normally use to hang themselves out of my head and close the head back. He said immediately from that moment he does not feel like dying again. Raise up your right hand and prophesy life unto every dead blessing in the name of Jesus.

I want you to look into the life of somebody called Daniel in the bible. God had the power to prevent Daniel from being thrown into the lion's den, God was not asleep when they were conspiring against him, God was not asleep when they cast him inside but they had forgotten that God created the lion, the men have forgotten that when you throw a child of the Lion of Judah they have forgotten that lion does not eat lion, they have forgotten that God has the supreme power. When Daniel got to the lions' den what did he do? The Bible said he prayed. So there are some prayers that can now withhold the mouth of the lion. When Daniel prayed in the lion's den, did God come late? Never, God never comes late, He may not come when you personally want Him but He comes at the right time. A certain fact about Daniel was not clear to the enemy, they didn't know the person they were throwing in. God permitted the enemy to try so that they can know that God is great. The Bible says *many are the afflictions of the righteous but the Lord delivers him from it all.* The affliction may be many but He will deliver you, you may pass through the fire, the rivers and the waters. So it is very dangerous to give up when your miracle is around the corner. The Bible says, the hairs of our head are numbered, if God says He knows the number of hair on my head, how about my life? Remember the widow of Zarephath she was at the end of the road completely helpless until Elijah came along. I decree by the decree of heaven that as from today the people who had been looking on you shall look up to you in the name of Jesus.

WHAT IS YOUR WEAPON DURING THE TIME OF HELPLESSNESS?

1. **Stubborn praying:** catching the horns of the altar and not letting the horn go until you hear the good news. That was what Hannah did, she calls the horn of the altar and say you are not going anywhere until Eli said okay woman go in peace. The example is Luke 11:5 *and he said unto them which of you shall have a friend and shall go unto him at midnight and say unto him friend lend me three loaves for a friend of mine in his journey is come to me and I have nothing to set before him and he from within shall answer and say trouble me not the door is now shut and my children are with me in bed I cannot rise and give thee, I say unto you though he will not rise and give him because of his importunity he will rise give him many as needeth.* Here we have two stubborn men one man is trying to get bread, the other determine not to give it but persistence won the battle. Persistence involves shameless praying, perhaps you are here you have the symptoms of defeat, depressed mood, sadness feeling of hopelessness and worthlessness, inadequacy, dwelling in the past, perplexity, lack of confidence, inability to concentrate, anger and anxiety, these are symptoms of defeat. You wake up in the morning you feel reluctant to get up, not able to sleep, sad meditation, suicidal thinking, rejected and discouraged appearances, frequent desire to cry, withdrawal from people, lost of self confidence, lost of initiative, inability to accept mistakes. You need a holy stubborn praying for something to happen. Jacob was a man down below the ladder but one day something happened he started his prayer meeting at 10p.m and he continued till 5a.m very interesting competition, a man was wrestling with an angel and he said unless you bless

me, am not going. I want you to say this with holy anger, my father I receive strength for the battle, deliver me from my strong enemy. I retrieve my times from the hands of the enemy, my father my times are in your hands, deliver me from the hands of my strong enemy. My father deliver me from the hand of my strong enemy. My father rescue my destiny from the hands of the wicked. My father let every gadgets of darkness that is monitoring my life be roasted completely. My father remove my name from any demonic calendar. My father, I destroy the program of the enemy for my life. My father I pray while I am yet speaking let heaven open in the name of Jesus.

PRAYER POINTS

1. Every arrow of untimely death fired into my life, die, in the name of Jesus.
2. Any power that is troubling my star, die, in the name of Jesus.
3. Any power assigned to kill me, die in the name of Jesus.
4. Every heaviness in my body, be shifted away in the name of Jesus.
5. Network of witchcraft from my place of birth, scatter in the name of Jesus.
6. Every strong man assigned to my breakthrough, die, in the name of Jesus.
7. Thou power of queen of heaven, thou power of queen of the coast, assigned against my life, die, in the name of Jesus.

The Serpent In The Family Line

Vol. 6. No. 3

Nahum 3:3-4 says; **The horseman lifteth up both the bright sword and the glittering spear: and there is a multitude of slain, and a great number of carcases; and there is none end of their corpses; they stumble upon their corpses: Be cause of the multitude of the whoredoms of the well-favoured harlot, the mistress of witchcrafts, that selleth nations through her whoredoms, and families through her witchcrafts."**

Today, I would like you to specially pray about your family. The prayers at the end of this message are designed to deliver families. I would like you to read on with a rapt attention so that, you will know how to key in. The first thing that you need to understand is the fact that, the family is a divine institution- the Almighty God created it. The second thing that you need to know is the fact that, the family is the first established human institution. The family was instituted even before the church. It has some powers that cannot be gotten from anywhere else. Each person is a leaf from a family tree. That is why a happy family is like heaven on earth. God is interested in the issue of the family and so also is the devil interested in it. The enemy knows that once the family is destroyed, everything else is. Everything that we are complaining about in the society is as a result of the decay in the family. That is why today, we not only have juvenile delinquency but more of adult delinquency. When something goes wrong in the society, it is because something had already gone wrong in the family.

Every family has a destiny, a purpose and a divine agenda. God purposely put you in your family for a purpose. If God wanted you to come from another family, He would have organised it. One way or the other, the situation is such that, no one has the power to decide which family he or she would come from. If some people had had the chance of choosing their heritage, they would not have chosen Africa.

The devil is specifically set out to deal with the family. The text we read in the book of Nahum shows the agenda-of the devil for the family. If you can stand in the gap for your family today, you will be amazed at what God will do amongst them. Perhaps that is why God allowed you to get born-again. Perhaps, that is why you are reading this particular edition of "Sound The Battle Cry'" Perhaps, it is for you to become the deliverer of your family. The verse above shows the trade of families through witchcraft. This implies that many people have already been sold out to the enemy and many, donated to the powers of darkness; powers of the rivers or forests or rocks.

Many years ago. a woman was having problems in her marriage. Her husband who was a Sunday-School-Teacher in their church, came home one evening with a lady and he said that she was his convert and would be staying with them. The woman found out that her husband was actually having an affair with the lady and he sleeps in the guest-room with her, every night. The woman protested but her husband did not stop. She threatened to tell their pastor and he threatened to stop going to church, if she reported him. Somehow she realised that it was a spiritual battle and she began to pray. The Lord revealed to her that, her mother did something many years ago which was now manifesting in her marriage.

She traveled to the village to ask her mother and the mother confessed that when the woman was young, she failed her school certificate examination four times and she (her mother) went to a herbalist for help. The mother was made to consult the river goddess who demanded some sacrifices. She got everything the goddess asked for and they threw the things into the river. The rule was that, the mother should renew the sacrifice every year, otherwise the girl would have problems getting married or keeping her marriage. The mother did it for some years and later forgot about the whole thing. Of course, the girl did not know anything about what her mother did, she found out that she passed her examination at the fifth attempt. This means that the woman's marriage had been sold out to the gods of the river, even before she got married. There are many people today in this kind of situation. My prayer today is that, the Blood of Jesus, shall recover any aspect of your life that has been sold out to any power of darkness, in the name of Jesus.

In many families, there are evil agents planted there to destroy them. One of such strategy that the devil uses in destroying family is by implanting a serpent there. Once there is a serpent-person in the family line, it is enough to destroy the whole family structure. Gehazi was the serpent in his family line. He had ancestors that had no problem, but he went to look for trouble and he got a curse, which placed leprosy on him and his descendants forever. Gehazi became a serpent in that family and put the whole structure in trouble.

FAMILY SERPENTS:
1. **Strange Children**
These are children who have been sent by the devil, to come and scatter everything. It could be a very serious matter. Many years ago, a fourteen-year-old boy was brought to us. Although he was 14 years old, he said he had been in existence hundreds of years ago; he talked about Noah and Methuselah. He said he was the one that prevented his mother from having another child and made his father to fail his professional examinations several times. He made sure that no one had a car in that family and the one that managed to buy one, drove himself into a river in the car. It was by God's grace that he did not die. Many families have such children planted there and they are putting the whole family in trouble.

2. **Cursed Ancestors**.
Sometimes, when a person does something wrong and he is cursed, those curses do not stop on him. They are carried over down the family line. This single person has become a serpent that is pouring venom into the family line and it goes right down even to the children that are yet unborn.

Are you from a family where no woman gets married? Or a family where no one is making it in life? Or everyone is fighting each other? Or no man ever gets a good job and it is their wife that works and feeds them? In some families, all the men as a matter of necessity, must marry witches. In some families, there must be one of them in jail, at one time or the other. In some, people die untimely. In some, anyone who dares to start building a house, will not live to finish it. In some, the girls are put in the family way at the age of eighteen, without being married.

I have seen a family, where all the girls get pregnant at a tender age and most of the time, the men responsible deny them. They later got married to other men, leaving their first children in the family house because they had no specific fathers. I pray that every serpent in your family line shall scatter today, in the Name of Jesus.

Many years ago, a woman dragged her husband to me. She said he did not want to work at all. He would sit in the parlour and watch CNN from morning till she returns back from work. She would prepare breakfast and lunch and if she would come home after 5p.m, she had to prepare supper also. All he needed to do was warm up the food and eat. During Christmas, he would ask her to buy him new clothes, if she did not want him to go to the church in shorts with her. The woman got fed up brought him to me. Looking at the situation ordinarily, one would say that the man had problems. But as a counselor, I have learnt to ask the Holy Spirit what to do. We started praying and the Lord said I should ask the woman, how many women were in her family and how many of them that were of marriageable age and are actually married.

She told me that there were six ladies in her family and she was the only one that was married.

This means that, by getting married, she had broken a rule. The powers that were warring against the family ensured that her marriage looked as if there was no marriage at all. It was when she was prayed with and the bondage broken, that her husband became serious. When prayer started and we sought the face of God, He revealed that, one of her ancestors who was very rich had oppressed people and took any woman that pleased him as a wife, whether she was someone else's wife or not. One day, he bought a slave who had a beautiful wife. The rich ancestor confiscated the woman and made her his wife and in anger the slave cursed him and said none of his female descendants, would ever get a man to marry them.

Take this prayer point:
* **Boasting serpents of my family line, I bury you today in the Name of Jesus.**

3. **Those with witchcraft powers.**
A single witch in a family is enough to sell everyone off.

4. **Familiar spirits.**

5. **Marine powers.**
If any of your ancestors was a river priest or priestess, the person would have probably sold out the whole family to a river or married them off to marine spirits.

6. **Lodge membership or any occult society.**
They all end up putting the whole family structure in a serious trouble. It is a serious situation, to be put in trouble for what you did not do, or what you are not aware of.

7. **Entry into evil covenants by an individual for the sake of the family.**

8. **Idol worshiping.**
These are very serious matters. What I am trying to explain is the fact that, a single person can put a whole lineage in bondage. King Jeroboam in the Bible offended God and that put the generations after him in trouble, they suffered for it. A person could enter into an evil covenant and put a whole race in trouble. Likewise, a single individual can magnetise misfortune into the family. An idol worshiper in a family, can make the family suffer woe for four generations. The presence of a serpent person in a family line, will cause: disintegration, demotion, poverty, backwardness, general failure, marital disturbance and all kinds of terrible things.

What to do
1. **Engage in spiritual warfare.**

2. **Identify and deal with the serpents.**

3. **Take over the ground the serpent had won.**
This is why you are going to pray aggressively today. Many families are already in trouble. Many people are not finding things easy today, because of the kind of place they come from. That is why it is good to know your family tree; if you do not know where you come from, you do not know anything.

Many years ago in the university, there was a beautiful girl who came from a rich family and never lacked anything. However, this girl was a thief. She steals even under wears from poor students who could only afford second-hand clothing. Later, it was found out that her grandfather was an armed robber in his life time and he was shot.

There was a family of five girls who grew up and got married one after the other. Some years later, each of them had one problem or the other with her husband and came back to live with their father, until all five were back. For some strange reasons, their father had five rooms in his boys'-quarters and they came back and occupied those rooms. Their grandmother too was living with their father in the main house. One way or the other, the last born got to know MFM and she was given the book titled: **Pray Your Way To Breakthroughs**.

She prayed fervently that night for about one hour.

The following day, her grandmother asked her the kind of prayers she was praying the previous night; she advised that she should go back to the former orthodox way of praying. The lady said she had heard. That made it clear to her that her prayers were making an impact but she was surprised at her grandmother's reaction. Anyway, that night, she prayed from midnight till 3a.m. The following morning, her grandmother warned her not to pray those prayers if she did not want anyone to die. That night the sister prayed all the prayers in the book, even those that were not relevant to her situation; she prayed from midnight till 6a.m. That morning, the grandmother did not wake up she was found dead on her bed.

Later, as they were going through the grandmother's belongings, a strange padlock was found under her bed, which surface looked like the skin of a baby-rat. Clamped into the padlock, was a piece of cotton wool with a drop of blood on it. Under it, was a tiny sheet of paper on which the names of the five sisters were written? That meant that their marriages were locked up as long as they were still menstruating. By the evening of the following day, the husband of the first-born came to beg his wife to go back home with him. By the end of that week, all five ladies were back in their matrimonial homes. Who would have linked their marriages with a padlock or a grandmother? God is the revealer of secretes and He is the one, who can break every bondage.

Today, I would like you to examine your life. If you are not yet born again, you cannot pray for your family line. It will be a suicidal mission, if you ventured it.

This bulletin is called: **Sound The Battle Cry"** A cry to battle, is neither silent nor gentle. The prayers that I am suggesting below are meant to be prayed, until something happens. Do not joke with these prayers because, as you begin to pray them, the power of God will move into your situation. Do not say that the words of these prayers are too harsh; you are fighting with merciless enemies so, you cannot show them any mercy. When the enemies eventually got Samson, they did not show him mercy at all. When the enemy was able to get at Judas, he did not show him mercy; he dealt with Judas and made him to kill herself. When the enemy got at Korah, Dathan and Abiram, he did not show them any mercy at all. Saul the king too, was pushed by the enemy unto destruction. You have no business showing mercy to the spiritual enemy of your soul. The angels of the living God shall be dispatched to do their work in your life today in Jesus' name.

The reason why I want you to pray these prayers is because, in those days, Daniel began to pray and right from that first day and God sent an answer which was delayed by a principality in the heavens called, the Prince of Persia. On the 21st day, it took a more powerful angel that was dispatched to the rescue of the one that was bringing the answer. So also are there principalities in the personal heavens of some people which must be dismantled for any progress to be made. Everyman and woman has an air space over his or her head. You have your own personal heavens, which is over your head likewise I too. That is why the Bible says: *"Thy heavens over thine head..."*

Therefore beloved, you will take these prayer points, with holy aggression, with fire and thunder in your voice. Do not just read them, pray them violently. Do not negotiate with the enemy. **You must get results!**

If hitherto, you have not surrendered your life to the Lord Jesus Christ, I would advise that you do so right away. All you need do is acknowledge the fact that you are a sinner and that you cannot approach God in your sinful state. Right there where you are and in total submission of yourself to Him; confess your sins to Him, name them one by one and ask Him to forgive you and cleanse you from all unrighteousness. Claim the redemptive power in the Blood of Jesus, that was shed on the cross at Calvary for the remission of your sins. Renounce the world and the devil and turn to the Lord. Invite the Lord Jesus Christ into your life and ask Him to become your personal Lord and Saviour. Enthrone Him over your life and ask Him to take over all that concerns you, Surrender your totality to Him and ask Him to have His way in your life.

If you just took that decision, I congratulate you for it. It is the most important decision in life and I pray that it shall be permanent in your life, in the Name of Jesus. I pray that the Lord will uphold you with His right hand of righteousness and keep you from falling. I pray that your name will be written in the Book of Life and nothing shall by any means rub it off, in the Name of Jesus. Now, think deeply about your own family line, so that you will know what to address when the time comes. Do you come from a family where people do not move forward? Or a family, where people are operating under curses? Have you noticed an evil trend in your family line? Have you noticed that women become widows in the early stage of their lives? Have you noticed that women in your family line get married very late in life? Have you noticed that men in your family line are always very poor? Do you notice any trend that you want the Lord to deal with today?

If you want God to deal with these evil trends in your family, everything now depends on the way you pray the following prayer points. I can assure you by the grace of God, that immediately you start praying these prayers, something concrete will happen in the spiritual realm. In spiritual warfare, what you see is not what you fight. Sometimes, what you are fighting is different from what you should actually fight. Sometimes, you pray some prayers which may be far from the difficulties that you are experiencing. That is how God operates and when He wants to start answering prayers, God can start in a very strange way. When God began to answer the prayers of the Israelites to get delivered from the bondage of Egypt, He started with the episode of the burning bush. Who would have related a bush somewhere, with the deliverance of some people from bondage? That is the way God operates. His ways are not our ways because His ways are past finding out.

Get ready to get really aggressive and pray these prayers until something happens. This should mark the beginning of a new era in your family line.

1. Every serpent in my family line, loose your power in the Name of Jesus.
2. O arm of God, strong to deliver, deliver my family line in the Name of Jesus.
3. Every activity of spiritual robbers in my life, die! in the Name of Jesus.
4. Every power assigned to make my family to expire, die! in the Name of Jesus.
5. Every Uzziah assigned to my family line, die! in the Name of Jesus.
6. Poverty serpent in my family line, die! in the Name of Jesus.
7. Every serpent of death in my family line, die! in the Name of Jesus.
8. Every marine altar, raised against my family, scatter! in the Name of Jesus.
9. Every evil pattern in my family line, die! in the Name of Jesus.
10. Every power assigned against the star of my life, scatter! in the Name of Jesus.
11. Any evil water that has flowed into my life, dry up! in the Name of Jesus.
12. All the witches in my family line, be exposed and be disgraced! in the Name of Jesus.
13. Every strongman assigned against my family line, die! in the Name of Jesus.
14. Every traffic of bad luck in my life, scatter! in the Name of Jesus.
15. Any power sitting on my joy, scatter! in the Name of Jesus.
16. Spirit of favour, overshadow my life, in the Name of Jesus.
17. Every rope, dragging me away from my prosperity, break into irreparable pieces! in the Name of Jesus.
18. By thunder, by lightning, by fire, I possess my possession, by fire, in Jesus Name.
19. Every power contesting with my angel of blessing, scatter! in the Name of Jesus.
20. Every power contesting with my angel of breakthroughs, scatter! in the Name of Jesus.
21. Thou power of the night, assigned against my breakthroughs, die! in the Name of Jesus.
22. Every power defiling my body, die! in the Name of Jesus.
23. Thou serpent of darkness assigned against my breakthroughs in life, roast to ashes, in the name of Jesus Christ.
24. Every serpent of

darkness assigned to monitor my progress in the spirit realm, what are you waiting for die, by fire! in the name of Jesus.
25. Blood of Jesus separate me from every family idol, in the mighty name of Jesus Christ.
26. God arise and disgrace every serpent of affliction in my life, in the name of Jesus.
27. My Father! as You killed the first-born sons in Egypt, kill every power that is working against my joy, in the Name of Jesus.
28. Every power that is mocking my prayers, die! in the Name of Jesus.

The Raging Altars Of Your Father's House

Judges 6:25-26; *"And it came to pass the same night, that the Lord said unto him, Take thy father's young bullock, even the second bullock of seven years old, and throw down the altar of Baal that thy father hath, and cut down the grove that is by it: And build an altar unto the Lord thy God upon the top of this rock, in the ordered place, and take the second bullock, and offer a burnt sacrifice with the wood of the grove which thou shalt cut down."*

There were altars in Gideon's father's house and God asked him to pull down the altar of the enemy in order to be able to raise an altar unto the Lord. He even used the wood that he had pulled down, to make fire unto God.

WHAT ARE ALTARS?
Genesis 8:20;
"And Noah builded an altar unto the Lord; and took of every clean beast, and of every clean fowl, and offered burnt offerings on the altar."

Altars are indispensable in a place of worship. They are means by which sacrifices are offered in worship. It could be a location or it could be a place. Initially, altars originated from the worship of God as seen by the first man that built one for the Lord; but nowadays, it has been polluted by the enemy. Altars are spiritual powers that bring a covering over a land. If a sacrifice is placed in front of a person's house, that place has become an altar and there will be a traffic of evil spirits there, except the person deals with it accordingly.

Altars are entities that control a land and the people inhabiting it. An altar is a place of sacrifice; a place of spiritual dedication, a place of covenant making. It is a place of communion with spirit beings.

A woman noticed that, every morning at 4.am, her husband would get up and go out. She did not suspect anything because he was a Christian and even a Sunday-School teacher. So therefore, she could not question him. Later, she became curious and followed him one morning, as he headed for the Lagoon. She hid in a bush and was looking at him from afar. Something came out of the waters and was talking to him; it said someone had followed him there and he said no.
The covenant was that, any day the secret leaked, the man would not go back home. Before the wife knew what was going on, he had disappeared. The woman ran back to town and reported to the Police, but her story was not believed. There was an altar at that lagoon; it was where the man communed with an evil spirit. An altar is a place of slaughter, for something that is worshiped. It is a place of spiritual exchange; spiritual dining place. It is a place of spiritual traffic of spirits either good or bad.

When Jacob got to Bethel, he slept and used a stone as pillow. He saw the vision of angels descending and ascending. He then concluded that "Surely, the Lord was in that place." If you look back into history, you will discover that, Abraham had earlier on erected an altar unto the Lord there - Genesis 12:8; *"And he removed from thence unto a mountain on the east of Bethel, and pitched his tent, having Bethel on the west, and Hai on the east: and there he builded an altar unto the Lord, and called upon the name of the Lord."*

If Abraham had been a witch doctor or a demonic person and had raised an evil altar there, it would have been a traffic of demonic spirits that Jacob his grandson would have seen and not angels. Altars are so important that, about 20 people in the Bible erected altars to God: Noah, Abraham, Isaac, Jacob, Moses, Balak, Manoah, Samuel, Saul, David, Jeroboam, Manasseh, Ahab, Elijah, Urriah, Zerrubabel, etc.
When Elijah confronted the

prophets of Baal, the first thing he did, was to repair the altar of the Lord that was broken down. Then he prayed and fire came down. Altars erected unto God are very powerful and the ones erected unto the devil are very wicked.

Altars have an agenda; a voice, a domain, a file of people dedicated to them, a memory, an armory, where they keep their weapons. Many of the problems in our communities, can be traced to the altars raised by our forefathers. Many of them lie dormant now, but the spirits behind them are active; some are being re-activated occasionally and when some are neglected, they could cause bloodbaths through wars and unexplainable accidents to collect blood for themselves. All the evil altars that our forefathers erected then, are a hindrance to our prayers today. They hinder our walk with God. Before a person can fulfill his destiny, those altars have to be dealt with because, most of them are altars of affliction and slavery.

Many are suffering from the influence of these evil altars and they do not know what to do. The altars are passed on from generation to generation. Even if the present generation is not re-activating these altars, the people are still under their influence, until it is broken and neutralised by the blood of Jesus.

To deal with altars, you need to cry against them to leave your life alone. This was what a Prophet of Judah did against the altar that Jeroboam built.

1 Kings 13:1-2;
"And, behold, there came a man of God out of Judah by the word of the Lord unto Bethel: and Jeroboam stood by the altar to burn incense. And he cried against the altar in the word of the Lord, and said, O altar, altar, thus saith the Lord; Behold, a child shall be born unto the house of David, Josiah by name and upon thee shall he offer the priests of the high places that burn incense upon thee, and men's bones shall be burnt upon thee."

When the altars of affliction are raised, they can contact the spirit world to report you. They can raise up a traffic of evil spirits to trouble the life of a person. Many factories will not function until some foundational and territorial altars are dealt with. You might not have access to your correct destiny, until you deal with these altars. You may not be able to deal with your troublesome marriage, until you have dealt with foundational altars.

1 **Shrines:** These are specific locations in a compound or house or village, town or country, where an idol is set up and then sacrifices are offered there unto the idol by a priest. Everyone from a family that has a shrine, automatically comes under their influence, until it is broken by the power of the living God. When a person that is under the cover of a satanic altar, goes where he or she should not go or do what he or she should not do, the person will get into serious trouble in the hands of the evil spirits that are operating in the altar. That is why anyone from such a family who gives his or her life to the Lord Jesus, has to get delivered from their grip.

A man was born into a Muslim family, but he wanted a change of religion. So, he joined the Catholic church. There, he saw people making obeisance to a statue of Mary and they were using beads like Muslims. He got fed up and wanted something more lively. He left and joined a white-garment gathering. The altars of his father's house were crying against him, so he was going from one bondage to the other. They did not allow him to go to a Bible believing church; a place where he would hear the true Gospel of our Lord Jesus Christ. **When your parents and ancestors have shrines, you have a lot of prayers to pray.**

One day, we were praying for a young man and it was taking quite some time and there was no result. Suddenly, a voice spoke through his mouth and asked why we were praying for him. It said we should not waste our time, but go and attend to other people. He said we should ask the young man for his name. We stopped and asked the man what his name was and he said; "Iwin wa mi wa" (i.e. spirits are looking for me), It was a strange name which I had never heard before. Of course, with a name like that, there would be a traffic of evil spirits in the life of that person.

2. **Images:**
Images in form of statues, pictures, to which people make obeisance.

"Deuteronomy 5:8-9 says;
"Thou shall not make thee any graven image, or any likeness of any thing that is in heaven above, or that is in the earth beneath, or that is in the waters beneath the earth: Thou shalt not bow down thyself unto them, nor serve them: for I the Lord thy God am a jealous God, visiting the iniquity of the fathers upon the children unto the third and fourth generation of them that hate me,"

3. **Cauldrons:**
These are pots in which people's lives and destinies are cooked or covered up in the spirit realm.

4. **Forests:**
Which are dedicated to evil spirits.

5. **Rivers/Seas:**
Sometimes one would find dead chickens, birds, floating on rivers.

This means, people have gone to appease the water spirits. Sometimes, they use fruits.

When the altars of your fathers house are raging against you, you are in a serious trouble, except you wage war against them in the power of God's might. They will rage against you, once you are bent on fulfilling your divine destiny.
If your ancestors were witch doctors and herbalists, and your father is or was a demonic hunter, you have a lot of bondage in your cupboard.

If you now decide that you want to be a child of God and then become a pastor, they will surely rage against you. They will bring out your family file and rage against you; that you want to soil your family pattern. If you decide not to be part of your evil family pattern and stand out, there will be a rage and they will not let go easily. There will be a rage, when you decide to be the head and not the tail; when you decide to move forward in spite of all odds, when you decide not to serve the strange gods that are demanding worship.

Beloved, I would like you to pray today like you have never prayed before. Pray them very well. There is a need to cry against all these altars. The devil has made counterfeits of altars, just as he does to other divine institutions and ordinances. The devil has stolen the blueprint of altars and has sold it to evil spirits. He has stolen the ministry of altars and has turned it upside down.

WHAT TO DO

1. Surrender your life to the Lord Jesus Christ.

2. Repent from known sins.

3. Prayerfully and spiritually pray against any curse or curses, the evil altars of your father's house has placed upon you in the name of the Lord.

4. Send the fire of God to consume them.

5. Destroy the satanic priests that are ministering there.

6. Withdraw your name from their file and cleanse yourself of the consequences of the altars.

However, if you have never at one time or the other accepted the Lord Jesus. Christ into your life as personal Lord and Saviour, you cannot deal with these altars, because they still have a grip on your life. All you need to do, is to cry unto the Lord, right there where you are. Confess your sins and those of your ancestors to Him and ask Him to forgive you and cleanse you from all unrighteousness. Claim the receptive power in the Blood of Jesus that was shed on the cross at Calvary.

Invite the Lord Jesus Christ into your life and ask Him to become your personal Lord and Saviour. Enthrone Him to take control of all that concerns you. Surrender your totality to Him.

I congratulate you for this decision that you have just taken. It is the most important decision in life; I pray that it shall be permanent in your life, in the name of Jesus. I pray that the Lord will uphold you and keep you from falling and your name will be written in the Book of Life in the name of Jesus.

You can now pray the following prayers with all the aggression that you can gather. If you pray them seriously, certain things will give way.

These are:
1. **The enemies that are crying against your moving forward.**

2. **The ladder that the enemy is using to climb into your life and gain access into your destiny.**

3. **Anything the enemy has planted inside you, that is contesting with your greatness.**

Many people who would have been great, have been sent into the position of demotion, by the powers of their fathers' houses and, their altars.

4. **The demands of the evil altars.**

They could demand for money, blood, human lives and all sorts of things.

Make sure you pray until something happens. Until Gideon pulled down the altars of his father house, he could not do what God wanted him to do. Until you pull down the altars of your father's house, you may not be able to fulfil your destiny.

PRAYER PPOINTS
1. Every altar of my Father's house, release me by fire! in the mighty name of Jesus.
2. Altars of demotion of my father's house, die! in the name of Jesus.
3. My blood, depart from every evil altar! in the name of Jesus.
4. Altar of poverty, die, in the name of Jesus.
5. Every foundational altar, bringing failure into my life, die! in the name of Jesus.
6. Thou altar of darkness fashioned against my destiny, die, in the name of Jesus.
7. I shall arise above my roots whether the enemies like it or not, in the name of Jesus.
8. God arise and move my destiny forward seven times faster, in the name of Jesus.
9. Thou umbrella of darkness, covering the glory of my family line, catch fire! be roasted! in the name of Jesus.
10. Every familiar spirit claiming ownership of my life, release me and die, in the name of Jesus.
11. Every power that have refused to let me go, die, in the name of Jesus.
12. Let the anointing for total breakthroughs, fall upon me now! in the name of Jesus.
13. Let the road of breakthroughs, open unto me today! in the name of Jesus.
14. My head, reject curses! in the name of Jesus.
15. Every covenant of suffering of my father's house in my life, today is your expiry date; therefore, die! in the name of Jesus.
16. God arise! and let my stubborn enemies scatter, in the name of Jesus.
17. Every embargo on my prosperity, your time is up; therefore, die! in the name of Jesus.
18. Every power that is against my promotion, die! in the name of Jesus.
19. Every obstacle on my way to greatness die, in the name of Jesus.
20. Every harassment of the enemy shall bring me testimony, in the name of Jesus.
21. The enemy servant, riding on my horse of destiny shall fall, in the name of Jesus.
22. The power, that does not want me to lift my head shall die, in the name of Jesus.
23. Begin to thank the Lord for the blessings you have received from Him.

Dealing With Poverty Magnets

It is not important for a person to do what people or he himself wants to do. The most important thing in the life of anybody, especially a Christian, is to do what God wants him or her to do. The most important thing for you as a person is for the Lord to have His way in your life.

Pray like this:
* O Lord, whether I like it or not, whether the devil likes it or not, have your way in my life in the name of Jesus.
* Every satanic storm, working against my life, be silenced forever! in the name of Jesus.
* Every satanic alliance against me, scatter! in the name of Jesus.
* Today O Lord, I must touch the hem of Your garment, in the name of Jesus.

The purpose of this message to you is that, poverty in your life, hiding under any mask, should be located and buried, in the name of Jesus.

What Is A Magnet?
A magnet is a device that draws metals to itself. No matter how hidden, once a magnet runs through a place that a metal is, it finds it out. When Jesus shall appear in heaven, He shall be a magnet and pull all the people that are like Him, unto Himself. I pray that anything in your life that will debar you from being magnetised to Jesus on that day, shall be destroyed today, in the name of Jesus.

Poverty may be sitting on its own but the magnet in the life of a person will attract it to him. The secret behind great deliverance is locating the magnet hiding in people's lives: You may have gone through deliverance several times and find out that the problem still persists; it is because there are some powers hiding in your life, that are magnetising the demons of this problem to you.

I have a friend who was shocked when he went to a naming ceremony. As they were about to serve people food, the baby's father came out with a notebook. He ticked the names of those who gave his wife money when she had their first baby. My friend was fidgeting because he did not remember if he gave her money then or not. It happened that he did and he was served food. Some people were given only a bottle of soft drink. I don't know if the baby's father was joking or not, but you would agree with me that to some extent, he was serious about it and it was poverty that pushed him to it. The naming ceremony was turned into a debt-collecting session which planted a seed of poverty into the life of that baby. A woman who feeds her baby on food bought on credit, is planting a seed of poverty into its life. Those who use things like rat at the naming ceremony and give a piece of it to the mother to chew and a piece on the baby's tongue, are planting life seed of poverty because, rat represent poverty in the spirit world.

There are many people with these magnets in their lives.

POVERTY MAGNETS:
1. **THE SPIRIT OF BONDAGE.**
Romans 8:15 says; *"For ye have not received the spirit of bondage again to fear; but ye have received the Spirit of adoption, whereby we cry, Abba, Father."*

Doors of Entry:
(i) Unrepented sin of the lust of flesh.

(ii) Generational sins of parents' ancestors.
If the children get born again, they can be washed of these sins, by the Blood of Jesus as they go through deliverance,

Manifestation Of This Spirit:
1. Lack of faith.
2. All forms of addiction.
3. Habitual sins.
4. Uncontrollable lust, sexual looseness.
5. Greed, over ambition.
6. Roots of bitterness, unforgiving heart.

7. Captivity to satan.
8. Fear of death.

Take this prayer point:
* I bury every bondage in my life today, in the name of Jesus.

2. THE SPIRIT OF DOUBLE MINDEDNESS (CONFUSION)
JAMES 1:5-8 has it that:
"If any of you lack wisdom, let him ask of God, that giveth to all men liberally, and upbraideth not; and it shall be given him. But let him ask in faith, nothing wavering. For he that wavereth is like a wave of the sea driven with the wind and tossed. For let not that man think that he shall receive any thing of the Lord. A double minded man is unstable in all his ways."

Doors of Entry:
(i) Lack of faith.
(ii) Lack of Bible knowledge.
(iii) Refusal to accept sound doctrines of the word of God
(iv) Illicit sexual relationships.

Manifestation Of This Spirit:
(i) Lack of assurance of salvation.
(ii) Uncertainty in the spirit realm and indecision.
(iii) Inability of victory over sin. Paul says in 1Cor. 9:26; *"I therefore so run not as one uncertainly; so fight I not as one beateth the air:"*

Take this prayer point.
* *Every spirit of hopelessness, come out with all your roots in the name of Jesus.*

3. SPIRIT OF FEAR.
2Tim. 1:7 says;
"For God hath not given us the spirit of fear; but of power, and of love, and of a sound mind."

Doors Of Entry:
Sin.
i. Generational sins of parents and ancestors.
ii. Bad experiences during childhood.
iii. Parental neglect.

Manifestation Of This Spirit
(i) Fearful behaviour.
(ii) Profound anxiety and worry.
(iii) Inability to relate to God as father.
(iv) Nightmares.
(v) Heart failures.
(vi) Lack of trust, doubt.
(vii) Torments.
(viii) Mismanagement and investment in wrong things.

This spirit is an old demon which started operation in the life of Adam in the garden of Eden, after he had sinned against God. Genesis 3:9-12;
"And the Lord God called unto Adam, and said unto him, Where art thou? And he said, I heard thy voice in the garden, and I was afraid, because I was naked; and I hid myself. And he said, Who told thee that thou wast naked? Hast thou eaten of the tree, whereof I commanded thee that thou shouldest not eat? And the man said, The woman whom thou gavest to be with me, she gave me of the tree, and I did eat."

Take this prayer point:
* *Every spirit of fear, depart from my life! in the name of Jesus.*

4. THE SPIRIT OF PRIDE
Proverbs 16:18-19 read thus;
"Pride goeth before destruction, and an haughty spirit before a fall. Better it is to be of an humble spirit with the lowly, than to divide the spoil with the proud."

Doors Of Entry:
(i) By inheritance.
(ii) Gossip
(iii) Boasting.
(iv) Envy.

Manifestation Of This Spirit:
(i) Snubbing.
(ii) Unteachable spirit.
(iii) Rebellion.
(iv) Argumentative nature, contentious spirit.
(v) Rejection of God's counsel.

5. THE SPIRIT OF HEAVINESS (DEPRESSION).
Hear what God says about this spirit in Isaiah 61:3; *"To appoint unto them that mourn in Zion, to give unto them beauty for ashes, the oil of joy for mourning, the garment of praise for the spirit of heaviness; that they might be called trees of righteousness, the planting of the Lord, that he might be glorified."*

This is the lot of Christians and many are going about with depressed hearts, not knowing that it is a magnet for pulling unto themselves, wicked things. God cannot be found in this kind of situation. It is a magnet of poverty. The idea of being happy on one or two days of the week and being depressed in the days that follows should be dropped. It magnetises arrows from the enemy.

Doors Of Entry:
(i) Tragic loss of loved one or things.
(ii) Sins of parents and ancestors.
(iii) Lack of contentment either in family life or business.

Manifestation Of This Spirit:
(i) Sadness.
(ii) Despair.
(iii) No urge to praise God.
(iv) Root of bitterness that cannot be pacified.
(v) Loneliness or wanting to be alone.
(vi) Gluttony.
(vii) Sleeplessness.
(viii) Self-pity.
(ix) Hopelessness.
(x) Broken heart.

Take these prayer points:
* **(Put your name here), reject every spirit of heaviness! in the name of Jesus.**
* **Whatever will hinder the joy of the Lord from being my strength, fall down and die! in the name of Jesus.**

6. SPIRIT OF INFIRMITY.
Luke 13:11 records that; *"And, behold, there was a woman which had a spirit of infirmity eighteen years, and was bowed together, and could in no wise lift up herself."* Hospitals are helpless when it is the spirit of infirmity that is dealing with a person. No microscope can detect a demon. No injection can chase out a demon; it will even get fertilised by it the more.

Doors Of Entry:
(i) Sin.
(ii) Unhygienic situations.
(iii) Satanic attack.
(iv) Heredity.
(v) Evil dedication before, during or after birth.
(vi) Insane conditions of living.
(vii) Ignorance.

You don't have to offend anyone or be wicked to anybody before they are wicked to you. You may be one of those who do not believe in the existence of witches and wizards. You may have to find out in a hard way that they exist. Even Europeans now know that they exist. You could be likened to a person who does not believe in the existence of hell, until he dies in his sins and finds himself there.

Manifestation Of This Spirit:
(i) Chronic illness or deformity.
(ii) Bent body or spine
(iii) Chronic cold and asthma.
(iv) Disorder in the body.
(v) Cancer.
(vi) Depression.

Take these prayer points: **(Insert your name), reject the spirit of infirmity! in the name of Jesus.**

* **Every arrow of infirmity, go back to where you came from in the name of Jesus.**

7. THE SPIRIT OF JEALOUSY.
Numbers 5:14 recounts; *"And the spirit of jealousy come upon him, and he be jealous of his wife, and she be defiled: or if the spirit of jealousy come upon him, and he be jealous of his wife, and she be not defiled:"*

Doors Of Entry:
(i) Sexual defilement.
(ii) Rage or anger.
(iii) Lack of discipline.
(iv) Strife.
(v) Parents Preference

Manifestation Of This Spirit of Hatred.
(i) Cruelty or murder.
(ii) Competitive spirit.
(iii) Causing division.
(iv) Revenge.
(v) Covetousness.
(vi) Greed.

8. THE SPIRIT OF LIES.
Deformation of the truth or outright untruthfulness, either to cover up or to deceive.

Doors Of Entry:
(i) Seeking enjoyable or flattering prophesies.
(ii) Hatred for constructive criticism.
(iii) Sin of parents.

Manifestations Of This Spirit
(i) Compulsive, habitual lies.
(ii) Deception, operating under delusion.
(iii) Flattering and insincere praising.

(iv) Wishing evil, while pretending to be friendly.
(v) Spirit of religion, pretending to be holy, over-spirituality, hypocrisy.
(vi) Excessive talking, idle gossiping, slandering.

All these hinder God from bombarding people with wealth. You have to deal with them and chase them out.

9. PERVERSE SPIRIT.
Isaiah 19:14 says;
"The Lord hath mingled a perverse spirit in the midst thereof: and they have caused Egypt to err in every work thereof, as a drunken man staggereth in his vomit."

Doors Of Entry:
(i) Following false prophets/priests.
(ii) Idolatry.
(iii) Generational sin.

Manifestation Of This Spirit:
(i) Sexual perversion.
(ii) Addiction to pornography.
(iii) Repeated disobedience to God.
(iv) Twisting the Bible to suit one's purpose.
(v) Ingratitude.
(vi) Filthy mind.

10. SEDUCING SPIRIT
These are powers that lure people into untruth or sin; they work in subtle ways and the person does not realise their presence until he or she falls into sin.

Doors Of Entry:
(i) Consulting false prophets and teachers.
(ii) Worrying about problems.

Manifestation Of This Sprit:
(i) Searing of conscience.
(ii) Double-mindedness.

11. THE SPIRIT OF SLUMBER.
There are powers that weaken and render a person useless. Romans 11:8 says; *"(According as it is written, God hath given them the spirit of slumber, eyes that they should not see, and ears that they should not hear;) unto this day."*

Doors of Entry:
(i) Spiritual carelessness.
(ii) Neglect by parents.
(iii) Wordless and prayerless life.

Manifestation Of This Spirit:
(i) Not knowing right from wrong.
(ii) Not loving others.
(iii) Stagnation.

12. SPIRIT OF THE DEVOURER.
These are the powers that eat up good things unto destruction. They waste good things and dismantle any height. Malachi 3:8-11; *"Will a man rob God? Yet ye have robbed me. But ye say, Wherein have we robbed thee? In tithes and offerings. Ye are cursed with a curse: for ye have robbed me, even this whole nation. Bring ye all the tithes into the storehouse, that there may be meat in mine house, and prove me now herewith, saith the Lord of hosts, if I will not open you the windows of heaven, and pour you out a blessing, that there shall not be room enough to receive it. And I will rebuke the devourer for your sakes, and he shall not destroy the fruits of your ground; neither shall your vine cast her fruit before the time in the field, saith the Lord of hosts.*

Doors Of Entry:
(i) Disobedience to God.
(ii) Not paying tithe and offering.

Manifestation Of This Spirit:
(i) Chronic poverty.
(ii) Financial calamity, natural disaster.
(iii) Inability to save money.

12. LEGION-UNCLEAN SPIRITS.
This is the multiple bombardment of evil spirits.

Doors Of Entry:
(i) Sin.
(ii) Idolatry, occultism.
(iii) Satanic attacks.

Manifestation Of This Spirit:
(i) Sleeplessness.
(ii) Suicidal tendencies.
(iii) Supernatural strength.
(iv) Enjoying seeing death or blood.
(v) Sadism.
(vi) Nightmares.
(vii) Self exhibition.
(viii) Extremism.

14. SPIRIT OF IDOLATRY.
An idol is anything that takes the place or position of God in a person's life. The spirit of Idolatry is responsible for some of the deeply rooted

problems people experience especially Africans, due to the idol worship their ancestors engaged in, which some of them are still practicing till today.

Doors Of Entry:
(i) Worship of false gods.
(ii) Offering- sacrifices.
(iii) Inherited family satanic worship.
(iv) Unholy addiction and reverence to something.

Manifestation Of The Spirit:
(i) Conscious or unconscious covenants.
(ii) Adultery.
(iii) Prostitution of the soul and the body.
(iv) Love of the world and money, food, glamour etc.
(v) Sexual confusion- equating sexual activities with love; sexual abnormality.
(vi) Marriage destruction.

The prayers I will ask you to pray are both curative and preventive. So, do not say you are not concerned.

BUT, you cannot pray these prayers if you have not surrendered your life to the Lord Jesus Christ, therefore I would advise you to do so right there where you are. Confess your sins to the Lord, name them one by one, ask Him to forgive you and let Him know that you will not go back to them again. Renounce the devil and the world and turn totally to the Lord invite Him into your life as your personal Lord and Saviour. I congratulate you for the decision you have just taken, and pray that the Lord will establish and uphold you till the end.

Now pray these prayer points:
1. Every gadget of poverty in my life, be roasted by fire! in the name of Jesus.
2. Every spirit of pocket with holes in my life, fall down and die! in the name of Jesus.
3. Every witch or wizard sitting on my money, be unseated by fire! in the name of Jesus
4. I reject, every rearrangement of my life by household wickedness in the name of Jesus.
5. Let every magnet of prosperity, be deposited in my hands now, in the name of Jesus.
6. Tell the Lord the kind of prosperity you want:
   (i) the one that will dumbfound your enemies,
   (ii) the one that will amaze and shock your friends,
   (iii) the one that will swallow up your poverty forever.
7. Lord, let Your boldness enter into my life, in the name of Jesus.
8. Every familiar face, harassing me in the dream, be defeated in the name of Jesus.
9. My life will not accept any satanic arrow, in the name of Jesus.
10. I refuse to sit for any satanic examination, in the name of Jesus.
11. I refuse to be spiritually stagnant, in the name of Jesus.
12. Every clever devourer, loose your hold! in the name of Jesus.
13. I don't want small breakthroughs, I want giant breakthroughs, in the name of Jesus.
14. My life will not follow any evil family pattern, in the name of Jesus.
15. I withdraw my progress from every evil altar, in the name of Jesus.
16. Any power paralysing my prayer life, fall down and die! in the name of Jesus.
17. I possess my foreign benefits, in the name of Jesus.
18. Every curse issued against me by satanic prophets, fall down and die! in the name of Jesus.
19. Every mark of poverty upon my life, be rubbed off by the Blood of Jesus, in the name of Jesus.
20. Every spirit of leaking pockets, fall down and die! in the name of Jesus.
21. Every problem, mocking my prayers, fall down and die! in the name of Jesus.
22. Every stone, blocking my progress, be buried permanently, in the name of Jesus.
23. Every witchcraft decision against my life, be buried permanently! in the name of Jesus.
24. Every satanic gathering concerning my

progress, be buried permanently! in the name of Jesus.
25. Every 'Pharaoh' and 'Goliath' harassing my life, be buried permanently! in the name of Jesus.
26. Every satanic prophet boasting against me, be buried permanently in the name of Jesus.
27. Every satanic angel troubling my life, be buried permanently! in the name of Jesus.
28. Every spirit of marriage destruction, be buried permanently! in the name of Jesus.
29. Every satanic joy concerning my life, be buried permanently! in the name of Jesus.
30. Every satanic poverty, be buried permanently! In the name of Jesus.

Thank the Lord for answering your prayers.

Release From Evil Covenants

Psalm 25:14; *"The secret of the Lord is with them that fear Him; and He will shew them His covenant."*

Jeremiah 34:18-20;
"And I will give the men that have transgressed my covenant, which have not performed the words of the covenant which they had made before me, when they cut the calf in twain, and passed between the parts thereof, the princes of Judah, and the princes of Jerusalem, the eunuchs, and the priests, and all the people of the land, which passed between the parts of the calf; I will even give them into the hand of their enemies, and into the hand of them that seek their life: and their dead bodies shall be for meat unto the fowls of the heaven, and to the beasts of the earth."

Many people have been involved in strange things in the past and as long as those things or the aftermath of those things are still in place unaddressed, such people will remain in bondage.

Some of the greatest problems that are putting the Blackman under bondage today are:
1. **Evil Spirits.**
2. **Curses.**
3. **Covenants.**

Let it be known to you today that, if you are committing sin willfully or you are in any wrong company, or you have worshiped idols before, or consulted herbalists before, or you have incisions on your body, or you have worshiped the sun or moon before, or you have consulted star-gazers, or read **'The Secrets Of The Psalms'** and have been praying to angels, or have been burning incense or candles, or gone for bloodbath, it means you have grave-clothes on and you have to remove them today. If any of your ancestors was a witch-doctor, magician, masquerade, or you have ever taken part in cultural dances, know for sure that you have spiritual grave-clothes on and they must be removed today.

Every involvement in immorality or pornography, is an invitation to grave-clothes in the life of a person. Many people do not know that they are forming covenants with evil spirits by watching films where the characters are chanting incantations and are portraying idol-worship and sacrifices. Subconsciously, the words are being registered in their brains and as they reiterate these words, they are forming covenants with those evil spirits without knowing it. If you have Indian films in your house and you watch them, be sure that you have invited some demons into your life with your own money. Some religion impose grave-clothes on people through infant baptism and dedication, wedding ceremonies and doctrines and so on.

My prayer today is that the power of God shall erase them in the name of Jesus. Many people are under curses. When evil people want to curse others, they first of all chant incantations. In chanting incantations, they are evoking demonic assistance so that, the words that they will utter, will work against the person and it will not backfire. All such curses shall be broken today in the name of Jesus.

WHAT IS A COVENANT?
Although this is a subject that is not commonly addressed, it exists in all possible spheres of life. A covenant is a strong agreement between two strong parties. It is like a contract, which terms are well spelt out and are binding between two or more parties. If such a covenant is broken, it is a very serious matter because, it is virtually a spiritual thing to form a covenant.

It is considered to be a sacred thing in the Bible. When God wants to commit Himself to something for someone; He forms a covenant with the person. When God has committed Himself to doing something, it is final and irrevocable. A covenant is like a chain that is binding two or more people together. It is like the yoke on two oxen ploughing a field. It drags one with the other, wherever it goes. An evil covenant binds a person to things that are not of God. It drags a person along, wherever it goes. Many today, have such evil covenants binding them.

When you look through the Bible, you will find out that God formed covenants with people. He formed a covenant with Abraham and gave him a condition, which was the circumcision of male children on the eight day after birth. That is why even till today, Jews are circumcised. When there was war in Israel, one of the ways they recognised spies, was by checking if they were circumcised or not. They believed that an uncircumcised man cannot be a Jew. God through Abraham, formed a covenant with the children of Israel that, if anyone curses them, the person would be cursed and if anyone blesses them, he or she would be blessed. That covenant is still binding till today.

There could be a covenant between two people. For example - marriage; which is a common covenant. God is against anything or anyone, who tries to separate two people that are married.
"What God has joined together, let no man put asunder." When a man and woman stand before a priest, and vow to take each other as husband and wife, they are forming a covenant. The difference between the marriage covenant and any other one is the fact that, it is a covenant between the man and the woman and between both of them and God.

Some people form covenants with the devil in order to get money or power or position and they could make an exchange with their lives. They could go to any length, even sleeping in burial grounds.

Exodus 23:28-32; *"And I will send hornets before thee, which shall drive out the Hivite, the Canaanite, and the Hittite, from before thee. I will not drive them out from before thee in one year; lest the land become desolate, and the beast of the field multiply against thee. By little and little I will drive them out from before thee, until thou be increased, and inherit the land. And I will set thy bounds from the Red sea even unto the sea of the Philistines, and from the desert unto the river: for I will deliver the inhabitants of the land into your hand; and thou shah drive them out before thee. Thou shalt make no covenant with them, nor with their gods."*

Isaiah 28:18;
"And your covenant with death shall be disannulled, and your agreement with hell shall not stand; when the overflowing scourge shall pass through, them ye shall be trodden down by it."

Some people promise to die on their wedding day. The most dangerous covenant is the unconscious one, which is made on behalf of a person, without him or her being involved in it. When a person is in such a covenant, he or she is bound to the effects and consequences. If the person is vigilant, he or she will notice that the things that are happening or that he or she is doing, are not normal and are not from him

The aim of this bulletin is to specifically address evil covenants.
When you get incision on you, you have entered into a blood covenant. It is one of the most stubborn covenants and is not easy to break it. The person cutting the incision, usually chant incantations and would invoke certain spirits. Tattoos, tribal marks or decorative marks, are doors to evil covenants and must be seriously dealt with. They are an indication that a person is covenanted to something.

The dark cannot fight the dark. It is not possible for an herbalist to chase out familiar spirit, or witchcraft. All they do is to hide them cleverly, while the name is still in the register and it is usually for a while. Logically, how could the eating of sugarcane or banana, set a person free from familiar spirit? There is no way that a girl who was dis-virgined by a demonic man, would live a normal life until she breaks the blood covenant that the intercourse put her into.

Sometimes, there is a covenant behind the evil dreams that people have. For example, eating with the dead, serving people, swimming in water, playing with snakes, etc. All these things cause all kinds of problems and setbacks. Those covenants shall break today in the Name of Jesus. It is wrong for a believer to accept any chieftaincy title; not only is it a demotion, it is also, an invitation to evil spirits and forming a covenant with them. **It is also a demotion to be called 'chief when the Bible says we are kings and princes.** Eating or offering sacrifices directly to idols or indirectly or symbolically, are the things that make people get involved in what they should not be involved in. If you are in such covenants, consciously or not, they will know if there is a door unconsciously, you will get out today in the name of Jesus.

Violent prayers.
(Violence is the language that the devil understands.)

Way Out Of Evil Covenants.
1. **Complete repentance**
You have to confess all sins and repent of them and ask the Lord to forgive you.

2. **Renounce every covenant step by step**

3. **Bind the Spirits attached to the covenant.**

4. **Command the Spirits to leave and then forbid them from returning.**

5. **Decree what you desire by aggressive faith.**

Many people inherited a lot of evil things from their parents that have put them in trouble. When parents are slack with their children and they allow them to smoke, keep bad company, stay out till late in the night or early hours of the morning; they are exposing them to demonic forces. When there is friction between parents during pregnancy or there is betrayal and denial or rejection, evil spirits will have a free access into the life of that child.

There are steps through which a person can be free. Many people need to go home and do a lot of work and research on their lives and that of their parents, to know what is open to the enemy in any way. Such doors must be closed. You should know for sure that, the enemy does not want you to locate such doors. He will keep you away from sitting down to think about it or finding a solution to it.

John said about Jesus; *"I indeed baptise you with water unto repentance: but He that cometh after me is mightier than I, Whose shoes I am not worthy to bear: He shall baptise you with the Holy Ghost and with fire. "* Mark 3:11

When you start calling the fire of God against any covenant, it will be roasted. If you know that you are the one in charge of your case, do not pray because, fire does not recognise the person that starts it. What you should just do is repent other wise, the fire will actually come and there will be trouble. If you fear the devil or you are having pity for him, then, you cannot break any covenant. Whatsoever will hinder you from praying the prayers I am suggesting below, or coax you to pray them gently, is your enemy and you must get rid of it. It will be very sad, for a person to come in close contact with the power of God and then allow Him to pass over his or her head. Concentrate and pray these prayers very seriously.

If you are reading this book and are the friend or child or spouse of the devil, you cannot break any covenant. If you are sorry for him, you cannot break any covenant that is binding you to him. The Psalmist says;*"When my enemies, even my foes came against me, to eat up my flesh and drink my blood, they stumbled and they fell. "*

If hitherto, you have not surrendered your life to the Lord Jesus Christ, I would advise that you do so right there where you are. He is there with you and is ready to set you free. All you need do is, acknowledge the fact that you cannot approach God in your sinful state. Confess your sins and repent of them. Name them one by one; ask Him to forgive you and cleanse you from all unrighteousness. Claim the redemptive power in the Blood of Jesus that was shed on the cross at Calvary, for the remission of your sins. Renounce the devil and all his works. Say bye-bye to sin and the world. Come into the marvelous light of the Lord Jesus.

Invite the Lord Jesus into your

life. Ask Him to become your personal Lord and Saviour. Enthrone Him over your life and hand over all that concerns you to Him. As from today, do not allow sin to have dominion over you again.

I congratulate you on this decision that you have just taken, it is the most important decision in life. I pray that it shall be permanent in your life in the name of Jesus. I pray that your name will be written in the Book of Life, in the name of Jesus.

Say this confession out loud.
Galatians 3:13-14
"Christ hath redeemed us from the curse of the law, being made a curse for us: for it is written, Cursed is every one that hangeth on a tree: That the blessing of Abraham might come on the Gentiles through Jesus Christ; that we might receive the promise of the Spirit through faith"

Col. 2:14-15
"Blotting out the handwriting of ordinances that was against us, which was contrary to us, and took it out of the way, nailing it to his cross; And having spoiled principalities and powers, he made a shew of them openly, triumphing over them in it.

PRAYER POINTS
1. I take back all the grounds given to satan by my ancestors, in the name of Jesus.
2. I curse you spirit enforcing evil covenants in my life and I command you to release me, in Jesus' name (when you have said this three times, begin to say 'Release me, in the name of Jesus'.
3. Let everything that has been transferred into my life by the demonic laying of hands, loose its hold right now, in the name of Jesus.
4. Let every serpentine poison, that has been passed into my life, get out now, in the name of Jesus.
5. Let the fire fall on every spirit of death and hell fashioned against my life, in the name of Jesus.
6. I break the head and crush the tail of every serpentine spirit, in the name of Jesus.
7. Let the spiritual bat and spiritual lizard, that have been introduced into my head, receive the fire of God, in the name of Jesus.
8. Let the sword of fire begin to cut off every evil parental attachment, in the mighty name of Jesus.
9. Father Lord, reveal to me any hidden covenant that the devil might have arranged against me, in the name of Jesus.
10. Every tree that the Father did not plant in my life, be uprooted, in the name of Jesus.
11. Father Lord, I electrify the ground of this place now, let every covenant with the feet begin to shattered now, in the name of Jesus.
12. Let every evil hidden covenant break, in the mighty name of Jesus.
13. I apply the blood of Jesus to break all consequences of parental sins.

Sing this song: "There is power mighty in the blood (2ce) of Jesus Christ. There is power mighty in the blood."

14. I apply the blood of Jesus to break all consequences of parental sins.
15. Lord, turn all the evil directed against me, to good, in the name of Jesus,
16. I command all powers, of evil directed against me to return, directly the sender, in the name of Jesus.
17. God, make everything the enemy has said is impossible in my life, possible, in the name of Jesus.
18. I release myself from any inherited bondage, in the name of Jesus.
19. Lord, send Your axe of fire to the foundation of my life and destroy every evil plantation.
20. Let the blood of Jesus., flush out from my system, every inherited satanic deposit in the name of Jesus.
21. I release myself from the grip of any problem, transferred into my life from the womb, in the name of Jesus.
22. Let the blood of Jesus, and the fire of the Holy Ghost cleanse every organ in my body, in the name of Jesus.
23. I break and loose myself

from every collective evil covenant, in the name of Jesus.
24. I break and loose myself from every collective curse, in the name of Jesus.

Take these prayer points with violence

25. Whatsoever is not of God in my life, come out and die! in the name of Jesus.
26. Every evil covenant, binding any part of my life, release, me and die! in the name of Jesus.
27. Every demon that has been summoned against me through curses, be roasted! in the name of Jesus.
28. Every demonic handwriting against my life, be cancelled! in the name of Jesus.
29. Every evil tenant in any department of my life, quit now! in the name of Jesus.
30. I terminate, every evil assignment fashioned against me from the headquarters of evil, in the name of Jesus.
31. I break the head of every serpentine spirit, dispatched against me, in the name of Jesus.
32. Every demonic transaction and contract against my life, be cancelled! in the name of Jesus.
33. I cancel every covenant of evil marriage upon my life, in the name of Jesus.
34. I cancel every covenant of late marriage upon my life, in the mighty name of Jesus.
35. Every unprofitable covenant upon my life, break! in the name of Jesus.
36. Every unprofitable covenant that has been binding me right from the womb, break! in the name of Jesus.
37. Lord, baptise me with Your fire, in the name of Jesus.
38. I vomit every evil consumption that I have been fed with as a child, in the name of Jesus.
39. I command all foundational strongman attached to my life to be paralysed, in the name of Jesus.
40. Let any rod of the wicked rising up against my family line be rendered impotent for my sake, in the name of Jesus.
41. I cancel the consequences of any evil local name attached to my person, in the name of Jesus.
42. I refuse to drink from the fountain of sorrow, in the name of Jesus.
43. I take authority over all the curses issued against my life, in the name of Jesus.
44. Ask God to remove any curse He has placed on your life as a result of disobedience.
45. I command any demon attached to any curse to depart from me now, in the mighty name of Jesus.
46. Let all curses issued against me be converted to blessings, in the name of Jesus.
47. You will now place blessing on yourself by saying There shall be no more poverty, sickness, etc. in my life in Jesus' name.
48. I release myself from the bondage of evil altars, in the name of Jesus.
49. I vomit every Satanic poison that I have swallowed, in the name of Jesus.
50. Every owner of evil loads, carry your load, in the name of Jesus, (if it is sickness or bad luck, let them carry it.)
51. I render every aggressive altar impotent, in the name of Jesus.
52. Every evil altar, erected against me, be disgraced, in Jesus' name.
53. Anything done against my life under demonic anointing be nullified, in the name of Jesus.
54. I curse every local altar fashioned against me, in the name of Jesus.
55. Let the hammer of the Almighty God smash every evil altar erected against me, in the name of Jesus.
56. Lord, send Your fire to destroy every evil altar fashioned against me, in

When The Enemy Is Too Strong

Psalm 18:17; *"He delivered me from my strong enemy, and from them which hated me: for they were too strong for me."*

This verse shows that it is possible to have an enemy that is strong and this is a terrible situation. That is, to face an enemy that is strong. When the Bible describes an enemy as being strong, it is referring to helpers. two powers as identified in:

Isaiah 49:24-26; *"Shall the prey be taken from the mighty, or the lawful captive delivered? But thus saith the Lord, Even the captives of the mighty shall be taken away, and the prey of the terrible shall be delivered: for I will contend with him that contendeth with thee, and I will save thy children. And I will feed them that oppress thee with their own flesh; and they shall be drunken with their own blood, as with sweet wine: and all flesh shall know that I the Lord am thy Saviour and thy Redeemer, the mighty One of Jacob."*

These two powers are:
1. The mighty and,
2. The terrible.

It is a terrible and dangerous thing to be in the custody of these two dangerous powers. No wonder the Psalmist prayed and praised God saying; *"He delivered me from my strong enemies which strong for me."*

'THE MIGHTY'

By 'The Mighty', the Bible means the forceful, the powerful and the enormous. They are strong forces that scare helpers.

Many years ago, I was invited to a place to pray and went with a brother. However, I did not know that he was afraid. When we got to the first room in that house, we found an idol with palm-oil all over it; the second room had a snake in it, with all sorts of things thrown at it on the floor. The third one had a live vulture in it. I then asked why the woman was living in such a house with those things. She said she inherited the house and found them there and did not know how to deal with them. That, that was why she came to the church to ask people to pray on the building. She said she could not abandon the house.

I assured her that we would pray to destroy those things and then, burn them to ashes. I then asked her to bring kerosene, matches and her anointing oil. All of a sudden, the brother that went with me started to speak in tongues and began to prophesy. He said "Thus says the Lord: "My servants, run out of this place you are not supposed to be here!" I was surprised but since he said it was the Lord speaking; I had to comply. Our camp was already divided and the enemy could take advantage of the situation. So, we had to leave

Later, the brother confessed that it was not the Lord but fear that gripped him and he develop a cold feet. What happened there? That is what I call the forces of the mighty.

They scare your potential helpers away. They also create terrible darkness that is difficult to penetrate.

Many years ago, a man said he needed help and consulted herbalists here and there, all to no avail. He then started to look for the high witch coven around. For three years, he sought to go to the highest witchcraft meeting in the land. Eventually, he was taken there and the witches told him that they could not help him because, the powers that were in charge of his case were too strong for them. They said those powers were the ones that normally gave them assignments. He then asked them to go to those powers and plead with them on his behalf. They laughed and asked him to get out of their coven. He said he was asked to walk out with his back. That man's enemies were strong.

The strong enemies are the powers that are contending with a person's angel of blessing. They contend with helper angels, just like the Prince of Persia that contented with the angel that was dispatched to answer the prayers of Daniel. They are not the small demons that anyone can just command to come out and they will obey. The strong and mighty are the forces that argue with deliverance ministers.

They all say that they will not get out. Sometimes, they say that their stay in the life of that person is not the business of the deliverance minister. They sometimes attack ministers or their family or property.

They are the senior serpents and scorpions, the Goliath-like and Pharaoh-like forces. They are forces that scare small prophets, scare even native doctors and high-level witchcraft. They are the aggressive strongmen.

THE TERRIBLE
They are powers that are fearful and formidable in nature. They ere extremely bad, frightful and horrible. Very violent lion-like enemies. I want you to understand that, if these forces are after you and you do not cry the correct cry, you will remain in bondage forever. They do not like to release their captives at all.
Isaiah 14:15-18;
"Yet thou shall be brought down to hell, to the sides of the pit. They that see thee shall narrowly look upon thee, and consider thee, saying, Is this the man that made the earth to tremble, that did shake kingdoms; that made the world as a wilderness, and destroyed the cities thereof; that opened not the house of his prisoners? All the kings of the nations, even all of them, lie in glory, every one in his own house."

A woman had seven children and each of them died at the age of thirteen. It was at the time that she was left with the last-born, that she came to MFM. Could you believe that the first person that made the attempt to pray for that boy, lost his voice instantly. Brethren had to rally round the person, to pray for him himself, for his voice to be restored.

The terrible powers are drinkers of blood and eaters of flesh; they are occultist powers, the spirit of death and hell and they are the spirits of the rock. That is why you will find out that, in places where there are rocks, there resides iron-like strongmen.

If you find out that, those who would normally have prayed for you are scared away, you need to cry out. If your former friends have become aggressive against you, or that you have life-threatening conditions, helpers come under attack, you have horrible dreams, regular accidents, you see dead relatives, ghosts, you notice a chain of bad luck, evil family patterns, it means you need to deal with these powers. Fortunately, the Bible says: *"The captives of the mighty shall be taken away and the preys of the terrible shall be delivered."*

HOW TO DEAL WITH STRONG ENEMIES:
1. Complete repentance is required.
2. Complete deliverance is also required.
3. You need to wage war against them.
4. You need to cry to heaven for help.
5. You must pray confrontational prayers

If you take these steps, you will see that, great things will begin to happen.

A brother noticed that he always had bad dreams. He would always see a woman harassing him in the dream. He had been born-again for many years and was an usher in his church. He told his Pastor but he did not respond. The harassment continued and he reported it to the Pastor again. To get rid of his pestering, the Pastor told him to go and shoot whoever was troubling him in his dream.
That night, he had another terrible dream and he got up to pray. He remembered what his Pastor told him and he began to say: "All you powers that are troubling me, I shoot you in the name of Jesus." He went on for about thirty minutes. After a while, he heard the footsteps of people going up and down the stairs. He opened his door and asked what was going on and he was told that his landlady was at the point of death. He rushed upstairs and he said he wanted to pray for the woman. To his utter amazement, the woman said; "what prayer? are you not the one that shot the bullet?" It was then that the brother understood what was going on. Are you ready to shoot prayer bullets at your strong enemy? Get ready to pray. However you cannot shoot any bullet and cannot be a victor, if you are still in the camp of the enemy. You must

be born-again and you can take that decision right there where you are right now. Jesus is waiting for you and He wants to set you free. All you need do, is acknowledge the fact that you are a sinner and that you cannot approach God in your sinful state.

Right there where you are, go to the Lord in prayer. Repent of your sins, confess them to Him, name them one by one and ask Him to forgive you and cleanse you from all unrighteousness. Claim the redemptive power in the Blood of Jesus that was shed on cross at Calvary, for remission of your sins.
Invite the Lord Jesus into your life; ask Him to become your personal Lord and Saviour. Surrender your totality to Him and ask Him to take control of your life and all that concerns you.

I congratulate you on this important decision that you have just taken. I pray that it shall be permanent in your life in the Name of Jesus. I pray that the Lord will uphold you and keep you from falling in the name of Jesus.

Take these prayer points with all the aggression that you can gather, so that, your stubborn, strong enemies will be disgraced and their efforts upon your life shall be wasted. Pray, so that they will not prosper in attacking your life.

1. Father Lord, create headaches for my stubborn, strong enemies, in the name of Jesus.
2. Let the efforts of my enemies be wasted, in the name of Jesus.
3. Every mountain, boasting against me, scatter! in the name of Jesus.
4. My days of affliction, expire now! in the name of Jesus.
5. Every power that must die, for my breakthroughs to manifest, die! in the name of Jesus.
6. The mighty and the terrible assigned against me, die! in the name of Jesus.
7. Every enemy that is too strong for me, die! in the name of Jesus.
8. Every power, that has formed a covenant to die instead of releasing me, die! in the name of Jesus.
9. Every owner of evil load, assigned against my destiny, carry your load! in the name of Jesus.
10. Anti-prosperity powers of my father's house, die! in the name of Jesus.
11. Anti-prosperity powers of my mother's house, die! in the name of Jesus.
12. Wealth of the Gentiles, be transferred into my hands! in the name of Jesus.
13. Every arrow of witch-craft, fired unto my destiny, die, in the name of Jesus.
14. Internal padlock, break, in the name of Jesus.
15. Every power, gathered to demote me, scatter, in Jesus' name.
16. Thunder, lightening, fire, locate my Pharoah. in Jesus' name.
17. Every stranger in the darkroom of my life, get out and die, in the name of Jesus.
18. Today, every witchcraft power gathered against me, fight it out in the name of Jesus.
19. Evil shall not locate my dwelling in the name Jesus.
20. I shall drink the milk and honey of this land.
21. Let every spirit of Goliath receive the stones of fire, in the name of Jesus.
22. Let every spirit of Pharoah fall into the Red Sea of their own making, in the name of Jesus.
23. Let all satanic manipulations aimed at changing my destiny be frustrated, in the name of Jesus.
24. Let all unprofitable broadcasters of my goodness be silenced, in the name of Jesus.
25. Let all leaking bags and pockets be sealed up, in the name of Jesus.
26. Let all monitoring eyes fashioned against me be blind, in the name of Jesus.
27. Let every effect of strange touches be removed from my life, in the name of Jesus.
28. 1 command every blessing confiscated by witchcraft spirits to be released, in the name of Jesus,
29. I command every blessing confiscated by ancestral spirits to be released, in the name of Jesus.
30. I command every blessing confiscated by envious enemies to be released, in the name of Jesus.
31. I command every blessings confiscated by

familiar spirit to be released, in the name of Jesus.

32. I command every blessing confiscated by satanic agent to be released, in the name of Jesus.

33. I command every blessing confiscated by rulers of darkness to be released, in the name of Jesus.

34. I command all the blessings confiscated by evil powers to be released, in the name of Jesus.

35. Let all drinkers of blood and eaters of flesh hunting for my life begin to stumble and fall, in the name of Jesus.

36. I command all the blessings confiscated by spiritual wickedness to be released, in the name of Jesus.

37. By fire, by thunder, by lightning, I possess my possessions, in the name of Jesus.

38. I command all demonic reverse gears installed to hinder my progress to be roasted, in the name of Jesus.

39. Any evil sleep undertaken to harm me, should be converted to death sleep, in the name of Jesus.

40. Let all weapons and devices of oppressors and tormentors, be rendered impotent, in the name of Jesus.

41. Let the fire of God, destroy the power operating any spiritual vehicle working against me, in the name of Jesus.

42. Let all evil advices given against my favour, crash and disintegrate, in the name of Jesus.

43. Let all eaters of flesh and drinkers of blood, stumble and fall, in the name of Jesus.

44. I command stubborn pursuers to pursue themselves, in the name of Jesus.

45. Let the wind, the sun and the moon, run contrary to every demonic presence in my environment, in the name of Jesus.

46. You devourers, vanish from my labour, in the name of Jesus.

47. Let every tree planted by fear in my life, dry up to the roots, in the name of Jesus.

48. I loose myself from any power of witchcraft and bewitchment, in the name of Jesus.

49. I bind every strongman over my family, in the mighty name of Jesus.

50. I bind the strongman over my business, in the mighty name of Jesus.

51. I bind the strongman over my blessings, in the name of Jesus.

52. I command the armour of the strongman to be roasted completely, in the mighty name of Jesus.

53. I command all curses issued against me to be smashed and broken, in the name of Jesus.

54. I separate my life from all evil idols present in my place of birth, in the mighty name of Jesus.

55. I separate myself from every evil streams present in my place of birth, in the name of Jesus.

56. I separate my life from all evil shrines present in my place of birth, in the name of Jesus.

57. Let all the agents banking my blessings and breakthroughs release them now, in the name of Jesus.

58. I cancel all enchantments, curses and spells that are against me, in the name of Jesus.

59. Let all iron-like curses break, in the name of Jesus.

60. Let divine tongue of fire roast any evil tongue against me, in the name of Jesus.

61. Let all pronouncements uttered against me by poisonous tongues, be nullified, in the name of Jesus.

62. I cut myself off, from every territorial spirit in the name of Jesus.

63. My Father! arise by Your fire, and pursue my pursuers, in Jesus' name.

64. Uncommon breakthroughs, manifest in my life, in the name of Jesus.

65. Let every power of the oppressors rise up against each other, in Jesus' name.

66. Let the joy of the enemy upon the progress of my life be turned to sorrow, in the name of Jesus.

67. Angels of breakthroughs, locate me, in the name of Jesus.

68. Every territorial spirit, in my life, die, in the name of Jesus.

69. I loose myself from every satanic bondage, in the name of Jesus.

70. Any power that wants to wage war against me as a result of these prayers, fall down and die, in the

When Your Battle Is From Home

Before we start this message, let us take these prayer points with holy aggression:
* **Thou that troubleth my Israel, my God shall trouble you today, in the name of Jesus.**
* **Anything that will make me remain empty handed, die! in the name of Jesus.**
* **Every 'Goliath' that troubleth my destiny, die! in the name of Jesus.**

STATEMENTS OF FACT:

If you are fighting an enemy whom nothing can pacify except your blood, then, you should be very careful not to give such an enemy the chance of getting at you. You should not give that kind of enemy any advantage at all. I want you to know that, the Bible refers to the enemy of our soul as the dragon; which represents malice and that makes him a malicious enemy. The Bible refers to him as a serpent; which represents deception. He is referred to as a scorpion; which signifies poison. He is also referred to as a lion; which represents strength, i.e he is powerful. Therefore, we have a malicious, deceptive, poisonous, strong enemy. If the enemy were not strong, the Bible would not have asked us to be strong in the Lord. The enemy has built factories in many families, which if not dismantled, will make people continue to struggle in vain.

I would like to re-narrate a proverb, which you might have read in one of our books and I would leave you to dissect it yourself. It goes thus; A man fell into a pit and could not get out of it. Whilst in the pit, he received twelve visitors.

1. Visitor number one: **Brother Sympathy** - he came and said; "I am sorry you fell into the pit" and he walked away.

2. Next came **Brother Logic** - he said it was logical that someone falls into the pit, since it was there.

3. Next **Brother Condemner** - who said it was because the man was a bad man, that he fell into the pit and that, that was the reward of his wickedness.

4. **Sister Mathematician** - she calculated the radius and circumference and depth of the pit and then walked away.

5. **Sister Journalist** - with her microphone, asked questions on how he fell into the pit and how he was feeling inside it and then walked away.

6. **Sister Self-Pity** - she told the man not to cry too much because the pit was not as big as another one.

7. **Brother Charismatic** - he said; "Shout Halleluiah! Brother, begin to confess that you are out in the name of Jesus" The man shouted halleluiah and chanted, "I am out in the name of Jesus!" He said it several times, but nothing happened.

8. **Brother Holiness** - he told the man that he was a sinner and that his sins made him fall into the pit.

9. **Brother Hope** - he encouraged him to stay there, that being out could even be a greater problem.

10. **Brother Faith** - he said the man fell into the pit for lack of faith.

11. **Sister Prophetess** - she told the man that the Lord said there would be mosquitoes that would trouble him in the pit.

12. Lastly, **Brother Prayer Warrior** - he prayed for him and passed down a rope for the man to grab and commanded him to come out of the pit in the name of Jesus, the man grabbed the rope and he pulled him out.

The church of God is like the Army, where there are different categories of soldiers. Some are drivers; who transport people and goods, some are doctors and nurses; they take care of the sick and the wounded, some are cooks; who prepare food, musicians; who blow the trumpet during the parade or in the mess, for relaxation. Some are Aide de Camps; who accompany their commandant, some are motor mechanics and so on. When there is war, it is a different category of soldiers that are deployed. These are the militant soldiers. This is the category that the Mountain of Fire and Miracles Ministries belong to, i.e the Army of God. We belong to the combatant arm of the army of the Lord. We do not blame those who are dancing or those who do not understand what we know. We just maintain our own position and carry out our duty as expected.

A woman went to farm and on her way back home, she found something on the ground which looked like a toy. She put it in her basket of yam hoping to give it to her children. She never got home because it was a grenade, which blew her head off. A soldier would not have touched it at all. Sometimes, when we see some Christians toying with dangerous weapons, we make them drop it. Some ladies grew up with two holes pierced into their ears as babies but they have added more, to take more earrings all in the name of fashion. Some will not desist from the use of hair attachment and ornament because, they do not understand the significance in the spirit realm. Some of them dress exactly like the queen of heaven. Many do not even understand the inscriptions on their jewelry.

There was a woman who was being prayed for and the Holy Spirit exposed the inscription on her pendant as being, a curse. She did not know the meaning. She bought it only because she thought it was beautiful. That is why there is a saying that: "Ignorance destroys." Ignorance can cause trouble. Your belief or disbelief of what you read in this message does not change its effect.

Spiritual warfare and the battles of life, can be fought at seven different levels:
1. Internal.
2. Family.
3. Place of origin.
4. Environmental.
5. Ground.
6. Waters.
7. Heavenlies.

The most serious battle is the one that comes from home. Many people come from backgrounds where their ancestors had raised evil altars, which are now speaking against them. The altars in your background are terrible and hazardous and it is a very serious issue. When Jacob was going back home after many years of sojourning in a foreign land, he stopped at a place and he slept off. He did not know that his grandfather Abraham, had been there too in his lifetime and had built an altar there unto the Lord. Jacob in his sleep had a dream wherein he saw angels going up and down. When Abraham was erecting the altar, he did not know that one day, his grandson would find himself weary from a long journey and sleep at that spot. If Abraham had been an occultist evil man and had erected an evil altar there, Jacob would not have seen angels. Instead, he would have seen the traffic of demons.

One day, a young man had a dream where his male organ was pulled by someone. He woke up and found out that the thing had disappeared. He was living in Europe and the first instinct was to go to the hospital. He found it difficult to convince the doctor that he was not born like that. The white-man said it was a genetic problem. He could not tell anyone. It bothered him for a long time and when he managed to voice it out, people avoided him like a pest. Later, he was taught how to pray fire prayers and as soon as he started praying there in Europe, his grandmother in Nigeria started to confess to witchcraft as she was about to die. She said the man should be summoned to come home to take his 'thing' from the garden. He came and she repeated it. He went to the garden and at the particular spot that she described, he found a male organ as if freshly cut with blood dripping from it. As soon as he brought it out, he felt his male organ come back to his body physically. It means there was an altar in that compound that was swallowing the members of that family

Take this prayer point with aggression:
* **Every family altar, in the**

yard where I was born or brought up, die! in the name of Jesus.

The existence of evil altars in a person's foundation is a very serious matter. Just as an altar is a meeting point for spirits, it is also a point for demonic traffic and an evil open door. I want you to know that, if you stubbornly address these altars, you will be amazed at what will happen. There is hardly any African family without an evil altar in the background. What we are struggling with today in our individual lives is the result of the altars that our forefathers erected. They know what they were doing, but most of us today do not know what we are doing. Our forefathers had so much demonic wisdom that in those days, if any pastor wanted land, they would give him their forbidden forests to build his church, with the hope of seeing his congregation tormented by demons and then, they will take over the people. That is why, many Orthodox churches remained the way they were in size and number for many decades. They had no fire, so very soon, the members got initiated into the lodge fraternity and other occult groups.

Judges 6:11-17; *"And there came an angel of the Lord, and sat under an oak which was in Ophrah, that pertained unto Joash the Abi-ezrite: and his son Gideon threshed wheat by the winepress, to hide it from the Midianites. And the angel of the Lord appeared unto him, and said unto him: "The Lord is with thee, thou mighty man of valour. And Gideon said unto him: "Oh my Lord, if the Lord be with us, why then is all this befallen us? And where be all His miracles, which our fathers told us of, saying: "Did not the Lord bring us up from Egypt? " But now the Lord hath forsaken us, and delivered us into the hands of the Midianites". And the Lord looked upon him, and said: "Go in this thy might, and thou shalt save Israel from the hand of the Midianites: have not I sent thee?" And he said unto him: "Oh my Lord, wherewith shall I save Israel? Behold, my family is poor in Manasseh, and l am the least in my father's house". And the Lord said unto him: "Surely I will be with thee, and thou shall smite the Midianites as one man. And he said unto him, If now I have found grace in thy sight, then shew me a sign that thou talkest with me*

Verses 25-26;
"And it came to pass the same night, that the Lord said unto him, Take thy father's young bullock, even the second bullock of seven years old, and throw down the altar of Baal that thy father hath, and cut down the grove that is by it: And build an altar unto the Lord thy God upon the top of this rock, in the ordered place, and take the second bullock, and offer a burnt sacrifice with the wood of the grove which thou shalt cut down."

The position of the Israelites had become so bad that, the Midianites would come to destroy their crops and food. Here was Gideon, stylishly and ticklishly threshing wheat by a wine press, so that, the Midianites would not know what he was doing. An angel came and addressed him as "a mighty man of valour." The angel addressed him according to the way his correct destiny was supposed to have been. Gideon had a very poor idea about himself; he said he came from a small, poor family. His background of idolatry did not allow him to have faith in God, so, he did not believe what the angel said and that made him ask the angel for a sign. He later saw that it was an angel of the Lord. Gideon was suffering, although he was a mighty man. He was powerless, until God came in. The altar of his father's house hindered him from fulfilling his destiny. It bound him and hindered God from identifying himself with him. God had to ask him to destroy it and build another one unto Him.

Beloved, until these altars are completely destroyed, many people will continue to retrogress and stagnate. That is why many people dream of seeing themselves in their old primary schools or former compounds etc. They see themselves going back. These are dreams of stagnation and retrogression. God saw the problems of Gideon but could not help because, there was an altar in his family which held him and his family captive. The altar sold everybody to satan, including Mr. Gideon.

Take these prayer points with aggression:
* I decree that, every altar

binding me to my father's compound or village should be broken, in the, name of Jesus.
* Every covenant, binding my destiny to the evil altars of my father's house, be broken! in the name of Jesus.
* Every evil connection between my placenta and any evil tree, be broken! In the name of Jesus.

Many people are not aware that some things in their lives have been locked up in witchcraft covens. For some, it is their career. For some, it is marriage or wealth or children. Most of the time, their own ancestors, parents or relatives took the things to these covens. This is one way that a person could be engaged in a battle without knowing it.

A family had five girls who got married one after the other. It happened that each of them got pregnant and never gave birth to any living child. They all had still-born births. The youngest of them got born-again and she began to pray specific fire prayers. The Lord revealed to her that her grandfather who was an occultist, had many slaves. One day, one of his slaves gave birth to a set of twins and he took the day-old babies and pounded them in a mortar, to make fetish concoctions. As they were being pounded, the slave was crying and issuing curses on the man and his descendants. She said that they would never have living children in that family again. It was during these prayers that the youngest of them addressed this issue and broke the curse. Take this prayer point with violence in your heart:
* *Every curse in my family-line, break by fire! in the name of Jesus.*

Matthew 15:22-28; *"And, behold, a woman of Canaan came out of the same coasts, and cried unto him, saying: "Have mercy on me, O Lord, thou Son of David; my daughter is grievously vexed with a devil". But He answered her not a word. And His disciples came and besought Him, saying: "Send her away; for she crieth after us". But He answered and said: "I am not sent but unto the lost sheep of the house of Israel". Then came she and worshipped him, saying: "Lord, help me". But He answered and said: "It is not meet to take the children's bread, and to cast it to dogs. And she said: "Truth, Lord: yet the dogs eat of the crumbs which fall from their masters table". Then Jesus answered and said unto her: "O woman, great is thy faith: be it unto thee even as thou wilt. And her daughter was made whole from that very hour."*

This woman cried to Jesus for help, but He did not answer her a word. Why? Although the Lord Jesus went about doing good, even to those who did not ask Him; like the man at the pool of Bethesda, yet He did not answer her. Even the disciples wanted to drive her away. It was because, she belonged to a tribe that had been cursed by Noah their forefather.

Genesis 9:22-27; *"And Ham, the father of Canaan, saw the nakedness of his father, and told his two brethren without. And Shem and Japheth took a garment, and laid it upon both their shoulders, and went backward, and covered the nakedness of their father; and their faces were backward, and they saw not their father's nakedness. And Noah awoke from his wine, and knew what his younger son had done unto him. And he said: "Cursed be Canaan; a servant of servants shall he be unto his brethren ". And he said: "Blessed be the Lord God of Shem; and Canaan shall be his servant. God shall enlarge Japheth, and he shall dwell in the tents of Shem; and Canaan shall be his servant."*

Deuteronomy 7:19-20; *"The great temptations which thine eyes saw, and the signs, and the wonders, and the mighty hand, and the stretched out arm, whereby the Lord thy God brought thee out: so shall the Lord thy God do unto all the people of whom thou art afraid. Moreover the Lord thy God will send the hornet among them, until they that are left, and hide themselves from thee, be destroyed,"*

Deuteronomy 29:18-22; *"Lest there should be among you man, or woman, or family, or tribe, whose heart turneth away this day from the Lord our God, to go and serve the gods of these nations; lest there should be among you a root that beareth gall and wormwood; And it come to pass, when he heareth the words of this curse, that he bless himself in his heart, saying, I shall have peace, though I walk in the imagination of mine heart, to add drunkenness to thirst: The Lord will not spare him, but then the anger of the Lord and his jealousy shall smoke against that man, and all the curses that are written in this book shall lie upon him, and the Lord shall blot out his name from under heaven. And the Lord shall separate him unto evil out of all the tribes of Israel, according to all the curses of the covenant that are written in this book of the law: So that the generation to come of your children that shall rise up after you, and the stranger that shall come from a far land, shall say, when they see the plagues of that land, and the sicknesses which the Lord hath laid upon it."*

Deuteronomy 29:24-27; *"Even all nations shall say: "Wherefore hath the Lord done thus unto this land? What meaneth the heat of this great anger? " Then men shall say: "Because they have forsaken the covenant of the Lord God of their fathers, which He made with them when He brought them forth out of the land of Egypt: For they went and served other gods, and worshipped them, gods whom they knew not, and whom He had not given unto them: And the anger of the Lord was kindled against this land, to bring upon it all the curses that are written in this book,"*

These curses on Canaan made them become dogs in the spirit realm. God could not relate with them and they could not receive the baptism in the Holy Ghost. They could not become ministers and could not enter into the holy place. All because, thousands of years before Jesus came, there was a curse on them. The woman that went to meet Jesus was affected by this. Thank God for the faith of that woman and the holy madness that she exhibited by continually screaming and shouting for help, until the Lord answered.

I want you to know that the altar in your background must be broken. The altar in the background of many people is anger. When everything is going on well, someone will get angry and rain curses which will send him or her back to square one. Anger has demolished many colourful destinies. You might have to go back to your mother's womb and disconnect yourself from the genes of anger. There is power in the Blood of Jesus to deliver you from every foundational altar. There is power to save you from every oppression of the enemy.

A lady had a special spirit husband who would mess her up and leave money under her pillow. She did not know what it meant. She only saw her self having sex with someone in the dream and she was never short of money. Thank God she was introduced to M.F.M and as deliverance prayers were going on, she screamed that, the ring on her finger was becoming hot. She was able to pull it off and she explained that, that was the only thing that she inherited from her grandmother. That was a covenant wedding ring with the spirit husband without her knowing it. It was an evil foundation which had to be broken to pieces.

Many people have to go back to the time that they were a foetus in their mothers' womb, and cut off their problem from that evil root. If your battle is from home, there are many things that you will notice:

1. **Internal Burial** - The person would be buried spiritually and all the good ideas that he or she has will not materialise. They could make more money than those in vigour now, but they will not come to fulfillment. You need to pray hard against that today.

2. **Frustration Syndrome.**

3. **Scape-Goat Syndrome** Always being blamed for what the person did not do. Would always be a candidate for misfired aggression.

4. **Displacement Syndrome** - Satanic substitution which allows children of darkness to be promoted but the person would be left floating.

5. **Destiny Reversal** - Being directly opposite of God's original intention for the person.

6. **Resistance Syndrome..**

7. **Evil Transfer** - Something good, that is meant

for the first born, would be given to the younger ones; the firstborn becomes poor and other siblings in the family become rich. It could be so bad for some people to the extent that, even poor people will refer to them as being poor.

8. **Personality or Character Disorder -** Such people could be very talented, but their character comes in to spoil what they are doing.

9. **Evil Spiritual Pressure-** The person does abominable things.

10. **Blockage or Dead-End Syndrome-** There would be blockage from progress.

11. **Attack of the Emptiers.**

12. **Overload-** A small person will bear many burdens and will not be able to enjoy himself or herself. Others go and put themselves into trouble and put the load on the person.

13. **Paralysis of Progress, Prosperity etc.**

14. **Stubborn Pursuers.**

15. **Harassment from Spirit of Death.**

WHAT TO DO:
i. **Break down every evil altar in your foundation.**

ii. **Repent from all known sins.**

iii. **Build an altar unto the Lord through prayers.**

A girl was asked to run to the market to buy crayfish. As she was coming back, she was confronted by a masquerade. So she ran to take refuge on a rock. The masquerade came closer to her and was about to whip her with his cane when she commanded his hand to hang in the air, in the name of Jesus. To the surprise of everyone, the masquerade could not bring down his hand. There was confusion and people were wondering what kind of girl she was, to have spoken to such a powerful masquerade. Meanwhile, she got down from the rock and went home to deliver the crayfish to her mother. She narrated what happened to her mother but she thought it was a child's play. The mother continued cooking and after about thirty minutes, the girl insisted that her story was true. Reluctantly, the mother followed her to the scene. As the girl was approaching, some of the on-lookers ran away. She jumped on the rock and looked at the masquerade. With her arms akimbo, she commanded him in the name of Jesus, to put down his hand and he did. That is the kind of power that you and I should and can exhibit. The altars in the foundation of Gideon, terribly affected his destiny. He was a mighty man of valour, but unfortunately, he could not move forward. The altar in his father's compound was speaking against him.

Beloved, there could be an altar in your family compound now, speaking against your marriage and you do not know. There could be an altar in your family compound that is screaming into your ears, that you will fail, that none succeeds in your family. It is time for you to speak against such altars and command them to be silent, that even if others are failing, you will succeed.

Right now, I want you to take a look at your family line, see if there is any altar erected there. Confess the sins of your ancestors to God and ask Him to forgive you their sins and abominations, because of the sacrifice that Jesus made of Himself on the cross at Calvary. Hand over your own life to Him and ask - Him to become your personal Lord and Saviour.

The prayers I am suggesting below, are going to cause chaos and confusion in the kingdom of darkness. If you want powerful and distinct breakthroughs, I want you to pray violently. They will provoke the power of God to move forth and sicknesses will disappear and destinies will change.

1. Evil altars of my father's house, die! in the name of Jesus.
2. Evil altars of my mother's house, die! in the name of Jesus.
3. Every altar, speaking against my career, shut up and die! in the name of Jesus.
4. Every altar, speaking against my marriage, shut up and die! in the name of Jesus.
5. Every altar, speaking against my business, shut up and die! in the

6. Every altar, speaking against my prosperity, shut up and die! in the name of Jesus.
7. Every grave-cloth in my family line, roast! in the name of Jesus.
8. Every altar, hiding the keys of my promotion, release it and die! in the name of Jesus.
9. Every altar, hiding the keys of my marriage, release it and die! in the name of Jesus.
10. Every altar, hiding the keys of my business, release it and die! in the name of Jesus.
11. Every altar, hiding the keys of my prosperity, release it and die! in the name of Jesus.
12. Every altar, hiding the keys of my health, release it and die! in the name of Jesus.
13. Every power, sitting on my breakthroughs, be unseated! in the name of Jesus.
14. Ancestral witchcraft embargo upon my life, break! In the name of Jesus.
15. Failure magnets in my life, die! in the name of Jesus.
16. Power of unprofitable struggling, die! in the name of Jesus.
17. Every power, collecting satanic power against me, die! in the name of Jesus.

Begin to thank the Lord answers to your prayers.

Holy Rebellion

1 Samuel 17:38-40; *"And Saul armed David with his armour, and he put an helmet of brass upon his head; also he armed him with a coat of mail. And David girded his sword upon his armour, and he assayed to go; for he had not proved it. And David said unto Saul: "I cannot go with these; for I have not proved them". And David put them off him. And he took his staff in his hand, and chose him five smooth stones out of the brook and put them in a shepherd's bag which he had, even in a scrip; and his sling was in his hand; and he drew near to the Philistine."*

The Philistine forces: As we had boasting Philistines in the time of David, so also we have modern-day Philistines now. They are the forces threatening the people of God, harassing them and vowing to cause tragedies in their lives. They do not hide their evil intentions, they say it openly just as Goliath was an open enemy.

Hear him in 1 Samuel 17:10-11; *"And the Philistine said: "I defy the armies of Israel this day; give me a man, that we may fight together." When Saul and all Israel heard those words of the Philistine, they were dismayed, and greatly afraid."*

1 Samuel! 7:41-46: *"And the Philistine came on and drew near unto David; and the man that bare the shield went before him. And when the Philistine looked about, and saw David, he disdained him: for he was but a youth, and ruddy, and of a fair countenance. And the 'Philistine said unto David: "Am I a dog, that thou comest to me with staves?" And the Philistine cursed David by his gods. And the Philistine said to David: "Come to me, and I will give thy flesh unto the fowls of the air, and to the beasts of the field". Then said David to the Philistine: "Thou comest to me with a sword, and with a spear, and with a shield: but I come to thee in the Name of the Lord of hosts, the God of the armies of Israel, whom thou hast defied. This day will the Lord deliver thee into mine hand; and I will smite thee, and take thine head from thee; and I will give the carcasses of the host of the Philistines this day unto the fowls of the air, and to the wild beasts of the earth; that all the earth may know that there is a God in Israel."*

What David did at the battlefront is what could be called 'Holy Rebellion.' After all, his real mission to the war front was to deliver food to his elder brothers. But when he got there and saw someone boasting and threatening the Israelites, he began to ask questions: "Who is this man threatening the armies of the living God?" He carried out a holy rebellion and what happened? Goliath fell. The man had a big head and a big sword too. David therefore took the sword of Goliath and with it, cut off the head of Goliath. This means that, the weapon that the enemies have fashioned against you shall he used against them, in the name of Jesus.

Difficult circumstances are a fact of life and there is no human being that can ever be useful without passing through some obstacles. Jesus Himself had to pass through the cross to receive glory and honour. The Bible says that He was despised, forsaken and counted unworthy to live. He was a man of sorrow and acquainted with grief. His face was not an object that anyone would like to look at because it was badly spoilt. They plucked off His beards. He passed through agony while on His way to receiving glory and honour. Inquire from anointed men of God and talk to people who have achieved something for God. They will tell you stories of what they had to pass through.

Some years ago, a relative of mine brought a girl who had just arrived from the village to my house to help in the household chores. The first night, she talked throughout in her sleep. I got angry in my spirit that day but I had to keep quiet as a matter of courtesy since that was her first night. The following morning, I confronted her and told her that if she dared have any conversation in her sleep again, both herself and her invisible partners would be imprisoned and caged. Behold, that particular night she did not make a single sound while she slept. By the following morning, she carried her things and left, my warning destabilised her.

The Apostles of old had cause to report some people to God. They said, "O Lord, behold their threatening." Many of us reading this message have been threatened in the past while some are now living under the threat of their enemies. What a big insult to the children of the living God to be living under such a condition. Therefore, I want you to get angry in your spirit and fire these arrows before you read further.

* I destabilise every witch or wizard, warring against my life, in the name of Jesus.
* Let every serpent dispatched against me, begin to bite itself, in the name of Jesus.
* Every enemy of my breakthrough, become blind! in the name of Jesus.

I am always amazed at the story of Elisha. Here was a man who followed Elijah and they worked together for some time. The first thing that would surprise a careful student of the Bible is the fact that, there were many students in the school of the prophets, how come at the crucial stage of Elijah's ministry, the only person he could see was Elisha? There must have been something special about him. He followed his master to the end. When they passed through Gilgal, Elijah asked him to wait there for him but he said, "No, as the Lord lives, where you go, I will go. I am not waiting." As they got to Bethel, Elijah again asked him to wait but he refused; and on getting to Jericho, when Elijah saw that Elisha was going to carry out a holy rebellion and was not going to let him go, he asked what he wanted from him.

If Elisha had turned back at Gilgal, there would have been no opportunity for Elijah to ask him that question. You may say that he was stubborn but he knew what he was looking for. When eventually he told his master that he wanted a double-portion of his anointing, his master said, *"You have asked for a hard thing. However, if you are able to see me when I am being taken away, it shall be so; otherwise, the request cannot be met" Elisha's final examination was to be able to see Elijah on the heavenly chariot physically, and he saw him. I am convinced in my spirit that prior to that day, Elisha must have fasted and prayed for days because he had not wanted to miss that golden opportunity. He had holy rebellion inside his blood. When the chariot came, he saw it and screamed,* *"My father, my father, the chariot of Israel and the horsemen thereof."* He took a further step of rebellion by not sitting and watching the chariot; rather he held on to his master and got his garment. That is a typical example of holy rebellion.

If you are a minister with a compassionate heart, sometimes you find out that people are going through unbearable things. When you hear or see the agonies some people are passing through, you will thank God for your own situation. Many often would soak 'gari' (cassava meal) in water and drink it with some groundnuts and they would not have health problems, yet they will complain of being poor. But there are thousands of people who dare not put one spoon of gari in their mouth, because if they do, they will land in an hospital.

Beloved, many people have serious problems. What do you make of that man whose wife asked for money for soup and he said he did not have. The next thing the woman did was to take a whip and beat him twice. From that day, he lost his mind and started dancing in the streets. People who did not know the genesis of the problem would not know what he was passing through. There are problems but Psalm 34:19 says: *"Many are the afflictions of the righteous: but the Lord delivereth him out of them all."* This verse does not say few are the afflictions but many, yet the Lord delivers him out of them all.

Verse 20 *says:* "*He keepeth all his bones; not one of them is broken.*" In essence, the Bible is reawakening that consciousness in us again that, there would be opposition and obstacles but at the same time there would be deliverance for God's children. It does not matter how long the problem has been in existence or what medical doctors have diagnosed.

I read an article in an international magazine that, scientists have discovered that prayer is a form of medicine. A medical doctor who had one particular patient in the ward with his two lungs already eaten up by cancer said that, from all indications and as far as his knowledge of science could go, that patient was not supposed to live for more than two weeks but he noticed that everyday, his church members gathered around him to sing and pray. In his anger, he had suggested to them to start practicing songs for his funeral, instead of wasting their time praying. He said that surprisingly, the man did not die and the way he got out of that sickness beats his medical knowledge.

One year later, the man paid him a visit. That made him to decide to carry out a research on prayer as medicine. He did the work in a hospital where about 300 patients were on admission. The names of some of them were listed without mentioning their ailments and some were passed to a church for prayers. They picked them at random. After six months, they checked the records and found out that about 80% of those they prayed for, survived; while only 25% of those that were never prayed for, survived. When the man found out that more people recovered on the prayer list, he was convinced about the power of prayer.

Some people cry everyday because of their problems. They forget that many are the afflictions of the righteous but the Lord delivers him from them all. The only person who can prevent you from being delivered from them all is not the devil, neither is it your pastor, nor your enemies, but you yourself. **So, whatever circumstance you are facing, the way you respond to it will determine whether you will be delivered or not. If you decide to respond by exercising holy rebellion, you will get out of it. It may not come quite easily but you will get out.** The circumstances or whatever you face can either make you a better person or a very bitter person. It can either make you or break you. Nothing can break those who exercise holy rebellion. What the devil wants people to be doing is to be crying everyday while his demons dance to the music to their crying and weeping.

Psalms 92:12 says: "*The righteous shall flourish like the palm tree: he shall grow like a cedar in Lebanon.*"

What does this mean? We shall be able to understand this question by taking a closer look at the life of a palm tree.

In the Bible, the palm tree is a symbol of victory. Let us, see Revelation 7:9 "*After this, I beheld, and lo, a great multitude, which no man could number of all nations, and kindreds, and people and tongues; stood before the throne, and before the lamb, clothed with white robes, and palms in their hands.*"

Also John 12:12-13; *On the next day, much people that were come to feast, when they heard that Jesus was coming to Jerusalem took branches of palm trees, and went forth to meet him, and cried Hosanna; Blessed is the King of Israel that cometh in the name of the Lord.*"

That was a day of victory, The Palm Tree: Scientists tell us that it has a lot of uses. For example, the fruit is the daily food for millions. What people call palm-wine is from the palm tree. Fresh palm-wine that is dropping from the palm tree is not intoxicating. It becomes intoxicating when it is stored and fermented. It is those that want to destroy themselves that store it to turn it into a chemical. It is the same thing with all of God's creation. Human beings are the ones who turn a useful thing into something harmful. The seed from the palm tree is used to produce animal feed for so many animals. Those who went to traditional schools know that ropes can be made from the palm; leaf called raffia. Part of it is also used to make brooms. The trunk is a valuable wood. Palm oil, palm kernel and palm kernel oil; coconut and coconut oil come from the palm tree. The wonderful thing about the tree is that although it stands with its feet inside undrinkable waters and with its head in the sun, yet men can drink the sweetest juice from it, eat sweet coconut from it and get some other useful products from it. Therefore, the palm tree through its inner life, can change the elements in the bad soil so that, it can minister growth and strength to it and it will bear fruit.

The righteous is likened to it. It means that although you and I have our feet or root in various unfavourable environments and situations, or come from families of cannibals or from places where anybody who builds a house dies or we come from an environment of bitterness and discouragement, the Bible says we are like the palm tree. In spite of all odds, we should grow and grow strong. We should reject the evil and assimilate the good. Many modern-day Christians are suffering from spiritual diabetes; too much sugar. They prefer the couch to the cross. They want to see the ladder descend from heaven like it did for Jacob, but they are not interested in putting their heads on the pillow of stone. They want to put their heads on nice foam pillows and they want the ladder of heaven to come down.

So, when they have a problem or encounter an obstacle, they make a big show of it. A lot of parents have pampered their children unto failure because they don't understand that, that which makes a person great, is that which hinders him.

Psalm 66:9-12;
'Which holdeth our soul in life, and suffereth not our feet to be moved. For thou, O God, hast proved us: thou hast tried us, as silver is tried. Thou broughtest us into the net; thou laidst affliction upon our loins. Thou hast caused men to ride over our heads; we went through fire and through water: but thou broughtest us out into a wealthy place."

We have to pass through all these rough roads that the Bible has mentioned before God can put us in a wealthy place. Before anyone can become anything in life, one way or the other, he or she must have been kicked around, discouraged and oppressed. There is no easy way to winning a crown. **Some people say that they want to grow and become powerful but when they are tried, they fail. God tries you with one problem or the other to see how you stand. If He discovers that you fail or you are unable to withstand the stress of the test, He may withhold the power. Therefore, the land of opposition is the land of opportunity. The food of victory is unfavourable circumstances. So, all the problems you think you are facing now should be seen as an opportunity to grow into maturity. They should be seen as an opportunity for you to advertise God's power in your life.**

We have a deliverer who is monitoring our lives and He will not test you beyond what you can bear. The world as it stands, is managed by God the greatest designer. He is the great Lord of lords. If you believe that this God is your Father, then you are stronger than any terrible circumstance and obstacle. When you face an obstacle, your purpose as somebody who is reigning like a king, should be to make the obstacle your servant. Don't make your obstacle your master for too long. Unbelief makes many people to be slaves to their obstacles and problems. Always believe that you are the master of your problem. As you grow older in the faith, are you becoming better or are you allowing the enemy to blackmail you?

There was the story of Ayo and Ojo who were in the boarding school. They were put in care of a teacher. In those days, when a student was put in care of a teacher, he or she was in trouble because as far as the teacher was concerned, anything short of first position would not do. Ayo and Ojo were supposed to look after the ducks owned by the teacher. One day, Ayo mistakenly killed a duck. He decided to eat the duck, as a way of hiding the mistake. His morning work was to sweep the sitting room, clean the kitchen, wash the plates, warm the soup and dress his master's children for school before he himself would get ready for school. The work of Ojo was to make sure that the grass around the house was cut and the flowers were all watered. The first day after Ayo ate the duck, he woke up at 6a.m. and woke Ojo up too but Ojo told him that he would wake up by 7a.m. and that Ayo should make sure he helped him with his morning work if not, he would tell their master that he had killed a duck.

From then on, Ojo did nothing in the house. Ayo was doing all the work and was growing lean. Sometimes, when they were served their meals, Ojo would eat all the meat. When the teacher noticed that Ayo was getting lean, he asked him what the problem was. Ayo denied having any problem but one day, he could no longer bear it so he went to confess to his master and asked for forgiveness. The master asked him how long ago it was he killed the duck and he said, "nine months ago." The master said, "Don't worry. I have forgiven you." So, Ayo slept happily for the first time in nine months. The following morning, Ojo, who did not know that Ayo had sorted himself out, woke him up as usual and said, "Have you forgotten that you killed a duck?" Ayo told him to go ahead and report because he was no longer afraid, having confessed his sins. This is how problem blackmails many people. It just dictates to them how to live their lives. Until you carry out a spiritual rebellion against an obstacle, it will continue to blackmail and harass you.

There is also negative rebellion. One day in my school, some of my classmates decided to stage a coup against a student-teacher. My protests did not count as I was voted out. In those days, when student-teachers went for teaching practice, their inspectors sometimes stood by the window to observe how they went about their work. The observer this time was a white man. These mischievous students got ready for the student-teacher. They were following the lesson and co-operating with the teacher until the white man turned up and they carried out their plan. The teacher said, "Boys, my boss is by the door, stand up and greet him." None of them stood up. He asked, "Are you deaf?" One of them said: "Your father is deaf." He felt insulted and took a whip and said. "Stand up all of you." The first boy he tried to beat took the whip from him, cut it to pieces and ran away. The rest ran out to call the principal. Before the principal came, they had started to sing: "We don't want him, he should go. All we are saying, he must go." That is what we call demonic rebellion. We are not talking about this type of rebellion but one targeted at satanic works.

When you are constantly getting worried about a particular problem, it shows that you are the servant of the problem not its master. If you are feeling that the situation will never come to an end, then you become the servant of the problem. If the problem becomes your major pre-occupation and is ordering you around like a military officer, it has become the master. If it takes away your happiness then it has become the master. If you are ready to try ungodly things, the problem has become your master. Some people go to church; for prayers and when the desired solution does not come as envisaged, they backslide. The truth is that the problem has become their master and they the servants. When a problem is allowed to dominate the mind, it will paralyse one's prayer life and make the person an obedient servant, for it will then start dictating all sorts of commands to the person.

You have to carry out a spiritual coup today and overthrow the king in charge of the problem by disagreeing with any obstacle you have been agreeing with.

THE WAY OUT:
1. Rebel against the obstacle with the word of God and prayer.

Decide that it is not going to push you around any longer; instead, you will be pushing it all over. One thing some people don't know about the devil is how to resist him. The Bible says, ***"Resist the devil and he shall flee from you."*** You will not recognise that the devil is a coward until you resist him and you will be amazed at seeing him run away.

2. Take your mind completely off the problem. Kick the thought of it out of your mind anytime it tries to

comeback. Replace it with the thoughts of the Scriptures.

3. Treat the obstacle like a dog without teeth. Do this by telling it that the Lord has defeated it on the cross. Tell it that He that is in you, is greater than he that is in it.

4. Rejoice in the Lord always. Do not let any moment of sadness cross your spirit. Encourage yourself with Psalms and hymns.

5. Fill your spirit with the word of God. God can never lie and as such - His words can never lie too. Learn to meditate upon the word of God, personalizing them to your situation. This is how you can turn the obstacle to your servant now!

6. Avoid faithless people who talk failure and discouragement. Avoid them because they will drag you further down.

7. Rebel aggressively against the problem, putting your faith into full use.

8. Make positive confessions everyday.

Faith without works is dead. So, you must put your faith to work. Faith says I am going to fight this battle and I will return. Faith also says, it is well. So, when you really have faith, you would have won the fight before starting. David killed Goliath before he slew him. How did he do that? He said to him, "You come against me in the name of your gods but I come against you in name of God of hosts. He exercised his faith.

So, I ask you a question: Are you reigning in life as a king according to Romans 5:17 which says *"For if by one man's offence death feigned by one, much more they which receive abundance of grace and of the gift of righteousness shall reign in fife by one, Jesus Christ."* Or have you allowed your life to be fully overtaken by problems? Wake up and challenge the problem. Say no to its continual existence in your life and carry out a holy rebellion. You will succeed, in the name of Jesus.

However, if hitherto you have not surrendered your life to the Lord Jesus Christ, I would advise that you do so right there where you are. The Lord is there with you and is ready to take you into His household. All you need to do is, acknowledge the fact that you are a sinner and that you cannot approach God in your sinful state. Confess your sins to Him; name them one by one and ask Him to forgive you and cleanse you from all unrighteousness. Say bye-bye to the devil and the world.

Invite the Lord Jesus into your life; ask Him to become your personal Lord and Saviour. Enthrone Him over your life and hand over your totality to Him.

I congratulate you on this decision that you have just taken; it is the most important decision in life. I pray that it shall be permanent in your life, in the name of Jesus. I pray that the Lord will uphold you with His right hand of righteousness and will not let you fall. I pray that your name will be written in the Book of Life and you will not by any means, rub it off in the name of Jesus.

Take these prayer points with all the aggression that you can gather. Make sure that your prayer stones, locate the unprotected fore-head of the 'Goliath' that has been harassing your life:

1. I challenge all obstacles before me and command them to be dismantled, in the name of Jesus.

2. All unprofitable trees, growing in my life, be uprooted by fire, in the name of Jesus.

3. I breathe in the healing power of God. (When you say it three times you take a deep breath into your system. Do it in faith and as you are breathing out. infirmities will go back to the sender, in the name of Jesus.

4. I reject every spirit of error, in the name of Jesus.

5. I refuse to fail in every area of my life, in the name of Jesus.

6. Begin to praise the name of the Lord for the miracle He has done in your life.

The Wind Of The Holy Spirit

Genesis 1:1-2; *"In the beginning God created the heaven and the earth. And the earth was without form, and void; and darkness was upon the face of the deep. And the Spirit of God moved upon the face of the waters. And God said, Let there be light: and there was light."*

In the beginning, the earth was shapeless; had no direction and was empty. That is also the state of the lives of many people today. There was darkness upon the deep. So also, the lives of many people are being caged by darkness; the power of darkness has put them into bondage. The Spirit of God later moved and it was after that move, that God commanded light into being and there was light.

The text above is an introduction to the Holy Spirit. It means that, right from the word 'Go' in the Bible, the Holy Spirit had been introduced. Also, the Trinity was introduced. Also, introduced. God created the Spirit moved and the 'Word' was manifested. God said; "Let there be light" and there was light. Wherever you see one, you will see the other entities of the Trinity.

Ezekiel 37:1-10.; *"The hand of the Lord was upon me, and carried me out in the spirit of the Lord, and set me down in the midst of the valley which was full of bones and caused me to pass by them roundabout: and, behold, there were very many in the open valley; and, lo, they were very dry. And he said unto me: "Son of man, can these bones live?" And I answered: "O Lord God, thou knowest". Again He said unto me: "Prophesy upon these bones, and say unto them: "O ye dry bones, hear the word of the Lord: Thus saith the Lord God unto these bones" "Behold, I will cause breath to enter into you, and ye shall live: And I will lay sinews upon you, and will bring up flesh upon you, and cover you with skin, and put breath in you, and ye shall live; and ye shall know that I am the Lord".*

So, I prophesied as I was commanded: and as I prophesied, there was a noise, and behold a shaking, and the bones came together, bone to his bone. And when I beheld, lo, the sinews and the flesh came up upon them, and the skin covered them above: but there was no breath in them. Then said He unto me: "Prophesy unto the wind, prophesy, son of man, and say to the wind: Thus saith the Lord God; Come from the four winds, O breath, and breathe upon these slain, that they may live". So I prophesied as He commanded me, and the breath came into them, and they lived, and stood up upon their feet, an exceeding great army.

The breath of the Holy Spirit came upon the dry bones and they came back to life. The Holy Spirit is a subject that many people do not understand. The Holy Spirit is a Personality; a Person to be experienced. The greatest thing that can happen to you in life is, for the power of the Holy Spirit to descend upon you. Whenever the Holy Spirit is given a free access to move in, poverty disappears. The earth was in a form of poverty, until the Spirit moved in. Once the seat of spiritual poverty is destroyed, the physical one disappears quickly.

The Earth was in a state of wasteful poverty, until the Spirit of God moved in. There are many people today, who need the move of the Holy Spirit in their lives. When the wind of the Holy Spirit blew into the city of Samaria, the Bible says there was much joy in that city because, wherever the wind of the Holy Spirit blows, He brings abundance, multiplication, food, water, healing, as a result of that flow. That is why Jesus says in John 3:6-8; *"That which is born of the flesh is flesh; and that which is born of the Spirit is spirit. Marvel not that I said unto thee, Ye must be born again. The wind bloweth where it listeth, and thou hearest the sound thereof, but canst not tell whence it cometh, and whither it goeth: so is every one that is born of the Spirit."*

Anywhere in the Bible where the Holy Spirit is mentioned, you will notice that there is or was a problem there. Let us now see a few examples in the Scripture of the move of the Holy Spirit in the lives of God's people and how these problems were solved and they in turn did great exploits for the Lord.

Judges 3:7-10;
"And the children of Israel did evil in the sight of the Lord, and forgot the Lord their God, and served Baalim and the groves. Therefore the anger of the Lord was hot against Israel, and he sold them into the hand of Chushan-rishathaim king of Mesopotamia: and the children of Israel served Chushan-rishathaim eight years. And when the children of Israel cried unto the Lord, the Lord raised up a deliverer to the children of Israel, who delivered them, even Othniel the son of Kenaz, Caleb's younger brother. And the Spirit of the Lord came upon him, and he judged Israel, and went out to war: and the Lord delivered Chushan-rishathaim king of Mesopotamia into his hand; and his hand prevailed asainst Chushan-rishathaim."

Judges 6:33-34;
"Then all the Midianites and the Amalekites and the children of the east were gathered together, and went over, and pitched in the valley of Jezreel But the Spirit of the Lord came upon Gideon, and he blew a trumpet; and Abiezer was gathered after him".

Judges 7:24-25;
And Gideon sent messengers throughout all mount Ephraim, saying, Come down against the Midianites, and take before them the waters unto Beth-barah and Jordan. Then all the men of Ephraim gathered themselves together, and took the waters unto Beth-barah and Jordan. Andthey took two princes of the Midianites, Oreb and Zeeb; and they slew Oreb upon the rock Oreb, andZeeb they slew at the winepress of Zeeb, and pursued Midian, and brought the heads of Oreb and Zeeb to Gideon on the other side Jordan."

Judges 11:28-29;
"Howbeit the king of the children of Ammon hearkened not unto the words of Jephthah which he sent him. Then the Spirit of the Lord came upon Jephthah, and he passed over Gilead, and Manasseh, and passed over Mizpeh of Gilead, and from Mizpeh of Gilead he passed over unto the children of Ammon".

Verses 32-33;
So Jephthah passed over unto the children of Ammon to fight against them; and the Lord delivered them into his hands. And he smote them from Aroer, even till thou come to Minnith, even twenty cities, and unto the plain of the vineyards, with a very great slaughter. Thus the children of Ammon were subdued before the children of Israel"

Judges 14:5-6;
"Then went Samson down, and his father and his mother, to Timnath, and came to the vineyards of Timnath: and, behold, a young lion roared against him. And the Spirit of the Lord came mightily upon him, and he rent him as he would have rent a kid, and he had nothings in his hand: but he told not his father/or his mother what he had done....

Judges 15:14-15;
And when he came unto Lehi, the Philistines shouted against him: and the Spirit of the Lord came mightily upon him, and the cords that were upon his arms became as flax that was burnt with fire, and his bands loosed from off his hands. And he found a new jawbone of an ass, and put forth his hand, and took it, and slew a thousand men therewith

Judges 16:27-30;
"Now the house was full of men and women; and all the lords of the Philistines were there; and there were upon the roof about three thousand men and women, that beheld while Samson made sport. And Samson called unto the Lord, and said, O Lord God, remember me, I pray thee, and strengthen me, I pray thee, only this once, O God, that I may be at once avenged of the Philistines for my two eyes. And Samson took hold of the two middle pillars upon which the house stood, and on

which it was borne up, of the one with his right hand, and of the other with his left. And Samson said, Let me die with the Philistines. And he bowed himself with all his might; and the house fell upon the lords, and upon all the people that were therein. So the dead which he slew at his death were more than they which he slew in his life."

CHARACTERISTICS OF THE WIND THAT CAN BE SEEN IN THE MANIFESTATION OF THE HOLY SPIRIT:

1. *The wind is mysterious in action*

You cannot predict when the wind will start blowing, or when it will cease. Sometimes, you will hear the move of the wind, sometimes, you will wonder if it is blowing at all. When a ship is assailed, sometimes, it would toss here and there; it is the mysterious activity of the wind blowing upon it. Sometimes, an aeroplane swerves here and there when there is a windstorm. Until it passes that particular place, it will not be stable. When the wind of the Holy Spirit blows upon your life you will become a mystery to the enemy. You will become like Peter, who was like a grain of corn in a bottle. The hen can only stare at it and salivate but it cannot eat the corn.

I want you to understand this fact beloved, the Bible says; "The wind blows wherever it wants." When the wind of the Holy Spirit blows upon your life and there is an inflow of His power into you, no power can cage you. It will no longer be possible for anyone or any power to hypnotise or charm you. It will no longer be possible for a strange woman to sweep you out of your matrimonial home. It will no longer be possible for anyone to include your name in the list of people to be given the sack from work. Other people could be selling wares that no one is buying not you, if the wind of the Holy Spirit is blowing inside you. You will become a mystery or as the Bible puts it "a spectacle." People will just be watching what is going on in your life.

They would not be able to understand what is happening and will not know what God is doing in your life.

Do you want to experience the power of the wind of the Holy Spirit? Get ready to pray. Today, you will be set free from every cage and any charm that has hitherto prospered in your life; for it will backfire and catch the sender. It will surely happen in the name of Jesus.

There was a brother whose wife was living abroad. For fives years, he made attempts to go there to join her, but was denied a Visa into the country. When he learnt warfare prayers, he started praying seriously. The wind of the Holy Spirit blew on him and he went back to the embassy. It happened that, the Whiteman who denied him the Visa five years earlier was the one who interviewed him again. The Whiteman told him that something had noticeably changed in his life, that he, the Whiteman, could not place his finger on what it was but that, something had actually changed in his life. He granted him the Visa, This is the move of the Holy Spirit; it is mysterious in action. God had to bring the same man that interviewed the brother five years earlier, to reverse what he had done.

2. *The wind is powerful in movement.*

Once the wind begins to blow, nothing can stop its activity. Once the wind of the Holy Spirit blows upon you, every obstacle on your way will be bulldozed away.

3. *The wind is independent in action.*

When the wind of the Holy Spirit blows upon you, your hands are taught to war and your fingers are taught to battle. Whether there is a Pastor around or not, you should be able to operate on your own and dismantle anything that the enemy has planted against you.

4. *The wind is invisible in action.*

It can be felt but cannot be seen. When the wind of the Holy Spirit blows upon your life, you will operate in a way that no one can understand or predict. The power of God will just move on your behalf and fight your battles in a way that you do not expect and men that you do not know, will campaign and fight for you.

5. *The wind clears away things.*

It is cleansing in service. Likewise, when the wind of the Holy Spirit blows upon your life, He will clean away every junk of the enemy from the laboratory of your destiny.

6. ***The wind is varied in direction.***
The wind can blow in every and any direction, that is why the Bible says that; "***It bloweth where it listeth.***" When the wind of the Holy Spirit blows upon you, no one can cage you. Your miracles will come from different directions.

7. ***The wind is penetrating in action.***
When the wind of the Holy Spirit blows upon your life, many wonderful breakthroughs that will affect generations after you will take place in your life.

WHAT TO DO, TO HAVE THE MOVE OF THE HOLY SPIRIT IN YOUR LIFE:

1. **Recognise the fact that the Holy Sprit is a Personality.** The Holy Spirit is not a thing, but the "Third Person of the Trinity.

2. **Recognise that He is God's executive agent in the world today**
There was a time in the Old Testament when God the Father operated. Later, God the Son came to planet earth and moved about physically. Now, we are in the age of the Holy Spirit, when God the Spirit is moving to break yokes, to deliver from bondage and to set the people of God free form the hands of the devil.

3. **Invite Him into your situation.**
Miracles will begin to happen in your life, when you invite Him into your situation. He is the same Holy Spirit that raised Jesus from death and He still helps our infirmities.

The Bible says that we do not know how to pray, it is the Holy Spirit who teaches us correct praying. The Bible says it is the Spirit of God that searches all things. It is His power that restrains the power of Satan. The Bible also says; "***When the enemy shall rise against you, like a flood, the Spirit of God shall raise a standard against him.***"(Isaiah 59:19) Halleluyah Amen!

The enemy has locked many people up and they do not know who they are. Many people sleep but do not dream at all. Their spirit has been made deaf, dumb and blind. When the wind of the Holy Spirit blows upon you, He opens prison doors and satanic challenges against you will be frustrated. You need to understand this today and then decide to daze the enemy now. Through the help of the Holy Spirit, you can overcome the enemy. The Holy Spirit cannot be trapped; He is the power of God to deliver to the uttermost.

A man of God gave the testimony of how during his Bible lecture one day at the Bible School, a man ran into his classroom naked. He had nails all over his body but there was no blood gushing out. He said he had drank the blood of a tiger and he was challenging them to use the power of their God to remove the nails. The students told him to come back at a later date. They saw it as a challenge and they prayed. Suddenly, one of the students felt the move of a wind like the one that blew on the day of Pentecost. He got up and commanded the man to be bound and he fell flat on the floor. He started to vomit blood and all the nails on his body fell off. In the presence of all the on-lookers and his fellow occultist men, the man surrendered his life to the Lord Jesus Christ.

Beloved, do not close this book without a fresh experience of His power. Tell Him to forgive you all your sins. What is the use of living a life of sin that will hinder you from experiencing your breakthrough? Maybe your own sin is stealing, or fornication, or talkativeness, or anger, etc. Ask Him to forgive you and tell Him that you want to experience what the Apostles experienced. Make up your mind that you want to have the story of a divine visitation; an encounter to tell everybody very soon. The wind of the Holy Spirit will blow across that place where you are and things will begin to change. Miracles will happen and your life will experience a change. Strange miracles and powerful breakthroughs both announced and unannounced, will begin to take place in your life. Talk to God your Father, right there where you are.

If you have never at one time or other surrendered your life to the Lord Jesus Christ, I would like you to do so, right there where you are. The Lord Jesus is right there with you and is ready to accept you into His household. All you need do is to repent of your sins and confess them to Him. Ask Him to forgive you and cleanse you from all unrighteousness. Claim the redemptive power in the Blood of Jesus, which was shed on the Cross at Calvary for the mission of your sins. Renounce the devil and the world of sin and make up your mind that you will never go back to them again.

The decision that you have just taken is the most important one in life, I pray that it shall be permanent in the name of Jesus. I pray that the Lord will uphold you with His right hand of righteousness in the name of Jesus. I pray that your name will be written in the Book of Life, and you will not by any means, rub it in the name of Jesus. Go! and sin no more.

Take the following prayer points with all the aggression and determination that you can gather. Pray them fervently until you feel the move of the wind of the Holy Spirit in your life. You will never remain the same again.

1. Lord, create in me a clean heart and renew a right spirit within me by your power, in the name of Jesus.
2. I renounce my right to my anger, in the name of Jesus.
3. Lord, remove from me the root of irritation that keeps anger alive in me, in the name of Jesus.
4. I reject all thoughts that I will never change, in the name of Jesus.
5. Spirit of God, cleanse and control anger in my life, in Jesus' name.
6. Lord, produce in me the power of self control and gentility in the mighty name of Jesus.
7. I reject all that robs me of the joy of my inheritance in Your kingdom in Jesus' name.
8. I speak to all evil mountains and break their powers over my life, in the name of Jesus.
9. Lord, enable me to hear Your voice in the name of Jesus.
10. Lord, let me know Your mind, in the name of Jesus.
11. Lord, by the power of the blood, remove from my life, any hindrance of the enemy, in the name of Jesus.
12. Every evil garment of shame, be roasted! in the name of Jesus.
13. Every evil garment of filthiness, be roasted! In the name of Jesus.
14. Every evil garment of spiritual laziness, be roasted! in the name of Jesus.
15. Every evil garment of dishonour, be roasted! in the name of Jesus.
16. Every evil garment of physical and spiritual depression, be roasted! in the name of Jesus.
17. Every evil garment of evil confessions, be roasted! in the name of Jesus.
18. The miracle of come and see, baptise my life in the name of Jesus.
19. By thunder, by lightning, by fire, I possess my possession, in the name of Jesus.
20. Every power contesting with my angel of blessing, scatter! in the name of Jesus.
21. Power of the untouchable, fall on me in Jesus' name.
22. God arise, manifest Your power in my life in the name of Jesus.
23. Power to do exploits for the Lord, possess me by fire in the name of Jesus.
24. Holy Ghost fire, cook me to the glory of God, in the name of Jesus.
25. I reject the spirit of the tail, I choose the spirit of the head, in the name of Jesus.
26. Lord, let the anointing of the Holy Spirit break every yoke of backward movement in my life, in the name of Jesus.
27. Every power contesting with my angel of break-throughs, scatter! in the name of Jesus.
28. Thou power of the night, assigned against my breakthroughs, die! in the name of Jesus.
29. My Father! as You killed the first-born in Egypt, kill every power that is working against my joy, in the name of Jesus.
30. Every power that is mocking my prayers, die! in Jesus' name.

The Eternal Destiny

1 Peter 4:17-18; *"For the time is come that judgement must begin at the house of God; and if it first begin at us, what shall the end be of them that obey not the gospel of God? And if the righteous scarcely be saved, where shall the ungodly and the sinner appear?"*

Now that we are here on earth, what next? It is good to prosper here; to locate what God wants you to do, but at the end of the day, a time will come when all of us with no exception, shall pass through what is in Psalm 23 (the valley of the shadow of death). In the valley of the shadow of death, Daddy or Mummy will not be there; you shall be alone as you walk down.

There are two eternal destinies facing everybody:
1. The destiny of damnation.
2. The destiny of life.

This means that, as you are right there where you are, you are on a journey either to eternal life or eternal damnation. Everybody is travelling on one of these two journeys.

There was a prostitute in the North. A pastor saw her and asked what she was doing out there at night. She said she was doing 'business'. The pastor preached to her and for the first time in her life, she heard a clear presentation of the word of God that, anyone who does not find life, will go into eternal death. She was afraid and wanted to make her way right with God. She was asked to kneel down and say the sinner's prayer. As she was repeating the words after the pastor, all of a sudden, there was silence for about 10 minutes. Then she was begging uncontrollably to be left alone, that she did not want to go to that place. After a while, she calmed down and when asked what happened, she said as she was repeating the sinner's prayer, she saw something that looked like a stage where the curtain was drawn and she saw many men and women in the fire. They were hanging and she saw that some were hung by their breasts or private parts, yet some by the legs, etc. They were inside a fiery furnace and were screaming. She said she had never heard that kind of horrible noise before in her life. Then an angel moved close to her to ask if she wanted to go to that place and she said no. The angel explained why those people were hung by the organs of the body; he said that those were the organs with which they sinned against God and it sent them to hell. That was what she saw that made her say she did not want to go to that place.

If God shows you the vision of heaven or hell, your life will no longer remain the same. A man of God was woken up from sleep one day and he saw himself being pulled out of his body. He was taken to a beautiful city where the streets were made of gold and there were beautiful mansions. He felt like staying on but was taken to another place, where he saw people wailing and gnashing their teeth in a fiery furnace. He said he saw worms of fire as described in the Bible, going through their noses and coming out of their mouths. It was a terrible sight. The Lord told this man to go back and tell his people not to come to that place.

We all have an appointment with God, which must be kept. An earthly appointment could be missed but it is not possible to miss this one. It does not matter if you are young or old. John in the Book of Revelation, saw the young and the old before the judgement seat of Christ. The only people who are not liable to God's judgement are babies. As soon as a baby grows wise enough to tell lies, steal, or do anything that is not right, he or she is liable to judgement. It means no one is free until he or she follows the path that God wants.

Many years ago, a man of God died and everybody was unhappy and depressed. He was a loving pastor who would st and pray for many days for people's problems to get solved. The prayer warriors decided that they would not agree with that death and they began to pray. They commanded him to come back to life; they sweated for hours and even removed their shirts. After four hours, the man opened his eyes. He asked them why they brought him back to earth. He was given food but he refused to eat saying that it was sand. For four days, he did not eat. He called every type of food that was set before him sand. That is why the Bible says; *"Eyes have not seen, nor ears heard, what the Lord has prepared for those who love Him."* The man died again on the fourth day as he could no longer conform to this world.

Beloved, it will be a tragedy to miss heaven. The Bible says that it would be better not to have been born, than to miss heaven. It means that the person would have lived a wasted life on earth, which is a gradual wastage and then the final wastage is when he or she gets to hell. That is, the life of the person is completely finished, wasted forever.

Many Christians will have to work harder if they plan to make the "Rapture." This is the message that the Lord wants me to portray in this issue of 'Battle Cry.' The Bible reading that you are neglecting and the fireless prayers must stop. The unserious abuses, boy/girl friendship, lust of the heart and of the flesh, must stop. Many people have seen the Rapture but were not taken up. The patience of God, is exhausting gradually. People are dying like houseflies; the end is drawing nigh and anything can happen at anytime. The millennium is here and there is nobody alive now that has lived up to a thousand years. Anything can happen even before the end of this year.

We had an Indian teacher who used to address those who were repeating the School Certificate Examination, Lazarus. He said they were like the rich man in hell, who wanted Lazarus to dip his hand in water to quench his thirst, or to go back to earth to warn his brethren not to come to hell. People are more ready to tell others of love and faith but do not warn them that, there is hell and they should not go there. They do not tell people that God is a consuming fire and that once His anger goes out, nobody can stop Him. Many people have a distorted picture of God. God does not do anything that is not necessary. When God wants to act, nobody and nothing can stop Him. He can give you several opportunities, but it will get to a stage where He will withdraw every assistance, if you refuse to come out of your sinful ways. It is like giving someone a slap on the face and apologising and repeating the slap. It will get to a stage where the person will either react or run away.

As far as God is concerned, He wants quality and not quantity. 600,000 men left Egypt and only 2 of them entered the Promised Land. 32,000 people volunteered to fight for Israel but only 300 were chosen to go with Gideon. God did not mind when all the inhabitants of the earth refused to join Noah and his family in the ark, they perished in the floods. If every Christian wants to make Heaven, God is ready to accept and accommodate us all. If only one person is ready and everyone else refuses to go, God does not mind.

As you are there right now, what is your position? God cannot allow sin to go unpunished. God wants to use some people, but they are running away. This is why hellfire is meant for rebellious people that are not ready to listen to God. Once a person gets to hell, there is no way out. It is better not to go there at all.

Today, I would like you to think very deeply about your life. You must realise the fact that those things that are in your life, that will not allow you to get to heaven, are the same things that will paralyse your destiny. The things that will not allow you to hear the trumpet sound, are the same things that will also disturb you from achieving your destiny.

This is not a matter to take jokingly. I am not trying to entertain you in any way. Some people have been playing games with the Lord and He has been warning them. If you are one of them, I will advise that you should not live a life that is not really pleasant here on earth, and then end up in hell again. It does not make sense at all; it is spiritual foolishness.

"If the righteous shall scarcely be saved, where shall the ungodly appear?" Those who do not want to know what the Lord is saying now, will soon find out that the truth about His word will soon catch up with them. Hellfire is worse than any picture that anybody can paint of it. That is, if a painter uses his discretion to describe hell on paper, it cannot be as real as hell really is. The picture that people have, will only provide fuel for the fire there. Abraham told the rich man in hell that it was too late. You brought nothing into this world and cannot take anything out of it. You are in the world now and as such you can still make changes. In hell, the murderer will look at his victim but cannot do anything to him or her. The cheat will see the face of those he or she has cheated, the student will see the question papers that he or she cheated in the examination with; every sin will be brought into the open. Death is the exit from life; it is the door to eternity. Jesus came from heaven, Moses and Elijah too came from there on the day of Transfiguration. No one has ever or can ever come from hell. Once a person is there, that is it.

Speak to the Lord right there where you are; ask the Lord to help you, that you do not want to go to hellfire.

If an ant is to empty the sand on the beach by carrying it in grains to Kaduna, the time that it will take it is still less than eternity. Do not toy with sin. There is no way out of hell. Unforgiveness, bitterness and every other sin should be banished from your life. A time will come when there will be nobody to warn you of the dangers of sin. Once the period of warning expires, the gate of grace will be closed and that will be the end. It might not happen generally but individually. There is a song that says; If the Lord comes today, will He meet you watching? Waiting for when the Lord shall come?"

God will call us home one by one. I believe that you are not reading this message for fun, neither have you picked up the bulletin by chance. There is an exit from the earth but none from hellfire. The Bible says the fire there shall never be quenched; that it is very hot and tormenting. If you put your finger in the flame of a burning candle for a few minutes, it will be very painful and the skin on the finger will burn. Can you imagine a person's whole body in a furnace where the fire is burning and the person is not roasting to death? The rich man found hell to be tormenting and he longed for water. He asked Abraham to tell Lazarus to dip a finger in water and place it on his tongue. Hell is a place of unending, unquenchable thirst. Many people are already heading for there. Even churchgoers are nicely and neatly going there. If you do not check yourself and ask God to forgive you, you might be heading there too. So, make up your mind to tread the path that He wants you to tread. All hypocrites, liars, are heading for hell.

Some Christians are advocating for liberty; they want to be free to do whatever they like, they do not realise that each person came to this world as an individual and will leave as an individual. If you continue to tread the path of hell with your unbeliever friends who do not know the Lord, you too will land in hell. Some people claim that there are foreign female ministers who paint their faces and wear trousers, using them as a yardstick, not knowing that we have to give account to God as individuals. They have not seen the Book of Life, so they cannot say that the name of such people are there. The issue of heaven is much more serious than appearance. The Bible says, *"no unclean thing shall enter into heaven."* If you are still watching pornographic films or are engaging in premarital or extramarital sex, you are heading for hell. If you are shy or ashamed to preach the Gospel, you are treading the path of hell.

The parable of the talents, recounts the detail of 3 servants that were given talents to work with. Two of them worked hard and got theirs multiplied, but the third one buried his and he was thrown into hell. If you are burying your talents, you are heading for hell. Isaiah 5:14;
"Therefore hell hath enlarged herself, and opened her mouth without measure: and their glory, and their multitude, and their pomp, and he that rejoiceth, shall descend into it."

It means hell has been enlarged to take more people. It is unfortunate to find out that more people are longing to go there. **Must you go there?** Do you want to perish? Do you want your eternal destiny to be in the place of fire? Do you want to discover the truth too late? Many people laugh and ridicule the existence of hellfire. It is unfortunate, that it will be too late by the time they get there, to find out that it is real.

There was a man who never, liked the Bible and detested God. He shunned every call to accept Jesus Christ as personal Lord and Saviour. Soon he took ill and just before he died, he cried out on his hospital bed that there we're some dark, strange-looking creatures in the room, that they had come to take him away. He called out for the nurse but she could not see what he was seeing. He lamented that he was just discovering that the Bible is real. He saw the messengers of death that came to take him to hell. He died immediately. The enemy harvested him without giving him the chance to repent even as he was realising the truth. The world is like a farm, ripe for harvest and there are gardeners there. The Holy Spirit and demonic spirits are harvesting people and throwing them where they belong.

We were preaching the Gospel to a man but he refused to surrender his life to the Lord Jesus. Suddenly, his wife died and the family of the defunct, reminded him of the fact that he got the woman through pregnancy, that he did not marry her legally. They asked him to go and buy a wedding gown for the corpse. He did, thinking they just wanted it for encasing the corpse. To his amazement, he was told that a wedding ceremony would be performed on that day. He thought it was a joke but they insisted and said they would not bury the corpse, if he didn't allow them to perform the wedding rites. They promised to deal with him if he runs away. Of course, he ran away and came to MFM for deliverance. This man is an example of those who criticize us and hate the cautions that we take in MFM, but when trouble comes, they come running for deliverance!

It is a terrible thing to discover the truth only when it is too late. If a person faces the judgement seat of God unsaved and unrepentant, the person's blood will be on his or her head because, the person has refused to accept the truth. One thing that always bother me is the fact that, some of the people that I have preached the Gospel to, will still land in hell. It is because they have heard and rejected the Gospel. They want to copy and remain in the world. How can a King or Prince marry a servant? It is a demotion of the highest order. Therefore brethren, I must warn you that hell is not a place that you should plan to go to. It is a place meant for those that have abandoned their God. The Bible calls it fire; the pit, prison, second death. It is a situation where a person tails into the hands of an angry God. It is outer darkness where there is weeping and gnashing of teeth; it is the bottomless pit.

If you make up your mind that you will not be harvested by the enemy and will not go to hell, you can make that decision solid today. You can make a covenant with the Lord. If you are already getting weak, you might need to rededicate your life to Christ. In hellfire, there will be no room for excuses. No one will claim that God is unfair to him to her, or that God gave him or her a raw deal.

One day, I was invited to a birthday ceremony. Everybody went there with the mind of eating and drinking. When I took the floor to preach, I asked them to open their Bible to a verse but I discovered that I was the only one that had a Bible there. I read it out loud and preached. There was a man in the front that was staring at me with disdain; had he had a gun, he probably would have blown out my head. He refuted the Gospel. He did not know that the devil was lurking around to harvest his life. A short while later, I heard that this man a professor, was caught by his wife having sexual intercourse with their house-help in the boys quarters. In order to spite the wife, he eloped with the house-help leaving the wife to go through pains. If he had listened to the word of God on that day, he would not have ruined his marriage, thereby his heaven.

Many people think that prayer should not be a rigorous affair. They do not know that if they leave it till they get to hell, they will cry out for help but will not be answered. Why must a person decide to perish? Why should anyone choose death? You have the choice of life now. Jesus has already died for you. If you want to see the hypocrisy of man, it is at a funeral that you will see it expressed. Everyone will be sober; they will wear sad faces, many will even weep. They will be confused and serious. Some will be waiting for the ceremony to be over so that they can eat the food provided by the family. Some will be waiting for the will to be read so that they can know what comes to them. Many will look blank. Highly intelligent people who are not born-again, get confused at such times. They keep wondering what has really become of the person that died. They would wonder what is happening to the person at that time. Some will reflect on their own live and decide to change for the better there and then.

At an interment service one day, a mad man came into the midst of the people at the cemetery and talked about the futility of life. He told them to bury the man with his big cars, if it was possible. He called the widow a fool for crying and asked her to jump into the grave with the coffin. He told them that the judgement of God was upon them. This was a mad man, but there was some sense in what he said.

Beloved what excuse will you have? Will you say you did not hear the truth? Will you say you did not get a sound Christian doctrine? At least you are reading this message now, so you have been told. You should get serious with God and pray hard. Read your Bible every day and claim His promises. Live a life of holiness. It will be very sad, if God tells you that you cannot enter His Kingdom because you have anger and impurity in your heart. If you are filling your heart with romantic stories and carrying worldly novels about, under the pretext that you want to improve on your spoken English, you are treading the path of hell.

The Almighty is watching and asking why you are occupying space for nothing. Do not allow the cry "*replace him...*" to go forth. If He cries out that you should be replaced, you will be in serious trouble. That is why you should pray hard that God should not replace you with a stone. Do you know that God can raise an atheist or Muslim that surrenders his or her life to Christ? He can make the person His oracle and he or she will go about preaching the Gospel and will be filled with the Holy Spirit. He will then place the person in a position where people who knew Christ before him or her, will run after the person seeking counsel. That is what it means to raise a stone in the place of a child of God. Think about it beloved!

A person could be smiling while committing sin, but when the repercussion comes, there will be no smiles. Anyone who goes to hell is actually trespassing because, the Bible says it is meant for the devil and his fallen angels not for you. Even today, judgement is going on somewhere. There are some natural laws that you should not violate. Hospitals are filled with people who have violated some natural laws and are suffering from the consequences. For example; if you jump down from a 3-storey building; you could break your legs and end up in the hospital. If you put your hand in the fire, it will burn. If you decide to go about sleeping with men or women, HIV/AIDS or any other disease will infect you. This means that, there is judgement all over the place. **Some people think they are not committing sin if they have only one boy-friend or girl-friend. They would compare themselves with others saying that, those ones have many but they have only one. Some even say that they do not commit fornication but they kiss each other. They consider themselves as not being bad. There is greater judgment for the person who knows the truth and goes against it.** Anyone who sows - the seed of sin, will reap the harvest of sorrow. That is what the Bible says and even in the court of law, ignorance is no excuse. You could get a lawyer to get you "off the hook" here, but not in the court of the Almighty.

You have an opportunity today because, the payday is coming and you need to repent and find the kind of life that God wants you to find. God has a way of monitoring us; He sees our heart. Your life does not belong to you so you have no right to live it your own way. In a Bible college, the students were taught that sin has three stages:

1. Seeing,
2. Touching,
3. Acting.

The theory of these three stages stuck to a man of God, until he saw a blind man give his life to the Lord Jesus Christ at a Christian meeting. The blind man wept bitterly for his sins. This man of God then understood that sin emanates from the heart and not from the eyes. God looks at the intent of the heart. Your life is not your property. Jesus was crucified naked; He died of a broken heart. Do you know what it means to die of a broken heart? It means to die of disappointment, sorrow, etc. The Bible calls Jesus, a "Man of sorrow and acquainted with grief." All His friends and disciples ran away; even Peter that went all the way to the courtyard denied Him and even cursed himself that he did not know Jesus. Even His Father forsook Him because of our sins. God cannot behold sin and so, He does not joke with anyone who is a sinner because, He has already given His only begotten Son as a once-and-for-all sacrifice for the sins of the world.

If you are reading this massage and you are still toying around with sin, it is very sad. The end of all things including Man's occupation of the earth, is approaching. The final destiny of man will then be determined. Then, there will be a separation. Those with the spirit of the goat will be taken to the left and those with the spirit of the sheep will be taken to the right side with God. He will take those with the spirit of the sheep into His kingdom and those with the spirit of the goat will be sent away.

One day, a woman who had two degrees from a Bible School was arguing with me about the Holy Spirit. She said we are no longer in the era of the Apostles, where they received the baptism in the Holy Ghost. I did not want to argue with her so I asked if she was ready to experience the infilling of the Holy Ghost. She said there was no harm in trying. I prayed for her and she started to speak in tongues. I left her there to attend to other matters and for about one hour, she was just speaking in tongues. Later, she told me that she saw an angry-looking angel who rebuked her and showed her a report sheet where she scored 22%. In God's Arithmetic 99½% is failure. She asked what it meant and the angel told her that she could not enter the Kingdom of God. She was worried on another occasion; she dreamt that the Rapture came and she saw people being taken up into heaven but she could not go. She tried to jump up but it did not help. She thought it was because she was fat but she saw fat people in the air, being taken up. When she recounted these experiences, I told her that God was opening her spiritual eyes to show her, her position.

When God shows you your position, you do not need a preacher to tell you that you are a sinner. You will know where you are and you will adjust your life. What marks do you score in God's report sheet? If your name is in worldly or occultist groups, it will not take you anywhere.

A songwriter says;
"Lord, I do not care about riches,
I don't care about silver and gold,
But I will make sure of heaven.
I will enter the gates.
In the book of your Kingdom,
Is my name written there?"

A man who was heading for eternal damnation, was shown his score sheet.

Love	0 %
Pride	90%
Prayer	10 %
In filling of the Holy Spirit	05 %
Internal Sexual Sins	100%
Zeal	0%
Patience	0%
Worldliness	98%
Lying	95%
Evangelism	06%
Gossip	80%
Word of God	01%

The remark below the score sheet reads: **Lost in the church**.

You need to realign and readjust your life beloved, so that you do not live a wasted life. Many Christians live in sin and are comfortable with it. The purpose for which God suspended His Son in midair, between heaven and earth is not a joke. Heaven and earth rejected Him. The Bible says: **"Though hand be joined in**

hand, no sinner shall go unpunished." You have to talk to the Lord and cry to Him, that you do not want to perish; that you do not want the enemy to harvest your life. You should not find yourself in hell, where witches and all workers of iniquity will be. The thought of having lost heaven will torment anyone that goes to hell.

My advice and counsel to you right now is that, you go on your knees and make things right with the Lord. Ask Him to forgive you all your sins. There are areas where you have failed Him; the things that He asked you to do and you did not do. How can you say that you go to church and are still living in sin? Throw out those sins and cry to the Lord today. Maybe God has been showing you the Rapture and you are not taking Him serious; cry unto Him for mercy. Ask Him to deliver you from the bondage of sin. Be determined not to allow sin to harvest your life. Surrender everything to Jesus. Do not joke with your eternal destiny. Drop all your evil friends and friendship, all the evil programs that you watch on TV. Beloved, this is a very serious matter. It is a matter of grave magnitude because it is about eternity.

Some years ago, some scientists in Norway were digging the ground. They continued digging into thousands of feet below the ground. At a stage, they heard voices of people crying. They could not believe their ears. They decided to let down a microphone to capture the sounds. To their amazement, they heard real human voices, lamenting and wailing in agony and pain. At that stage, these scientists who did not believe in any religion or God, realised that what the Bible says about crying and anguish in hell fire, is true. Many of them surrendered their lives to the Lord Jesus Christ right there and then.

If hitherto, you have not surrendered your life to the Lord Jesus Christ, I would advise that you do so right now without wasting time. You have the opportunity of asking the Lord to save you today. If you say that you are born-again and you are still in love with sin, you are toying with hell fire. Do not allow yourself to be hung by your reproductive organ or mouth or legs. Do not allow any ephemeral enjoyment to lead you to hell.

Right there where you are, call upon the Lord; repent of your sins; confess them to Him, name them one by one and renounce them. Makeup your mind that you will never go back to them again. Say bye-bye to the world of sin and to the devil.

Invite the Lord Jesus Christ into your life, ask Him to come in and become your personal Lord and Saviour. Enthrone Him over your life and all that concerns you. Ask Him to take a total control of your life.

I congratulate you for this decision that you have just taken. It is the most important decision in life. I pray that it shall be permanent in the Name of Jesus. I pray that the Lord shall uphold you with His right hand of righteousness and will not let you fall. The Lord will write your name in the Book of Life and you will not by any means, rub it off in the Name of Jesus.

Now, take these prayer points with all the aggression and determination that you can gather:

1. Hell fire will not harvest my life, in the mighty name of Jesus.
2. Every enemy of the kingdom of God in my life, loose your hold! in the name of Jesus.
3. I will not allow myself to perish; so help me Lord, in the name of Jesus.
4. Lord, dethrone me from the center of my life and enthrone Yourself, in the name of Jesus.
5. Lord, I will no longer disobey You. I will do what You ask me to do, in the name of Jesus.
6. I destroy the power of any satanic arrest over my life, in the name of Jesus.
7. Every emptier, targeted against my life, fall down and die! in the name of Jesus.
8. I refuse to be shaken by the enemy, in the name of Jesus.
9. I regain my balance today, in the name of Jesus.
10. I reverse every damage done to my life from the womb, in the name of Jesus.

11. I bind and bring to naught, all evil counsels and imaginations against my life, in the name of Jesus.
12. Anything planted by the enemy into my life to destroy me, receive the fire of the Holy Ghost and be roasted, in the name of Jesus.
13. Let the blood of Jesus, cleanse me from head to toe of every evil mark, in the name of Jesus.
14. You windows of heaven, open to me now! in the name of Jesus.
15. I trample upon scorpions and serpents, in the name of Jesus.
16. Let the power to pray above my normal level, fall upon me, in the name of Jesus.

Begin to thank the Lord for what He has done in your life, in Jesus name.

The Fresh Fire

God is not looking for bosses; He is interested in those who will serve Him will all humility

Isaiah 64:1-2; *"On that Thou wouldest rend the heavens, that Thou wouldest come down, that the mountains might flow down at Thy presence, as when the melting fire burneth, the fire causeth the waters to boil, to make Thy name known to Thine adversaries that the nations may tremble at Thy presence!"*

More than at any other time beloved, we need the 'Fresh Fire of the Holy Ghost' upon our lives today. Nothing can answer the confusing questions that the enemies are raising today, than the Fresh Fire of the Holy Ghost. When that Fresh Fire falls, the waters will boil. The Bible says: *"Out of your belly shall flow rivers of Living Waters."* When this water is flowing in you, and the Fire of God falls upon it, it will boil and the name of the Lord will become known to His adversaries, and nations will tremble before Him.

This is the secret of the lives of the Apostles; they had fresh fire in them and every prayer meeting was an opportunity to get refreshed and filled again. There was power and fire in the way they moved, in their evangelism and ministrations, and in everything that they did. No wonder, they were accused of turning the city upside down. It would be good if we too can be accused of turning the world upside down for Jesus.

If you want the Fresh Fire of God upon your life, you have to allow the 'Living Water' in you to boil. You have to be on fire at all times. The enemy will not come against you when you are on fire; he will only come when the fire goes down. That is why he is always trailing the children of God so that, he can get hold of them at thier unguarded hour. When you find out that as you are praying, you doze off and you wake up as your Bible is slipping off your hand; you can only spend a few minutes before the Lord or you find out that you can hardly sit to read the Bible, or you find out that you hardly witness to people- it means that the enemy is round the corner. You must be careful. The enemy wants to box you to a corner and you must not allow it: If you do not set yourself loose, the enemy will take an advantage of you.

KEYS TO RECEIVING THE FIRE OF GOD:
1. Hunger and thirst for the word of God.
When a person is hungry or thirsty and he or she sees food or drink, the person grabs it quickly and would almost finish it before he or she realises it. Both hunger and thirst are feelings that will insist on being satisfied before they leave a person in peace. A Christian cannot get very far with the Lord, if all that he or she does is to read a verse of Scripture per day and if what the person reads is not even understood and digested.

Deuteronomy 8:3; *And He humbled thee, and suffered thee to hunger, and fed thee with manna, which thou knewest not, neither did thy fathers know; that He might make thee know that Man doth not live by bread only, but by every word that proceedeth out of the month of the Lord doth Man live."*

Here what Jesus told Satan in Luke 4:4; *"And Jesus answered him, saying: "It is written, That man shall not live by bread atone, but by every word of God."*

Some people are depending on what they learnt in the Sunday School when they were young. Many claim that their brain is getting old and cannot retain anything. It is a pity that God will not take such excuses from anyone. At the same time, the devil will take an advantage of their ignorance of the word of God to deal with them. Many Christians are lazy when it comes to reading the word of God. Some cannot even be bothered. Many feed their bodies with all kinds of nourishing food but when it comes to feeding the spirit with the word of God, they start to slow down. Some people do not even read the Bible, all that they read is a pamphlet that talks about Bible stories daily? They prefer watching movies that will not help them in any way. Some of the movies or television programs that they watch are produced by some people who have openly declared that they are not in God's camp.

The devil knows that the more of the word of God you have in you, the more powerful you are. He knows that there is power in the word of God and he can weigh a person's word level. A pastor used to tell those who find it difficult to sleep at night to take their Bible and read; before long, they would be fast asleep. It works as sleeping drug for those people because the devil does not want them to read the word of God in the first place. When you are hungry and thirsty for the word of God, there is an indication that things will get better, Some people do not have a complete Bible: all they have is a small collection of the New Testament which they carry about without reading. When such people get to the church with their incomplete Bibles, they are lost when the sermon is taken from the Old Testament. It also means that, they cannot examine what they were taught at home. Those who were serious with the Lord as we were growing in the Christian faith are doing something tangible for the Lord now. Those who just attended fellowship for the sake of it and had no time for the word of God. are still patching up with life today

2. **Become a prayer addict.**
The Bible says; *"Pray without ceasing."* Prayer is the means by which we communicate with God and He is never tired of listening to his children. Although He wants us to avoid vain repetitions, still, He does not want us to stop praying. Prayer is power. The Bible says: *Ye who remember the name of Jehovah, give Him no peace until He establishes Jerusalem and makes it a praise in the earth."*

3. **Live a life of holiness.**
The Bible says; *"Without holiness, no man shall see the Lord."* Live a sinless life in words, thoughts and deeds.

4. **Be completely obedient to God.**
Whatever God asks you to do personally or through His words must be done without questioning. Do not argue with God when He asks you to do anything. It might not sound logical, just do it.

5. **Have a great desire for the return of the Lord.**
1 John 3:1-4; *"Behold what manner of love the Father hath bestowed upon us, that we should be called the sons of God: therefore the world knoweth us not, because it knew Him not. Beloved, now are we the sons of God and it doth not yet appear what we shall be: but we know that, when He shall appear, we shall be like Him; for we shall see Him as He is. And every man that hath this hope in Him purifieth himself, even as He is pure. Whosoever committeth sin transgresseth also the law: for sin is the transgression of the law."*

You have to be expectant of His coming that, He could come back at any time. By so doing, you will not mind the things of the world, you will not do anything that would displease the Lord.

6. **Have violent faith in God.**
Take God for His word. Do not be the kind of Christian that would grumble and cry whenever there is a problem. The Apostles knew God and took Him for His word.

7. **Love sacrificially.**
Love everybody. It is an act that depicts our adherence to the Lord. He says: *"By this shall men know that ye are My disciples, if ye have love, one for another."*

With these keys, we should be able to walk towards the fresh fire that is needed in these 'Last-Days.' God Himself has called us. However, the extent to which He uses an individual depends on the extent to which the person yields himself or herself to God. The reason why we are reading about the Apostles today is because they yielded their totality to God. The space that you give to the Holy Spirit is the space that He will occupy. Instead of asking what we can do for God, we are more interested in what God can do for us. We have turned

God into 'a big errand boy' who is to give this or bring that. If we seek God first and allow His Fresh Fire to get into us, things will work out well for us and the Lord will do more than we can ask or expect from Him that is what the Bible says. All we need do is put ourselves in the centre of the will of God. That is why we need the Fresh Fire of God.

The truth of the Bible is that, when God sets out to do something, nothing and nobody can stop Him. He will do what He wants to do. You may ask Him for anything as long as you have faith- He will do it. You have to set your priorities right. What you want might not necessarily be what you need. The Bible says that God showed His works to the children of Israel but He showed His ways to Moses. God spoke to Moses face to face. When God wanted to talk to the children of Israel, they sent Moses to be their interlocutor. They said he should go to God and hear what He has to say and then transmit it to them. They lost the opportunity of hearing God directly. God wants to talk to us as individuals but the choice is ours.

The prodigal son got his inheritance, lavished it and came back. He satisfied himself and was taken back into the household but he did not really know his father. I am exposing these things because you need to reorganise your spiritual priorities and allow God to do the main thing in your life. **it is possible to claim everything in the Bible and even have it but one should first ask what God wants one to have and then be sure that it is used to the glory of His name. Ask where He wants you to go, rather than just claim the word that says**: *"He shall give you any where that the sole of your feet shall tread."* **Do you know where He wants you to tread in the first place? Do you know that it is possible to obtain from God what He does not really want for you? It is possible if you do not allow Him to have His way in your life. It is possible when you squeeze it out of His hands. However, it is better for you to wait for God to give you that which pleases Him, that which He knows is good for you at the right time and to the glory of His name.** You need His Fresh Fire, to be able to know and remain where He wants you to be.

Psalm 106:13-15; *"They soon forgat His works; they waited not for his counsel: but lusted exceedingly in the wilderness, and tempted God in the desert. And He gave them their request; but sent leanness into their soul."*

The last part of this text is sad but true. Many people go about consulting herbalists and when they see that they are not making a headway, they will now go to the church and instead of waiting on the Lord, they want to use Him as a more powerful fetish. That is why you will see some people who are living in sin but have 'holy water' anointing oil and even their Bible under the pillow for protection. Such people want the gift of God but are rejecting the giver Himself. There was a herbalist who recommended M F M stickers to motorcyclists. He asked them to stick it on their machines that they would make good sales and would not be involved in accidents. Of course it will work for them. "He is out there, not accepting Christ into his life but he is serving as signpost; pointing the way out and not getting out himself.

It is possible, for a person to perform wonders without being pure. The Bible says that many people will get to the gates of heaven and they will say that they prophesied and worked miracles in the name of the Lord but the Lord will turn them down and call them workers of iniquity. **It is possible to see visions without wisdom; experience the manifestation of God's power in a gathering without having a penetration of heart. It is possible to seek popularity without having a depth in the things of the Lord.** All these amount to nothing without you having the Fire of God in your life. It is possible for a person to have anointing but be without character. It amounts to nothing. Character is who you really are in the depths of your inner being in the dark. It is possible to listen to different messages and different preachers but if you do not obey what the Lord ministers to you through those messages, its a waste of time. It is possible to sing about the power of God but the most important thing is to get that power in you.

HINDRANCES TO RECEIVING FRESH FIRE:

1. Pride.

It is the first sin. It made Lucifer fall from heaven. It is the exaltation of self. The focal point is 'I', 'Me'. That is why the Bible says we should not seek great things for ourselves. Seek what God wants you to be and be contented with it. You will see that things will begin to happen. The Bible asks why a person should be proud, when what he has is not even his but was given to him.

Romans 12:10 says; *"Be kindly affectioned one to another with brotherly love; in honour preferring one another"* Romans 13:7 further says; *"Render therefore to all their dues: tribute to whom tribute is due; custom to whom custom; fear to whom fear; honour to whom honour."*

Many workers in the church are proud; they do not see their work in the church as a privilege to serve the Lord but they see it as an opportunity to suppress others, seeing themselves as being superior. The Bible says we should have respect, one for another. The fact that you are a leader does not mean you should denigrate other people. In John 13, Jesus did something outstanding, that we need to emulate; He washed the feet of His disciples. He demonstrated love in all humility. He, the Creator, the Master, took up towel and basin and washed the feet of His followers. God is not looking for bosses; He is interested in those who will serve Him with all humility. That is why we always pray in MFM, that God should provide ministers that would help to tend the flock; those who will see their positions as an avenue to serve and not those who will see themselves as being better than every other person.

Many people have invited trouble into their lives by not being the servants that God wants them to be.

Many through pride, have missed out on their calling. They forget that God is able to raise stones to replace anyone who refuses to serve Him. God does not tolerate any vacuum at all. If you are one of those who do not want to do anything in the house of God, just because you have not been made the leader of the place, you had better repent now, before God replaces you with a stone. It is pride that leads to boasting; it drags down power and quenches the Fire of God in the life of a Christian

2. Lack of love.

The Lord likens the household of God to a flock of sheep. A sheep behaves like a little child who is simple-hearted, loving and obedient, A sheep does not criticise but could make suggestions. Instead of criticizing, why do you not pray for that person?

Titus 3:2; *"To speak evil of no man; to be no brawlers, but gentle, shewing all meekness unto all men."*

Do not become 'old wine in new skin'- be transformed; change and let God remold you. It is change that brings progress.

3. Lack of dedication.

When you are not committed to the cause of God, He cannot confide anything in you.

Galatians 6:9; *"And let us not be weary in well doing: for in due season we shall reap, if we faint not."*

Many people are not patient enough to see what God wants to do in and through their lives. When they get to a gathering, they are quick to drawing conclusions and giving up. If you notice that some things are not going on the way they should, the best thing to do is pray, it is not the time to give up and leave.

4. Not seeking the Glory of God.

Isaiah 42:8; *"I am the Lord: that is my name: and my glory will I not give to another, neither my praise to graven images."*

There was a misunderstanding in a church group and the leader said he was leaving. The man with whom he had the controversy got up and bid him good riddance and encouraged the others that he would now be their leader. As the former was leaving, he came to the window and told the latter that he would not sit on that seat of leadership. He thought it was a joke until the following day when he could not get up from his bed. He was paralysed. Someone brought him to MFM for prayers and I asked him why he was that confrontational. I asked him if he could be a leader in a paralysed state. If we are seeking the glory of God, there will be no leadership struggle.

It will not matter if it is A that leads or if it is B. God would just stand aloof and watch when people want to share His glory with Him.

One of our fathers-in-the-Lord told us that he went to a church and met the people at a meeting. There was a hot argument and when he could no longer bear it, he asked them to excuse him for a while. He asked them to open their Bible to the Book of 1 Corinthians 10 verse 31, which says: *"Whether therefore ye eat, or drink, or whatsoever ye do, do all to the glory of God,"* He asked each of them to read it out loud and then said they should continue their argument. They could not. That marked the end of the hot argument.

5. **Unclean life and secret;** Psalm 66:18; *"If I regard iniquity in my heart the Lord will not hear me."*

God sees the heart. He knows it. He knows who is faithful *to* Him and who is not; He works through the heart. The kind of fire God wants us to carry about is such that, no witch or wizard will be able to withstand. They should not even be able to pass through our environment to attend any witchcraft meeting.

One night, a vigil was going on in MFM and suddenly, a woman, landed in the compound from the sky. When the prayer warriors moved close, she told them that she was flying across the premise in form of a bat but was arrested by the fire of God and she dropped and transformed into a human being. She was told that having seen the power of God and what it can do, would she surrender her life to the Lord Jesus Christ? She said she had gone too far with the devil, that she could not surrender her life to Christ. The fire that we should have should be such that, when an occultist person shakes our hand, they should be electrocuted.

A brother thought he had a lot of problems and a friend said he would take him to an elderly man who would look into his matter. The brother was born-again but he had come to his wit's end. He wanted someone who could see vision. When they got there, he discovered that the elderly man was a herbalist. As soon as the herbalist shook his hand, he asked him what he wanted; that he had 'that thing' in him. The brother asked what that thing was and he got to understand that it was the Holy Ghost. It was ridiculous to discover what he had, in the house of a herbalist. This is often the case with the children of God. The powers of darkness know who we are but we ourselves do not know who we are. This is a serious pity.

There was a woman who knew who she was. One day, she was going to the market and she bumped into an occultic man who harassed her and threatened to deal with her. She said she was sorry but he said he would show her his power. People around were afraid because the woman was pregnant and they thought she would die. The occultic man started to chant incantations and fire came out of his mouth. The woman commanded the fire to quench in the name of Jesus, and it did. People were amazed and the occultic man prostrated, rendering homage to her. She told him that her own power was not occultic but that she had Jesus in her. That is the kind of Christian that God wants each of us to be. I know that some sisters would have ran away frightened and could even decide not to ever go to that market again. They would have been looking for their Pastor or General Overseer to pray for them.

Today, you will have to pray for the Fire of God to come into your life. If God calls you, He will empower you to do that which He wants you to do. It is good for people to see you and give glory to God. The Lord is the one of whom the Bible says, every knee shall bow at the mention of His name. Every knee whether in heaven or on earth or underneath the waters, must bow at the mention of the name of Jesus.

However, if you are not yet born again, there is no way the fresh fire can come into your life, therefore, I would advise that you take the decision to surrender your life to the Lord Jesus right now, right there, where you are. All you need do is, confess your sins to the Lord, name them one by one, repent of all those sins, and ask Him to forgive you and cleanse you from all your unrighteousness. Claim the redemptive power in the Blood of Jesus, that was shed on the cross at Calvary for the remission of your sins. Renounce the world and the devil and make sure you do not go back to them anymore. Say bye-bye to the devil and all his works.

Now, invite the Lord Jesus Christ into your life and ask Him to become your personal Lord and Saviour. Open your heart and enthrone Him as the Lord of your life. Ask Him to take total control of your life and all that concerns you. This is a very important decision that you have just taken. I congratulate you and pray that it shall be permanent in your life, in the name of Jesus. I pray that the Lord will uphold you with His right hand of righteousness and will not let you fall. I pray that the Lord will take control of all that concerns you, in the name of Jesus.

Take these prayer points beloved:

1. Lord, baptise me with Fresh Fire from above, in the name of Jesus.
2. Lord send Your Fire just now and baptise me, in the name of Jesus.
3. Lord, turn me into untouchable and unquenchable fire, in the name of Jesus.
4. Every power, challenging the authority of God in my life, die! in the name of Jesus.
5. Lord, connect my life to your socket of power, in the name of Jesus.
6. Father, make me to hunger and thirst for righteousness in Jesus' name.
7. Lord, grant me victory over temptation and satanic devices in the name of Jesus Christ.
8. Let the multiple strongmen, operating against me be paralysed in Jesus' name.
9. Let all strangers flee my spirit and let the Holy Spirit take control in Jesus' name.
10. I decree the joy of the oppressor over my life to be turned into sorrow in the name of Jesus.
11. Anything in me, quenching the fire of God, die! In the name of Jesus.
12. Holy Ghost fire, purge my life of every filthiness debarring me from hearing God, in the name of Jesus.
13. My life! Become too hot for the enemy to handle, in the name of Jesus.
14. Fresh fire of revival, fall upon my life, in the name of Jesus,
15. Let the chariots of Fire; pursue the enemies of my soul into the 'Red Sea', in the name of Jesus.
16. Let the chariots of Fire pursue the enemies that are like the sun, like the moon, like serpents, like scorpions, like dragons into the 'Red Sea', in the name of Jesus.
17. Father Lord, help me to retain and maintain the anointing of fire that I have received, in the name of Jesus.
18. Give glory to God for the fresh fire that you have received.

Paralysing Progress Arresters - 1

First of all, I would like you to turn the title of this message into a prayer by saying; "*I paralyse every progress killer in the name of Jesus.*"

Our text for today is taken from the Book of Isaiah 52:2;
"Shake thyself from the dust; arise, and sit down, O Jerusalem: loose thyself from the bands of thy neck, O captive daughter of Zion."

You will see in this passage that, the onus to shake oneself from the position of the dust, lies on the person himself or herself.

Take this prayer point.
* **Let the anointing that breaks yokes, fall upon me now! in the name of Jesus.**

FACTS:
God will not force anyone to live a victorious Christian Life. The person has to make a personal decision and be determined to arise from a particular position and get into another one. The time is gone, when a person would wail and weep over situations.

Some sisters cry and brood over the fact that they were raped 15 years ago and remain morose for the rest of their lives. Do not allow your past to ruin your present and future; arise and shake yourself out of the dust and start moving.

This message is not for those who are satisfied with a defeated and sub-standard Christian life, like we see around these days. If you are happy with your spiritual level or attainment and are content with maintaining the status quo, then this message is not for you. If you decide to do nothing about your life. God too will just be looking at you.

The prodigal son would have died a pauper if not for the fact that, at one time in his life, he came to his senses. The King James Version of the Bible says; "*He came to himself.*" In our local English translation, this can mean the same thing as 'his head became correct.' He said to himself that, there are countless servants in his father's house who have enough to eat and drink and he was there suffering in the midst of pigs. He then made up his mind and said: "*I will arise!*" His breakthrough started at that very moment. Do not allow the enemy to keep you in the back room. You have to make a decision to arise.

This message is for those who are thirsty for God's best. It is for those who want God to destroy every idol that is pulling them backward. It is for those who want God to cut off the spiritual cancer and diarrhea that are inhibiting their progress. It is unfortunate to find out that, many people are limiting God and by so doing, they are limiting their own lives. There are many Christian traders who have been managing the same rat-shed for many years and they have no plan for progress; they have no vision. When you ask some people when they will leave their petty-trading for something bigger, they will ask you where the money to start something good will come from. Thus, they limit God and limit themselves. God too will take their decision as final since that is what they want.

Psalm 78:41 says;
"Yea, they turned back and tempted God, and limited the Holy One of Israel.".

This is limitation. The people of Israel turned God into a limited liability company with fixed assets. Many people today, who have very fine professional certificates have with their own hands, signed evil agreements with the devil. They declare that the certificate is no longer worth it and they dump it, thereby limiting God. The way God operates is this; If He has to go into a rock to bring out honey for His children, He does not mind doing it. He does not mind two countries going to war because of His own child. If you limit Him, He will remain where you put Him.

Cry unto the Lord right there where you are and ask Him to forgive you for limiting Him.

If as a trader you have no plan; no vision or prospects, no faith, where will he land? Have you been buying soap at N50 and selling it at N55? When do you hope to move to the level of wholesale? When do you hope to open a supermarket? Some people say that they are in their present state because they have no helper. I wonder where they put our heavenly Father? Is He dead or alive?

A man wanted a top post in the government and lamented that he did not know anybody up there. He said a person needed to know those that matter in government to get that post. I asked him if he knew the Lord God Almighty and he said he did. I told him that if he knows God, he knows everybody. I gave him some prayer points and a few weeks later, he came to testify that he got the job.

Some people say that they do not have funds but they forget the One, Who provides capital. This is how many people commit spiritual suicide. Many condemn themselves and declare that they are poor. How is this? When they want to pay their tithe, they limit themselves to 10% and calculate it to the exact nearest Kobo. They are limiting God to their salary. Are you like that? When do you wish to move away from that level? Are you a petty tailor, whose shop is on his shoulder? Are you a cut and sew tailor? When do you want to leave that level and own a sewing institute? This is what is called spiritual suicide and many believers do it everyday.

Many people do menial jobs and have no intention of progressing. Many are at the apprenticeship level, yet they become masters of themselves and do not make progress. Whereas, God has deposited many things in them but they are not making use of those things. Many have talents, gifts and potentials that God has deposited into their lives, but they are not making use of them; they put a limit on themselves and so, they are not progressing. It could be in academics or in business, crafts and so on, but they declare that they are limited and so, they cannot move. In this kind of case, the person himself made the declaration and the devil stamped it. Such people blame their misfortune on people or forces, without knowing that they had first drawn a conclusion for the devil to sanction.

Take these prayers points:
* **I command all the forces limiting my potentials to be paralysed, in the name of Jesus.**
* **I refuse to enter into the waste bin of life, in the name of Jesus.**

WHAT ARE POTENTIALS?
1. **Hidden Talents.**
You might be surprised to find out that the thing that is making you prosperous now, is the least of the things that God would like to bestow upon you. The superior one that would make you burst forth into your breakthrough, could still be hidden. So, you need to take time out to find out what your hidden talents are. How do you know them? Simple. What are those things you enjoy doing, or those things that give you satisfaction or inner joy? *Note they have to be good and positive things.

2. **Reserved Power.**
It is in your life but you are not making use of it.

3. **Unused Success.**

4. **What you can do, but you have not done and are not doing.**

5. **How far you can go, but you have not yet gone and are not going.**

6. **Hidden or latent ability or power.**

7. **What you can accomplish, that you have not yet, accomplished.** It is an egg that is incubating but not hatched. Whatever you have already accomplished is no longer a potential, it has been achieved.

8. **The height to which you can climb, but that you have not yet attained.**

God in His mercy and wisdom, created everything with potentials. God did not give you your potentials to deposit it in satanic graves. It is a pity that many people die without exploring the potentials and abilities in them. Many lives, including those of Christians, are like batteries in a torch. As long as the torch is there unlit, the batteries are there unused. If care is not taken, they will leak and cause corrosion in the torch and everything will be wasted.

Take this prayer point:
* **I paralyse, all powers assigned to waste my abilities, in the name of Jesus.**

If you allow your potentials to be paralysed, you are committing spiritual suicide.

DESTROYERS OF POTENTIALS ARE:
1. **Sin.**
It is the biggest paralyser, aborter and killer of potentials. It blocks potentials and spoils God's plan for the life of a person. It kills a person internally and buries him or her while still alive. A sinner is in a dark end and so cannot see God and God is not looking at what the person does. Everything that such a person does is done in darkness. There are many people who would have been extremely useful to God, but they are living in sin. For some people, it is drunkenness; for some, anger or impatience. Sin is a spiritual coffin which buries potentials.

Some are living in sin and are suffering from its consequences, but they are blaming their predicament on other people. They are just wasting their time. Many people who are supposed to be leaders have been turned to servants by cigarettes, alcohol, etc. Could you imagine a whole President, who got to that position with God's consent, sleeping in a gutter because he was drunk? Some people say they drink in moderation, but they cannot be wiser than the devil.

One day, during a funeral service, the preacher gave an unusual sermon. He said the man that died was most likely in hell. He said he the preacher, was called upon several times to remove the man from the gutter whenever he got drunk. He told the widow to stop crying, that he knew how she cried all the time whilst the man was alive and was misbehaving. That was a strange sermon but it was the blunt truth. When people are told the truth, they do not like it.

When MFM started in one of our branches abroad, the sisters at first found it difficult to comply with our principles. They did not know that holiness is not just within a person, but also without. They found it difficult to accept the fact that trousers are for men and not for women. They found it difficult to do away with their make-ups, jewelry and attachments. So, many of them left.

Some out of those that left, came back after realising the usefulness of staying away from those things. As a student in England, I attended a church where majority of the population were white. The sisters did not wear trousers and they tied a scarf on their heads when coming to church. So, it is not a matter of colour or location. It is a thing of the mind.

Many people who are supposed to be first class students, have been paralysed by Indian Hemp and Cocaine. Some ladies who are supposed to be top class students got pregnant in Form 3. Accidental pregnancies have been used to paralyse their careers and lives.

Many people struggle throughout life and never make it because of sin. Sin destroys divine fertilizers. Sin has the potential to paralyse the potentials of the practitioners. It blocks the divine flow of God's power and locks up the person's potentials. It causes untimely death and all that people can do for the dead person is to write an epitaph on his or her grave that he or she 'died untimely' while stating all the degrees that the person acquired and did not make use of. Take this prayer point aggressively.

* **O Lord, if there is any sin in my life, remove it far away from me, in the name of Jesus.**

When I was a student in the secondary school, there was a girl who could speak English like a Briton. She was a Christian and had always passed her examinations with brilliant colours. The least mark she ever got was 96%. One day, a Yoruba man wanted to discuss with an Edo woman, but the woman did not understand Yoruba and the man too did not understand English. So, he called this girl to interpret his intentions- he wanted to commit fornication with the woman. The girl too sat there and was interpreting. As a Christian, she should have refused point blank but she conveyed the immoral message. Soon, she sat for the School Certificate Examination and everybody was expecting a Grade 1 distinction. To our utter surprise, this girl failed woefully. When she went to check her results, she burst out crying that she knew what she had done, that the devil crept in through the sinful interpretation that she did. She went to the Lord in total repentance and retook the examination the following year and she came out with a Grade 1 Distinction.

She did not have to loose one-year just like that, but she did because of her involvement and compromise with sin. You might say that she was not the one that committed fornication but it was through her that the message was conveyed. This shows that children of God should not compromise with sin in any way. Beloved, you have the chance today of making up your mind that, sin wilt not have dominion over you.

2. **Unbelief**.
There are many miracles that God cannot do because of unbelief Let us see Mark 6:5-6;
"And he could there do no mighty work, save that he laid his hands upon a few sick folk, and healed them. And he marveled because of their unbelief. And he went round about the villages, teaching."

Also Mathew 13:58;
"And he did not many mighty works there because of their unbelief."

This is a sad story. As powerful as the Lord Jesus is, He was limited by the unbelief of the people. He could not do much there to help them; right in His home town. Unbelief ties the hands of the Almighty God so that, He cannot do that which He intends to do in the life of a person. A person could fast and pray, but until he or she starts believing, nothing happens. Satan knows that a person cannot get anything from God except through faith, so he struggles to fill the hearts of people with unbelief. Sometimes, unbelief could do more harm than lying or adultery because it is not easily detectable. Many men of God in the Bible changed their destiny by faith in God, and by unbelief, many buried themselves alive. Hebrews 11 gives an account of those who walked with God by faith and quenched the rage and fire of the enemy.

Take this prayer point: **Every spirit of unbelief, pack out of my life in the name of Jesus.**

Beloved, keep this message in your heart it will transfer you from minimum to maximum.

3. **The spirit of 'Herod'**
If Herod had succeeded in killing Jesus in infancy, Jesus would not have died for the whole world on the cross at Calvary. The spirit of 'Herod' is the spirit of abortion. It terminates life before the full potentials are realised. It aborts people's potentials and kills them in infancy; not allowing them to go further than they should go. This spirit has many children:

i. Untimely death,
ii. Insanity- being alive but dead,
iii. Incurable and terminal diseases.

Although there are many ways through which Satan kill people, but, he does not have the power to take life if the person does not allow him.

Ways Of Killing Oneself:
1. **Suicide**.
Some people decide that they are fed up with life and decide to end it by jumping into a river or hanging themselves etc.

2. **Fear**
One day, during a practical chemistry class, a student mixed some chemicals and there was an explosion. Before we knew what it was, everyone had sought refuge here and there. Suddenly, we noticed that our lecturer was nowhere to be found; he had jumped out of the window. Later he came in and we confronted him that he had the spirit of fear in him. He defended himself by saying that if anything bad had happened, that was how he would have escaped. At the same time, if that professor had knocked his head on hard concrete, he would have died. The truth is that, he had the spirit of fear in him. Fear makes people to kill themselves by their own hands. People die by the hands of other people, while some die by breaking natural laws. Some die by fearing death. Some die by getting old. By sickness or diseases. All these things could be used by the

Spirit of Herod against anybody.

Take this prayer point seriously.
* **Every "Herod" operating in my life and that of my husband/wife and children, be roasted! in the name of Jesus.**

Beloved, this topic is so important that I would not like to rush over it. Therefore, I would like to stop here for now. We shall continue next time by the special grace of God.

If hitherto, you have not surrendered your life to the Lord Jesus Christ, I would advise that you do so right away, right there where you are. The Bible says that the eyes of God cannot behold sin; therefore, repent and confess your sins to Him. Name them one by one and ask Him to forgive you and cleanse you from all unrighteousness.

Claim the redemptive power in the Blood of Jesus that was shed on the cross at Calvary, for the remission of your sins. The Lord is ready to save you; all you need do, is come to Him humbly and surrender your totality to Him. Renounce the devil and the world; say bye-bye to them and make sure you do not go back to those things that you have left behind.

Invite the Lord Jesus into your life; ask Him to become your personal Lord and Saviour. Open the door of your heart to Him; enthrone Him over your life and hand over all the affairs of your life to Him.

I congratulate you for this decision that you have just taken. It is the most important and I pray that it shall be permanent in the Name of Jesus. I pray that the Lord will uphold you with His right hand of righteousness and will not let you fall in the name of Jesus. I pray that your name will be written in the Book of Life and you will not by any means, rub it off in the name of Jesus. Take the following prayer points with all the aggression that you can gather:

1. Any herbalist, searching for my star, receive blindness! in the name of Jesus.
2. My God shall arise and my enemies shall scatter, in the name of Jesus.
3. My God shall arise and miracles shall manifest in my life, in the name of Jesus.
4. Spirit of promotion, fall upon me! in the name of Jesus.
5. Every power of sorrow and tragedy in my life, die! in the name of Jesus.
6. Every witchcraft Pharaoh, stubbornly pursuing my life, die! in the name of Jesus.
7. Lord, smoothen my way to the top, by Your hand of fire, in the name of Jesus.
8. Lord, help me to identify and deal with any weakness in me that can hinder my progress, in the name of Jesus.
9. I bind, every strongman delegated to hinder my progress, in the name of Jesus.
10. Let every evil records planted by the devil in anyone's mind against my advancement, be into shattered to pieces, in the name of Jesus.
11. Lord, transfer, remove or change all human agents that are bent on stopping my advancement, in the name of Jesus.
12. Let all adversaries to my breakthroughs be put to shame, in the name of Jesus.
13. Let the anointing of the overcomers fall upon me, in the name of Jesus.
14. Let all negative word and pronouncement against my success be completely nullified, in the name of Jesus.
15. Every arrow of the enemy fired against my life, to slow down my progress in life, die, in the name of Jesus.
16. Every satanic bondage in my life, that is limiting my progress break by fire, in the name of Jesus.
17. Let every satanic barrier on my way of progress be dismantled, by the thunder and fire of the Holy Spirit, in the name of Jesus.
18. I paralyse every progress arresters fashioned against my destiny, in the name of Jesus.
19. Every Goliaths, of ungodly delay, what are you waiting for, die, in the name of Jesus.
20. You my life, climb by fire, to the mountain top where you cannot be afflicted again, in the name of Jesus.
21. I receive the anointing to move from minimum to maximum today, in the name of Jesus.

22. My life, become too hot for the enemy to handle, the name of Jesus.
23. Every power, calling me from the mountain top to the valley, die, in the name of Jesus.
24. Every wall of Jericho barring my promise land, incrumble by fire, in the name of Jesus.
25. Lord anoint me to excel above my counterparts, in the name of Jesus.
26. Every satanic summon of my head, back fire! in the name of Jesus.
27. God arise in my life and let my enemies know that You are my God, in the name of Jesus.
28. I shall be the head and not the tail, in the name of Jesus.

Paralysing Progress Arresters - 2

Isaiah 52:2 *"Shake thyself from the dust; arise, and sit down, O Jerusalem: loose thyself from the bands of thy neck, O captive daughter of Zion."*

Last time, we started this important topic and we adjourned, in order to be able to go into more details. We mentioned the fact that shaking the dust off a person depends on the person concerned. In other words, the onus has to come from him or her. We discussed the relationship between progress and the potential that God deposits in an individual. We also saw the elements that could destroy these potentials; with or without the person's consent. We mentioned the fact that it is possible for a person to kill those potentials by himself whether consciously or unconsciously, and we termed this as being suicidal. As we continue this topic, I advise that you read with a rapt attention and pray the prayers that follow, with all the seriousness that you can gather.

PROGRESS ARRESTERS:
These are elements in the life of a person that put a person in a state of unseriousness with God. Many people are students in 'The School of Those Who Take The Word of God Lightly.' Beloved, God says what He means and means what He says; that's who He is. God would not speak if He didn't mean it. If you therefore take God's word lightly, it means you do not fear Him. The Bible says: *"The fear of God is the beginning of wisdom."* You could call yourself the greatest professor in the world, as far as the Bible is concerned, if you do not fear God, you are not wise at all, because the starting point towards wisdom, is the fear of God. The Bible says something in Matthew 12:34: *"O generation of vipers, how can we, being evil, speak good things? For out of the abundance of the heart the mouth speaketh."*

To buttress some important points, let's also see some other Bible verses in correlation with the above verse. Luke 6:45: *"A good man out of the good treasure of his heart bringeth forth that which is good; and an evil man out of the evil treasure of his heart bringeth forth that which is evil: for of the abundance of the heart his mouth speaketh."* Matthew 12:36: *"But I say unto you, that every idle word that men shall speak, they shall give account thereof in the Day of Judgment."*

Matthew 12:37:
"For by thy words thou shalt be justified, and by thy words thou shalt be condemned."

The verses above are pointing to the fact that the heart is involved in what a person says. It means, it is what you have in your heart that you speak out; nothing comes out accidentally. The way a person uses his or her tongue is a clear indication of the person's spiritual condition. If you are the kind that just says anything without thinking deeply, the Bible says all the things you say, are being saved into the heavenly computer and will be replayed before you on that day of judgement; and you have to answer to each of them. The Bible says if you call your brother a fool, you are going to hell-fire. You have to give an account of every word and if you take it lightly, there will be trouble. If you are a person who decides to pick and choose which of God's commands you want to obey, it means you are not thinking of serious spiritual breakthroughs.

A man of God noticed that nothing was happening in his ministry. He locked himself up in his room for three days. He told his wife not to open the door until he says he has seen Jesus. He was there for three days and on the third day, he saw the Lord; The Lord told him that he had 13 things in his life that he had to correct, for power to fall upon him and then his ministry would prosper. He wrote down these 13 things and found out that the last two were too shameful to admit to his wife; he had to remove these two things from the entire list, though he worked on them secretly.

This shows that God knows every tiny detail of our life that other people might not know. It is like a rat hiding under a cupboard; it thinks the cupboard is fixed like a mountain, so it feels its hiding is secure. It would be surprised one day, when the owner of the house decides to move the cupboard from that location to another. The rat will be exposed and probably killed with all its kitten.

When God ministers to you through His Word in the Bible or through a message, you have to act accordingly, in the Mountain of Fire and Miracles Ministries, we talk a lot about brokenness. It is possible for a Christian to err, because he or she is human but if such fails to acknowledge the wrong doing, it means he or she is not ready to repent. A sinner with pride and dry eyes cannot be forgiven. A sinner who admits that he or she has sinned and breaks down mourning, crying before God, knowing that he or she has failed Him, will find favour with God. God will forgive such a child and hear his or her supplication. A sinner that is not sorry for his or her sins and just continues life as if nothing happened is taking God's word lightly and such is wasting time.

The Bible says: "Blessed are those who mourn, for they shall be comforted. Why do they mourn? They mourn over their inefficiency, their failure and sinful conditions. When you fall short of God's expectation, you have to repent and mourn and take God's word seriously. Do not compare yourself with the people that are still in the world. Do not say that you are better off. You might be shocked to find out on the day of judgement that your name is not in the Book of Life; though your father had been a catechist and you were dedicated and baptised on the eighth day. It will be too late to realize that all the singing in the church choir, all the meetings you have been attending, amount to nothing on the day of judgement. It would only mean that church attendance and the display of Christian slogans on stickers are all vain. I pray that it shall not be so for you, in the name of Jesus. But then, all His words must be taken seriously; do not be in the company of 'Executive Sinners' who commit fornication in the office without anyone's knowledge; yet, they come home in good time, perform their duties as husband and father, attend church services and put up a Christian front. If nobody knows, God sees them, and all these things are being recorded. Therefore beloved, if you want your potentials to grow, you must take the word of God with all seriousness.

One day, a sister got home and found her husband in their matrimonial bed with a strange woman. She just sighed, went into the sitting room and started to pray that God should deliver her husband and the woman because they were unconsciously possessed. When the husband came out of the bedroom with the strange woman, they were shocked to find the wife just sitting there, not saying anything. Later, the strange woman turned to the man and called him an animal, that he had such a beautiful, well-behaved wife at home and was still playing pranks with her. She immediately vowed never to see him again. That incident brought the husband to the Lord, and he is now a member of M.F.M. In fact, he now prays harder than the wife. I really know that some sisters would not have taken that kind of incident lightly; they would have fought ruthlessly on that day and would have brought more trouble into their lives and home. The man would not have had the opportunity of surrendering his life to the Lord Jesus Christ.

Have you decided to be serious with God? The Bible says: 'Man shall not live by bread alone, but by every word that comes out of His mouth." The Bible says EVERY WORD, not SOME,

One day, a sister said the Lord spoke to her, that if she wanted to be useful in His vineyard, she had to do away with her jewelleries. She removed her necklaces and others but left the earrings. One day, she was in a bus, when a man gave her a slap on both cheeks and her earrings disappeared. She actually thought the man was a robber. When she told me, I said it was possible that the man was an angel sent by the Lord; The Lord saw that she was not helping herself so, He sent an angel to help her. Some people sometimes need such a help, in order to be what God wants them to be. This also means that it is possible for satanic powers to cage a person's potentials and star, so that such that he will not move forward.

Take this prayer point:
* **O Lord, I will take every word from Your mouth serious in the name of Jesus.**

SATISFACTION WITH PAST ACHIEVEMENTS:
People have the tendency to settle for what they have accomplished, even when these achievements are stale. One of the greatest enemies of progress is: Previous Success. Although you could be pleased with what or where you are now, I am telling you that you are not yet where God wants you to be. It is a tragedy, to accept your present state as being final. It should not be so; your present state is just a stage. If you are going to attain the level that God intends for you, you should not be the same as you were last year, and you should not remain as you are now, next year. The moment you settle down and are satisfied with what or where you are now, you are closing the door of the possibility of exposing what God had deposited in your life.

The Apostles received a matching order that they should remain in Jerusalem until the Holy Ghost came upon them, that they would receive power and become witnesses in Jerusalem, Judea, Samaria and the uttermost parts of the earth. After the Holy Ghost had come upon them, they still sat in Jerusalem and only a few people got converted. When persecution started, they realised that they had to move and do what the Lord asked them to do. Many Christians are like that; they are content with being born again. If you are saved, you have to seek to be sanctified, if you are sanctified, you must seek to be baptised in the Holy Ghost, seek to prophesy, seek the other gifts, seek to speak in tongues and interpret the tongues. Similarly, if you are a petty trader, move to a kiosk or shop, then move to your complex; do not slaughter the 'Moses' that God has given to you, on the altar of your present satisfaction.

Pray like these:
* **I refuse to be stagnant in the name of Jesus.**
* **I refuse to remain in the same condition, in the name of Jesus.**

COUNTERFEIT BAPTISM!
Before a car battery can be useful, it needs acid. The Holy Spirit is the key that supplies the water of life into your life, to release your potentials. Without the infilling of the Holy Spirit, a person cannot function to his or her fullest potentials. If you are not yet a Christian, it means you do not know who you are yet; you belong to the 'Endangered Species.' It is like the decrees that have gone out against the killing of animals like the elephant, hyena and a few others. They are termed. 'Endangered Species' because of the rate at which they were being killed either for food or other purposes; they are likely to become extinct, if care is not taken. They are endangered because, if they finish, future generations of children will not know what they are. There is a possibility of them disappearing forever. Anyone who does not know or accept the Lord is an 'Endangered Specie'; there is the possibility of him or her dying and perishing; nobody will see such again.

When you become born again and you receive the Lord Jesus Christ as your personal Lord and Saviour, the power of God comes upon you and the Holy Spirit will reveal to you, who you really are. Your physical eyes cannot see your true potentials or who you really are. Your physical ears cannot hear what the Holy Spirit is saying; your mind cannot perceive it. Unless the Holy Spirit reveals it to you. He is the only One Who goes deep into a person and captures the wealth of the potentials inside him or her and then brings them to the surface.

If you have been going about with the kind of spirit that came upon you through blabbing or through some strange words that were written on paper which you were asked to learn by heart then you have a counterfeit spirit which you must get rid of, and then seek the Spirit of the Living God. Some people think that their ability to dream and see visions, is the baptism in the Holy Spirit but it is not so. Cornelius saw a vision without sleeping but he did not have the Holy Ghost, until Peter went to him. Some people speak in the tongues that they heard from preachers on television, which they have memorised.

A 17-year-old girl told me she received the baptism in the Holy Ghost and as she started speaking, I found out that they were empty blabbing. Some people say: "Eli. Eli, Eli" or "Ma ma ma." These are empty words. The Bible says we should speak as the Holy Spirit gives us utterance. If a person says he speaks French and all he can say is "Merci beaucoup" to every question asked him. It will be discovered that he cannot speak the language. Some people roll on the floor whilst saying strange things and regard it as the manifestation of the Holy Spirit.

I was invited to a white garment church to preach and the Spirit of God asked me to go. During the service, a woman started to manifest; she banged her head on the floor, rolled from one end of the room to the other and her garment almost came off her. I was wondering what was going on and suddenly, someone went close to her and said; *"Speak Lord for your servants heareth."* I knew that was not the Spirit of God but the people did not know it.

Maybe the kind of spirit you received is the one that makes you hop on one leg or makes you bend double. You have to seek the true baptism in the Holy Ghost, for your potentials to be exposed. There is no one who receives the genuine baptism in the Holy Ghost that does not experience a change in his or her life. If your life remains the way it has always been, without fresh fire to pray or to witness or to read the Bible, you have to examine the kind of spirit that you received.

AVOIDING CHALLENGES:

One of the best ways of keeping holy is witnessing to others. If you go to the streets to witness, it will be difficult for you to engage in any thing that does not edify. I remember the day I found out that I could actually climb a tree. On that day, a friend asked me to go to the Railway Compound with him, in order to pluck fruits. We got to an unusually clean house, with a clean surrounding and we started plucking fruits. Suddenly, we heard a wild dog barking and heading towards us. My friend quickly jumped and climbed a tree. I had never done it in my life, but that was the only way out, if I did not want to be bitten by the dog. I jumped and discovered that I could actually climb the tree. I thank God for that dog, because it made me know how to climb a tree. It also made me to pray hot prayers on the tree. It refused to go; it was pacing up and down. So, I had to pray that the Lord should make it forget about us. Eventually, God answered my prayers and it left.

The same holds true for each and everyone. You could be the way you are now, because there are no challenges. Do not wait for a dog to chase you; challenge yourself to praying your way through. Take a look at yourself now; decide to be the best at what you are doing. Be sure you are even better than those that got there before you. Do not wait for challenges. Do not run away from challenges. If you are a student, study hard. If you want to be the best student, then study harder than any other person and then pray for God's blessings on what you have read.

LIVING A PLAN-LESS LIFE:

Jesus asked if there was a person who would want to build a house that would not first sit and calculate all that he needs for the construction. If he does not do his calculations well, he could find out midway, that he is not able to complete the building, and people will mock him for it. A lot of Christians live plan-less, order-less lives. They do a lot of talking without doing anything; these people have failed to plan.

Beloved, do you have a notebook where you have written out the things that you would like to do in the next five years or even five months?

If you are confused about your life now, it means you do not know what is going on in it. Are you living your life day by day without a concrete documentation by which you live? You could say that your life is in the hands of God but you must note that He wants you to plan your life. Have you been struggling with the same issues for years? Do you move three steps forward and four steps backwards? If there is no good thing that you are pursuing now, you will be dragged back to demotion. Progress requires planning. Some people have food timetables, to manage their feeding but have nothing for their life. When you have no plan for your life, you cannot check your progress. You must have some raw materials for God to work upon.

Many people ask God to bless them without plans. They wake up and say they want to do one thing or the other, without having specific plans on how they want to go about it. What raw materials do you want God to work upon? Plan who you want to be and God will then begin to soak that plan in the Holy Spirit. If He does not like it He will ask you to change it to something else. You must have a plan.

LAZINESS:
You have to put hard work in whatever you are doing. A lazy man cannot expect food on his table. God detests the lazy spirit.

SATANIC FORCES:
These are powers that destroy people's potentials.
A brother did not know what was wrong with his life, until he started to pray fire prayers. During a 'Power Must Change Hands' Programme, as he was praying, he saw himself taken out to a grave, by an angel. The angel tapped the grave and called the name of the brother's grandmother. An old woman came out and the angel ordered her to return what she had stolen from the brother. She looked here and there and said she could not find it but the angel insisted; until she brought out a parcel and handed it over to the brother. This brother did not know his grandmother physically; she died before he was born, but she had already finished his life. Thank God that he prayed those prayers. It was after that incident, that he started to experience breakthroughs and the success story of his life began.

This is to show that satanic powers can cage a person's potentials and consequently cage his or her star, so that the person will not advance. Maybe you are in that kind of state, where the agent who had done any evil to you is dead, I declare to you, that power must change hands in your life today, in the name of Jesus.

WHAT TO DO TO TAKE AUTHORITY:
Stand against these evil powers and forces behind abnormalities in your life, and pray them out of your way. Many Christians do not understand what it means to take authority. Some only say it without knowing what it means.
Taking authority means:

1. **To command:** James 5:14-15: *"Is any sick among you? Let him call for the elders of the church; and let them pray over him, anointing him with oil in the name of the Lord: And the prayer of faith shall save the sick, and the Lord shall raise him up; and if he have committed sins, they shall be forgiven him."*

2. **To decree:**
Establishing a thing militantly.

3. **To allow:**
That which should be given the chance of taking place. Many times in the Bible, we read "And it came to pass..." Allow the word of God to be established in your life, as He has promised,

4. **To disallow:**
You must disallow negative things like poverty, hardship and all evil things against God's plan for you. Paul was in a shipwreck and he declared that no life shall be lost in the ship and it was so.

The word of God, prayer, fasting, and holiness form the power base of Christians; these form an important source through which Christians can operate. You have to start taking action as from today. Get out of the school of wishful thinking. Put your pen to paper, take down plans and take them to the Lord. Refuse to remain in your present position. Do not say you are not doing too badly; look ahead of that position. If your business is little, turn it into a giant. If it is already a giant, make it become a situation, where your absence will subject people to restlessness; make it an essential thing. We have the God who says: "Behold Silver and Gold are mine." He says

He can teach your finger to battle and your hands to war. We have the God who can give you power to leap over a wall and run through a troop and capture your oppressors.

Are you ready for some serious praying on this message? I do not expect your life to remain the same after this. We are going to start with household wickedness because that is where the potentials of most Africans are buried. You have to pray with holy madness so that the way will clear for you in everything.

However, if hitherto, you have not surrendered your life to the Lord Jesus Christ, you are not born again, and you would need to do so, before you pray the prayers that I am suggesting below. The Bible says that, God cannot behold sin. You cannot approach the throne of grace in your sinful state. All you need to do is acknowledge the fact that you are a sinner. Repent from your sins, confess them to Him, name them one by one and ask Him to forgive you and cleanse you from all unrighteousness. Claim the redemptive power in the Blood of Jesus that was shed on the Cross, at Calvary, for the remission of your sins. Say bye-bye to the world and the devil. Then invite the Lord Jesus Christ into your life. Ask Him to become your personal Lord and Saviour. Enthrone Him over your life and ask Him to take control of all that concerns you. Surrender your totality to Him and do not go back to the world any more.

If you just took this decision, I congratulate you. It is the most important decision in life. I pray that it shall be permanent in the name of Jesus. I pray that the Lord will uphold you with His right hand of righteous and will not let you fall in the name of Jesus. I pray that your name will be written in the Book of Life and you will not by any means, rub it off in the name of Jesus.

This is no joke at all; take these prayer points with holy madness:

1. I refuse to wear the rags prepared by household wickedness in the name of Jesus.
2. I exhume all my potentials buried in the ground; come out to me now! in the name of Jesus.
3. I break every curse, working against my progress in the name of Jesus.
4. I shall reach my goal whether the devil likes it or not, in the name of Jesus.
5. The plan of God for my life shall not be aborted, in the name of Jesus.
6. Lord, open my eyes to see my divine destiny, in the name of Jesus.
7. Every evil driver in the vehicle of my destiny, get down now! in the name of Jesus.
8. Holy Spirit, be my destiny driver in the name of Jesus.
9. Lord, remove me from every diverted path in the name of Jesus.
10. I shall reach my promised land, by fire, in the name of Jesus.
11. Societal hindrances shall not know my destiny, in Jesus' name.
12. Where is the Lord God of Elijah, arise and destroy whatever does not glorify you in my destiny, in Jesus' name.
13. I refuse to tread the path of failure, in Jesus' name.
14. Lord, give me the opportunities that will promote my destiny forever, in Jesus' name.
15. My God, arise and silence the mouth of the enemy speaking against my destiny, in Jesus' name.
16. I shall arise and no man shall be able to stop me, in Jesus' name.
17. The star of my destiny shall shine brightest, in Jesus' name.
18. Powers of my father's house, release me by fire, in Jesus' name.
19. Powers of my mother's house, loose your hold on my glory, in the name of Jesus.
20. Every voice of my family idol, crying failure on me, die by fire, in the name of Jesus.
21. I am for success, I am not for failure, in the name of Jesus.
22. I am an opportunity to my generation, in Jesus' name.
23. I refuse to be wasted, in the name of Jesus.
24. Marital failure, loose your grip and die, in the name of Jesus.
25. Let every evil marriage conducted for me under the waters, hindering my progress, be annulled in the name of Jesus.
26. I release my potentials

hidden in the body of any water in the name of Jesus.

27. Lord, promote me from minimum to maximum in the name of Jesus.

28. God arise and let me experience Your raw power in the name of Jesus.

29. I seal all my prayers with the Blood of Jesus and they shall become testimonies in the name of Jesus.

The Way Of Wholeness

Luke 17:11-19: *"And it came to pass, as he went to Jerusalem, that he passed through the midst of Samaria and Galilee. And as he entered into a certain village, there met him ten men that were lepers, which stood afar off: And they lifted up their voices, and said, Jesus, Master, have mercy on us. And when he saw them, he said unto them, Go shew yourselves unto the priests. And it came to pass, that, as they went, they were cleansed. And one of them, when he saw that he was healed, turned back, and with a loud voice glorified God. And fell down on his face at his feet, giving him thanks: and he was a Samaritan. And Jesus answering said, Were there not ten cleansed? but where are the nine? There are not found that returned to give glory to God, save this stranger. And he said unto him, Arise, go thy way: thy faith hath made thee whole."*

Ten men in this story were healed but it was only one that came back to give thanks to the Lord Jesus. Jesus immediately marvelled at this man's faith and blessed him the more, saying that his faith had made him whole. It however would signify a total restoration of everything in him; the parts or organs of his body that were eaten up by leprosy, were replaced with new ones.

Wholeness means a complete, full or joyful state of the mind, spirit, soul and body of an individual.

The keys to the way of wholeness are outlined in the above passage; they are:

1. **Whole-hearted prayers**: The lepers called upon the Lord in verse 13. Their heart were not divided, they were with a deep concentration. It is advisable when you approach the Lord in prayer; to do it with your whole heart.

2. **The word of God**
Read, digest, regurgitate on His Word. You must be able to quote the Scriptures for every situation. Sometimes, when a person is attacked in the dream, all that is needed, is the application of the Word of God. Psalm 138:2 *"I will worship toward Thy holy temple, and praise Thy Name for Thy loving kindness and for Thy truth: for Thou hast magnified Thy word above all Thy name"*

Psalm 107:20: *"He sent His word, and healed them, and delivered them from their destructions."*

These texts show the position of the Word of God; He magnifies His Word. In the beginning, every thing was in a confused state until God said: "Let there be light" and there was Light.
I will not cease to say that believers should memorise the Word of God. Anyone who has been born again for up to one or two years, should have memorised at least 52 verses of the Bible. That is an average of one verse a day. You must fill your heart with the Word of God. If the level of the Word of God in a person is high, sickness will be far, and demons will flee. If the level of the Word of God in a person is low, problems and pains will gain an upper hand. This is the stand of the Scriptures. Jesus spoke to those lepers and they were healed. God could speak to us through His written word or/and directly, and the onus is on us to listen to His voice.

3. **Obedience**
The lepers obeyed; they did not argue. Many people come to God and they are not really searching for something good. Many are really planning to fail. It is surprising to note that many people get to the place of power, with the plan to fail. They will get to a place where God is moving and all they are looking for are faults. They actually find these excuses and always end up not receiving anything for themselves. Some people are busy searching for hypocrites in the midst of the Children of God and they will find them there. In a crusade, where God is healing people, some people would be on the look out for those who will not get healed and they will see at least one;

since that is what they are looking for. These people would now use that as a standard.

It is God's will for everyone to be in good health; obedience to His Word is very important. Many people receive healing through the reading of His Word, or by listening to it being read. They key in to His injunction and obey what He says and miracles happen. When Naaman went to God's prophet and he was given instructions, he first argued. Thank God he eventually obeyed; he would have gone back home with his leprosy.

A man was referred to me for prayers because he had stroke. We prayed and for the first time in several months, he slept that night. He did not wake up until 12 noon the following day. Gradually, strength came back to his hand and he began to write with it. Later, he was able to move his leg and then started to walk. After a while, he resumed work. He was the Principal of a school and he was surprised that his assistant was shocked to see him back on his feet. (I declare today, that where you are not expected to reach, you will get there. Where you are not expected back at your rightful position, you will not only get there, but your enemies will bow to you in the Name of Jesus.) God is a God of wonders. This man regained his health perfectly, but the enemy was not happy. He came to see me one day, to say that his wife wanted him to go to the hospital for medical check-up. I told him not to go that the illness and the healing were not physical, that the Lord had done it and he had to stick to his testimony. The wife continued to pressurise him and eventually, he went to the hospital and of course, he was told that his blood pressure was high. He was admitted immediately and he never got down from that hospital bed.

The Bible says that obedience is better than sacrifice and to hearken, than the fat of rams. Jesus told a man to go to the river of Siloam to wash his face that he would be made whole. The man did not argue that it was on a Sabbath; he obeyed and was made whole. When we obey God, things will happen.

4. **Joy and gratitude**

A lot of people are experts at complaining; they forget the goodness of God in their lives. All they see is the bad side of life and the bad things that are happening to them. They are like the man who was always complaining that he had no shoes. He murmured and asked why God did not provide shoes for him. One day, he saw a man praising God that he was alive. The man praising God had a smile on his face and looked contented. Looking closely, the man that had no shoes saw that the man praising God had no legs; his legs had been amputated. Thus, this prompted the complainer to henceforth stop grumbling and murmuring and to start praising God; if for nothing but that he had legs with which he could walk by himself.

The Bible says; "Rejoice in the Lord always." There should be no room for sadness in our lives at all. He says Rejoice in the Lord always and again, I say rejoice. Therefore with Joy shall you draw water from the well of Salvation."

If a person wants to go about with anxiety and with the burden of sorrow, wholeness will be far from him. People who wear the garment of melancholy are always sick, because it invites all the negative things. Worry, anxiety, depression etc invite sicknesses and destroy the internal system; making wrong things happen.

Scientists have discovered that the number of muscles that are needed for a smile are not as many as the ones put into action, when a person frowns his or her face. When the frowning muscles are in action, things begin to go wrong. You do not have to be a frowning person to show that you are holy. Some people wonder why others are happy and are smiling, despite all odds. These category of people see the world as being upside down. They do not know that wholeness does not come that way. It is a vicious cycle. A person who worries does not see miracles happen and before long, fear sets in and problems begin. As a child of God, you should be happy in any situation that you find yourself. You might not know what will happen tomorrow, but you have a Father who holds tomorrow in His hands and know what it holds. You should know that even though you do not know tomorrow, He knows; therefore, there is nothing to worry about.

I have a friend who says: "Why pray, when you can worry?" This is to provoke people to pray and see the futility in worrying. The Bible says: **"Cast all your burdens on Him, for He cares for you."** In everything: marriage, business, career, finances, choices, work, etc; cast them on Jesus, drop everything there; do not go back to take any thing. Can you imagine the dilemma of a motor mechanic, who has a client that keeps coming back to check the car that he (the client), brought for servicing. If the client keeps checking and testing the car every hour, the mechanic will not be able to do a proper job on the car; he will be disturbed and distracted and the work will not move forward.

When you drop your burden of problems at the feet of Jesus, and you keep picking out one item or other from the total burden, to worry about, you will be disturbing God. It could be that the moment you came to your marriage from His feet, was when He was going to start work on it. That means you have postponed your marital breakthrough.

Those who desire wholeness must have the joy of the Lord in their hearts. All Christians are supposed to have joy in their hearts not because they have money or riches, but because their names are written in the Book of Life. The Bible says if it is in this World alone that we have hope, then; we are of all creatures, most miserable. We thank God that we have hope here now and in eternity. Some people address themselves as 'miserable sinners. Beloved, it is bad enough to be a sinner, but is it even worse, if the sinner is miserable.

Many Christians are guilty of borrowing today's problems and transferring them to tomorrow's load. Many bring yesterday's problems and add them to today's.

Many years ago, a man was angry with another, saying that the other man's father offended him many years ago and did not apologise before he died. The other man said his father was dead, and wanted to know if the man wanted to go to the grave to still show his annoyance to the dead person. Such issues should not come up at all, anything that went wrong in the past, is gone. It is only the consequence that should be checked and prayed about, so as not to spoil today. If someone offended you two weeks ago, it should not make you worry today, otherwise wholeness will be far from you. When you encourage worry, anxiety, grumbling and complaining, you grow older than your age. You should be grateful to the Lord, for all that He has done for you and avoid this life shortener and heaven hinderer called worry.

The Bible says: *"Looking unto Jesus, the Author and Finisher of our faith."* If you go to the church and remove your attention from the Lord Jesus, you are likely to carry an unwanted luggage. The devil will give you many diversions; there will be many things to look at, so that you do not see Jesus. It rests on you not to look at the ugly situations around you; not to fix your attention on the strife or problem around you but to fix your gaze upon Jesus, and Jesus alone. Peter made that mistake; he took his eyes off Jesus to study his problems. He had a good start when he saw Jesus walking on the water; he asked Jesus, if it was truly Him and asked Jesus to tell him to come, if He was the one. Jesus then assured Peter that He was the one and asked him to come. He got up, stepped into the water, and began to walk. But immediately Peter removed his gaze from Jesus, he began to sink.

Many people today, would have asked Jesus to come and meet them where they were. One could give credit to Peter for attempting to walk on the sea. He is the first and only person to have done it so far because even Moses that parted the Read Sea walked on dry land. As Peter was sinking, he cried out for help and Jesus saved him; and asked why he doubted calling him a man of little faith. That simple doubt was enough to sink Peter.

Many people today, study the circumstances and storms around them; they reads conclusions on their situations, leaving Jesus out of them. Jesus grabbed Peter by the hand and drew him to safety. The faith of Jesus made Peter to walk back to the boat. Those who fix their gaze on Jesus, do not go about looking for mistakes in other people. They do not pass comments on the other people's behaviour or dressing; they look unto Jesus.

John 3:14-15:
"And as Moses lifted up the serpent in the wilderness, even so must the Son of man be lifted up: that whosoever believeth in Him should not perish, but have eternal life."

This is a simple fact about being made whole.

If you want to be made whole, the following ingredients are necessary and should be regular:
1. Repentance
2. Fasting and prayers

The day a Christian gets to the level of committing sin and not feeling sorry, the person has really started to decay, and is giving an urgent invitation to sickness, diseases etc.

Some people say that their God is not wicked, using this as an opportunity to commit all kinds of sin. An unmarried lady was brought to me for prayers and the Lord told me that she was sleeping about with men and still did so a few days before then. I then told her that I could not pray for her; that she needed to sort herself out with God. She said I was being too rigid, that God is not that harsh. I said that her own god must be different from the living God. who destroyed Sodom and Gomorrah executed the sons of Aaron because of their sins.

Hindrances to Wholeness

1. **Lack of knowledge of The Promises of God, to Make Whole and Deliver His People.**

Ignorance is a very terrible school. It is unfortunate that ignorance, as it is in every human court of law, is not an excuse. God has set the world in order and has laid down some rules. He says: *"Thou shall not do this or that"* Behind every 'Thou shall not ..." (which God has no obligation of explaining to you), there are punishments and repercussions attached; there are ready-made consequences of breaking the laws. Immediately a person breaks God's laws, a repercussion follows. It does not have to wait to be manufactured. If you get into trouble because you lack knowledge, that does not mean that you will not suffer for it; the punishment will come. The Bible says: *"The servant who knows the will of the Master and does not do it, shall receive many stripes but the servant who does not know, shall receive few."* It means that at the end, both of them shall receive stripes.

Do not say that you did not know what you were doing. When a law has been broken, punishment follows; that is why God is just and righteous. He says: "Though hand be joined in hand, no sinner shall go unpunished," though the Bible says: 'The times of ignorance, God over looks."

Beloved, no one can have faith in what he or she has never heard about. The first day I heard about the Anti-Christ, I was shaken to the roots. The preacher showed me many verses of the scriptures. In my church then, all we were taught was; singing and dancing. We were not taught about sin and its consequences, neither were we taught about the End Times. And if I never heard, how would I take action? The Rapture could have come and one would have been left behind. Ignorance of these things would not have disrupted God's programme. Many people are hearing the Good News and are not doing anything about it. Let such know now that God's word has no respect for persons and that ignorance is never an excuse.

I would also like you to retain the fact that wholeness is part of your birthright as a Christian. Sickness does not glorify God. If you however do not know about God's promises that none of these diseases of the Egyptians which you know shall come upon you, you may suffer ignorantly from an affliction which should have been sent to the sender.

2. **Sin**
God will not heal a sinner, so that he or she can continue to sin. See what John 3:36 says:
"He that believeth on the Son hath everlasting life: and he that believeth not the Son shall not see life; but the wrath of God abideth on him."

A white preacher once said that if you educate a sinner, you are producing a clever devil or an academic sinner. The way of the transgressor however is hard; it is not easy. God has no pleasure in the death of a sinner but wants him or her to repent because He knows that anything you sow, you will reap.

Sin will destroy your wholeness. Your faith cannot make any impact when there is disobedience to God's clear commandments. Many people collect prayer points but these prayers do not have any effect because they have not allowed God in every area of their lives; God's mercy can only work when the wicked forsakes his wicked ways.
When you allow lies, deception, envy, greed, crooked business, the sale of harmful and sinful substances like alcohol, stimulants, condoms, cigarettes, etc into your hands, you are sinning against God. If you have a supermarket or restaurant, you should not sell or serve alcohol to please customers. If you do, the devil will have reasons against you and will quote the Scripture that says: *"Woe unto him that gives his neighbour drink."* He will say that a person that is under God's 'Woe' cannot be made whole.

3. Unforgiving Spirit
Some people have someone or people that they have vowed not to ever forgive.

4. Friendship With The World
James 4; *"Ye ask, and receive not, because ye ask amiss, that ye may consume it upon your lusts. Ye adulterers and adulteresses know ye not that the friendship of the world is enmity with God? Whosoever therefore will be a friend of the world is the enemy of God."*

If you act, talk like the people of the world, or work for the same purpose for which they are working, you are friendly with the world and that brings trouble.

5. Failure To Make Restitution
If you have done anything wrong to anyone, you have to put it right. Failure to make wrong things right has led many people to their graves early. Often, people excuse themselves in things that they accuse others of. If you have taken anything that does not belong to you, return it. If there is someone that you are quarrelling with, settle it today. If you have anything that you got through manipulating other people, take it back and then wholeness will be yours.

6. Impatience
This hinders people from persisting in prayer; because with consistency at times, comes receiving from God. Some people stop attending church services because nothing happened on the first day that they went there. They forget that no preacher can preach everything that is needed in one night. Some people take time to go to the hospital, but cannot take time off to listen to the Word of God. Many people take 'sick leave' to go and relax on a hospital bed, but cannot ask for permission to go for deliverance. Many cannot persist before the Lord and have faith in God.

7. Unbelief
Mighty miracles will be stopped if you do not believe God. Jesus was unable to do anything in His hometown because of their unbelief.

Today beloved, I would like you to pray fervently. Those lepers called upon the Lord and He answered them. You too can call upon Him today. However, if you have not yet surrendered your life to the Lord Jesus Christ, I would like you to do so, right there where you are. He is waiting to take you in His arms. All you need do is repent of your sins and confess them to the Lord. Name those sins one by one and renounce them. Ask Him to forgive you and cleanse you from all unrighteousness. Claim the redemptive power in the Blood of Jesus that was shed on the Cross at Calvary for the remission of your sins. Open your heart and let the Lord Jesus Christ come in. Invite Him unto your life and ask Him to become your personal Lord and Saviour. Enthrone Him over your life and ask Him to take absolute control of all that concerns you. Make sure you do not go back to the world of sin and the devil.

I congratulate you for taking the decision to surrender your totality to the Lord. It is the most important decision in life and pray that it shall be permanent in your life, in the name of Jesus. I pray that the Lord will uphold you and keep your feet from falling. I pray that He will write your name in the Book of Life and you will not by any means, rub it off in the name of Jesus.
Beloved, I advise you to take

these prayer points with all the aggression and determination that you can gather:

1. Lord Jesus, baptise me in Your fire, and let it burn away every rubbish in my life in the name of Jesus.
2. Lord Jesus, purify me with your fire in the name of Jesus.
3. I command every spiritual dog, barking against my health to die in the name of Jesus.
4. Every hidden infirmity in my body, come out and die in Jesus' name
5. Wherever I have been deceiving myself, O God arise and deliver me in the name of Jesus.
6. Anything in my life resisting the touch of God, catch Holy Ghost fire in the name of Jesus.
7. Anything in my life resisting marital breakthrough, come out and die, in the name of Jesus.
8. Anything in my life resisting career and academic breakthroughs, scatter by fire, in Jesus' name.
9. Anything in my life terrorising my testimonies, receive fire, die, in Jesus' name.
10. The head of failure in my destiny, melt by the fire of the Holy Ghost
11. I receive wholeness in my spirit, soul and body, in Jesus' name.
12. Anything introducing pain into my life, your time is up. Die, in Jesus' name.
13. Today, my God shall arise and deliver me from my enemies, in Jesus' name.
14. The powers of death and hell, release me, die, in Jesus name,
15. Owners of evil load in my family, carry your load, and die in Jesus' name.
16. Any power introducing coffin spirit into my affairs, what are you doing there, die! in the name of Jesus.
17. I refuse to die prematurely, in Jesus' name.
18. The eagle of my destiny, arise and soar greatly, in Jesus' name
19. I shall not miss heaven, in the mighty name of Jesus.
20. You the tailors of the garments of infirmity, wear your garments in the name of Jesus.
21. Father, You are the God of wholeness, make me whole in the name of Jesus.
22. I command every part of my spirit, soul and body to receive wholeness in the name of Jesus.

The Tongue Of Power

In Isaiah 6:1-8, we read the account of how Isaiah's tongue received power;
"In the year that king Uzziah died, I saw also the Lord sitting upon a throne, high and lifted up. and his train filled the temple. Above it stood the Seraphims: each one had six wings; with twain he covered his face, and with twain he covered his feet, and with twain he did fly. And one cried unto another, and said, Holy, holy, holy, is the Lord of hosts: the whole earth is full of his glory. And the posts of the door moved at the voice of him that cried, and the house was filled with smoke. Then said I, Woe is me! for I am undone: because I am a man of unclean lips, and I dwell in the midst of a people of unclean lips: for mine eyes have seen the King, the Lord of hosts. Then flew one of the seraphims unto me, having a live coal in his hand, which he had taken with the tongs from off the altar: And he laid it upon my mouth, and said. Lo this hath touched thy lips; and thine iniquity is taken away, and thy sin purged. Also heard the voice of the Lord, saying. Whom shall I send, and who will go for us? Then said I, Here am I; send me."

Isaiah was a prophet of the Living God recounts his encounter with the Lord. A Seraphim of the Lord picked a live coal fire and placed it on the tongue of Isaiah. Note that the Seraphim picked the live coal with a tong; he did not pick it with his hand because it was hot. It was as a person would pick a hot slice of yam from a pot on fire. The Seraphim placed the hot coal on Isaiah's tongue and the tongue became pure. It was then that he could answer the call to be sent by God. Immediately Isaiah saw the Lord, the trouble with his life and the reason for his powerlessness was revealed to him. His lips were unclean and his tongue was polluted, therefore, his words carried no power.

This incidence took place in Jerusalem around 742 BC. Isaiah was a middle-aged man. He was in the midst of worshipers in the temple whilst the evening sacrifice was taking place. Uzziah King of Judah, one of the best kings around had just died.

2 Chron. 26:1-5;
"Then all the people of Judah took Uzziah, who was sixteen years old, and made him king in the room of his father Amaziah. He built Eloth, and restored it to Judah, after that the king slept with his fathers. Sixteen years old was Uzziah when he began to reign, and he reigned fifty and two years in Jerusalem. His mother's name also was Jecoliah of Jerusalem. And he did that which was right in the sight of the Lord, according to all that his father Amaziah did. And he sought God in the days of Zechariah, who had understanding in the visions of God: and as long as he sought the Lord, God made him to prosper."

2 Chron. 26:21-23;
"And Uzziah the king was a leper unto the day of his death, and dwelt in a several house, being a leper; for he was cut off from the house of the Lord: and Jotham his son was over the king's house, judging the people of the land. Now the rest of the acts of Uzziah, first and last, did Isaiah the prophet, the son of Amoz, write. So Uzziah slept with his fathers, and they buried him with this fathers in the field of the burial which belonged to the kings; for they said, He is a leper: and Jotham his son reigned in his stead.

Uzziah was a powerful wise king who became very strong and was feared by neighbouring countries. His strength got into his head and he became proud. Before then, he was really a better king than many; his reign was golden, money and splendour corrupted the hearts of the people. God's people forgot their calling as a holy nation. They were no longer living in conformity with the statutes of the Lord. They no longer trusted in God to protect them and provide for them. They conformed to the unholy ways of the nations around them. Their bellies and ears became heavy; they were unable to speak the Word of God. They could not even hear from God. Isaiah too was like that until he saw the Lord and his life changed. He realised that he had unclean lips i.e. his tongue had no power. A tongue can either carry power, discouragement, defeat or failure.

1. **Encounter the Power Giver.**
The Bible says; "Death and Life are in the power of the tongue." Your tongue can carry power or weakness, disease or discouragement. God however, wants our tongue to carry power. It is amazing to discover that the children of the devil do not mind doing anything to get power. Some sleep in the burial ground for 201 nights, some fast for many days, while others memorise many incantations because they want power. On the other hand, it is discouraging to note that, the children of God find it difficult to memorise the Word of God or fast and pray for many days.

2. **Allow God's coal of fire to drop on your tongue to purify it, and your sin will be wiped away.**
Do not be like the sons of Sceva, who were trying to cast out a demon in the name of Jesus that they heard Paul preach. They themselves did not know Jesus, so, the demon revolted; saying that it knew Paul and Jesus but did not know them. It pounced on them and dealt with them seriously.

Acts 19:13-16; *"Then certain of the vagabond Jews, exorcists, took upon them to call over them which had evil spirits the name of the Lord Jesus, saying, We adjure you by Jesus whom Paul preacheth. And there were seven sons of one Sceva, a Jew, and chief of the priests, which did so. And the evil spirit answered and said, Jesus I know, and Paul I know; but who are ye? And the man in whom the evil spirit was leaped on them, and overcame them, and prevailed against them, so that they fled out of that house naked and wounded."*

Hear the excuse Moses gave to God when He called him to go and deliver Israel from the hand of Pharaoh, king of Egypt. Exodus 4:10-12; *"And Moses said unto the Lord. O my Lord, I am not eloquent, neither heretofore, nor since thou hast spoken unto thy servant: but I am slow of speech, and of a slow tongue. And the Lord said unto him, Who hath made man's mouth? or who maketh the dumb, or deaf, or the seeing, or the blind? have not I the Lord? Now therefore go, and I will be with thy mouth, and teach thee what thou shalt say."*

Another typical example in the Bible is Prophet Jeremiah, when he too was called to the Lord's service. Jeremiah 1:6-10; *"Then said I, Ah. Lord God! behold. I cannot speak: for I am a child. But the Lord said unto me, Say not, I am a child: for thou shalt go to all that I shall send thee, and whatsoever I command thee thou shalt speak. Be not afraid of their faces: for I am with thee to deliver thee, saith the Lord. Then the Lord put forth his hand, and touched my mouth. And the Lord said unto me, Behold,, I have put my words in thy mouth. See, I have this day set thee over the nations and over the kingdoms, to root out, and to pull down, and to destroy, and to throw down, to build, and to plant."*

When these men experienced the touch of God's hand on their mouths, their tongues received power and they were able to do exploits for the Lord.

HOW TO EXPERIENCE THE TONGUE OF POWER:
1. **Your 'King Uzziah' must die**
Anything blocking you from seeing the Lord is a 'King Uzziah'; It is that thing which prevents you from seeing divine revelation; **It is the thing that makes you so comfortable that, you do not have time to pray or work for God again. It is the thing, which occupies your time at the expense of your prayer life and Bible study.**

Take this prayer point seriously.
* My 'Uzziah' must die today!, in the name of Jesus.

It does not make sense for anyone who says he or she wants to reign with Christ, to have strange dreams where he or she is having sexual intercourse or is being pursued or is flying. This is not God's plan for His children. Your Uzziah must die.

Uzziah stands for pride, over-confidence, etc. Isaiah could not see anything or move forward until King Uzziah died.

2. Have a personal encounter with the Lord

You should be able to say clearly and with certainty, how and when you met God. If you cannot remember when you got born-again, it is unlikely that you are. If you are not sure that you are born-again, it shows that you are not. Some people say they got born-again several times. It is not possible; you are either born-again or you are not. A person who gives his or her life to the Lord Jesus, changes. The Bible says he becomes a new creature, old things are passed away and all things become new.

3. **Do not deceive yourself or compare yourself with other people.**

Peter had fished all night, and Jesus came to tell him where to throw his net to catch fish. He did and he caught a lot. It was then that he realised that he was a sinner. He saw himself the way he was. Do not look in the mirror of someone else to see yourself. Know who you really are. When you see the real you, you will know who you really are and God will drop His coal of fire upon your tongue, and He will destroy the things that have been limiting His power in your life.

4. **The Bible says: "Walk in the Spirit and you will not fulfil the desire of the flesh."**

You must lay down all your weapons of rebellion and give full control to the Holy Spirit.

5. **Ask God to purge your life and purify you.**

This is a practical message; your tongue is either dead or alive. There is no middle camp; you have either seen the Lord or you have not. You either see yourself the way you are or, you do not see anything.

Right there where you are, ask the Holy Spirit to shine His light upon your life and reveal every hidden sin. Every sin of pride, malice, unforgiveness, sleeping with men or women to whom you are not married; i.e fornication or adultery, etc. All these are signs of rebellion and until they go, not much can happen.

Uzziah must die, but before that happens, you have to open your life before the Lord. Tell Him who you are; tell Him what you are thinking about. Be sincere with yourself so that God can touch you today.

It will be sad beloved, if you take this message lightly and not allow God to touch your life. There is anointing to break every yoke of sin, destroy every bondage of bad habits and remove every cataract from your spiritual eyes so that, you too can say that you have seen the Lord. When you see the Lord, your life will no longer be the same. For your eyes to see the King of Kings, something must happen.

LESSONS FROM ISAIAH'S EXPERIENCE:

1. He saw the Lord.

When you see the Lord, something must happen. The picture remains indelible in your heart. No matter where you are or how far you have roamed away, the picture stays there unforgettable.

2. He became aware of his spiritual state.

When you see the Lord, nobody needs to tell you your sin; you will see yourself the way you really are. You do not need a preacher to tell you what is wrong with you. You will know your position. If you have been faking, you will know. If you are a pretender or a glorified hypocrite, you will know. You will see yourself plainly when you see the Lord.

However, you cannot see the Lord, if you do not surrender your totality to Him. This means that you have to decide to be born-again. All you need do is repent of your sins, confess them to the Lord and ask Him to forgive you. Name those sins one by one, renounce them and ask God to cleanse you of all unrighteousness. Claim the redemptive power in the Blood of Jesus that was shed on the Cross at Calvary for the remission of your sins. Say goodbye to the world of sin and the devil.

Open your heart and ask the Lord Jesus Christ to come into your life. Ask Him to become your personal Lord and Saviour. Enthrone Him over your life and hand over all that concerns you to Him. Let Him take over all that concerns you.

If you have just taken this decision. I congratulate you. It is the most important decision in life. I pray that it shall be permanent in your life in the name of Jesus. I pray that the Lord will write your name in the Book of life and you will not by any means rub it off in the name of Jesus. I pray that the Lord will keep your feet from falling in the name of Jesus.

Take the following prayer points with all the aggression that you can gather:

1. Holy Ghost Fire, purge my eyes! in the name of Jesus.
2. Lord, make Your way plain before my face! in the name of Jesus.
3. You my eyes, receive divine revelation! in the name of Jesus.
4. The Bible says bitter and sweet water cannot come from the same source Death and life are in the power of the tongue. I do not know what your tongue is carrying right now, but I know that God wants it to carry power. Oh Go, let my tongue carry fire in the name of Jesus.
5. Lord, purge my tongue with your fire, in the name of Jesus.
6. Anything in my life making my word ineffective against the enemy, get out now! the name of Jesus.
7. Satan, you are a liar, what you are saying about my life will not happen to me, in the name of Jesus name.
8. Lord let every barrier between me and You be removed by fire, in the name of Jesus.
9. Let utterance be given unto me to make known the mystery of the Gospel, in the name of Jesus.
10. Lord let me be filled with the knowledge of your will, in the name of Jesus.
11. Let the word of the Lord have free course and be glorified in me, in the name of Jesus.
12. Lord fill me with the food of the champion, in the name of Jesus.
13. Father Lord, inject your fire into my tongue, and fill it with power from on high, in order for me to make exploits for you, in the name of Jesus.
14. Lord, inject into my tongue divine immunity that will kill every spiritual germ and deposits, in the name of Jesus.
15. Let every sickness in my tongue receive termination now by fire, in the name of Jesus.
16. My father, purge my heart with your fire and let every word that comes out of my mouth be pure, and godly, in the name of Jesus.
17. Lord deliver me from every spirit of talkativeness that saps away the power of God in the lives of people, in the name of Jesus.
18. Let every spiritual poison I might have eaten that has rendered my tongue polluted, be purged out by the blood of Jesus in the name of Jesus.
19. Let every bewitched material that have entered into my mouth catch fire and burn to ashes, in the name of Jesus.
20. Father Lord, let me be who You want me to be, in the name of Jesus.
21. Lord, make me Your worthy ambassador here on earth in the name of Jesus.
22. Lord, forgive me for every corrupt and unclean words that I have spoken with my mouth, in the name of Jesus.
23. Heavenly Father make me Your oracle, in the name of Jesus.
24. Lord, make me useful to You in every area, in the name of Jesus.
25. Lord, let my tongue be under the control of the Holy Spirit, in the name of Jesus.
26. Any power planning to eat my children, eat yourself and your children! in the name of Jesus.
27. Every embargo on my spiritual upliftment, be destroyed, in the name of Jesus.
28. I will arise above powerlessness by the power in the blood of Jesus.

29. Every satanic mission against my calling, be paralysed! in the name of Jesus.
30. Let all satanic success on my life, be turned to defeat for the devil, in the name of Jesus.
31. I trample upon all my personal Jericho, in the name of Jesus.
32. Any blessing of mine, locked up in the heaven, in the earth or underneath the earth, be released! in the name of Jesus.
33. Let every hindrance to my breakthroughs, be melted away by the fire of the Holy Ghost, in the name of Jesus.
34. Every organ of my body, stored in the bank of the enemy, be released now! in the name of Jesus.
35. My body, reject every satanic arrow! in the name of Jesus.

Begin to bless the Lord for the blessings you have just received.

The Evil Manipulators

Obadiah 3-4 says; *"The pride of thine heart hath deceived thee, thou that dwellest in the clefts of the rock, whose habitation is high; that saith in his heart: "Who shall bring me down to the ground?" Though thou exalt thyself as the eagle, and though thou set thy nest among the stars, thence will I bring thee down, saith the Lord."*

Anything that can cause failure for Man, was completely conquered when Jesus died on the cross at Calvary and rose again. Before then, the devil was very powerful but when Jesus came, He overpowered the devil. That is why the Bible says, one cannot enter into the house of a strongman, except a stronger man first binds him. We have a Stronger Man that has taken care of the devil. Jesus is that Stronger Man. It is a sad thing that today, many believers are living inside smoke instead of being in the fire. The unbelievers are supposed to see the glory of God around and within us. The aim of this message is to make you get out of the smoke and get into the fire. One particular character of the devil that many people overlook is found in John 8:44; **"Ye are of your father the devil, and the lusts of your father ye will do. He was a murderer from the beginning, and abide not in the truth, because-there is no truth in him. When he speaketh a lie, he speaketh of his own: for he is a liar, and the father of it."**

I would like, you to read this statement aloud, **"There is no truth in the devil"**, that is what Jesus said. The devil is the master of lies and deception.

In 1979, I was living in a house with other tenants. One day, a fight broke out and I went to pacify the two fighters, but they did not listen. As a matter of policy, if I try to pacify people and I am told to get lost, I will take precaution and leave. That day, I tried to talk to the two fighters but the fire that started gradually broke out into a big one and these two girls beat each other up mercilessly and tore each other's dress. Women around had to give them wrappers to cover their nakedness. I later learnt that the cause of the terrible fight was their boyfriend.

One of them was in the room with the young man when the other one came and the fight broke out. I thought it was an ordinary fight until I slept in the night, and the Lord showed me a vision where I saw these two girls being sent specifically to destroy the man. Both of them knew exactly what they were doing. People thought they were fighting because they loved him. The truth is that, the devil had finished the voucher of that young man and had sent the two people to finish him up. Whilst they were fighting, he was begging them to stop and wanted them to resolve the matter amicably and that he loved them both. This is a case of evil manipulation which the devil set up so that, the young man would feel he is so handsome, that ladies are quarrelling over him. They are meant to collect materials from his body and take them to the demonic world. They were meant to levy accusations of unfaithfulness against him in their meeting and to lead him to a point of no return.

When the devil wants to manipulate a person, he could start organising it right from the person's adolescence. If he has a particular event in mind or he could start organising the manipulation two or three years earlier. He would groom different people up, bring them together and they will eventually manipulate the person. Many people are under the umbrella of such manipulations; the enemy has moved them from the fire into the smoke and they have allowed evil pronouncements and prophecies to work against them. Maybe you are one of those that have allowed evil prophets to prophesy evil against you and you stuck to it. That is evil manipulation. You have to reject it and declare that it does not belong to you.

Many years ago in Akure, we had a stubborn woman who got pregnant. One day, she went to the market and a white-garment prophet accosted her and said she would die with the unborn baby, except she gave him certain things. The woman got angry and grabbed the man by his garment and asked him to revoke the statement. He said it was a prophecy from the Lord, that he could not revoke it. The woman became more aggressive and held his garment. People gathered round them and asked her what the problem was. The woman told them and everybody said the man had to revoke what he had said. When the so called prophet saw that the people were ready to lynch him, he revoked the statement. It was then the woman left him and departed. A few months later, she gave birth safely to a bouncing baby. Thank God she stubbornly rejected the evil prophecy. Maybe it would have come to pass if she had accepted it. Fear would have gripped her and it would have followed her to the labour room. That is an evil manipulation.

Many people have been deceitfully moved away from their place of destiny to the wrong place. From the right wife to the wrong one, from the right job to the wrong one, from the right profession to the wrong one. Many have been led to praying wrongly. Many have quarrelled with the right friends and are clinging to the wrong ones. My prayer today is that, every manipulation of evil control will be broken today, in the name of Jesus.

These forces have destroyed so many lives. The unfortunate thing is that, some people actually hand over their lives to manipulators. The purpose of manipulation is to give the person an inferior or bad life and eventually send him or her to hellfire.

TOOLS OF MANIPULATION:

1. *Anger*
If you find out that anger has overcome your life, I would like you to know that it will open the door of your life to evil spirits to manipulate. There are some miracles that will not happen in the life of a person who gets angry. It is against the rule, no matter how hard the person prays, the road remains blocked by anger; no matter how hard the person prays for miracles, they will not come until anger leaves. It is a great manipulating tool that the devil is using and I want you to take it serious.

2. *Sexual force*.
Illicit sex is the highest power that the devil uses in manipulating, dominating and controlling people and it has destroyed many lives. When you are not able to control your sexual appetite, it is a sign of evil manipulation and the devil will use it to push you where you do not want to go.

3. *Evil Inheritance*.
Many mothers have used their children as torch lights; by initiating them into witchcraft whilst in the womb. If such people become born-again, they would need to pray seriously against the powers of the manipulators; otherwise, they will continue to operate under their influence. They have to command the chain to break. If at the time the mother is using her own child as a torchlight, a physical problem manifests, no prayer will work against such manifestations.

A woman was praying for the fire of God to fall on the troublers of her soul because, a strange woman was troubling her marriage. She did not know that she herself was the one that had evil manipulators in her, that sent her husband towards strange women. She has become a torchlight without knowing it.

4. *Lust of the Eye*.
There are women and men who seduce people. Samson saw Delilah and fell headlong in love with her. He insisted on having her as a wife contrary to the will of God for his life and she manipulated him unto destruction. Proverbs 6:25-26 warns that; *"Lust not after her beauty in thine heart; neither let her take thee with her eyelids. For by means of a whorish woman a man is brought to a piece of bread: and the adulteress will hunt for the precious life."*

5. *Strange Children*.
When household enemies want to deal with a family, they program strange children into it in order to use them as agents. Many people do not know that there are powers around us that can force a person to do what he or she does not want to do. A person that has been manipulated in the dream to marry a spirit, is likely not to be able to get a

physical husband or wife to marry on earth.

6. *Money*.
A person's finances could be siphoned through demonic money given to the person by evildoers.

7. *False Prophets*.
Matthew 7:75; **"Beware of false prophets, which come to you in sheep's clothing, but inwardly they are ravening wolves."** There are wolves in sheep's clothing- devils in disguise. They put people inside spiritual boxes and lock them up and sit on them. Many people have become slaves to their fellow men because of spiritual laziness and curiosity about the future. Perhaps you have allowed a false prophet to lay hands on you - or given you a bath by the stream, or given you 'holy water' to drink; it means you have become a candidate for manipulation and you need to get out of it. Many people go about with the spirit of death. It makes them feel lifeless or feel as if they are dying, it makes people go where they are not supposed to go. It means the spirit of manipulation is already at work and must be dealt with.

8. *Thoughts*.
Many people cannot think straight because their thoughts have been manipulated. They cannot think the way other people are thinking. Some have been forced not to even think at all. Thinking could look easy to you, but it is hard work. Only a few people do good or sound thinking- it is manipulation. Get your thought life out of evil manipulation!

9. *Food*
A man of God went to the interior of the country for a crusade. During the deliverance session, a girl came forward and was delivered after confessing to witchcraft. She was a 'moin-moin' (steamed bean paste) seller. She confessed that she used to go about at night to spiritually collect people's blood and she prepared her 'moin-moin' with these blood. That was why hers was the most solicited for 'moin-moin' in town. She said she manipulated people's lives through it. Until hers finished, no one bought from any other 'moin-moin' seller. Many people at the crusade recognised her and regretted having eaten her 'moin-moin. Some cried, many coughed in disgust as if they could cough out the 'moin-moin' that they had eaten. The girl said she however noticed that when some Christians ate the 'moin-moin', she could not manipulate their lives or subject them to her control.

10. *Rejection*.
If a pregnant woman does not want an unborn child and tries to abort it and fails, when the child is born, he or she automatically comes under the influence of manipulators. Such a child could experience unexplainable fear and always see everyone else as being against him or her. Sometimes, during hot prayers, some people start to manifest. It is because they are under the influence of some powers which have been challenged by the prayers. We shall do that kind of challenging today, through the prayers that I am suggesting below. Spies plant things in the rooms of people to be able to see what they are doing. So also spiritual manipulators; they plant things into the lives of people in order to spy and control their lives.

One day in France, a man went to a primary school and held some children hostage in a hall. He had dynamite tied around his waist and threatened to ignite it if he was not given a huge amount of money. Everybody was under tension. Parents were outside the school weeping. The police too were there. After many hours, the children were tired and hungry and the police asked if the man would allow the children to be given food to eat. He agreed but said he would not eat. He was served a meal and a glass of juice anyway but he did not touch them. After some hours, he drank the juice without knowing that it had a sedative in it. A video camera was planted in a plate of food and through it, the police monitored the man. As soon as he drank the juice he became drowsy and dozed off. That was how the police grabbed him and liberated the children. So also, something could be planted spiritually into the life of a person and any time he or she tries to make progress, the forces of manipulation will know and will hinder the progress. If he or she wants to start praying seriously, they will know and hinder him or her from praying, so that the person will not get to the level of a breakthrough.

11. *Evil Marks and wicked Incisions.*

12. *Satanic Deposits.*

13. *Satanic Guards.*

14. *Occultic Materials.*

15. *Jewellery.*

16. *Decorations*

If you have anything that you inherited, you had better check it very well and be sure that it is not an object of manipulation. Perhaps you even bought some strange objects yourself and you think they are souvenirs or decorations; you had better check them very well. Some of them are satanically inspired to monitor people's lives. If you have the game called 'Snake and Ladder' at home; you had better get rid of it because it has its origin in magic. Wicked people steal menstrual pads in order to manipulate people's childbearing. They steal wedding rings and they manipulate homes through them. We have heard of wedding rings being exchanged, without the couple realising it. In MFM we do not join people with rings rather, we use the Bible. So, this kind of thing cannot happen to our members. Some people put on crosses that they were given by false prophets, thinking that it would help them to overcome evil forces. They do not realise that some of them are objects of manipulation.

Types of crosses:

(i) **Simple Cross** - A straight board with another one placed on it as seat on which they put a culprit with his hands and legs tied.

(ii) **St. Anthony's** - It is like capital letter 'T'

(iii) **Rail** - It is like letter 'X'

(Iv) **Italian** - Like small letter 't' the one on which the Lord Jesus was crucified.

(v) **Ankh** - It has a hole on it. It is a combination of the first two with a hole on it. Witches use it.

If you have any of these items in your possession, you had better flush them out. Plead the blood of Jesus on them and get rid of them.

17. *Self.*

A person could be under the bondage of SELF. Such people deceive themselves; they are selfish, they tell lies, praise themselves and are over-sensitive. They are being manipulated internally. Jesus says if anyone wants to follow Him, the person should carry his or her cross and follow Him, In other words, Jesus wants us to be crucified with Him on the cross. Paul says in Galatians 2:20; *"I am crucified with Christ: nevertheless I live; yet not I, but Christ liveth in me: and the life which I now live in the flesh I live by the faith of the Son of God, who loved me, and gave himself for me."*

A lot of problem that people have with their bones, intestines, are evidences of evil manipulation. Many people are under evil designs. Sometimes, this is the fault of parents who want their children to become what they want. They take the unfortunate licence to control the lives of these children. They take the driver's seat in the child's life and place the child in a profession that has nothing to do with his or her inborn talents. This makes the child to operate under the design of the parents. Some children are born with the traits of the opposite sex. For example; maybe a couple wanted a girl and the baby turns out to be a boy, there is the tendency of treating him as a girl and gradually, the child becomes a female-boy or vice-versa. Any design that it not from God is a way of manipulating a life to go the way that it should not. We have to pray against all these devices.

18. *Lying.*

If you attempt to build anything on the foundation of lies or half-truth, it will not stand. Lying will disturb God's guidance for your life; it will make you to take the steps that you should not take. It will produce greater loss than whatever savings you gained through it.

Proverbs 19:9 says;
"A false witness shall not be unpunished, and he that speaketh lies shall perish."

Also Proverbs 12:2;
"A good man obtaineth favour of the Lord: but a man of wicked devices will He condemn."

RESULTS OF LYING:

i. You make yourself a child of the devil, who is the father of liars. John 8:44.
ii. You are building a foundation of sand.
iii. You are heading for hell. Revelation 21:8 says; *"But the fearful, and unbelieving, and the abominable, and whoremongers, and sorcerers, and idolaters, and all liars shall have their part in the lake which burneth with fire and brimstone: which is the second death."*
iv. You will attract lies and liars to your life and handwork.
v. You will lack understanding.
vi. You will fail to enjoy God's blessings.
vii. You will fail to enjoy God's permanent blessings.
viii. You will end up in bondage,
ix. You will be punished,
x. Lies will come back to you.
xi. You will become a fool.
xii. You will send bad signals to your offspring.

Lying is a serious power of manipulation. Every lie needs another one to back it up, or accompany it, or cover it up. When a lie sees the truth, it creates distress for those who harbour it. It is a coward and it collapses before a single truth. I would like you to take note of these things. If a person tells a lie, something is planted in that life and through it, the spirit is manipulated into other dangerous areas.

19. *Ignorance*.
The devil uses the tool of ignorance and the thought of having no enemy, to manipulate people a lot. The truth is that, everybody has an enemy. Even our Lord Jesus Christ had; they hated Him so much that they condemned Him to die on the cross. As long as there is envy, jealousy and strife in the world, there will be enemies. As long as human beings are friends with the devil, there will always be enemies. As a Christian, you are not supposed to fight human beings but the evil spirits behind their actions. That is why the text in Obadiah cited above talks about the pride of the heart.

We are in the last days wherein many people are being manipulated and the materials of manipulation must be destroyed. If you are being used against yourself, you must let go and let God deal with you. Reject every manipulative material and pray sincerely in real stubborn faith. However, if you are not born-again, these prayers might not be of help to you. Whereas, I would like you to get the maximum from them. God has a purpose for your life and He wants you to fulfil it.

Therefore, if you have never at one time in your life, surrendered your life to the Lord Jesus Christ you have never asked Him to come into your life, I would like you to do so right there where you are. He is there with you and wants to set you free from every bondage. All you need to do is acknowledge the fact that you are a sinner and that you cannot approach God in your sinful state. Repent of your sins right there where you are. Confess all your sins to Him, name them one by one and ask Him to forgive you and cleanse you from all unrighteousness. Renounce the world of sin and the devil Claim the redemptive power in the blood of Jesus that was shed on the Cross at Calvary, for the remission of your sins.

Open your heart and ask the Lord Jesus to come in. Ask Him to become your personal Lord and Saviour. Surrender your totality to Him; enthrone Him over your life and ask Him to take control of your life and all that concerns you. Hand over all your affairs to Him and let Him take pre-eminence in your life.

If you sincerely took this decision, I congratulate you. It is the most important decision in life. I pray that it shall be permanent, in the name of Jesus. I pray that the Lord will uphold you and keep you from falling in the name of Jesus. I pray that the Lord will write your name in the Book of Life and nothing shall by any means, rub it off in the name of Jesus. Go and sin no more!

Take these prayer points with all the aggression that you can gather and with violent faith in your heart:

1. I break the hold of all the forces of evil manipulators upon my life, in the name of

Jesus.
2. I reject every manipulative material planted in my body, contrary to the Holy Spirit, in the name of Jesus.
3. I reject every deceptive family control upon my life, in the name of Jesus.
4. Every witchcraft controlling force upon my life, be roasted! in the name of Jesus.
5. I disband every periodic problem in my life, in the name of Jesus.
6. I reject every evil leadership into wrong roads in my life, in the name of Jesus.
7. Any material, in my body, through which my life is being monitored, lose your hold and go back to your sender in the Name of Jesus.
8. I break every evil control over my life as a result of hands laid upon my head, in the name of Jesus.
9. I vomit every evil milk I drank as a baby in the name of Jesus.
10. Every manipulation of my life from the sea, the forest or the air, scatter! in the name of Jesus.
11. Lord, wherever I'm tied down in the spirit, loosen me with Your hand of fire, in the name of Jesus.
12. Every evil prophesy spoken into my destiny, die! in the name of Jesus.
13. My destiny, reject bewitchment in the name of Jesus.
14. Father Lord, wherever I am my own problem, save me from myself, in the name of Jesus.
15. Blood of Jesus, damage my ignorance and make me wiser than my enemies, in the name of Jesus.
16. My thought process, receive deliverance by fire! in the name of Jesus.
17. Holy Ghost fire, purify my life in the name of Jesus.

The Destroyers Of Potentials - 1

Isaiah 54:16: *"Behold, I have created the smith that bloweth the coals in the fire, and that bringeth forth an instrument for his work; and I have created the waster to destroy."*

Nahum 2:2
"For the Lord hath turned away the excellency of Jacob, as the excellency of Israel; for the emptiers have emptied them out, and marred their vine branches."

I would like to congratulate you for picking up this bulletin to read; it means God has a special purpose for your life. The topic is a very serious matter, so follow with a rapt attention.

When we say "POTENTIAL," what do we mean?
It means an unused success, a hidden talent, a sleeping ability or a reserved power. It is something that is there, but not being called into use. It is an untapped strength, which has got abilities but with bottled capabilities. It means the progress that a person is supposed to have, but which such does not yet have. It is something that is yet to be accomplished; it has been planted but has not germinated.

A seed is a potential tree; if it is planted and nurtured, it will become a tree. If it dies, or is eaten up, there will be no tree. A potential therefore in this case means something that may make one great but that needs to be worked on.

This message is referring more to the Blacks, than the Whites. There are two terrible potential-destroying powers that the enemy has unleashed on the Black Man; in Africa especially, you will notice that the good man is pulled down, while the wicked is exalted; the inferior is on top and the superior is below; the loser is riding the horse and the winner is sweeping the ground. The Bible calls these potential destroying powers the following names:
(1) The Wasters,

(2) The Emptiers.

To waste a thing means to use it wrongly or not fully. It also means to render worthless or useless. It could also be an excessive use of a thing in a way that it becomes useless or ineffective or the act of making a thing useless by damaging it. To waste could also mean a situation when a thing or person is not used at all, especially when such could have been employed for maximum breakthroughs.

Beloved, if you do not know how to pray in anger, I would advise that you learn it today, so that you can deal with the powers of the wasters and emptiers. What I am trying to explain is that, it is a futile effort to sit at home and cry because of the rage of these powers; this will not help you as it is only a waste of time. Beloved, I reiterate it: sitting down to grumble and complain is a waste of time, accusing one person or the other for your predicament, is also a waste of time; it is a useless exercise. But giving up is even a more foolish decision.

ANALYSIS OF THE POWERS OF THE WASTERS.
This power is a strong force that is working against many nations of the world, including ours. One of their strategies is to blind people from knowing these sets of various great opportunities that would change their lives forever. The victims will have opportunities but would not know that they do. These powers of the wasters are very deceptive in nature; they will not give the person a true picture of what they are about to venture into, and thus they end up causing failure, impossibilities, difficulties and setbacks in all kinds of areas of the lives of their victims. These powers make a person lose unrepeatable opportunities. It is so unfortunate that many people who should go on a three-day fast to address these powers are roaming about, saying: "It is one of those things," while

some say it is "bad luck." But as far as the Bible is concerned, there is nothing like luck: a person is either blessed or cursed. What many people call bad luck is usually the activity of the wasters. The wasters are also the powers that plant the spiritual disease called impatience into many lives. Of course, one cannot buy the gold of maturity with the currency of impatience.

Rushing and impatience have made many people to lose many things in life. This disease is everywhere: banks, schools, highways, homes, and even in the church of God. Know beloved, that impatience is a child of the wasters. If anyone seriously wants to rise from the level of poverty to prosperity; from defeat to victory, from failure to success, or from being a nobody to a somebody, he or she must deal with these powers, especially if the person is from the Black race. Many people think that money is their problem, but the truth is that, if they do not deal with the wasters, having more money will increase their problems.

It is the powers of the wasters that make people to give up when overtaken by a temporary set back. These powers make people to go about aimlessly; such people go about life without a defined purpose.

Do you know that there are some human beings who actually go through life with the expectation that the worst things will happen to them? Their characters and thoughts chase good things away from them, because they themselves internally push away good things; their minds have first rejected success, how would their person accept greatness? I do not want you to joke with the enemy; I would like you to first take this prayer point with a boiling anger:

* *I refuse all satanic manifestations, whether they come as roaring lions, or as angels of light in the name of Jesus.*

When the wasters are operating in a person's life, they will blind the mind of the person from understanding many things. For example, the Bible wants us to become champions. A champion is a person who has triumphed over great enemies. David was a champion because he faced and defeated Goliath but unfortunately, some people do not realise the fact that there is no champion without a fight.

If God has been allowing you to go through some painful training, it is possible that all He wants is for you to become a champion but the powers of the wasters will not allow you to know this; they will keep telling you different stories. People are said to be great because they have overcome great battles. It is usually the person who passes an examination that is promoted to the next class. God could be passing you through some training right now; so, do not faint and do not be discouraged. The Book of Proverbs says; "If you are weak or if you faint in the day of adversity, you strength is small."

God's test is an opportunity to become a spiritual giant. God tested Belshazzar; He put him on the scale and found out that he was unfit. God then told him that he had been found wanting; that means he just wasted his life.

When you do not test a product, it is as unreliable as the weather. Great spiritual assignments are reserved for the vessels that do not break under trial. If Meshach, Shedrach and Abednego had broken down, wept and grumbled before God; and lamented that they were serving God but He abandoned them, they would not have become the heroes of faith that we read about today. They would have wasted their lives, like those that bowed to the golden calf for fear of being thrown into the fiery furnace, at the expense of their relationship with God.

If you are the kind that always see a problem from beneath, then the problem will pull you down. If you stand tall and look at your problem from the top, from God's point of view, then the problem will become a testimony. The problem with Peter was that he looked at the storms from beneath.

When he was looking at them with the eyes of Jesus, he could walk on the sea but as soon as he looked at them from beneath, he began to sink. Think about it beloved! Even if some problems cannot be changed, they can be chained. It is possible that people misunderstand you, tell lies against you, reject you or deny you, do not worry, just stick to your God, but if you refuse to, you are heading on a final wastage journey that ends in hell-fire. I decided a long time ago, that I will not go there.

Why don't you take this prayer point?
* **I will not waste my life in the name of Jesus.**

When the wasters are in operation, they start in a little way; in bits, until the destruction becomes great.

THE THINGS THEY WASTE
1. Time
This is a moving element that does not wait for anybody. Time waits for no man; it is an unfavourable, selfish partner. It does not mind whether you are serious or not. It does not just wait; it will not hold on. You cannot go back to five minutes ago; it is gone forever. You cannot go back to yesterday; it is gone. Fools can waste money or other resources but the most foolish people are those that waste time. Many people also unfortunately waste their time on spiritually useless activities.

2. Money
Many people waste their money on useless projects. Many people have leaking pockets in the spirit; they keep losing money. These people have swallowers of blessings inside of them. There are also some people who use their money to bless those that God has cursed, not knowing that you cannot bless who God has cursed: of course nothing will work out from such giving because the principle does not work out that way.

3. Family
The wasters work on people from one home or family to the other: men or ladies over-due for marriage in some cases will not see themselves as wasting away, but will say that the men or women that they speak with concerning the marriage are bad. So, they keep leaving one person for the other, in criticism, not knowing that the powers of the wasters is at work in their lives.

We used to have a neighbour that made me realise that a person who has not read the Bible is not literate, even when he or she has big university degrees. Therefore a person could be, an illiterate even with 'a doctorate in theology'.

One day, a rich man drove a Mercedes Benz to the house of a couple and asked the woman to go in and pack her things, and follow him. The husband of the woman watched his wife in amazement as she went in and packed her belongings. When the husband asked what was going on, she said she had made up her mind, that she would not die in poverty and that was how a married woman left her matrimonial home. The husband on the other hand almost killed himself, but for some people around. Surprisingly, after three years, the woman came back in company of the members of her family to beg to be taken back as his wife. The husband reminded her of her unwillingness to die in poverty and informed her that he was still poor so, she should go back to where she had been.

Judging superficially, one would say that the woman was bad and mean, and she could be given all sorts of names. Her real problem was that the powers of the wasters were at work in her life.

There is nobody on earth that God created to be useless. In fact, nobody chooses to be useless but there are some powers that are stronger than these people and these powers are in operation in their lives, controlling and confusing them. Most of the people that do evil, do not really want to, but there are certain powers that are urging them up like people do to relay runners. To these satanically manipulated people, it is only at the end of the race when the devil disappears, that they will find out that they have been deceived.

It is one thing to have a spouse, it is another thing for him or her to be available. It is possible for a person to live with her husband or his wife for many years, and very possible for him or her not to be available to the spouse. Many relationships are like that today; it is the work of the wasters.

4. Opportunities (physical or spiritual)
When God wanted to talk to the Israelites on Mount Sinai, there was lightning, thunder; everywhere was shaking, they

were afraid and they said they did not want God to talk to them; that Moses should be their interlocutor. They sold their opportunity to Moses and he was the one that was talking with God; thus they lost the opportunity of talking to God directly. God never intended to have a middleman between Him and them; they made that decision. This is part of the reasons we in the Mountain of Fire and Miracles Ministries encourage people to learn how to pray to God directly; it is a do-it-yourself affair.

Many people get puffed up with power; they make themselves intermediaries between people and God, thinking that people cannot get to God except through them. Esau sold his birthright to Jacob; he was the firstborn, but he lost the opportunity of being God's reference point. Today, we refer to God as the "God of Abraham," "God of Isaac," and "God of Jacob, but you would hardly hear anyone call Him "God of Esau." Esau would have probably assured himself that he did not need his birthright, not knowing that there was the power of the wasters in operation in his life. If the wasters had got hold on Bartaemeus, son of Timaeus, he would have missed the opportunity of receiving his sight. If he had seen himself as a 'civilised man', and that it would not be necessary for him to shout in public, he would have remained a blind beggar. There are many people who vaunt themselves because of their educational qualifications, thereby refusing to do certain things which are simple, but which could have moved them forward. They should be reminded that the devil has no respect for anybody.

5. **Talents**

Many people waste their talents; some bury theirs and some sell theirs to the devil instead of using them to glorify God. Such people have a direct ticket to hell-fire because if there is any thing that God hates and that will take a person to hell-fire, it is a wastage of the talents that He gave the person. If you only watch people in the house of God, and you do not contribute positively to the spread of the Gospel, you are wasting away and could land in hell-fire

The young man that buried his talent, said he knew his master to be harsh; that he wanted to reap where he did not sow; he knew his master too much. Many people know too much; even more than their Creator as they suppose. When God asks them to do something in a particular way, they would insist on doing it in another way. People refuse to obey God in simple things and they insist on doing the ones that will land them in trouble. They keep looking for their 'class.' The young man that buried his talent was summoned to return it and he was thrown into utter darkness; where there is weeping and gnashing of teeth.

A woman came for prayers one day with her husband and the Lord showed me a crown of serpents on her head. I told her husband that the woman was not serious, and he told me to make her serious. During our discussion, she said she did not want a church where she would be sitting on the same bench with paupers. I reminded her husband of what I said earlier.

6. **Health**

When some people are strong and can work for God, they are busy not being serious; they are playing with time, thinking that God is a fool. The Bible says: *"Remember now, thy Creator, in the days of thy youth."* It is not when you are being carried to church, or when you cannot do anything on your own that you will serve God. Many people waste their energy on useless things; they run the race that nobody asked them to run; a lot do the business that nobody apportioned them to.

7. **Life**

Life is the worst thing that anyone can waste. If you do not know the purpose of God for your life, it means you do not know what God wants you to do with your life, it is therefore as good as saying that your life is in danger. Any life without a divine purpose is in danger; it is an experiment; a guinea pig for the devil, because evil spirits will try their new weapons on the body of the person, knowing that the person is just there, without knowing why.

Many people are in churches and they are very busy there, but as far as God is concerned, they are not doing anything; they are being effective in the wrong things. Many people add gossip and backbiting to the things that waste them. The fact that what you are doing is good does not mean it is right. If your life is an experiment, you had better pray hard today. It is a tragedy when a seed dies, without becoming a tree, or, if a girl dies without becoming a woman or if success dies in failure. That is what happens when a life is wasted.

I would like you to think deeply about these things because God has a purpose for allowing you to read this message.

Many people have been turned upside down and they are so used to it that they see the people walking upright as the ones that are not walking aright, and vice versa. It is like the first experience you have when you enter into a dark room; you will not be able to see anything for a few seconds or minutes. If you continue to stay there, your eyes will get used to the dark and you might be able to figure out some things and walk through, without falling or bumping into anything. Many people are used to darkness. I counsel you today to get out of that darkness and move into the glorious light of God because when you are used to darkness, you will get used to strange things, which you are not supposed to get used to.

At this juncture beloved, I would like to pause, so that you can think properly on what I have explained so far. We have seen just one of the destroyers of potentials. In the next bulletin, we shall focus on the second; The Emptiers. They are like their counterparts, the wasters that we have just seen; their mission also is to destroy, and I pray that you will not get into their web and if you are already in it, I pray that the Lord will set you free in the name of Jesus. I would like you to pray very fervently today, so that you will be set free from the pangs of "the little foxes that spoil the vine."

However, if you have never at one time or the other, surrendered your life to the Lord Jesus Christ, I would advise that you do so, right away. He is there with you, right there where you are, and is ready to save you. All you need to do, is acknowledge the fact that you are a sinner and that you cannot approach God in your sinful state. Repent of your sins, confess them to the Lord; name them, one by one and ask Him to forgive you and cleanse you from all unrighteousness. Claim the redemptive power in the Blood of Jesus that was shed on the cross at Calvary, for the remission of your sins, renounce the world of sin and the devil and make sure you do not go back to them again. Open your heart and invite the Lord Jesus to come in. Ask Him to become your personal Lord and Saviour. Ask Him to take control of your life and all that concerns you. Hand over your life to Him and surrender all that concerns you to His control.

If you took this decision, I congratulate you. It is the most important decision in life; I pray that it shall be permanent in your life in the name of Jesus. I pray that the Lord will uphold you with His right hand of righteousness and will keep you from falling in the name of Jesus. I pray that your name will be written in the Book of Life and nothing will by any means rub it off in the mighty name of Jesus.

Beloved, having gone through this message, I advise you to take the following prayer points with all the determination that you can gather:

1. God, ordain Your arrows against my persecutors, in the name of Jesus.
2. Let every pit dug by the enemy become a grave for the enemy, in the name of Jesus.
3. I render null and void the effect of any interaction with satanic agents moving around as men, in the name of Jesus.
4. I pull down the stronghold of evil strangers in every areas of my life, in the name of Jesus.
5. Any negative transaction currently affecting my life negatively, be cancelled, in the name of Jesus.
6. Every manifestation of the enemy whether as roaring lions or as angels of light, I conquer you, in the name of Jesus.
7. Every wolf in sheep's clothing, be disgraced, in Jesus' name,
8. God arise, with whatever that makes you God, and fight for my destiny in Jesus' name.

9. Every evil summoner of my destiny from the dream, fall and die, in the mighty name of Jesus.
10. Every power having negative awareness of my destiny, die, in the mighty name of Jesus.
11. Every secret of my destiny in the hand of the enemies of my life, become fire and destroy my enemies, in the name of Jesus.
12. The evil powers that have refused to let me go and fulfill my destiny, enough is enough, thus saith the Lord to you Pharaoh: "Let My people go," in the name of Jesus.
13. Let the powers supporting the enemies of my destiny, fail and scatter by fire in Jesus' name.
14. Associate yourself O ye people, and you shall be broken into pieces in the name of Jesus.
15. Take counsel together against me, it shall not stand, in Jesus' name.
16. Speak your evil words against me, and it shall not come to pass, in the mighty name of Jesus.
17. Let the powers that have vowed against my marriage, receive angelic slaps and die, in the name of Jesus.
18. Every mark of 'do not marry' upon my life, blood of Jesus wash it away, in the mighty name of Jesus.
19. The joyful height that none has reached, I reach by fire, in the name of Jesus.
20. I refuse to fail, in the name of Jesus.
21. My Father, I must make it, in the name of Jesus.
22. Let any personality that has vowed against my breakthrough fail, fail and fail forever, in the name of Jesus.
23. I refuse to fail at the edge of breakthroughs in the name of Jesus.
24. The single opportunity that my life has been waiting for, manifest and promote me now in the name of Jesus.
25. Opportunity that will change my life for the better, appear by fire, in the name of Jesus.
26. Let all incantations against me be cancelled, in the name of Jesus.
27. I command all oppressors to retreat and flee in defeat, in the name of Jesus.
28. I bind every strongman having my goods in his possession, in the name of Jesus.
29. I break the curse of automatic failure, working upon my life, in the name of Jesus.
30. Let the anointing to prosper fall mightily upon me now in the name of Jesus.

The Destroyers Of Potentials - 2

Isaiah 54:16 *"Behold, I have created the smith that bloweth the coals in the fire, and that bringeth forth an instrument for his work; and I have created the waster to destroy."*
Nahum 2:2;
"For the Lord hath turned away the excellency of Jacob, as the excellency of Israel: for the emptiers have emptied them out, and marred their vine branches."

Last week, we started this message and we explained what we meant by potentials. We said it is an unused success or a hidden talent; a sleeping ability or reserved power. It is something that is there, but not being called into use. It is an untapped strength, an able but bottled capability. We explained that it is the progress that a person is supposed to have but does not yet have. It is something that is yet to be accomplished. It is planted there but has not germinated. We established the fact that the destroyers of potentials operate through two agents and the Bible calls them:
i. The Wasters, and
ii. The Emptiers

We dealt with the wasters in the last bulletin. Today, we shall focus on the emptiers.

THE EMPTIERS:

In the olden days, there was a whistling kettle. The whistle blows as the water in the kettle is boiling. That whistle is the glory of the kettle and it distinguishes it from others. It can be likened to the glory of Man. When the emptiers come into operation, they will not put off the fire, neither will they remove the kettle from it. They would rather pour out the water in it. Emptiers do not hinder a cup from getting filled up to the brim; they will wait until it is full and then pour out the content. The emptiers will not hinder parents from training their children; they will wait for them to graduate and then cause an accident that ends their lives. They do not hinder people from going into business; they will wait until everything is done and then trip it over. Sometimes, they do not wait for good things to accumulate: once they see anything good, they eject it from the life of the person. All the money that some people are making or will ever make, have been spiritually bound and kept on top of an iroko tree or buried in the ground or under the sea or hidden in a rock. Your former boy or girl friend could be the emptier that was assigned to defile you at a tender age, so that your virtues will be siphoned and you will not attain your full potentials.

Many years ago, a young man was moving with a girl with the intention of marrying her. One day, he went to see a prophet who told him that the girl was a 'dangerous element' and that he should not marry her. The young man went to the girl and announced an end to the relationship. To his utter surprise, the girl told him that he could not leave her, that he was already hooked. He thought it was a joke and he left. The following day, he was given sack at work, and the company car and accommodation were withdrawn from him within few days. He became miserable and was jobless and homeless for many months. He was forced to go back to the girl to ask for forgiveness and reconcile with her. The relationship restarted and before he knew it, a dispatch rider brought a letter from his former office asking him to resume work. That man is in the web of the emptiers; in the form of a girlfriend that is of course likely to finish him spiritually when they get married.

The emptiers manifest themselves in dreams too. That is what happens when you eat in the dream or have sexual intercourse or see yourself getting married or seeing dead relatives or serpents. They are the ones responsible for incurable diseases, unexplainable setbacks in business, broken marriages, sexual drive that make people want a man or a woman, without wanting to get married.

When a person hears strange voices, the emptiers are at work. They make people find it difficult to read the Bible, pray or even attend church services. They are at work when a person perceives a strange odour that no one else perceives, or the feeling of a strange sensation; as if something is moving about in the body.

These powers manifest through anger and make a handsome person to become wild and fierce looking under the influence of anger. The person's body would be vibrating and at that moment, he or she could throw anything at anybody and could have a heart-attack. These powers introduce failure mechanism into the lives of people. They introduce a trap, and escort the person to the trap and make him or her to be caught in it and then bring the person back to square one.

Let this be clear to you beloved, there are powers that can remove good things from the lives of people. Such things could be stolen or transferred to other people. Naaman had leprosy and he got healed in the River Jordan. Do you know that, that leprosy was transferred to Gehazi and his family? That leprosy is actually an entity which existed as a spirit, otherwise, it would not have been possible for it to be transferred. The prophet said: "The leprosy of Naaman," it means he was referring to that particular one that came off Naaman. It had a name. It was not for Gehazi, it belonged to Naaman who got it removed in the River Jordan but the emptiers made Gehazi to receive an evil transfer and he was wasted with his descendants.

Jesus told His disciples to go and witness to others. He told them that they should go to houses and greet the inhabitants by saying: "Peace be unto this house." He said if a child of peace is there, the peace will stick to the person, otherwise, their peace would come back to them. This is wonderful. It means that peace too can be transferred. It can move about. The emptiers understand the fact that the things that people enjoy can be transferred but many people do not know. A person's brain can be spiritually transferred. A girl was being prayed for and she started to confess to witchcraft. She said she had changed the brain of her brother to that of a cow. When asked why, she said her brother was doing well at school and he got everybody's admiration, approval and gifts. After the exchange, he became dull and was failing his examinations. A person's heart could be spiritually transferred and he or she would be having heart problems. The hands could be transferred and there would be no prosperity; the legs could be transferred and there would be no progress.

Babies in the womb can be chased out and replaced spiritually. A midwife was on night duty and she noticed that the tummy of a pregnant woman had gone flat. She woke the woman up and asked her what was going on. The pregnant woman said her baby had gone for a meeting. By the following day, the tummy was big again. You might find it difficult to believe such stories but they are true.

Physical things can carry power; that is why Jesus could spit on clay and He rubbed it on the eyes of a blind man and the latter began to see. God is the Creator of heaven and earth and He created Man from clay, so He did the work of recreation on that man. Jesus healed this blind man who had no eyes at all. If the eyes were there and the devil was behind the blindness. Jesus could have addressed the spirit and cast it out. If the eyes were bad. He would have commanded them to be healed and they would have been. But Jesus knew that the man needed eyes and He moulded clay and spat on it and He made a set of eyes for the man. The saliva of Jesus carried power.

Physical materials can carry things from or into people's lives. When Peter was going about preaching, people got healed through the touch of his handkerchiefs. Peter's handkerchiefs carried sufficient power to heal the sick, likewise, just as these things carried good power, there are some materials that carry negative powers. Beloved, the truth is that, there are emptiers that are distributing materials that carry strange powers about. A single material of the emptiers in your house, can sap away the peace in it. Therefore, check your jewellery, where do they come from? Has God told you that there is nothing wrong with them? Are you basing your opinion on the pastor that says there is nothing wrong with adorning yourself with anything? Do you know that a single earring could sap out peace from your home? It could be empowered by the emptiers. Check that necklace or ring, does it bear the structure of a snake? Does it look like a snake or the skin of a snake? Check that ring, does it have the picture of the moon on it? Do you know that occultists use the picture of the moon to signify witchcraft? Check that thing in your house, does it have the engraving of a fish or an eye? Check that cross on your neck, are you sure it is Jesus that is represented on it or it is an ankh? Why do you have to wear a cross anyway?

Check those decorations in your house, do they have strange odours like that of fish or incense? Check those decorations, do they glorify the Lord? How could you hang the picture of a dragon or snake in your house and hope to be blessed? How could you have carvings of an idol in your house and not expect the presence of evil powers? When you know that personalities like Sango, Obatala, Ogun, Amadiora etc, in the myths or history of Yoruba or Iboland were mysterious or evil men and women, and they died mysterious deaths, why buy carvings of these personalities that have become idols to their worshipers? It means you are looking for trouble because, those carvings are an embodiment of their spirits and at night, they will hold their meetings in your sitting room. Perhaps you have the powers of the emptiers in your house, you have to really throw them out. It is only the power of the Cross that can empty the emptiers and make captivity captive.

How People Enter Into The Traps Of The Emptiers:
1. **Food.**
Many people eat anywhere and anyhow, not minding who prepared it and with what.

2. **Incisions And Tribal Marks.**
The Bible is against incisions. This is because the origin has a link with idolatry. It is highly demonic. They expose people to the idolatry of their tribes and should be seriously prayed about. It is an open door to the emptiers.

Leviticus 19:28; *"Ye shall not make any cuttings in your flesh for the dead, nor print any marks upon you: I am the Lord."*

Many ladies take pride in the incisions and tribal marks on their bodies, saying that they are meant to make them beautiful. If you have them on your body, you have to pray seriously today. Point at them and pray well especially if those who inscribed them on you are already dead. Find out how and why the marks were inscribed on you. Some people were born with some strange patches which they call 'birth marks' many of which are highly demonic; they are an invitation letters to the emptiers.

3. **Demonic Sex Partners.**
Sexual intercourse is meant to take place between married couples. It was ordained by God for a husband and his wife who have been legally and divinely joined together in holy matrimony. If you engage in illicit sex, you expose your life to the emptiers. If you are not married, you should not have sexual intercourse. If you are married, you should not have it with any other person than your spouse. When sex is done outside marriage, it exposes the lives of the people involved to the emptiers.

A lady going about with a married man is digging her own grave. Such people are exposing their lives to the powers of the emptiers. A married man that is going about with girl friends is digging his own grave. There used to be a man who always went to prostitutes whenever he collected his salary. He would not leave until he had exhausted all his money. He would then go home to his wife, a kerosene seller and would harass her every morning for transport fare to work. If you have a husband that is flirting about with 'assorted' girls, do not bother boxing his face, or that of the girls; pray and bind the powers of the emptiers and the powers that are pursuing him.

4. **Ancestral Spirits.**
If an emptier has been released into a family, it goes from person to person. Just as the umbilical cord transfers food from a pregnant woman to the

baby in her womb, so also are evil spirits transferred from mother or father to the child.

5. Contaminated Possessions.
Do you have bloody or unclean money? Carry out an inventory of your possessions; find out how you acquired them. If you are addicted to jewellery, you need to be very careful. Check out those things that you inherited. If your father was demonic or was possessed or was a wicked man. it means you have inherited some of those things that are or were in him. You would be harming yourself by using the things he left behind.

Have you noticed that you are always in debt? Check your possessions. When some people are advised to do away with such things, they proudly declare that there is no way they can do away with them. We do not force anyone to do away with his or her demonic possessions, we just advise and tell people the mind of God. Anyone is free to heed or not, our own mission is to tell people the mind of God and expose the devices of the enemy. A believer should not find it difficult to do away with anything. Anything that has the slightest possibility of affecting your life in a negative way should be done away with. It should not be difficult to part with such things. If it is difficult, then it has become an idol; you have become an idol worshiper.

I would prefer to be seen as looking dull than to go about with demons, in the name of fashion. Think about it, beloved. There are some people who have been given the emptier called alcohol. They drink to forget their sorrow but alcohol is such a waster that leaves a person in a worse situation than before. The problems remain when the effect is cleared off. They say they drink to drown their sorrow, they do not know that sorrow is a stubborn thing that alcohol cannot drown. It will only energise it. Anyone who drinks is wasting his time and life.

What To Do Against These Powers:

1. Recognise Their Operation
By acknowledging their existence, you are not confessing negative; you are being realistic. Some people are prompt to say; "I reject it" when the thing is already there.

There used to be a mad man whom I admired as I was growing up. He used to speak Queen's English. He played fantastic music; he could play a mouth organ with his nostril. The man was a genius; he knew mathematics. He had a lot of potentials but he was just there on the streets; wasting away. The emptiers and wasters have seen to it that he becomes useless to himself and to the society. He became a subject of entertainment to the enemy.

He had fantastic potentials, but they were destroyed. Think about it beloved.

2. Repent
Anything that you or your parents might have done to expose you to those evil powers, repent of them. In those days, young girls used to wear beads around their waists; as simple as it looked, it has destroyed the lives of many women today. They did not know that each of those tiny beads had significance in the demonic world. If you have ever worn it, you have to lay your hand on your waist and pray aggressively today.

3. Renounce these powers violently and aggressively,
Declare that you will not surrender your life to them.

Beloved, you should have understood by now what I meant at the beginning by "praying in anger" I asked you to learn it if you have never prayed in anger before. The fact that things look okay should not make you relax. In fact, that is when you should really pray harder. Our forefathers used to say that bad things need prayers, so that they can become good and that good things need prayers, so that the enemies will not spoil them.

If you pray aggressively today, you would be immunising yourself so that when those powers show up, they will not find a place to stay in you. Beloved, I would like to encourage you to allow the Holy Spirit to work in you today. Address this issue with all seriousness and power will change hands in your life from the hands of the destroyers of potentials, to the hand of the Lord.

However, if you are reading this bulletin and you have never at one time or the other surrendered your life to the Lord Jesus Christ, you cannot fight against these destroyers. They will report in your place and will refuse to be bound or leave. If you know that you are ready to be born again, wherever you are, I would like you to go before the Lord in total repentance. He is right there with you and is ready to set you free from all unrighteousness. All you need do is confess your sins to Him; name them one by one and ask Him to forgive you. Renounce those sins and ask the Lord to cleanse you with the blood of Jesus that was shed on the Cross at Calvary for the remission of your sins. Claim that sacrifice and ask the Lord to redeem you from your sins. Open your heart to the Lord; invite Him into your life, ask Him to become your personal Lord and Saviour. Hand over your life to Him and ask Him to take control of all that concerns you.

If you took this decision sincerely, I congratulate you. It is the most important decision in life. I pray that it shall be permanent in the name of Jesus. I pray that the Lord will uphold you and keep your feet from falling in the name of Jesus. I pray that the Lord will write your name in the 'Book of Life' and nothing shall by any means rub it off, in the name of Jesus.

The prayers that I am suggesting below are prayers that the enemy does not want you to pray, Jesus told Peter that the devil wanted to have and sift him like wheat but that He, Jesus, had prayed for him. That would have been a waste of the life of Peter if Jesus had not intervened. Samson had great potentials to succeed in life but, he was emptied and his life was wasted and he died with his enemies. The life of Saul as a king was worse, as he ended up his life consulting a necromancer. If someone told Saul earlier on that he would end his life that way, he would have rejected it and bound the person. The powers of the destroyers of potentials worked and succeeded in his life.

Take these prayer points with all the aggression you can gather:

1. You powers of the emptiers and wasters, dry to your roots! in the name of Jesus.
2. All destroyers, fashioned against my potentials, be destroyed! in the name of Jesus.
3. I recover my life, from the hands of the destroyers of potentials, in the name of Jesus.
4. I loose myself from any dark spirit, in the mighty name of Jesus.
5. Lord! restore all my potentials that the enemy has destroyed, in the name of Jesus.
6. Any power assigned to suffer me, you are a liar, receive the judgement of fire in the mighty name of Jesus.
7. Every power, denying me of my benefits, release everything now and die, in the mighty name of Jesus.
8. My long time benefits in the camp of witchcraft, become fire and locate me now, in the name of Jesus.
9. Let everything giving joy to my enemies in my life, begin to pour out sorrow for them in billions in Jesus name.
10. The joy of my life shall not turn to sorrow, in the name of Jesus.
11. Whether the devil likes it or not, my potentials shall make me great, in the mighty name of Jesus.
12. Let God arise and let my enemies be scattered, in Jesus' name.
13. Let every strange woman attached to my divine marriage, fail woefully, in the name of Jesus.
14. The problem of my divine marriage, receive the fire of God. in the mighty name of Jesus.
15. The financial breakthroughs that my destiny has been waiting for, where are you? appear by fire, in the name of Jesus.
16. Anything in my life that is keeping me waiting longer than necessary in the waiting room of God, come out and die, in the name of Jesus.
17. Father Lord, give me divine enablement to become what You have destined me to become, in the name of Jesus.
18. Anointing of the overcomers fall mightily upon me the name of Jesus.

19. Anything programmed into my life to manipulate me into error and failure, jump out and die, in the name of Jesus.
20. Association of witchcraft in my environment, be broken to pieces, in the name of Jesus.
21. Every close enemies, be exposed and be disgraced, in the name of Jesus.
22. Anything in me that will promote my generation, manifest by fire in the name of Jesus.
23. I will not labour for the enemy to eat, in Jesus name.
24. All my blessings roaming about, locate me now! in the name of Jesus.
25. Gift of God within me, burst forth! don't lie dormant in the name of Jesus.
26. I command all the dark works done against me in secret, to be exposed and nullified! in the name of Jesus
27. I reject every evil design for my life, in the mighty name of Jesus.
28. I recover all my potentials that have been buried, in the name of Jesus.

Bad Link, Label And Mark

Psalm 129:4 *"The Lord is righteous: He hath cut asunder the cords of the wicked."*

Certain things stick to some people who avoid deliverance. In other words, when some people pray fervently, nothing happens. Sometimes in these cases, things that have left, stage a come back. On another hand, there are some people who see some particular faces in their dreams, or who see some dead relatives pursuing them. Other times, some people dream of dangerous animals like lions, snakes, crocodiles, etc. Some people have a problem of attaching themselves to some people, even when the friendship is painful; they adamantly strive on in a maltreating and draining relationships.

There was a quarrel between a couple one day which I went to settle. The woman was bent on making the man kill her. She refused to leave his shirt. I tried to make her lose her grip on him but she gave me a thorough slap. The man said the wife's younger sister had to leave and the woman said "no;" that if her sister left, she too would leave. I saw that it was a serious case. The woman got married to the man; not the younger sister. Why did she insist at all cost that her sister had to stay? That is a bad link.

Why do some adults find it difficult to take decisions until they have sought advise from their father or mother? Why should an adult of 25 years, still be cuddling a teddy bear that she had since she was a toddler?

The cords of the wicked Isaiah 5:18; *"Woe unto them that draw iniquity with cords of vanity, and sin as it were with a cart rope."*

Why do all the things I listed above, happen to people? Why should they even happen to those who claim to be born again, spirit-filled, children of God? I would like you to read this message with a rapt attention and make sure you grasp what I am about to expose to you. Evil spirits propel most of the instances I listed above, and we have discovered that they happen to the children of God because there could be an evil link between them and some evil spirits.

There could be a conscious or unconscious evil link between a person and the family idol. Even if a child was born to churchgoers and on the eighth day, was given a Christian name, that does not break the link between him and the powers that are ruling the family. There are diverse kinds of evil links: there could be a link between a person and a family curse, there could be a link between a child and an evil person in the family.

These are some reasons why some people always dream about their former schools and schoolmates which is the reason why some people even though they are married, dream about their former boy or girlfriends to whom they wanted to get married but which for one reason or the other did not work out. It is why so people keep dreaming about the village or seeing themselves in midst of some strange friends, even when they have had no dealings with such over a long period of time.

Many people have bad communication systems, from where wrong messages pour into their souls. Wrong things that believers should not think about, keep pouring in. Some problems remain in place and keep coming back because of these links. Unfortunately, the problems continue until the links are broken. Some people have possessions that link them to evil; some of them could be in form of presents; that is why I would advise at this juncture, that if you have not unwrapped some of your wedding presents, you should do so prayerfully right away, because a link could be there.

There was a couple, who got married and when they came back from the honeymoon, were curious to see the content of a particular wedding present in a big carton. When they unwrapped it, they found a dry loaf of moldy bread! Another couple found a dead dry lizard in a wedding present. You might have any remote-controlling thing in your possession; you have to check it up and break that link.

It is possible for a person to have marks on the body. The painful thing is that it could be an evil link. A sister used to see herself in the dream, with her grandmother. She would just be going about with the grandmother. One day, she had a dream after she came for serious deliverance prayers. In the dream, she saw her grandmother asking her why she was following her about. The sister said she did not know and that she would prefer not to, because she, the grandmother was dead. The grandmother then told her that when the sister was born, she was given her placenta to bury, but she didn't; but cooked the placenta and ate it, and that is why the sister looks older than her age and talks like a sage.

Beloved sister, or brother, what happened to your placenta? Do you know where it was buried? Do you know what was done to it? I am sure you do not know. Electricity needs a source, in order to generate power. For you to be able to boil water in a kettle you need to connect the kettle to electricity, which is the source of power that generates heat. You would need to break loose from the source of evil linkage today. You might not be able to kill all the witches and evil spirits in the world, but you can break the link between you and them; the link through which they come to you. I would encourage you to pray fervently today, in order to break every link between you and any satanic power. All the evil phone lines must be destroyed; they are the powers behind wrong decisions that people take, and which leads them to destruction. They are evil communication links, You must break the wire, through which evil current flows into your spirit. The energy from the devil flows into people's lives. Today, there will be a spiritual surgery and all such evil spiritual links will be broken in the name of Jesus.

Many people are being pulled about, like an unwilling goat. This is because of the yokes linking them to evil things. Such yokes must be broken today in the name of Jesus. The enemy of our soul is always trying to connect his telephone and electric wires to people. If you allow him to plug one thing on you, he will establish a mini-electric station and turn you into a dumping ground. I refuse to be a dumping ground for the enemy.

A lot of people have tied their souls to all sorts of demonic souls. Sometimes, two souls are joined together for evil: this is called evil soul-linkage. It causes a person to follow another, even when such a person he is following does horrible thing on earth. It would strengthen the friendship and make a person to fulfill the bad desires of the other person. Such a person would even surrender his or her property to the person; and in no long a time, the person could experience the same problems as the person he or she is tied to.

Evil linkage causes false love; people lust after each other, and call it love. These oftentimes result in relationships that end up in bondage.

One day, a man came for prayers. He said whenever he was in bed with his wife; his mind would not be with her, but with his former girl friend. That is an evil link between him and the former girl friend. Until that link is broken, there will be no real marriage or peace between him and his wife because bad spirits can pass through such links to cause very serious problems.

It is possible for a child to be linked to his father or mother; this link could cause trouble for the child, especially if the father or mother is or was demonic or an occultist. It is possible to have an evil link with a former boy or girl-friend or acquaintance. It is possible to have a link with a false prophet that prayed for a person, or with members of demonic or lodge groups or with evil playmates. Some people would say that they left such friends, many years ago. It is true that the person has left them, but the question is, have they left the person? It is like registering a person in a school and paying the tuition fee. Even if the person does not attend lectures, he or she is a bona-fide student of the school and his or her name will be in the school register.

The mission of this message is to break all evil links. I want that to be clear in your spirit. When an evil link is in place and the person does not cut it off, the current will continue to pass through. Sometimes, when the person prays hard, and the body, soul and spirit are on fire, certain things will not be able to pass through that linkage at that time. However, if the person relaxes, the thing will come back. When a person fasts and prays and becomes too hot, the things could be around, but will not be able to pass, through the body. Beloved, if you break such links, the connection is broken.

Bad Label and bad Stamp
Ezekiel 9:1-5; *"He cried also in mine ears with a loud voice, saying: "Cause them that have charge over the city to draw near, even every man with his destroying weapon in his hand". And, behold, six men came from the way of the higher gate, which lieth toward the north, and every man a slaughter weapon in his hand; and one man among them was clothed with linen, with a writer's inkhorn by his side: and they went in, and stood beside the brasen altar. And the glory of the God of Israel was gone up from the cherub, whereupon he was, to the threshold of the house. And he called to the man clothed with linen, which had the writer's inkhorn by his side; And the Lord said unto him: "Go through the midst of the city, through the midst of Jerusalem, and set a mark upon the foreheads of the men that sigh and that cry for all the abominations that be done in the midst thereof". And to the others He said in mine hearing: "Go ye after him through the city, and smite: let not your eye spare, neither have ye pity."*

I want you to know that as we have physical labels and stamps, we also have spiritual ones. In the text above, God was angry at Israel and He decided to deal with them. Those who had the mark of God on their foreheads were spared, but the angel of destruction destroyed those without His mark. It means that God could put a label on a person, which might not be visible to the physical eyes. God's label and stamp are done with His own spiritual pen and cannot be seen with the physical eyes. He does it with the Blood of Jesus, the fire of the Holy Ghost and with the aid of His Angels. With these and others, He marks people out.

Contrarily, demonic people could put contrary marks, labels and stamps on a person. The same way, evil people can recognise the mark of God on a person and would avoid him or her, when they see such a person, they also recognise their own marks and labels on anyone when they see it. Therefore, no matter how far a person might roam, they will see the person through their monitoring gadgets. That is why some people who think they have problems because they are in Africa, will continue to have problems, if they go to Europe or anywhere in the world. Those powers see them, even though they are far away form home. Evil spiritual labels and stamps follow people like a stigma and wherever they go, the problem will continue there. God puts His own mark on people. If you are a careful reader of the Bible, you will note that He usually puts His mark on people's foreheads. Here are some examples in the Book of Revelation:
Revelation 7:3;
"Saying: "Hurt not the earth, neither the sea, nor the trees, till we have sealed the servants of our God in their foreheads."
9:4:
"And it was commanded them that they should not hurt the grass of the earth, neither any green thing, neither any tree; but only those men which have not the seal of God in their foreheads."
14:1:
"And I looked, and lo, a Lamb stood on the mount Zion, and with him an hundred forty and four thousand, having his Father's name written in their foreheads."

22:4:
"And they shall see His face; and His name shall be in their foreheads."
Paul says: *"Let no man trouble me; for I bear in my body, the mark of the Lord Jesus Christ"* it is not that he had the word 'Jesus' physically written on his body; but it is there spiritually. That is why the demons that challenged the seven sons of Sceva, said they knew Paul

and Jesus; but did not know those young men. This is because there was a mark of God on Paul, which they recognised.

A man of God went on a visit to a house, which happened to belong to a herbalist. As the man of God stood talking to him, the herbalist could not look straight into his eyes. As soon as the man of God left, the herbalist warned his tenant, not to ever bring that man of God to his house again. The herbalist said he saw two men standing by the sides of the man, with dazzling swords in their hands. Meanwhile the man of God did not see the men. This means that the doers of evil, recognise real servants of God and they know those who are not serious with God. They know those who are patching up and living in sin. They know those who are strong. They know those who are prayer warriors and those who utter empty words. They know those who speak theory and those who are practical. The devil also puts his marks on people. In Revelation 13, we are told that the anti-Christ will put his mark on people's hands. Such people will be monitored, no matter where they run. We have seen this all over the world. Many people spend years, struggling and then, they decide to travel out of the country. When they get there, they find out that the same problems persist. It is because there is an evil mark upon their life.

I had a friend who sat for one examination after the other, and failed. Somehow, he thought the solution to his problem would be to travel abroad. He was able to travel and one day, he went to the swimming pool. As he jumped from the diving board, he missed the water and landed on the concrete at the side of the pool. He hit his head and died on the spot. No one could explain how he missed the water. There is actually no other explanation than the fact that he had an evil stamp, with a mission to end his life at all costs. The evil mark sometimes makes people to be resistant to the Gospel. They might not even want to pray. It makes them consider how good a place looks, before they can pray there. All these marks, labels and stamps, are the ones responsible for the recurrence of bad things that were meant to have been solved and gone completely. Many people these days, are with their own hands, inviting such trouble into their lives by spoiling the image of God, and calling it fashion.

Leviticus 19:28; *"Ye shall not make any cuttings in your flesh for the dead, nor print any marks upon you: I am the Lord."*

Perhaps you have an evil stamp on your body, and you do not know how it got there; you have to pray seriously today. Some people draw flowers, birds, temples of idols, trees, on the body as tattoos for decorative purposes, but that could be a stamp of the enemy on their lives. When you do these things, you alter the image of God in your life and invite the label and stamp of the enemy. When you try to change the way God created you, it means you are inviting the stamp and the label of the enemy into your destiny. These are things that God wants us to look closely at, so that we do not invite any trouble upon our spirits. In the Mountain of Fire and Miracles Ministries, we have seen a lot of jewelries that have caused problems in the lives of many people. I do not know why people prefer to get into trouble than to avoid these things. If you find it difficult to discard something, then it has formed a link with you; and that link must be broken.

Jacob, on his way to Bethel, commanded his wives to bury their jewelries and idols, so that those things would not cause a hindrance to their resettlement. When the enemy sits quietly in his corner, some people go to look for his trouble; then the enemy starts to reclaim what belongs to him. You might wonder what belongs to the enemy that is in your possession; it could be anything and in any form. It could be that there is an evil mark upon you. I pray that those evil marks shall be rubbed off today by the blood of Jesus.

Some people go about with these evil marks without knowing it. A person could inherit the stamp and label of the enemy, from parents. It could be acquired by decision. The most pathetic is the case of those, who go about with stamps and labels, without knowing it. It gets to the extent that all their friends desert them.

I had a friend, who went for business with some people. They would fix a time to meet but before he gets there at that time, the others would have all gone. It happened twice and he decided to go to the meeting place at about 4a.m; instead of the 6a.m. they agreed on. He found out that they were just about to leave, when he arrived. He was surprised to find them getting ready to leave; he asked them why he was treated that way and only one of them opened up to him saying that, each time he went with them, they did not get good results, so they decided to go on their own without him. The problem of this young man is the fact that he had a bad label on his life; and so, wherever he went there was no prosperity.

If an evil stamp is on a woman, she could have marital distress; she would go from one husband to the other and would always end up being chased out, or would decide to leave one man for another. That was what happened to a woman who eloped with a rich man because her husband was poor. Three years later, the woman came back begging, but the former husband refused to take her back. She ran after money but unfortunately, the rich man treated her as part of his money.

We always tell unmarried women, that a nice man might not necessarily be rich and vice versa. Many women are on the look out for rich men but they end up getting more than they desired.

They are treated like a physical object and then, they start running around seeking a way out. Many ladies fall victims after they have decided to go for a man that would look after them and their relations. It is a sign that there is an evil label on their lives. All those are things that you should pray seriously about.

If you got a job somewhere and you were given the sack, you got another one, you were fired, you should know that there is something wrong somewhere. If at a particular time of the year, you have an ailment and you go from hospital to hospital and it cannot be diagnosed, meanwhile, a lot of money has been spent and then the sickness disappears on its own or reappears again, then know that there is a problem somewhere. It means there is a bad label, which must be removed and cleansed by the blood of Jesus. I would urge you to do some serious praying today.

Colossians 2:14:
"Blotting out the handwriting of ordinances that was against us, which was contrary to us, and took it out of the way, nailing it to his cross."
Jesus has already given us victory over all these things but however, do not joke with this issue. Pray the prayer points I am suggesting below, with all the seriousness that you can gather. It is important that you concentrate and pray these prayers with all the seriousness that you can gather. However, if you have never at one time in your life decided to be born again. I would advise that you do so right away. The Lord Jesus is with you where you are, and is ready to set you free. All you need do is acknowledge the fact that you are a sinner and that you cannot approach God in your sinful state. Repent of your sins. Confess them to the Lord; name them one by one and ask Him to forgive you and cleanse you from all unrighteousness. Claim the redemptive power in the blood of Jesus that was shed on the Cross at Calvary, for the remission of your sins. Invite the Lord Jesus into your heart and ask Him to come in and become your personal Lord and Saviour. Surrender your totality to Him, enthrone Him over your life and hand over your affairs to Him and ask Him to take control.

I congratulate you for this decision that you have just taken, it is the most important decision in life and I pray that it shall be permanent in the name of Jesus. I pray that the Lord will uphold you and will keep your feet from falling in the name of Jesus. I pray that your name will be written in the Book of life and nothing shall by any means, rub it off in the name of Jesus.

Take these prayer points with holy aggression.
1. I cut off, every conscious or unconscious evil spiritual link between me and any spirit in the name of Jesus.
2. Let every evil mark, label or stamp upon my head be rubbed off by the blood of Jesus.

3. I cut off, every evil link with any dark spirit in the name of Jesus.
4. I cut off every evil spiritual link between me and the dead, in the name of Jesus.
5. Let every evil spiritual link, label and stamp upon my head be washed off by the blood of Jesus.
6. Every bad link that I have with any living person, I cut you off in the name of Jesus.
7. I cut off every evil link with the past in the name of Jesus.
8. Every evil link, label and stamp upon my hands, be cut off in the name of Jesus.
9. Lord arise for my help and let my status change, in the name of Jesus.
10. Anyhow You will do it Lord, do it, and let my life move forward by fire, in the name of Jesus,
11. The miracle that my destiny has been waiting for, arise and manifest by fire, in the name of Jesus.
12. Lord I am tired of my situation, arise and change my life by Your power and by Your fire, in the name of Jesus.
13. Lord, use Your best to replace my worst in the name of Jesus.
14. By the Voice that calmed the wind and the seas, let my problems die, in the name of Jesus.
15. Every mark of "you shall not marry" on my forehead, blood of Jesus wash it away, in the name of Jesus.
16. Every stamp of marital failure glued to my destiny, tear off completely, in the name of Jesus.
17. Every stamp of "you shall not reproduce and replenish" upon my destiny, catch fire, in the name of Jesus.
18. Every link to financial poverty, break and shatter, by the hammer of heaven, in the name of Jesus.
19. Every stamp, label or link attached to any part of my body, be destroyed by the blood of Jesus.
20. Let all the destructive plans of the enemies aimed against me blow up in their faces, in the name of Jesus
21. Let my point of ridicule be converted to a source of miracle, in the name of Jesus.
22. Let every disappointment I have suffered in the dream be converted to divine appointment in the name of Jesus.
23. Let all powers sponsoring evil decisions against me be disgraced, in the name of Jesus.
24. Let every evil effect of any strange touch be removed from my life, in the name of Jesus.
25. I command all demonic reverse gears installed to hinder my progress to be roasted in the name of Jesus.

When The Winds Go Contrary

God says in Psalm 50:15, *"And call upon me in the day of trouble: I will deliver thee, and thou shall glorify me."*

Place your finger on that verse, close your eyes and pray like this;

* **God that answered Elijah by fire, answer me according to this Scripture, in the name of Jesus.**

Mark 4:35-41, *"And the same day, when the even was come, He saith unto them: "Let us pass over unto the other side," And when they had sent away the multitude, they took Him even as He was in the ship. And there were also with Him other little ships. And there arose a great storm of wind, and the waves beat into the ship, so that it was now full. And He was in the hinder part of the ship, asleep on a pillow: and they awake Him, and say unto Him: "Master, carest Thou not that we perish?" And He arose, and rebuked the wind, and said unto the sea: "Peace, be still". And the wind ceased, and there was a great calm. And He said unto them: "Why are ye so fearful? How is it that ye have no faith?" And they feared exceedingly, and said one to an-other: "What manner of man is this, that even the wind and the sea obey Him?"*

Jesus suggested crossing over to the other side of the river, so it means they were on a route approved by God. There is however one thing you must know; the fact that you are traveling on a route approved by God does not mean you will not have attacks. The storms were great and water began to sip into the ship. Some of the disciples of Jesus were great fishermen and so they were used to storms and things like that; at least, Peter was there. They would have started arguing saying: "Let's do this, let's do that.'" They would have tried everything before they now decided to go and wake Jesus up. Somebody would have said: "well, maybe this is how everybody will die," someone else would have said; "Let us steer the ship to this or that direction. All sorts of suggestions and counter suggestions would have been made but none of them remembered to pray. Immediately they woke Jesus, the Bible says: "And He arose." Say this to yourself: "Jesus shall arise for me today." When Jesus arose. He did some curious things:

He rebuked The Wind.

That word rebuke is the same thing as when a teacher is telling a student to put his two hands up and close his eyes for misbehaving. The teacher could add, "If I hear anything from you again you are in trouble." It is that kind of language that Jesus used in rebuking the wind. It is the same rebuke that Jesus used against demons. So it means that, there was a spirit behind the wind that arose; it was the wind that was causing the trouble therefore, He rebuked it. Then, He spoke to the sea too, He said; "Peace be still" therefore, the sea was not the one causing the problem, it was the wind that was making the sea to cause problem. That is why Jesus addressed the two of them differently. I pray that you will obtain a divine prescription today in the name Jesus. Jesus spoke harshly to the wind, He told it to be still. The Lord says; **"Call *upon me in the day of trouble: I will deliver thee, and thou shall glorify my name."*** in Psalm 50:15

Do you feel as if there is a force resisting you? Do you feel as if you are swimming against the currents and torrents of life? Are you concentrating on the problems instead of concentrating on God's promises? Maybe you have examined yourself and you know that you are in God's will for your life; you are not committing any known sin but things still look very rough. What do you now do? How do you pray when you are in that kind of position? Perhaps you are the kind of person that struggles and struggles before moving ahead, it is time for all that to stop; enough is enough. The disciples were in that kind of situation when Jesus said; "Let us go over to the other side." Therefore, while doing what Jesus commanded, they had problems. Meaning that, the land of opportunity is the 'land of opposition.' Any system that does not develop crises at all is dead. There is no human being who will not come across the time of Jacob's trouble; there is no one that the devil does not throw stones at, but it touches people in different areas.

How can you pray against satanic currents? What will you do so that you will not float like a dead fish? How do you pray when you feel caged? How do you pray when you know you are doing what you are supposed to do but you are not getting any result? That is why you are reading this message. "Let us go over to the other side" but then while doing that, some problems arose. The land of opposition is the land of opportunities. The land of adversity is the breeding ground for miracles. If you never had a problem, you will never know that God can solve it and you will not know what faith in God can do. There is no situation so terrible or so bad that God has never or cannot reverse. Nobody is beyond redemption.

If you are complaining that you have problems, you will be rolling on the floor and thanking God for your life when you see those who really have problems.
I want you to pray these prayer points like an angry lion;
* **I will reach my goal, no power shall defile me, in the name of Jesus.**
* **Every plan, desire and strategy of the enemy for my life, die! in the name of Jesus.**
* **Let the mantle of solution from the God of Elijah, fall upon me now! in the name of Jesus.**

We came across a strange case some years ago. A woman's husband ran away; not because the woman was not beautiful or was not cooking well but, there was a problem that he could not disclose to outsiders. The problem was that, there is no amount of food the woman will eat that would satisfy her because as she was eating the food, it was not landing in her stomach. It was as if something was collecting it. The woman would be crying of hunger even whilst eating. It is being siphoned away by unseen powers. I am sure your own problem is not as serious as that.

Note this great secret beloved, many people see the presence of the enemy but they are ignorant of the presence of God. No matter how educated you are, if you do not know how to experience the presence of God, you are a play thing in the hand of the enemy. In fact, the presence of God is more to be desired than university degrees or anything else. God was with the disciples but they were ignorant of His presence. There are thousands of people who have never felt the presence of God in their lives. I prefer to have the presence of God in my life than to be anywhere else. It is a wonderful thing to wake up at night and feel the presence of God around you. It does not matter which direction God is asking you to go as far as His presence is there with you. Once you get outside His presence, you will find demons, diseases, fear, death, discomfort and sorrow. The Bible says; *"Though I walk through the valley of the shadow of death, I will fear no evil, for Thou art with me; Thy rod and Thy staff they comfort me."*

STEPS TO TAKE WHEN THE WIND IS CONTRARY

1. **Confirm God's Presence In Your Life.**

In His presence, you will walk through the valley of the shadow of death, and there will be no problem. Therefore, when you are overwhelmed by contrary winds, the first thing to be sure of is that, you are in God's presence and He is still with you. The Bible says who can separate us from the love of Christ?" The only person who can separate you, is you yourself. Those who went out of the presence of the Lord in the Bible caused it by themselves. Adam ran away from the presence of the Lord, Cain, Joab and many others went away from the presence of the Lord. A person may decide like the prodigal son to walk away and leave God. Are you sure of being in the presence of God all the time? The first thing to do when you want to stand against contrary wind is to confirm God's presence in you; confirm that Jesus is still in the ship of your life. The devil has no power except the power you personally give to him. The devil cannot be a lion if you do not make yourself a lamb. Confirm God's presence; check up your own character, check up your own nature.

2. **Lay The Blame where It Belongs.**

The first thing people do when things go wrong is to look for somebody to blame. They hardly see their own contribution to what went wrong. The most difficult thing for a human being to do sometimes is to say; "I am sorry, I was wrong." Yet, this is what we must do if we want to identify and fight the contrary winds. Some people would say; "Brother A, Brother B is my stumbling block." No, If you are walking in the light, you cannot stumble. You cannot blame anybody; not your wife, or husband, or pastor, or girlfriend. No. The one to blame is you. When you begin to put the blame where it belongs and then come before the Lord in repentance, then, you will begin to move forward again.

3. **Learn To Praise And Worship God.**

Enter His gates with thanksgiving in your heart, and enter His courts with praise. Psalm 96:9 says; "*O worship the Lord in the beauty of holiness: fear before Him, all the earth.*"

Worship is not singing or chanting songs of praise alone; it is a direct acknowledgement to God for Who He is, His nature, attributes, ways and promises. Worship Him in the beauty of holiness.

4. **Pray The Binding Prayers.**

That is, bind the activities of the devil. Bind negative activities and the powers of darkness from your situation.

Matthew 18:18; "*Verily I say unto you, whatsoever ye shall bind on earth, shall be bound in heaven and whatsoever ye shall loose on earth, shall be loosed in heaven.*"

5. **Pray The Loosing Prayers.**

That is you bind the evil things and pull down strongholds. The Bible says; "*though we walk in the flesh, we do not war after the flesh. The weapons of our warfare are not carnal but they are mighty through God to the pulling down of the strongholds of the devil.*" Let doubt be far from your life. It may be terrible habits; it could be anything pull down that stronghold.

6. **Cast Down Imaginations And All The Vain Things.**

That is, those things that cement strongholds of the enemy together against your life, cast them down. Once you attack the enemy in the area of imagination, he cannot fulfill his mission anymore. If somebody is still imagining evil against you and you cast down that imagination, it will not come to pass.

What they are planning will be neutralized because it is the imagination that sponsors the action. Those are the kinds of prayers we are going to pray today.

7. **Bring All Negative Thoughts Into Obedience**

It means, throw out evil thoughts out of your system. All the thoughts that are not of God; all the thoughts of failure, throw them out of your system.

8. **Fight back.**

Take your revenge, according to Psalm 149:5-9;

"*Let the saints be joyful in glory: let them sing aloud upon their beds. Let the high praises of God be in their mouth, and a two-edged sword in their hand; To execute vengeance upon the heathen, and punishments upon the people; To bind their kings with chains, and their nobles with fetters of iron; To execute upon them the judgment written: this honour have all his saints. Praise ye the Lord.*"

It means you should take your revenge by commanding confusion upon your enemies; command them to eat their own flesh and drink their own blood. This is made possible because God Himself has promised it in the Book *of* Isaiah 49:24-26; "*Shall the prey be taken from the mighty, or the lawful captive delivered? But thus saith the Lord, Even the captives of the mighty shall be taken away, and the prey of the terrible shall be delivered: for I will contend with him that contendeth with thee, and I will save thy children. And I will feed them that oppress thee with their own flesh; and they shall be drunken with their own blood, as with sweet wine and all flesh shall know that I the Lord am thy Saviour and thy Redeemer, the mighty One of Jacob."*

These are the strategies to use when praying against contrary winds. I would like you to pray the prayers that I am suggesting below with holy aggression. Remember that this bulletin is called 'Sound the Battle Cry' you have to challenge the enemy to a fight, Do not play or joke with the enemy. You must make the time that you have spent reading this message worth the while.

However, if you reading this bulletin and you have never at one time in your life surrendered your life to the Lord Jesus Christ, I would advise that you do so right now, right there where you are. The Bible says, for you to enter into the kingdom of God, you must be born again. All you need do is acknowledge the fact that you are a sinner and that you cannot approach God in your sinful state. Confess your sins to Him; name them one by one, ask Him to forgive you and cleanse you from all unrighteousness. Let Him know that you will never go back to the world of sin again. Renounce the devil and his works. Invite the Lord Jesus Christ into your life; accept Him as your personal Lord and Saviour. Enthrone Him over your life and hand over all that concerns you to Him. Ask Him to take total control of your life and all that concerns you; surrender your totality to Him.

I congratulate you for this decision that you have just taken. It is the most important decision in life and I pray that it shall be permanent in your life, in the name of Jesus. It is the first step to becoming God's friend. I pray that the Lord will uphold you with His right hand of righteousness and will keep you from falling in the name of Jesus. I pray that your name will be written in the Book of Life and you will not by any means, rub it off in the name of Jesus.

Perhaps you have been so bombarded by the enemy that you are almost at the verge of giving up. Do not give up. It is your enemy that will give up in the name of Jesus. Perhaps your children seem not to be under control, as if nothing good will come out of their lives. Today, the basket cage on their heads shall be burnt to ashes in the name of Jesus. Perhaps you have good qualifications and certificates to show, but you have not been able to get a befitting job. Maybe the enemy has smeared those certificates with saliva or urine; that saliva and urine shall dry up today and the certificates shall be cleansed today, with the blood of Jesus.

Now take these prayer points with all the seriousness that you can gather:

1. Every wicked grip upon my life, loose your hold! in the name of Jesus.
2. I drink the blood of Jesus, to neutralise every satanic food that I have eaten in the dream, in the name of Jesus.
3. Every plantation of darkness in my life and body, be uprooted! in the name of Jesus.
4. Every plantation of sickness in my life and body, be uprooted! in the name of Jesus.
5. Every power, making me to labour in vain, die! in the name of Jesus.
6. Every Luciferian night worker, harvesting the fruit of my labour, be roasted! in the name of Jesus.
7. Anything planted in my life to make me go out of God's will, be destroyed by fire! In the name of Jesus.
8. Lord let me experience Your presence anew, in the name of Jesus.
9. Every opportunity that I have lost to the enemy, I recover you by fire.
10. You the power of affliction, swallow yourself! in the name of Jesus.
11. Holy Ghost fire; destroy every garment of reproach in my life! in the name of Jesus.
12. Just as the grave could not hold Jesus, O Earth, release my virtues! in the name of Jesus.
13. Any dead relative, sitting on my blessings, release them by fire! in the name of Jesus.
14. I bind every spirit of death; go back to your sender! in name of Jesus.
15. Every evil dream, I cancel you by the blood of Jesus. You my hands, you shall not co-operate with poverty. You shall cooperate with my prosperity, in the name

of Jesus.

16. This year, I shall reach my goal, in the name of Jesus.
17. Every power of sorrow and tragedy in my life, die! in the name of Jesus.
18. Every witchcraft Pharaoh, stubbornly pursuing my life, die! in the name of Jesus.
19. Every satanic summon of my head, backfire! in the name of Jesus.
20. God arise in my life and let my enemies know that You are my God. in the name of Jesus.
21. God arise, and let me experience Your raw power in the name of Jesus.
22. The peace of God that passeth all understanding, flow into my life in Jesus' name.
23. I cross over to my land of opportunity today and possess my possessions in Jesus' name.
24. I declare that my life is not for sale, in the name of Jesus.

Begin to give glory to God for what He has done in your life.

Deep Secrets, Deep Deliverance

We will start this message by first looking at some Scriptures.
Deut. 29:29; *"The secret things belong unto the Lord our God: but those things which are revealed belong unto us and to our children for ever, that we may do all the words of this law."*

Daniel 2:22;
"He revealeth the deep and secret things: He knoweth what is in the darkness, and the light dwelleth with Him,"
Jeremiah 33:3; *"Call unto me, and 1 will answer thee, and shew thee great and mighty things, which thou knowest not."*

There are some things that are deep and others are on the surface. When you want to get something that is deep, you have to dig deep below the surface level to find it out. Gold, oil and other minerals, are treasures and they cannot be found on the surface of the ground; you have to dig deep to find them. There are some deep secrets about life and the Bible tells us that, it is God that knows the things that are in secret and He can also reveal them. The word of God goes on to say that God knows the things that are in the dark. One fact about darkness is that the person in it can see the person in the light very clearly but the one in the lighted area would need special anointing to see the person in the dark. Until certain secrets are revealed, it might be difficult to receive some victories. The enemy of our soul fights a very terrible battle for the souls of men. The devil has no honour or integrity. He is the father of lies, so his tactics are very deceitful. As far as the devil is concerned there is nothing like fairness. If you want to destroy your enemy, you would need to know his secrets.

WHAT ARE THE DEEP SECRETS?

1. **Not everyone Who Calls God is calling GOD.**
You may be surprised to find out that some people pray to petty gods and if you are not careful, you will say Amen to what they are saying. Such utterances that they call prayers are actually incantations. In such utterances, you will never hear the name of Jesus and they will never address the God of Abraham. Isaac and Jacob. They will just say: "god. god."

1 Corinthians 8:5-6 the Bible says;
"For though there be that are called gods, whether in heaven or in earth, (as there be gods many, and lords many,) But to us there is but one God, the Father, of whom are all things, and we in Him; and one Lord Jesus Christ, by whom are all things, and we by Him."

Many people are being deceived every day. This was how a brother got into serious trouble one day. He thought he had problems and a friend took him to see someone who could give spiritual assistance. He said when they got there, he was taken to a room which was very dark whereas, it was just 11a.m. He also saw birds flying about and was hearing voices as if the birds were talking, he felt very uncomfortable and he got up to leave. Just then, he sighted a Bible on a table and he sat back, reassuring himself that the Bible meant the presence of God. Someone came to 'pray' for him and he noticed that the person was addressing the creator and never mentioned Jesus. He thought he was referring to God the Creator. He did not know that he was in an occultic place.

Before he knew what he had gotten himself into, all his three children were deported from abroad in one day. They were not living together but they all met at the airport in Nigeria. None of them brought back anything. They came back empty handed and could not explain why they were deported. That is why we should be careful where we go. If the Holy Spirit begins to rebel within you, it means you are not supposed to be where you are or you are not supposed to be doing what you are doing. If you stay on, you are looking for trouble and are likely to get it.

2. The Devil Has An Organised Kingdom.
The devil has followers and emissaries and he runs his kingdom contrary to the kingdom of God.

3. The Worst Attack Comes During Sleep.
Some of the problems that people are struggling with started at night, during the hours of 12 midnight and 3a.m. That is why it is advisable to stay awake and pray during these hours.

According to Matthew 13:25 the Bible says; *"But while men slept, his enemy came and sowed tares among the wheat, and went his way."*

4. If Food is Taken Out of Existence, Demonic Oppression Will Decrease.
A major part of the affliction of Man comes from the food that he eats. It is a serious thing to find oneself eating in the dream. Spirits do not eat food but when they force-feed a person in the dream, the person will experience different types of affliction.

5. There Are Some Creatures That Are Used By Witchcraft Powers, To Afflict People In Their Dreams.
If you see the following animals in your dream, you should pray seriously because, it means you are under witchcraft attacks: goat, cat, rat, bat, termite, serpent or mud-fish.

6. Agents of Darkness Like To Put On Black Clothes.
Beware of a person who is not mourning, but is always putting on black clothes.

7. People use candles to destroy others:
If you have ever been to a gathering where candles are lit to perform rites, you need to go through deliverance.

8. The Enemy Can Mix With The Wind To Afflict People.
Some people got paralysed or started to have serious ailments after a strange wind blew on them suddenly. I pray that if you have been afflicted that way, you shall be delivered today in the name of Jesus.

WHEN IS DEEP DELIVERANCE REQUIRED?
When a problem is on the surface, it is easy to get rid of it through prayers within a few minutes or hours; but when a problem is deeply rooted, it would need more effort to pull it out. Many people have confessed to witchcraft and one of them in particular was a small girl. She brought a clay pot in which she had seventeen padlocks. It was amazing to discover that she knew the function of each of the padlocks. Out of the seventeen, she had used twelve on her own father. She said she had locked up all the money that the man had, or would ever have in life.

It is clear that this kind of thing exists, therefore, it is then necessary to take spiritual warfare serious. Imagine a person at a prayer meeting, praying and then three of such padlocks get destroyed and the person is not even aware of their existence, not to talk of their destruction. If such a person is not serious, more wicked ones will replace those three that were destroyed. That is why you have to pray and be sure you pray through

I would like you to know that there are some problems that are deeply rooted. There are some problems that people can not discuss with others because they sound very strange. For example, **there is something called spiritual blockage**; where a person cannot connect to heaven; there is no vision, no dream, no prophesy, they see nothing from God. Everything, in the spirit realm is black, deaf and dumb. Anytime such people decide to fast and pray, it is a serious problem; whenever they pick the Bible to read, they fall asleep. Anytime they start to pray, their thoughts wander from one thing to another because it cannot concentrate. Sometimes, when they go through deliverance, they fall sick and land in the hospital. Any method they use in progressing spiritually, lands them in trouble. Such people need deep deliverance.

There is something called dry faith; the person prays but doubts God in the depth of his or her heart. They are the people who will cry and weep all the time despite the fact that they have prayed. They might even prophesy, but they still cry.

Some people have abnormal thoughts; dreadful things are always passing through their minds: strange thoughts about suicide, sex, cruelty, tormenting thoughts and so on. **For some people, everything would be going on well and they would almost be at the verge of their breakthroughs, then they would have a strange dream and the breakthrough will not come**; then there would be a lot of attack and strange things will happen to them. **For some people, there will be no problem when they have no money but as soon as they have, one thing will pile up after the other, until the money is exhausted.** Before money comes again, problems would have piled up, waiting to gulp it. Such people need deep deliverance.

There is something called prayer-blockage; that is, when a person cannot pray on his own. The only time that such people pray is when they are in the church, in the midst of other people graying. **Some people experience excessive tiredness**; they are exhausted beyond measure without doing any hard work. It means the devil is toying with their bodies. **Some people experience inexplicable hatred**; people are just hostile towards them without cause. They are not wanted around for any reason. All these people need very deep deliverance.

WHAT TO DO:
1. **Know that there is a problem.**
Know that something is wrong somewhere. Once you realise the fact that there is a problem, the solution has started.

2. **Pray with desperation.**
When a person becomes desperate, progress begins. Many people pray but they are not yet desperate and until you are desperate, some mountains will not move. God says in Psalm 50:15; *"And call upon me in the day of trouble: I will deliver thee, and thon shall glorify me."*

One day, a woman came to me crying that her husband was always beating her. He would beat her to the extent that she would faint and he would take her to the hospital. I told her that there were two ways to it. She had to pray for the salvation of his soul. The Lord told me that his salvation would come in a hard way and I told her. She agreed to pray those prayer points. On the second day of her prayers, her husband was arrested and taken to the police station and later to prison. He had been there for some weeks, when it dawned on him that the beggarly powers that he was depending on, could not help him. When the wife went to visit him the following day, he showed her the incisions on his back and said it was a useless effort. By the time he had spent two months in prison, the wife came to me again saying that she was tired of going to give him food in the prison everyday. She said she was ashamed of being referred to as the wife of a prisoner. I told her that the Lord had not finished dealing with him but she wanted him out of prison. We prayed and he was released. As soon as he came back home. the beating started again.

When you get desperate, there are some prayers that you will pray and they do not have to be long. There are many Christians who need to pray desperate prayers today. A brother explained his problems and I gave him some prayer points; I told him that the prayers were dangerous because anything could happen. He said he was ready for anything. Within five days of prayers, the Lord dealt with the 'Troublers of his Israel.'

If a human being makes a covenant with evil powers in the dark world that he or she would kill a person and the person happens to be a child of God, whatever they do to the person in the dark world will backfire. If the evil doer vowed that he or she would rather die than see the person alive and prospering, the vow will happen when the Lord arises on behalf of His own child. That is why some evil people that are unrepentant, experience strange things or even die when the children of God pray. It is as a result of their evil vow which cannot go back without fulfilling its mission. I tell you, some of us really need to pray some deep prayers today. There is nothing that prayer cannot do.

Prayer has brought down fire on soldiers before and roasted them.

2 Kings 1:11-12;
"Again also he sent unto him another captain of fifty with his fifty. And he answered and said unto him, O man of God, thus hath the king said, Come down quickly. And Elijah answered and said unto them: "If I be a man of God, let fire come down from heaven, and consume thee and thy fifty. And the fire of God came down from heaven, and consumed him and his fifty."

Prayer has sealed the mouth of lions before.
Daniel 6:7;
"All the presidents of the kingdom, the governors, and the princes, the counsellors, and the captains, have consulted together to establish a royal statute, and to make a firm decree, that whosoever shall ask a petition of any God or man for thirty days, save of thee, O king, he shall be cast into the den of lions".

Verse 10;
"Now when Daniel knew that the writing was signed, he went into his house; and his windows being open in his chamber toward Jerusalem, he kneeled upon his knees three times a day, and prayed, and gave thanks before his God, as he did aforetime".

Verse 16;
"Then the king commanded, and they brought Daniel, and cast him into the den of lions. Now the king spake and said unto Daniel, Thy God whom thou servest continually, he will deliver thee".

Verse 22;
"My God hath sent his angel, and hath shut the lions' mouths, that they have not hurt me: forasmuch as before him innocency was found in me; and also be-fore thee, O king, have I done no hurt."
Prayer has shut the heavens before.
1 Kings 17:1;
"And Elijah the Tishbite, who was of the inhabitants of Gilead, said unto Ahab, As the Lord God of Israel liveth, before whom I stand, there shall not be dew nor rain these years, but according to my word."

Prayers have introduced confusion into the camp of enemies before. Prayers have made owners of evil load to carry their evil load. Prayer has pulled down a witchcraft bird from the sky before and it became a human being. There is nothing that prayers cannot do. To be quite honest with you, anyone who can really pray has no problem. Many of the churches that did not believe in our kind of prayers have started praying them now; some are even asking for deliverance sessions to be conducted in their churches.

The prayers that I am suggesting below are not for gentle men; they are prayers for mad prophets. When a prophet prays in holy madness, fire falls. 1 Kings 18:36-38;
"And it came to pass at the time of the offering of the evening sacrifice, that Elijah the prophet came near, and said, Lord God of Abraham, Isaac, and of Israel, let it be known this day that thou art God in Israel, and that I am thy servant, and that I have done all these things at thy word. Hear me, O Lord, hear me, that this people may know that thou art the Lord God, and that thou hast turned their heart back again. Then the fire of the Lord fell, and consumed the burnt sacrifice, and the wood, and the stones, and the dust, and licked up the water that was in the trench."

Are you tired of the harassments of the devil and his cohorts? Then, you have to become desperate and pray with all the aggression that you can gather. I want you to pray and be expectant. Beloved, if you pray these prayers fervently and you lose your voice in the process, you would have made a good bargain because, you would have obtained your deliverance from those powers that are trying to prove stubborn. These prayers will cause a lot of havoc in the camp of the enemy. These were the kind of prayers that chased out demons and they were begging Jesus not to send them out.

However beloved, if you have not yet surrendered your life to the Lord Jesus Christ, you cannot really pray the prayers that I am suggesting below. If you are not born again, you cannot claim to be a child of God and He cannot reveal any secret to you. All you need do is acknowledge the fact that you are a sinner and that you cannot approach God in your sinful state, If you are ready, confess your sins to Him and ask Him to forgive you and cleanse you from all unrighteousness. Claim the redemptive power in the blood of Jesus that was shed on the cross at Calvary for the remission of your sins. Say bye-bye to the world and the devil and make sure you do not go back to them again. Invite the Lord Jesus Christ into your life and ask Him to come in and become your personal Lord and Saviour. Ask Him to take an absolute control of your life and all that concerns you.

I congratulate you on this decision that you have just taken. It is the most important decision in life; and I pray that it shall be permanent in your life in the name of Jesus. I pray that the Lord will write your name in the Book of Life and nothing shall rub it off in the name of Jesus.

Take these prayer points with holy aggression:

1. Every power, circulating my name for destruction, wherever you are, die! in the name of Jesus.
2. Every serpent of my father's house, today is your final day, die! in the name of Jesus.
3. My destiny, arise from the graveyard and shine!, in the name of Jesus.
4. Thou power of affliction, my life is not your candidate, therefore, scatter! in the name of Jesus.
5. Every power that wants me to remain in the valley all the days of my life, die!, in the name of Jesus.
6. Arrow of confusion in my life, backfire! in the name of Jesus.
7. Every owner of the load of oppression in my life, carry your evil load by fire, in the name of Jesus.
8. Blood of Jesus, arise in Your power and fight for me today! in the name of Jesus.
9. Every stubborn strongman in charge of my problem, die! in the name of Jesus.
10. Every power that has swallowed my virtues, vomit them and die! in the name of Jesus.
11. Every power assigned to cut my life short and add it to theirs, die! in the name of Jesus.
12. Every power assigned to steal my wealth, die! in the name of Jesus.
13. Every power shedding blood to destroy me, die! in the name of Jesus.
14. Power to pray prevailing prayers, fall upon my life, in Jesus' name.
15. Thoughts that do not conform to the word of God, my heart is not your habitation, in the name of Jesus.
16. Every spiritual blockage. clear away in the name of Jesus.
17. Anything in my life, making heaven to be closed to me, blood of Jesus, flush them out.
18. God, arise and do not pass me by, in the name of Jesus.
19. Thou power of the strange children of my father's house, die! in the name of Jesus.
20. Thou power of the strange children of my mother's house, die! in the name of Jesus.
21. Power to be lifted up, fall upon me now! in the name of Jesus.

Ten Truths The Devil Does Not Want You To Know (1)

Psalm 119:89; *"For ever, O Lord, Thy word is settled in heaven."*

The word of God is the only unchanging truth. The word of Man will forever change. Most of the science books that were written twenty years ago have been revised or changed. In Nigeria for example, we had storybooks which were compulsory for pupils learning English language, but today, they are no more in circulation. One of such books had the story of Abdul and the Angel, another one had the story of Shokolokobangoshe. Today, they are no longer in existence. The syllabus had changed repeatedly.

The Bible says God is the Alpha and Omega; that is the 'A' and 'Z'. If you look through the Alphabets, you will find out that there are many letters between 'A' and 'Z'.
John 18:37-39;
"Pilate therefore said unto Him: "Art thou a king then?" Jesus answered; "Thou sayest that I am a king. To this end was I born, and for this cause came I into the world, that I should bear witness unto the truth. Every one that is of the truth heareth my voice". Pilate saith unto Him: "What is truth?" And when he had said this, he went out again unto the Jews, and saith unto them, I find in him no fault at all."

Pilate did not know the 'Truth'. He did not understand the fact that the "Truth" is the word of God. Jesus is the word of God and He is the Truth. He was standing before Pilate but Pilate did not understand Him. Many people are like that today. There was a rich young man who came to meet the Lord Jesus Christ and asked Him questions on how to get eternal life. Jesus asked him what the Scriptures said and he answered correctly. When Jesus told him to do all that the law demanded, he said he had been doing those things since his youth. Jesus then told him to go and sell his property, distribute to the poor and follow Him. It was difficult for him to swallow and the Bible says the man went away with his head bowed. He was sad. He saw the Truth, but he did not recognise Him. He was a loser. He was far from the Truth, when he found Him and lost Him.

I would like you to pray like this:
* *Lord, I do not want to be blind to the truth, I do not want to be just near the Truth, but I want to be in the Truth, in the name of Jesus.*

The devil has already been defeated but he does not want people to know it. That is why he keeps the truth away from them. The devil also prevent people from using their spiritual weapons and keeps away useful spiritual information. Some people go to gatherings where there is no useful information for them. Normally, if a gathering is referred to as a fellowship of Christians, you should expect at least three things to happen there. You should expect that, some people would leave the place mad at themselves because they have been convicted of their wrong doings. Some would leave the place sad, because they have wasted time in the camp of the enemy; the others would leave the place happy because they, have received solution to their problems or are glad because they have received salvation, deliverance and healing. If none of these things happen to you, then, it had not been a useful gathering.

God has secrets, but everything is open to Him. The devil too has secrets, which the Lord has the power to reveal to His children.

Deuteronomy 29:29 says;
"The secret things belong unto the Lord our God: but those things which are revealed belong unto us and to our children for ever, that we may do all the words of this law."

Daniel 2:22;
"He revealeth the deep and secret things: He knoweth what is in the darkness, and

the light dwelleth with Him."

Psalm 25:14;
"The secret of the Lord is with them that fear Him; and He will shew them His covenant."

Jeremiah 33:3;
"Call unto me, and I will answer thee, and shew thee great and mighty things, which thou knowest not."

Life has secrets; the devil too has secrets that he does not want the children of God to know. One of the abilities of the devil is the fact that, he can remove the word of God from the hearts of people, as we saw in the parable of the sower. Many people can remember worldly songs but cannot remember Bible verses; this is why many churchgoers will find themselves in hell fire because, they allow the evil one to remove the fruit of the word of God from their hearts. He makes people to be ignorant of what the Bible says about them. He combats useful spiritual information that will move their lives forward. The devil even make people to forget their dreams when they wake up.

THE TEN TRUTHS HE DOES NOT WANT YOU KNOW

1. **The Devil Is A Liar.**
John 8:44-45;
"Ye are of your father the devil, and the lusts of your father ye will do. He was a murderer from the beginning, and abode not in the truth, because there is no truth in him. When he speaketh a lie, he speaketh of his own: for he is a liar and the father of it."

The devil lied to Adam and Eve and caused them to be chased out of the Garden of Eden. He came in form of a serpent and framed a question in a way that Eve got carried away. He knew what God said but asked if God had told them not to eat from the trees of the garden. He told her that they would not die if they ate the fruit of that tree. He is still using that method on people today by giving them false security. He makes them believe that they have no problem. In fact, they go to the extent of saying that it is only the people who have problems that go to church, so they do not need to go to church.

A sister came to see me one day and I asked what the problem was. She said she had no problem and I asked what she came for. She said she wanted me to pray for her. I asked on what subject and she said; "generally". I said we do not pray general prayers in MFM but 'specific' prayers. As we were praying, the Lord revealed the fact that her two legs were fish tail. There are many people like that today. There are some that the devil will convince that they are very intelligent and they know more than everybody else. In fact, he will tell them to do what their heart tells them to do. When you begin to listen to the lie of the devil, you will get into trouble.

Pray like this: **I refuse to listen to the lie of the devil, in the name of Jesus.**

One night, whilst prayer warriors were praying in the church, some birds came flying across the church premises. One of the warriors spotted them and pointed at them, commanding the fire of God to arrest them and one of them crash-landed and turned to an old woman. This was about 2 a. m. The prayer warriors tied her hands and made her sit on the floor, waiting for the morning. The security men said at a point in time, they were getting weak and were dozing off. At that very moment, the rope with which they tied her broke off. It was when they woke up that they retied the rope. When I got there in the morning, I asked her where she came from and she mentioned the name of her village.

I told her that having seen that the power of God is greater than the one she has, she should think about it and surrender her life to the Lord Jesus Christ. She said "No, that it was too late, that she had sold out her heart and life to the devil." She admitted that the airspace over MFM was not their normal route, that they were on their way to Unilag where they wanted to strengthen the cult there. Since she was not ready to surrender her life to the Lord Jesus Christ, we asked her to go and she left. It is the devil that tells people lies like this and make them belong to evil associations. It is when most of them land in hell that they will know the truth, that the devil had been deceiving them.

On another occasion, the president and secretary of an evil association were flying over the premises where prayer warriors were praying and the secretary dropped, but the president escaped. I pray that the wings of any evil power flying over your habitation shall break and be paralysed, in the name of Jesus. Beloved, if you are in any evil associations like witchcraft, familiar spirit, "Ogbanje". etc, you had better renounce them and come to Jesus before it is too late. Do not allow the devil to tell you his lies.

At a service one evening, a girl said she had a calabash in her stomach. As we were praying for her, she was groaning in pain and she started to speak a strange language. We asked her and she said she needed a bucket of water, in order to summon Mammy-Water. We got the bucket of water and she chanted some words and later sighed, saying that, the spirit could not come into the house because, there was an angel at the door with a sword of fire. That would have been the first time I would have seen Mammy Water had she appeared.

She was delivered but some time later, she listened to the lies of the devil that was making fun of her, that she had become poor and was no longer attractive. The devil tell lies everyday just to deceive people. He is the one who tells women that one man is not sufficient for them. He encourages men to take more than one wife; he has his own prophets who imitate the truth in order to deceive people. He prepares scotch-egg for them; the outer coat will be nice and attractive but the inner part will be bad; he knows how to coat lies with some truth; that is why fake prophets tell some truth, so that you would not find out that they are deceiving you.

Lying is an instrument of hypocrisy and deceit, and that is why the Bible is harsh on all liars. The Bible says they are of the devil and they will find themselves in the lake of fire. You can see this in the book of Rev. 21:8:

"But the fearful, and unbelieving, and the abominable, and murderers, and whoremongers, and sorcerers, and idolaters, and all liars, shall have their part in the lake which burneth with fire and brimstone: which is the second death."

It is the lie of the devil to give you a bad picture about your life and tell you that certain things are impossible. The devil will make you believe that an illness is incurable: the idea is to make you believe and then miss what God has for you. One thing that you can do about making the devil flee from you is talking back to him.

A preacher was driving on the highway and he heard the devil mocking him that he had been preaching for many years and had not gained anything from it. The brother packed his vehicle and commanded the devil to get out. Since then, the devil never molested him again. You too can talk back to the devil and he will flee from you. The doctors might have told you that your disease is incurable or that you would need a major operation before you are healed. These are lies of the devil; you should examine what God says about your health. He says no evil shall befall you, the Bible says none of the diseases of the Egyptians will come upon you. If you believe God for what He says, then what the doctors say will become lies. The devil has killed so many people with lies like these. When they are supposed to be claiming God's promises, they keep saying that it is a sign of old age.

Sometimes, the devil manufacture problems that make people think that the days of trouble will never end. The devil coaxes people about their beauty and make them think that they are meant for every man or woman. The devil encourages people to alter God's creation in them; he encourages people to be promiscuous, thinking that they are lucky whereas, that is the worst kind of luck that a person can possibly have. He also encourages people to look for evil means of keeping their spouses. The devil will make people listen to his lies and when trouble comes, he abandons them.

There was a professor in England in those days, who used to go about preaching in the open market place. He was the next qualified for the post of Vice-Chancellor but the council decided that they would not give him the post because he used to preach in public and that would make him a disgrace to the university. He was not bothered and he continued witnessing for Christ. When the council could not find a better qualified person, he was appointed as Vice-Chancellor of the university. He did not listen to the lie of the devil but continued steadfastly in his witnessing for Christ. Today, there are some people who argue against the word of God whereas; they have not achieved anything tangible in life. Some scarcely scale through university, yet they argue against the word of God, The devil make people equate themselves with God. Immediately a person realises that the devil is a liar, the chains binding the person begins to break and he will begin to obtain freedom. It shall be so today in the name of Jesus.

2. The Seniority Of Power.

The devil does not want people to understand the fact that the power of God is greater than his own. As far as the Bible is concerned, there are three that bear record in heaven; God the Father, the Son and the Holy Spirit. They form the 'Trinity' and they are in the 'third heaven.' The second power is the Church of Christ on earth. The next one is the power of God's angels, the lowest power is that of the devil and his demons.

Hebrews 12:23-24;
"To the general assembly and church of the firstborn, which are written in heaven and to God the Judge of all, and to the spirits of just men made perfect, and to Jesus the mediator of the new covenant, and to the blood of sprinkling, that speaketh better things than that of Abel."

Salient Facts:
Beloved, you should get these facts straight; the devil is not God and cannot be like Him. God did not create the devil; He created Lucifer who fell and turned himself into the devil. The devil is a creature and he is subject to the power of God and can only operate with permission; he cannot over-power God. The devil is not above judgment. The church of God is above the Archangels, Cherubim, Seraphim, and the innumerable company of angels. They share the authority of Christ. Ephesians 2:6; *"And hath raised us up together, and made us sit together in heavenly places in Christ Jesus."*

Jesus has been raised to the third heaven, and every other thing is under His feet. If the Church is His body, then, every other thing is underneath the Church. Jesus says; *"The Lord rebuke you Satan"* the Church would say; "I rebuke you Satan, in the name of Jesus. If you have been afraid of the devil, you should stop being afraid. The truth is that, if you know and stay in your position, the devil too will stay in his position, which is underneath your feet, not on your shoulder and definitely not on your head.

3. The Source Of The Problem.

Many problems will be solved as soon as the source is detected. A problem could emanate from any of the following sources:

i. **Sin**: God hates sin with perfect hatred. It opens people up to spiritual attacks and kills. It is spiritual leprosy. It is the greatest tragedy that has ever befallen Man. He who commits sin does not know God and is not known of Him. Willful sin is an attempt to overthrow God's kingdom and taking sides with the Kingdom of the devil. There is no small sin. It has the power to hinder God, that is why the Bible says in the book of Isaiah 59:1-2; *"Behold, the Lord's hand is not shortened, that it cannot save; neither his ear heavy, that it cannot hear: But your iniquities have separated between you and your God, and your sins have hid his face from you, that he will not hear."*

Anyone who knowingly practices sin is lost already. If God could discipline Moses, Ananias and Sapphira and the sons of Aaron who offered strange fire, then it shows that He hates sin; no matter how 'small' it looks and that He is a respecter of no one. The Bible says; *"Though hand join in hand, the wicked shall not be unpunished: but the seed of the righteous shall he delivered."*

(Proverbs 11:21) Whenever there is a problem, make sure you check your life and see if there is any sin lurking there.

ii. **Demonic spirits:** They

cause sleeplessness, horrible dreams, sicknesses and diseases, internal heat, things moving about in the body, hearing strange voices, etc. If you are being bothered by demonic powers, I would advise that you go for deliverance.

iii. **Self-inflicted problems**: It is an amazing fact but many people do things that run contrary to their own peace. They set battles in array and vigorously fight within themselves. The Bible talks about some people who fight against themselves. All the fornication and adultery, abortion leading to complications, all the drinking and smoking, means you are fighting yourself and it is a certificate in the school of self-destruction. All the anger, malice, impatience etc, will facilitate self-destruction. Are you fighting with yourself? Repent! before it is too late.

iv. **Accidental problems**: Some people go to places where they carry evil load of the enemy. When a person just walks into an environment where there is an epidemic, the person will be infected. There is an adage in Yoruba that says; "When a person is asked to help bring down a heavy load and he now lays claim to it, there is a serious problem somewhere."

The Bible says that: *"the angels of the Lord encamp round those that fear Him"* (Psalm 34:7). If your life is dirty, the angels will not be able to tolerate your smell. If your life is chasing away angels and there are arrows flying about, the arrows will enter into your life without hindrance.

v. **Inherited problems**: These are the problems that are transferred from parents to offsprings. It could be suicidal tendency, broken homes, insanity, poverty, and persistent problems. They are usually attached to the family roots. As soon as you can trace the history of a problem within a family, you should know, that ancestral spirits are there.

vi. **Curses**: These are evil, negative pronouncements against a person. It could result in, repeated chronic diseases, marital failure, financial insufficiency, unnatural death, etc

vii. **Spiritual carelessness**: Many people are proud and un-teachable. Sometimes the Holy Spirit would be speaking but many people do not listen to Him. Many are careless in the things that are related to holiness, they take many things for granted and some even underrate the devil.

1 Peter 5:8 advises on what we should do; *"Be sober, be vigilant; because your adversary the devil, as a roaring lion; walketh about, seeking whom he may devour."*

viii. **Evil covenants**: This is an evil agreement made with an evil spirit, it could be made on behalf of someone; it could be conscious or unconscious; it could be through rituals or sacrifices, blood bath or drinking of blood, bath at the river or beach, incisions, supply of materials to herbalists or false prophets, etc.

ix. **Possession of cursed or abominable things**: These are decorations, ornaments, jewelries, and carved woods dedicated to idols. You should know how the Holy Spirit talks to you. Learn how to hear from God so that, you will know what to do at every point in time. A spiritual inventory of your possession is necessary. People criticise us in MFM that we do not allow people to put on jewelry. It is because we do not want to take chances. Some of the jewelry on sale are items dedicated to idols. Some of them have diabolic inscriptions or images. Some have snakes drawn on them, half moon, eye, some look like a cross but at a closer look, one would see that they are hanks. If we find any door through which the enemy can 'Come in', we block it completely. We tell people the blunt truth because, we do not want their blood to be demanded of us. When the devil sees that his mission to a place is defeated, he tries to water down the efforts of the people there and antagonise them.

I read an article captioned "The man who refused to die". He was attacked in the dream by a snake; he struggled with the snake but could not get himself freed from it and he shouted "Jesus" and an angel came to his rescue. The angel hit the snake on the head and it died. The following morning, he got a message from his village that his father was dead and that he had a big cut in the head. He understood that his father was the snake that attacked him the previous night. There is an ancient songwriter who wrote a hymn, which says: "Jesus has conquered death; death is dead." Many people are toying with the enemy. You have to say "No, not me!"

Beloved, I would like to pause here for now. We shall conclude this important topic next week by the grace of God. Meanwhile, I would suggest that you regurgitate what you have read so far and redigest it. I pray that the Lord will minister to you more in the name of Jesus.

However, if you are reading this bulletin and you have not at one time in your life surrendered your life to the Lord Jesus Christ, I would ask that you do so now, right there where you are. The Lord is right there where you are and He is ready to set you free from every bondage. All you need to do is to acknowledge your sins and confess them to the Lord. Ask Him to forgive you and cleanse you from all unrighteousness. Claim the redemptive power in the Blood of Jesus that was shed on the cross at Calvary, for the remission of your sins.

Invite the Lord Jesus Christ into your life, ask Him to come in and become your personal Lord and Saviour. Ask Him to take total control of your life and all that concerns you. Subject your totality to Him. This is an important decision and I congratulate you for taking it. I pray that it shall be permanent in your life in the name of Jesus. I pray that the Lord will uphold you and keep you from falling in the name of Jesus. I pray that He will write your name in the Book of life and you will not by any means rub it off in the name of Jesus. Go and sin no more!

I would like you to take the prayers that I am suggesting below with all the aggression that you can gather. Be determined not to allow the devil to have the last say in your life.

1. I refuse to be devalued, in the name of Jesus.
2. Every evil utterance by satanic agents against my life, against my marriage, be nullified by the blood of Jesus.
3. Every evil dedication of my father's house working against my life, break and loose your hold upon my life, in the name of Jesus.
4. I cancel every evil ordination against my life, in the name of Jesus.
5. Every evil hold upon my life. break loose by fire, in the name of Jesus.
6. My life shall not be terminated by the wicked agenda of the enemy, in the name of Jesus.
7. Lord kill every ignorance working against me in the name of Jesus.
8. Lord, open my eyes to see every secret I need to know about my life, in the name of Jesus.
9. I refuse to hear the voice of the devil, in the name of Jesus.
10. I neutralise every satanic agenda for my life, in the name of Jesus.
11. I challenge my body with the Fire of God, in the name of Jesus.
12. Every negative vow that I have made with any man or woman that is affecting me negatively now, break and be cancelled by fire! in the name of Jesus.
13. Every citadel of the enemy in my home, break! in the name of Jesus.
14. I refuse to be a candidate of amputated breakthroughs, in the name of Jesus.

Ten Truths The Devil Does Not Want You To Know (2)

In the last bulletin, we started this important topic; on issues the devil would not want anyone to read. We said that the devil is a liar and the father of all liars. We also said that Jesus is the "Truth" and that it is very important to know Him and to have a personal relationship with Him. We enumerated some salient facts concerning problems and their sources. This week, we shall see the other truths that the devil does not want people to know, in other to remain under his bondage. Read on and allow the Lord to minister to you. God bless you in the name of Jesus.

4. Sin And Sinners Are Destroyers.

Ecclesiastes 9:18; *"Wisdom is better than weapons of war: but one sinner destroyeth much good."*

The Bible says "sin is the transgression of the law." This means sin is lawlessness. It is like a cloud covering the face of God's blessings. When God says you should not do something and you do it, it is a sign of lawlessness. No man can break God's law; the person will only succeed in breaking himself or herself. Sin is a sickness that contaminates the whole body. Whenever the enemy wants to get at a person, he manipulates him or her into the state of sinfulness, knowing that in that state, he or she cannot approach God and that God would not answer such a person's prayers. That is why one of the signs of the end of the age is that iniquity shall abound and the love of many shall wax cold.

Isaiah 59:1-3;
"Behold, the Lord's hand is not shortened, that it cannot save; neither His ear heavy that it cannot hear: but your iniquities have separated between you and your God, and your sins have hid His face from you, that He will not hear. For your hands are defiled with blood, and your fingers with iniquity; your lips have spoken lies, your tongue hath muttered perverseness."

Sin is a binding rope; it holds Man in its power. It is a slave-owner; it embitters the life of the slave. It is a disturber of rest; it causes disorder and anxiety. It is a robber of blessings; it starves the soul. It stabs from the back and overthrows the sinner. During the overthrow, many things will be destroyed. To worsen the case, sin is a keeper of records; it records all sinful acts and recalls them. It leaves its mark upon the path of the person. It is a detective; it will turn against the sinner, trail the sinner and find him or her out no matter how fast the person runs or how cleverly he or she hides, and then it will expose the person with the sin.

Numbers 32:23;
"But if ye will not do so, behold, ye have sinned against the LORD: and be sure your sin will find you out."

Sin is an accusing witness; it will accumulate evidence to the condemnation of the sinner. The Bible concludes by saying that the person that sins is of the devil: there is no neutral ground. There is no clever sinner; in fact, engaging in any sinful act is foolishness. What a sinner is doing now could afflict his or her children and it might go on for ten generations. Sin has a way of linking itself to other sins and it goes on expanding and gets to the biggest one that eventually leads to death.

Samson was a child of miracle; an angel prophesied his birth and gave his mother divine instructions on how to look after him. God said he was going to deliver his people Israel and he actually did exploits. He carried the whole gate of a city and put it aside. When the problem of Samson was going to start, it started with idleness; he had time to sit in the midst of people and tell stories and give them riddles, then, his eyes began to x-ray women; fornication set in and he began to behold prostitutes. He graduated into disobeying God's instituted law on marriage, which says His children should not be unequally yoked together with unbelievers. Samson went to his parents and begged them to marry Delilah for him. What was his reason? He said she pleased him well. Not because she was a child of God, but because he liked her. Delilah signaled the obituary of Samson. He played with his God given power; Delilah made him tell her the secret of his power and she sold him out to the enemy. He lost his power, became a grinder of pepper and then died with his enemies. He put the whole nation in trouble and it all started with 'just a little sin

Achan put the whole nation of Israel in trouble by stealing the forbidden thing. Sin destroys body, soul, and spirit and causes eternal separation from God. There is no small sin and all sinners shall be destroyed. Sinners in a fellowship will hinder the power of God. They limit the power of the Holy Spirit. It pains me to find out that when the angels of God come into a congregation, they sometimes go away from one person to another, because people are not ready to receive from God; there is sin in the camp. Sinners cause dishonour to the name of the Lord; they make God look powerless by hindering or diverting the route of God's communication with them.

Beloved, if you are living in any known sin, you will do yourself and your children, family, the church and the whole world a lot of good by repenting. Do not be the 'Achan' that will bring destruction upon your family because you are destroying yourself and it will affect them. The issue of sin is so serious that God had to send His Son to die for the world, in order to reconcile the world unto Himself. When Adam and Eve sinned in the Garden of Eden, they were chased out of the garden and that alienated Man from God. The Bible says; *"The wages of sin is death."* If you decide to collect 'salary advance' by thinking you are clever, you are playing with fire. Anything you are doing, that you will be ashamed of if people see or hear you do, is not worth doing at all. Those things that you cannot announce in public that you are doing because they are not edifying, stop doing them before you put yourself and other people in trouble. Depart from iniquity!

5. **Everyone Is Living A Borrowed Life.**
Romans 14:7;
"For none of us liveth to himself and no man dieth to himself."
What we do, could add to the sorrow or happiness of other people. Those who love you might suffer more than you, for your evil actions. Many people think they have the right to do what they like. They live their lives the way it pleases them. Some disregard the advice of their pastors, counselors, elders and parents. Some flout the rules of common sense so that they can feel important, but such people will soon discover that it is foolishness. The Bible says nobody has the right to use his or her life the way he or she pleases. You and I are living on borrowed time and we shall account for every minute and every second. The Bible says we must appear before the judgment seat of God, to give an account of everything we have done on earth, where we have been to, what we have said or ate, everything!

6. **The Secret Of The Power In The Blood Of Jesus.**
The Blood of Jesus is unique because the Holy Spirit, not man, conceived Him. His Blood was not contaminated; God Himself prepared the body of Jesus. Jesus is the word of God; so, His Blood is of God. Since blood carries life, the Blood of Jesus carries the eternal life of God. The Blood of Jesus spells defeat for the devil and paves the way to heaven for us; drives demons out of our way and brings judgment to stubborn sinners. The devil hates people making mention of or pleading the Blood of Jesus. The Bible tells us that the Blood of Jesus has redeeming power, that is, if a person has sold himself or herself to the devil, he can be bought back by the Blood of Jesus. The Blood of Jesus has forgiving and cleansing power, that is, through the Blood of Jesus, the sins of a person can be forgiven and all filthiness cleansed. The Blood of Jesus has the power to cover and to preserve, so that spiritual contaminators will not enter into a person, place, thing, or situation. The Blood Jesus has justifying and sanctifying power. You can plead the Blood of Jesus on any situation. Since there is

life in blood generally, the Blood of Jesus carries the life of Jesus. The Bible says that the Blood of Jesus speaks better things than the Blood of Abel, which was crying out unto God for vengeance. The Blood of Jesus has melting, pacifying and confirming power. It is through the Blood of Jesus that we can enter into the Holy of holies; the Throne of God. The Blood of Jesus has life-giving and overcoming power.

John 6:53;
"Then Jesus said unto them; "Verily, verily, I say unto you; except ye eat the flesh of the Son of man, and drink His blood, ye have no life in you". Revelation 12:11; **"And they overcame him by the blood of the Lamb and by the word of their testimony; and they loved not their lives into the death".**

The devil hides this information from believers so that they will not know the power in the Blood of Jesus.

7. Healing And Divine Health Is God's Will For Us.

Some people have become so used to sickness that, even when they are not ill, they look sickly. God wants you to be well and healthy; it is the devil that wants people to be sick. If you come to God and there is doubt in your heart as to being healed, you might never be healed.

A man of God was ministering at a crusade and he spotted a crippled man on a wheel chair. Occasionally, the cripple would make some noise with his stump. The minister sent an usher to tell the man not to disturb the audience. When the minister saw that the man kept shaking his body and it was as if he was trying to get up from the wheel chair, the man of God himself came close to him and said it was not yet time for him to pray for people to get healed, so, the man should be patient. The minister discovered that the man could not understand the language that he was speaking and the ushers got someone to interpret. The man said he came to the crusade to be healed and nobody would hinder him, not even the minister of God.

When the minister got back to the pulpit, he prayed and said, like Elijah: "If I be a man of God, arise and walk! Before he finished praying, the man got up from the wheel chair and started to walk. The man went there with faith in his heart, with the intention and expectation of being healed, that is all what God is looking for and he got his healing.

Sometimes, people attend prayer meetings because they were asked to come and nothing actually happens. If you go to the presence of God with expectation in your heart. knowing that God is the creator of heaven and earth and that the Bible says; *"In the beginning, God created..."* then, He must have spare parts. If what your health needs is a spare part, He will provide it. If what it needs is servicing, He will bring out all the dirt in you and all the evil food that you have eaten at the table of the devil and from the hands of night caterers. He will drain you, if it means turning you upside down. He will do it. The Bible says; *"He Himself bore our infirmities... and by His stripes we are healed."* God has done all the healing, all we need to do is claim and collect it. The will of God for His children is that we be in good health and be free from all sicknesses, pain, diseases and all physical sufferings. God has provided all the necessary weapons to defeat sickness and all the works of the devil.

John 3:8;
"He that committeth sin is of the devil; for the devil sinneth from the beginning. For this purpose the Son of God was manifested, that He might destroy the works of the devil."

The Bible says Jesus came to destroy the works of the devil and that He has given us victory over him. Two believers were being harassed at night by demonic forces; they saw scratches on their bodies and were always sick. One of them started to read Psalms but nothing happened and the other discovered what the Bible says about his health, that Jesus had already borne his sicknesses and diseases. He then prayed "THE PRAYER OF THE DESTROYER"; he prayed with all the aggression that he could gather, declaring that; "Any power that moves close to my habitation to afflict me, receive spiritual leprosy, in the name of Jesus." Those forces never moved close to him again because, he had discovered the right weapon.

God has given us weapons to destroy the works of the devil and He has given us abundant life too. If you allow the devil, he will come and give you lectures on how the disease that you have kills and will enumerate the number of people that it has killed. When you sit before a television set, he will show you how the disease is killing people day by day. When you pick up newspapers, he will show you statistics about the disease. All these programming are in a bid to get you discouraged and then make you give up. Tell the devil that he is a liar, so that he will not tell you more stories. Disagree with the negative things you have agreed with before; disagree with the picture on the X-Ray or Scan, or the tests that say this or that is positive or negative as the cases may be.

8 The Devil Is A Defeated Foe And He Can Be Frightened.

Colossians 2:13-15;
"And you, being dead in your sins and the uncircumcision of your flesh, hath he quickened together with Him, having forgiven you all trespasses; Blotting out the handwriting of ordinances that was against us, which was contrary to us, and took it out of the way, nailing it to His cross; And having spoiled principalities and powers, He made a shew of them openly, triumphing over them in it."

HOW TO FRIGHTEN THE DEVIL

a. **Have aggressive faith**
b. **Pray violent prayers.**
c. **Live a life of holiness.**

James 2:19 says;
"Thou believest that there is one God; thou doest well: the devils also believe, and tremble."

9. The Devil Has No Gift.

This particular point is very important and I would like you to take it serious because, the devil is succeeding through it in the lives of many people. The devil operates a simple primitive 'Trade by Barter' If he gives someone money or children, he will surely take something else in exchange for it. He will either make a person vomit what he gave him or her, or allow that thing to kill him or her. Since it is the devil that distributes sicknesses, he puts them on people and has the power to remove them when appeased; but be sure that he will take something back in exchange. He can operate through strange religions and doctrines; he will remove one problem and replace it with a wicked, clever, and subtle one. Some people will rush to some places because they have leaking pockets. There, they will help them to remove the leaking pockets but will replace it with an incurable disease. The devil would remove tuberculosis and replace it with fornication.

Many years ago, there was an article in the papers where a cemetery guard was asked what the secret of his wealth was, since his normal salary was meagre. He said his 'friends' the dead, gave him one thing or the other, whenever they went out in form of living beings. He accumulated such things for years but he died a tragic, mysterious death and all those things disappeared. You cannot collect something from the camp of the enemy and expect God to prosper it. If the money you possess is from the camp of the enemy, you have to do away with it. **Some people think they can bribe God after acquiring wealth from the camp of the enemy, they will now sign cheques and distribute money to religious gatherings. Some even build prayer houses; they do not know that the devil is still around and will reclaim what they owe him.**

If you have taken things from 'sugar daddies' and you still possess them after giving your life to the Lord Jesus Christ, they will serve as open doors to the devil; he will come back. Sometimes some people pray for the fire of the Holy Ghost to fall on them and the Lord wakes them up in the night to pray. As they start singing in praise and worship to the Lord, the devil can come and remind them of his things that are in their possession. In fact, he will say they have no right to pray because he has proofs that they are still in his camp. He can even go before God to accuse them and since God is righteous and just, He will check to see if the devil is correct and turn back with His blessings. **This is why, when some people get born again, God drains away whatever they brought from the world, before He gives them His**

own. The Bible says a man has nothing except it is given him from above. Whatsoever you have and you know that it is not from above and is from the devil, you had better spit it out, before the devil makes you vomit it the hard way.

The devil is a hard slave master; he does not tolerate nonsense at all. In the house of God, you will see people going late to services. It is not done in the camp of the devil without a punishment. It is not possible to go late to a demonic meeting and go scot-free. An offender could pay with the death of his or her first born or another child, or with one organ in his or her body. **Many people go to wolves to fight their battles for them; the truth is that there is no prophet that can fight your battles for you. You might wonder why some of them see visions or prophesy and it comes true; it is because people want to be deceived and the devil will bring out some seemingly true things about the person, so that he or she will continue to consult him. By running around prophets, you are inviting demonic prophesies into your life, instead of fighting for yourself. Do not sit tight in a gathering of dead people, saying that it is your 'family church' or that there are powerful prophets or prophetesses there.**

A sister was coming to our meetings and her mother did not like it; she said they had a prophetess in their church that could see visions and prophesy. When the sister told me, I asked her to invite the prophetess to our house and she did. When they came in, I asked them to stand as we prayed. The prayer point that I asked every one of us to pray was: **"O Lord, send Your Fire into my life, in the name of Jesus."** We had not prayed for long when the 'prophetess' screamed and started to roll on the floor, crying "Fire, Fire" and was wriggling like a snake. The sister then understood the kind of power that the woman had. As they were going back home, the sister asked the prophetess to go home with her and they were fortunate to meet her mother at home. The sister asked that they prayed the same prayer again and the woman demonstrated even worse than she did earlier on. The sister's mother did not need anyone to convince her that she had made a mistake all along.

Many people have received evil prophesies from evil and fake prophets like that. Some girls have become that kind of prophetess because they no longer have sugar daddies who can give them money. They have now turned prophesying into a moneymaking venture.

10. **God Has The Final Say.**
Proverbs 19:21;
"There are many devices in a man's heart; nevertheless the counsel of the LORD, that shall stand."

God is the Only One that has the final say on our lives and on things that concern us. Do you feel trapped in any way by a habit, a practice, a nagging thought, a problem, a sickness, and attacks by the enemy? I want you to know that these things do not have the final say concerning your life. Even if some people are planning to destroy you, whether they are your parents or friends, do you know that they do not have the final say concerning your life? Even if your parents are very demonic and they place a curse upon your life, do you know that God has the final say in and concerning your life?

The fulfillment of God's word in your life may take some time. Do not be discouraged; He is the God of the suddenly. When God decides to take action on your behalf, your enemies will be caught unawares; they will just find out that you are now enjoying life at its fullest. If God decides that you will be president of this country, you are president, right from the day He pronounces it. Any other person can canvas for it but He has already said it concerning you and it shall stand. Since God is the Alpha and the Omega, the beginning, and the end, it is what He says that matters. Other people might say or do what they like; what matters is what God says about you and your situation. The Bible says we should not accept defeat.
Proverbs 24:16;
"For a just man falleth seven times, and riseth up again: but the wicked shall fall into mischief."

Do not bow to the devil or his agents. Do not accept that the devil has the final say. If the Lord has decided that you have to pass through a specific fiery situation, you have to pass through it. You might have to pass through the waters; through the seas, through the valleys; you have no option, you have to pass through it. In every situation, God has provided a way of escape; without trial, there is no triumph. When Israel was before the Red Sea and Pharaoh was behind them with his army, God provided a way through the sea. When Goliath was bragging and boasting and threatening Israel, God provided David. When Ahab was troubling Israel. God provided Elijah. Jesus Christ Himself was led by the Spirit into the wilderness and was tempted by the devil and He overcame. Whatever you are going through now is for a while; it will not kill you. Without examination, there is no promotion. God has the final say on your life; not a human being, not a prophet, not a herbalist, not a star-gazer or palmist that has told you that your life will be short, not even your family record or village idol but God. God has the power to do whatever He likes and nobody can query Him.

Daniel 4:35 tells us;
"And all the inhabitants of the earth are reputed as nothing; and He doeth according to His will in the army of heaven, and among the inhabitants of the earth: and none can stay His hand, or say unto Him: "What doest thou?"

If you believe that God has the final say concerning your life, I would like you to re-examine these ten things that the devil does not want you to know and then put your knowledge of them into practice and put the devil to shame. The family unit is the nucleus of the society and that is the target of the devil. Once he has a hold on the family set up, he has a hold on the society. That is why you have to barricade your life and that of your family with the fire of the Holy Ghost and with the Blood of Jesus, and refuse the devil entry into any aspect of your life.

If you are reading this bulletin and you have not at one time in life surrendered your life to the Lord Jesus Christ, I would ask that you do so now, right there where you are. The Lord is right there with you and He is ready to set you free from every bondage. All you need do is to acknowledge your sins and confess them to the Lord. Ask Him to forgive you and cleanse you from all unrighteousness. Claim the redemptive power in the Blood of Jesus; that was shed on the cross at Calvary for the remission of your sins.

Invite the Lord Jesus Christ into your life; ask Him to come in and become your personal Lord and Saviour. Ask Him to take total control of your life and all that concerns you. Surrender your totality to Him and enthrone Him over your life. Say goodbye to the world of sin and satan and make sure you do not go back to them any more.

I congratulate you for this decision that you have just taken. It is the most important decision that you could ever take in life. I pray that it shall be permanent in your life in the name of Jesus. I pray that the Lord will uphold you with His right hand of righteousness and keep you from falling in the name of Jesus. I pray that He will write your name in the Book of Life and you will not by any means rub it off in the name of Jesus.

Here are some prayers that I would like you to pray with all the aggression that you can gather. Pray them from the depth of your spirit.

1. I refuse to yield to the commands of the devil, in the name of Jesus.
2. Blessings are supposed to pursue and overtake me, not evil pursuers in Jesus' name.
3. Stubborn pursuers; be chained, in the name of Jesus.
4. Every twin substitute in the spirit, stealing my blessings fail and die, in the name of Jesus.
5. Every testimony swallower, vomit my testimony and die in the mighty name of Jesus.
6. Lord arise and let my miracles appear now, in the name of Jesus.
7. Every evil gathering against my faith scatter by fire, in the mighty name of Jesus.
8. Testimony that cannot be covered, fall upon my life, in the name of Jesus.
9. Lord, be My God in every situation I pass through, in the name of

Jesus.
10. By faith, I go up Mount Zion and I possess my possessions, in the name of Jesus.
11. I shall not die unsung, I shall be celebrated, in the mighty name of Jesus.
12. The powers saying no to the joy of my life are terminated by fire and by force, in Jesus' name.
13. Lord, reveal Your Truths to me every moment of my life, in the name of Jesus.
14. Every spiritual summoner of my spirit, die, die, die, in the name of Jesus.
15. I break the hold of problematic powers upon my life, in the name of Jesus.
16. Evil powers in my environment; be roasted!, in the name of Jesus.
17. All evil delegates sent against me, be roasted!, in the name of Jesus.
18. Lord, speak Your words of fire into my spirit; and let them burn away every rubbish in my life, in the name of Jesus.

The Mighty Hand Of God (1)

1 Samuel 2:6-10 *"The Lord killeth and maketh alive. He bringeth down to the grave and bringeth up. The Lord maketh poor and maketh rich; He bringeth low and lifteth up. He raiseth up the poor out of the dust and lifteth up the beggar from the dunghill, to set them among princes and to make them inherit the throne of glory: for the pillars of the earth are the Lord's and He hath set the world upon them. He will keep the feet of His saints, and the wicked shall be silent in darkness; for by strength shall no man prevail. The adversaries of the Lord shall be broken to pieces; out of heaven shall He thunder upon them: the Lord shall judge the ends of the earth and He shall give strength unto His king and exalt the horn of His anointed."*

This is a wonderful text of Scripture and I would like you to apply it to your situation.

If God's little finger is pointed at a particular situation, it alters that situation in a dramatic way. It will surpass all imaginations and people will find it difficult to believe. No matter how long a person has been under pursuit, the day God decides to point just a little finger at their situation, it will confuse and confound the adversary. I pray that it shall be so in your case, in the name of Jesus. A little finger wrote the obituary of Belshazzar on the wall; he had been doing what God did not like, he had been doing abominable things that defied the name of God, and so he got what he deserved. Some people accused Jesus of casting out demons with Beelzebub, they did not know that it was the finger of God in action. Beloved if the finger of God can cast out devils, what happens when He decides to stretch out His arm?

Exodus 15:6:
"Thy right hand, O Lord, is become glorious in power: Thy right hand O Lord hath dashed in pieces the enemy."
Here, Moses was referring to what God did to the stubborn pursuers of the children of God.

Moses was reminding them that God parted the Red Sea for His children to pass, while He allowed the enemy to rush into it and perish.

1 Samuel 5:11
"So they sent and gathered together all the lords of the Philistines, and said: "Send away the Ark of the God of Israel, and let it go again to His own place, that it slay us not and our people: for there was a deadly destruction throughout all the city; the Hand of God was heavy there."

Beloved, I pray that the hand of God shall be very heavy upon your enemies today, in the name of Jesus.

Ezra 7:28:
"And hath extended mercy unto me before the king and his counselors and before all the king's mighty princes. And I was strengthened as the hand of the Lord my God was upon me. And gathered together out of Israel, chief men to go up with me."

The hand of God was upon Ezra and he succeeded. I want you to say this to yourself:
The hand of God is upon me, therefore, I shall prosper in the name of Jesus,

When the hand of God is upon you, you will find favour with men.
Joseph as an example, was thrown into prison and because the hand of God was upon him, he found favor with all men. A person that has the favour of God upon him or her has an enviable destiny and cannot live a pitiable life, neither can such be killed by any principality or power.

Ezekiel 40:1:
"In the five and twentieth year of our captivity, in the beginning of the year, in the tenth day of the month in the fourteenth year after that the city was smitten, in the self same day, the hand of the Lord was upon me and brought me thither."
It is a fact that when the hand of

God is upon you, you will see outstanding visions and wondrous things, as Ezekiel did.

Acts 4:29-31
"And now, Lord, behold their threatening; and grant unto thy servants that with all boldness they may speak Thy word, stretching forth Thine hand to heal; and that signs and wonders may be done by the Name of Thy holy child, Jesus. And when they were assembled together; and they were all filled with the Holy Ghost and they spake the word of God with boldness."

Acts 5:31:
"Him hath God exalted with His right hand to be a Prince and a Savior, for to give repentance to Israel and forgiveness of sins"

I pray that as the right hand of God exalted Jesus, you too shall be exalted in the name of Jesus.

When the Apostles were being persecuted, they asked God to stretch forth His hand into their midst, so that there would be signs and wonders, and as from then on, they became bold and did exploits for Him.

The Mighty Hand of God
For the mighty hand of God to operate in your life, you have to obey the following commands concerning God:

(i)   Knowing God
(ii) Love Him
(iii) Obey Him

Knowing God
Many people have heard of God by His name, they have heard that He is the Creator of the whole universe and the Father of Jesus. But they have never met Him personally; they have never had an encounter with Him; no intimate relationship with Him: that is why many people are going through the problems that they have now. If you know God, you will talk to Him and He will talk to you. If some people had known God, He would have warned them and they would not have been married to the man or woman that they are married to today and certainly, their lives would have been better off. Some would not have started the business that has wrecked them today.

Many years ago, I applied for a job at the University and was invited for an interview. I found out later that I had a trip scheduled for Cuba which clashed with the date of the interview. I then wrote a letter informing those concerned that I would not be able to attend the interview. I took the letter to the department by hand and met a woman who attended to me nonchalantly. When she heard me say: "I am Olukoya," she jumped to her feet and apologised; she said she was the Head of Department and was expecting me. What I want to stress here is that, though that woman was preparing for my arrival at the interview, she did not know me. Even when I introduced myself to her, she was surprised because she was looking forward to seeing a pot-bellied man with a pair of glasses on his nose! Many people are like that. They talk about God, pray to God, but they really do not know Him!

One day, a man, shabbily dressed with a hoe in his hand went to a five star hotel, to ask for a room. When he got to the reception, he was turned down. The owner of the hotel came out and told him that they did not want people like him in their hotel. The man turned back and left. Suddenly, someone came to tell the owner of the hotel that he had just turned down the Vice President of the country. He ran after the shabbily dressed man and apologised that he did not know that he was the Vice President. The man said he would not oblige to the welcome because, if it was not good enough for the farmer, it was not good enough for the Vice President! That was how the hotel earned itself a bad name in the country. This is because they did not really know the Vice President. They must have seen his photograph or seen him on television and would have known his name, but they did not know him. If you know a person, you will recognise him; no matter what kind of dress the person is putting on.

Many people have pictures of 'Jesus' hung all over the house but they have never met the Lord Jesus Christ on a personal note. They have not had an encounter with Him; so, they do no know Him. Are you like that? You had better come to the saving knowledge of the Lord Jesus Christ today, so that He can be your friend.

One day, I went to visit a brother and I met a lady seated on his bed. There was also a Christian music playing at the background to soften the atmosphere. When I asked what the lady was doing on his bed, the brother said that she came on a visit from Ibadan. I rebuked him and turned to the lady and asked who she was. She replied by asking who I was too. This brother had Christian music-playing, had stickers on the door and on the walls, which say: 'Jesus-Saves,' 'Angels on guard, keep off" etc, but He did not have Christ dwelling in him; He did not know Christ.

One day, the governor of a state in a country, went to a prison, with the intention of setting a condemned robber free on the eve of his execution. When he got to the jail the governor said: "My brother" before he could add anything else, the robber shouted at him and asked him to leave. The governor left and someone came to inform the robber that he had just turned down the governor who came to set him free. He wept sore but it was too late. The following day, he was executed.

Many of us have seen the President on television, many have seen his photograph but have never seen him physically. Some people are members of his cabinet; they attend meetings with him, discuss with him, sometimes dine with him. But in actual fact, they only know him to some extent. Some people are his friends, they visit him at home, and they discuss and joke with him, some people are his relatives, they go to his house, eat, sleep there etc; they knew him from birth and know his parents. These category of people are closer than his cabinet members or close friends. Then, there are members of his nuclear family; these would know him better than his relatives and all. They are his children; he brought them up; they see him everyday in all his moods. His wife should be the closest to him; closer to him than the children.

She knows who he is and can recognise him, even in the dark. She can recognise his voice amongst other voices. She knows him very intimately and well. All these people could be said to know the President, but at different levels. Those who are his are the ones that would know him best.

The question is: Do you know God? Do you have an intimate relationship with Him? As the world is running to a close, those who do not know God will suffer. Those who run from prophet to prophet, from guru to guru, from preacher to preacher, from church to church, in search of solutions, are just wasting their time. They need to know God on a personal note and they will stop running here and there. Many people would need to pray for three hours or even three days, before God reveals anything to them. Whereas, there are people who just talk to Him in five minutes, and they will know the mind of God on a given situation. Some people see visions, dream dreams, but cannot interpret them. They do not know what God is saying. This is because they do not know God Himself. Some people see visions whilst they are praying, some see things without closing their eyes, some people hear God's voice aloud, like Moses etc. God actually went to some people in the Bible, called them by their names, and told them what to do. Would it not be great to hear God call you by your name and hear Him tell you what He plans to do? It is possible, if you know Him.

A sister had problems with her husband. She went on a three-day dry fast. On the third day, the Lord revealed to her, that something evil had been programmed into her two-year-old son and the thing was meant to manifest at the age of 20; the Lord told her that He had set her son free. The Lord also informed her that her husband would increase the beating but that later, he would come back to his senses and would apologise to her and change for the better. It all happened that way; when the husband came to beg, the sister gave him some conditions, including the fact that he would allow her to go to church and he complied. This is what happens when God calls you by name.

God called Ananias by name and sent him to go and lay his hands on Saul. Ananias argued a bit, saying that Saul was a persecutor of Christians. Any way, he went. Some people pray and see the person that they are going to marry, sometimes, not everything is clear, sometimes, God speaks vividly and gives them the name of the person etc. You too can get to that level, if you want it, but you have to stop struggling with God.

Love God
If you love God, you will serve Him with all your heart; you will not allow His work to suffer. You will do all you can to further the cause of the Gospel. You will be His friend and will do all that He asks you to do. It should be like the relationship between two people, who are engaged to be married. They will visit each other, see each other off, the one will accompany the other to the end of the road and then back again, they will stand and talk, go forward, backwards, until they realise that time is far spent.

A boy was asked to explain the verse that says: "Enoch walked with God, and he was not..." The boy said, God and Enoch were seeing each other off; back and forth, until one day when Enoch was seeing God off and just decided to go to heaven with Him, and did not come back again.

If you begin to walk with God, you will communicate with Him. Have you ever noticed that the first problem that manifests when there is trouble between a couple is communication break down? They will not talk to each other and then, one will start assuming what the other thinks and then draw conclusions, which most of the time are not true. Those who love God, love talking to Him; they are prayer addicts. They are happy to talk to their Father and He talks to them too. God loves such people and is looking for them. It is unfortunate to note that many people hurry out of the presence of God. You must obey God, whether what He is saying is palatable or not. The Bible is not a book of suggestions; it is a book of commands. The Bible does not advise you not to run after men or women but commands you not to fornicate. The word of God has no respect for your opinion. It commands you. If you know God and you love Him, His mighty hand will come upon you.

I would like you to pray like this:

* *O Lord, let Your mighty hand come upon me; I want to know You, I want to love You, in the name of Jesus.*

God cannot be defeated and His methods are always perfect. His provision is always sufficient. No territory is outside His jurisdiction. This includes the heart of your husband that you think is too hardened. There is nothing beyond God's control; no event can escape or overrule Him. The little that you have is enough, if God is in it. Therefore, with God's hand upon you, His strength behind you, and His love within you, you are more than sufficient for the days ahead.
1 Kings 18:46:
"And the hand of the Lord was on Elijah; and he girded his loins and ran before Ahab to the entrance of Jezreel"

Elijah was a man of God. He called down fire from heaven, locked up the heavens and the rains and later opened them and killed all the prophets of Baal; all these, because the hand of God was upon Him. God created Adam, and Eve was his helpmate. Later, they fell and were driven out of the Garden of Eden. They had two sons Cain and Abel. Cain killed Abel and God put a mark on him; he became an outcast. Later, Adam had another son called Seth who gave birth to Noah, who had three sons Shem, Ham, and Japheth. God called out one man from the descendants of Shem, called Abraham. He called him out to form a nation for Himself, a nation that would be an example of the holiness walk with God. That nation is Israel.

Abraham gave birth to Isaac who gave birth to Esau and Jacob, Then, Jacob gave birth to 12 sons who were taken into captivity because of Abraham's complaint about childlessness. They were in Egypt as slaves for 430 years. After some time. God decided to take them out of Egypt. Before then, He performed many wonders. God collected their salary arrears and gave it to them in one day. Likewise, I prophesy unto you today, that any good thing that the devil has withheld from you, shall be restored in the name of Jesus.
God made them to cross the Red Sea without a bridge. He

turned bitter water into sweet water, and brought water out of the rock for them. He set a table for them in the wilderness. What a wonderful thing for God to set a table before you. They ate angelic food. Would you not like to eat such a food? He provided food for them by supernatural means. I know that I will get to heaven and will be fed with angelic food too. Would you not love the same?

Their shoes and clothes did not wear out, for 40 years. They obtained direct electricity from heaven. God was with them until they got to the Promised Land. God told them that they should not worship other gods that their neighbors were worshiping. Much later, the Israelites looked round and saw that some of their neighbors were worshipping Dagon, (half-man, half fish), others were worshipping Ashteroth, (under every green tree). They then concluded that they were fed up with worshipping a God that they could not see, so they started worshipping Baal. As they were doing this, they were committing immorality and God was not happy with them. He then sent prophet Elijah to them who decreed to them, that there should be neither rain nor dew for some years.

Does this not sound like the story of Nigeria to you? We are blessed in all areas, with everything; we have intelligent people, and our pilots are the best in the world. We send lawyers and professors to other countries to help them. We have uranium, groundnut, cocoa, and all kinds of crops. Unfortunately, some of people got up some time ago, and invited all the demons of Africa, to Nigeria, under the guise of a festival of arts and culture. All those countries came with their idols into this country and that marked the beginning of problems in Nigeria. The aftermath is still there today, and only the mighty Hand of God when called into operation can deliver us.

Elijah challenged the prophets of Baal to a contest and he won; fire fell and everybody acknowledged God as God. Then, he killed all the prophets of Baal. After that, they saw signs of rain after many years of drought and the king started to go back to his palace. The king's chariots were drawn by six horses and the distance from Mount Carmel, the place of the contest was about seven miles from Jezreel. Elijah outran the horses, because the Hand of the Lord was with him.

Beloved, I would like to stop here, we shall continue this message in the next bulletin, if the Lord tarries. However, if you have never at one time in your life, surrendered your life to the Lord Jesus Christ, I would advise that you do so, right away. He is there with you; all you need do, is acknowledge the fact that you are a sinner and that you cannot approach God in your sinful state. Repent of your sins; confess them to Him, Ask Him to forgive you and cleanse you from all unrighteousness, name those sins one by one, renounce them and forsake them. Make sure that you do not go back to them. Claim the redemptive power in the Blood of Jesus, that was shed on the cross at Calvary, for the remission of your sins.

Invite the Lord Jesus into your life. Ask Him to come into your life and become your personal Lord and Saviour. Enthrone Him over your life and ask Him to take total control of everything that concerns you.

I congratulate you on this decision that you have just taken. I pray that it shall be permanent in your life, in the name of Jesus. I pray that the Lord will uphold you with His right hand of righteousness and He will not allow you to fall but stand steadfast in His word. I pray that you will have a personal encounter with the Lord and I assure you that you will never be the same again.

Today, you have a wonderful opportunity before the Lord. Cry unto Him wholeheartedly and He will answer you and do great and mighty things in your life. First, ask Him to cleanse you from every filth that could cause a hindrance to the answers to your prayers.

Take these prayers with holy anger in your spirit:
1. Father Lord, let your mighty hand touch every inherited problem in my life in the name of Jesus.
2. Father Lord, touch me with you unchanging Hand, in the name of Jesus.

3. God, arise and promote me unto Your power house, in the name of Jesus.
4. God arise and surprise my enemies with my dumbfounding testimonies, in the name of Jesus.
5. My Father, by the thunder of Your power, arrest my arresters, in the name of Jesus.
6. The Hand of God that cannot fail, deliver me now by fire, in the mighty name of Jesus.
7. Lord, heal me and I shall be healed, save me and I shall be saved, deliver me and I shall be delivered, in the mighty name of Jesus.
8. Lord, deliver me from the powers that are stronger than I in the name of Jesus.
9. Swallowers of good things in my life, die! in the name of Jesus.
10. Every satanic twin stealing my breakthroughs in the spiritual, die, in the name of Jesus.
11. Ancestral yokes, break by the Hand of God, in the mighty name of Jesus.
12. Every power preparing failure for me, release me and die, in the mighty name of Jesus.
13. Every owner of evil load in my life., carry your evil load by fire, in the name of Jesus.
14. Let all my prayers bring me multiple breakthroughs, in the name of Jesus.
15. My Father, single me out for miracles this year, in the name of Jesus.
16. Lord, grant me the power of Your presence forever, in the name of Jesus.
17. Where is the Lord God of Elijah?, arise and change the story of my life, in the name of Jesus.

The Mighty Hand Of God (2)

Vol. 6. No. 26

I Samuel 2:6-10; *The Lord killeth and maketh alive. He bringeth down to the grave and bringeth up. The Lord maketh poor and maketh rich; He bringeth low and lifteth up. He raiseth up the poor out of the dust and lifteth up the beggar from the dunghill, to set them among princes and to make them inherit the throne of glory: for the pillars of the earth are the Lord's and He hath set the world upon them. He will keep the feet of His saints, and the wicked shall be silent in darkness; for by strength shall no man prevail. The adversaries of the Lord shall be broken to pieces; out of heaven shall He thunder upon them: the Lord shall judge the ends of the earth and He shall give strength unto His king and exalt the horn of His anointed."*

In the last bulletin, when we started this important message, we saw how the hand of God wrought wonders in the lives of individuals and in the lives of the people of Israel. We saw how the hand of God moved in their defense against their enemies.

We also mentioned the fact that "the hand of God makes a difference in our lives; it attracts favour and all the goodness that you can think of. Today, I would like you to read this continuation with all the seriousness that you can gather. I would like you to pray the prayers that follow with fervency and be determined that you must feel the touch of God's hand today. God bless you as you read on. Beloved, 1 would like you to ask the Lord at this point to touch you with His mighty hand, as you sing this song:

*"All I need is a touch of Jesus,
All I need is a touch of the Lord,
All I need is a touch of Jesus,
All I need is a touch of the Lord."*

When God touches a person, that life will never remain the same. Miracles must happen. When God's unfailing hand touches a sick person, that sickness must depart. We all need that touch today.

1 Peter 5:6 says; *"Humble yourselves therefore under the mighty hand of God, that he may exalt you in due time."*

Mark 10:13-16; *"And they brought young children to Him, that He should touch them, and His disciples rebuked those that brought them. But then Jesus saw it, He was much displeased and said unto them: "Suffer the little children to come unto me and forbid them not; for of such is the kingdom of God Verily I say unto you, whosoever shall not receive the kingdom of God as a little child, he shall not enter therein." And He took them up in His arms put His hands upon them and blessed them."*

The mothers of these children were very clever. They must have noticed that something good happened to those that the Lord Jesus touched, so they brought their own children too. The disciples tried to stop them but Jesus took them in His arms. Today, the Lord wants you to get that touch. You might say that you are not a child but many people are spiritual babies and Jesus even says that we should take the kingdom of God, as little children.

Matthew 8:1-3; *"When He was come down from the mountain, great multitudes followed Him. And behold, there came a leper and worshipped Him saying; "Lord if Thou will, thou canst make me clean. And Jesus put forth His hand and touched him saying; "I will; be thou clean." And immediately, his leprosy was cleansed."*

The touch of Jesus healed that leper. You might say that you are not a leper but the worst leprosy is sin; it is the leprosy of the soul and anyone going about with any form of sin is leprous and needs to be touched. When you are preaching to lepers, the message goes straight down. These people have been rejected by the society and cannot use their limbs effectively; they can hardly hold anything. When you preach at a funeral, it sinks in especially at the cemetery: when people see the reality of death. Beloved, if you refuse to leave the world, one day, the world will leave you. Some ladies have boyfriends or 'sugar-daddies', they vow that if the man leaves them, they will die. They forget that as soon as they die, the man will get another lady to replace them.

Some men have wives at home, yet, they will be calling other ladies their sweetie or honey outside. The time will come, when this sweetie will drink their blood and go to other men. The leprosy of sin must be flushed out of many lives today. You might have to call your husband or wife and tell him or her, some blunt truths today.

Mathew 8:14-15; *"And when Jesus was come into Peter's house, He saw his wife's mother laid and sick of a fever. And He touched her hand, and the fever left her and she arose and ministered unto them."*

Jesus touched the mother-in-law of Peter and the fever flew away. You might say that you have no fever but it could be that you are being cooked in a witchcraft pot, which is hotter than any fever. Some times, a person could have a dream where he or she sees another person sitting in front of a pot that is on fire; it could be the life of a person that is being cooked on fire. The worst fever is when every aspect of a person's life is windy and stormy and troublesome i.e. no breakthrough anywhere. Nothing works - marriage, business, career, work, etc. People hate the person for no obvious reason and then, the person is being cooked. The fire preparer must be sent packing, the fire must be quenched and then, the hand of God will be asked to come down and touch the person.

Mathew 9:27-30a;
"And when Jesus departed thence, two blind men followed Him, crying and saying: "Thou Son of David, have mercy on us." And when He was come into the house, the blind men came to Him and Jesus saith unto them: "Believest ye that I am able to do this? "They said unto Him: "Yea, Lord" then touched He their eyes, saying: "According to your faith, be it unto you" And their eyes opened."

At the touch of Jesus, the blind men began to see. You might say that you are not blind, but many people are spiritually blind. This is why many people develop high blood pressure. The way things are going on in the world today, those who do not have Christ, do not have rest and many are dying for nothing. Elisha's servant thought that, they were doomed when he saw the army that came against him and his master. Elisha had to pray that God should open his eyes. It was then that he saw that the host of heaven that was with them outnumbered their enemies. When God opens your spiritual eyes, you will discover that many people hate their friends and love their enemies because they cannot differentiate. This is the problem with many sisters; they like people that have sugar-coated tongues. They are bored with serious, sincere people and so, they fall into the snare of the enemy. When the liars come, they are carried away, not knowing that they are entertaining their enemies. Many people hate the things that will keep them alive and like things that will destroy their lives. Many people are beautifully dressed but under their beautiful clothes, are all sorts of sicknesses and diseases: diabetes, ulcer, cancer, strange sicknesses, and so on. All you need today is the touch of Jesus.

Mark 7:33-35:
"And He took him aside from the multitude and put His finger into his ears and He spit and touched his tongue; and looking up to heaven, He sighed and saith unto him: "Eph-Phatha", that is, "Be opened." And straightway, the string of his tongue was loosed and he spake plain."

Jesus touched the tongue of this dumb man, and he began to talk. You might say that you have no speech problem, but many people have sick tongues. There is a saying in German that qualifies a dull person as having an unscrewed nut. The first screw that looses when a person is getting out of proportion, is the one that ties the tongue in place. The sick tongue is the one that tell lies, curses, gossips, backbites, confesses negative things, etc. Some people do not need to think before they tell lies; it comes naturally as if the person were speaking in tongues. If you are in that category, you should ask the Lord to use His spittle to touch your tongue today. When some men are given invitation cards that read Mr. and Mrs. So, So and So, they conclude that their wife is too 'local' to be taken to such gatherings and so, they look for a 'modern lady' who will accompany them. Such men need the touch of Jesus to put in place, the loose nut in their thinking faculty.

Luke 7:12-15:
"Now, when He came nigh to the gate of the city, behold, there was a dead man carried out, the only son of his mother and she was a widow and much people of the city was with her. And when the Lord saw her, He had compassion on her and said unto her: "Weep not" And He came and touched the bier and them that bare him, stood still. And He said: "Young man, I say unto thee: "Arise!" And he that was dead sat up and began to speak. And He delivered him to his mother."

The woman had been tortured by the death of her husband and now, her son is dead. She was weeping profusely when Jesus came along and He said: "Weep not". Perhaps you are going through some hard times that are making you to weep. I want you to know that Jesus is passing by today, and He is saying: "Weep not". The Lord Jesus touched the coffin in which the boy had been put. ready for burial and the boy sat up. Today, all the dead organs in your life will receive the touch of the mighty hand of God. in the name of Jesus. When God touches anything dead, it comes alive. When God touches you, all those things that are medically, physically and or spiritually dead, will come alive. It could be a dead marriage, dead business, progress, anything at all. Today, I want you to stretch out your hand and touch the Lord. He is ready to touch you. Cry out to Him now.

There was a boy who was a dullard. His parents studied abroad and were lecturers in a university. He used to come last in the class; he came 30th in the examinations. When the number of pupils increased to 33, he came 33rd. Then, it gave his parents a lot of concern and they started trying all kinds of methods. They got him a teacher for each subject to teach him at home; they got him a computer, but there was no improvement. They tried every knowledge they got from the College of Education, but nothing worked. One day, they took the matter to God in prayers and the Lord touched the brain of the boy. To everybody's amazement, he moved up to the 1st (first) position. When the teachers saw the result, they said it was impossible. So, another set of questions were prepared for him alone and he was put in a classroom on his own, with all the teachers invigilating. This time around, he scored higher marks than before, in all the subjects. This is what happens, when God touches a person. God has not changed; He is still alive. There is nothing wrong in receiving a multiple touch from the Lord, When God touches you, all other strange touches will disappear.

There was a lady of 35 years old, who had never menstruated in her life. She attended one of our prayer meetings and a prayer point was raised:

Every owner of evil load in my life, carry your evil load! in the name of Jesus. She prayed fervently. In fact, she left her seat to go to the back of the auditorium so that, she would be able to fight it out properly. She prayed until her dress was soaked with sweat. Suddenly, a hand came upon her head and she felt a cold sensation, which ran through her body. The next thing she saw was blood flowing down her legs. That is what happens when God's mighty hand touches you.

CONDITIONS FOR GOD'S TOUCH:
1. **Repent From All Sins.**
As the Lord is bringing forth His hand, the accuser of the brethren (the devil), will oppose it and if there is sin in the life of that person, God will withdraw His hand because He is a just God. The sin could be pride, anger, hatred, backbiting, gossiping, malice, unforgiveness, envy, jealousy, stealing, alcohol drinking, smoking, gambling, greed, covetousness, bearing false witness, fornication, adultery, etc. You should not allow any

hindrance to God's touch. So, you must examine your life and repent from your sins.

2. *Humble Yourself Before God.*
I Peter 5:6; *"Humble yourselves therefore under the mighty hand of God, that he may exalt you in due time."*

3. *Be Determined To Feel The Touch Of God Upon Your Life And Situation.*

4. *Pray With Holy Anger And Fervency, Until Something Happens.*
I am proposing some prayer points to you that could actually sound very strange and I want you to pray them with great, thundering anger. If God would open your eyes to see the evil that polygamy has done in this country, you will know that 80% of the problems of this country come from there. There is an adage that says; "Many wives, many problems." "It is true and it also extends to the children. Most of the time, the rivals would have died and gone, but the children will linger on in these problems.

Now, I want you to begin to soak the remaining part of this year in the blood of Jesus. Declare that no weapon that the enemy has formed against you shall prosper and any power that does not want you to have peace this year, shall be buried today, in the name of Jesus. God shall restore to you, all your breakthroughs that 'the enemy has stolen away. There shall be a complete overthrow and any power that does not want you to move forward shall be arrested and summarily dealt with in the name of Jesus.

Take these prayer points with boiling anger in your spirit.

1. Blood of Jesus, flush out the leprosy of sin from my life, in the name of Jesus.
2. Any hidden sin in my life, robbing me of the special touch of God, die! In Jesus' name.
3. Let every physical and spiritual power, sitting on my progress, be uprooted! in the name of Jesus.
4. Let every spirit of Herod be disgraced, in the name of Jesus.
5. Let the angels of God roll the stones of fire to hinder every power hindering my upliftment, in the name of Jesus.
6. Lord release my mind from every image of Jealousy, in the name of Jesus.
7. Every confusing force I stand against your attacks over my life, in the name of Jesus.
8. Lord, make me uncomfortable until I get to the right track, in the name of Jesus.
9. Let hell open its mouth without measure and swallow every suckers of my peace, in the name of Jesus.
10. Let every enemy of my soul start their day in confusion and end it in destruction, in the name of Jesus.
11. Every evil hand, pointed at my destiny this year, wither by fire and die! in the name of Jesus.
12. My Father, show me Your way, in the name of Jesus
13. Angels of breakthroughs, encamp around me! in the name of Jesus.
14. Thou power of signs and wonders, overshadow my life! in the name of Jesus.
15. I receive the strength and power to be a warrior and not to worry, in the name of Jesus.
16. Thou mighty hand of God, deliver me from the strongmen from my father's house, in the name of Jesus.
17. Thou mighty hand of God, deliver me from the strongmen of my mother's house, in the name of Jesus.
18. Thou mighty hand of God deliver me from the strongmen from my in-laws' houses, in the name of Jesus.
19. Every agenda of the wasters for my life, die! in the name of Jesus.
20. Father Lord, let your mighty hand, touch every inherited problem in my life, in the name of Jesus.
21. Father Lord, touch me

with Your unchanging hand, in the name of Jesus.
22. God arise, and promote me unto Your power house, in the name of Jesus.
23. Let the mighty hand of God terminate every problem in my life now in the name of Jesus.
24. Let the mighty hand of God, terminate every sickness in my life now, in the name of Jesus.
25. Let the mighty hand of God change my situation to the best by fire, in the name of Jesus.
26. Let the mighty hand of God gather my blessings back to my life, in the name of Jesus.
27. Let the mighty hand of God destroy my weakness in the name of Jesus.
28. Let the mighty hand of God destroy every satanic ladder in my life, in the name of Jesus.
29. Let the mighty hand of God draw me back from every journey of destruction in the name of Jesus.
30. By the mighty hand of God, I shall excel in every area of life in the name of Jesus.
31. By the mighty hand of God, all my enemies shall be disappointed this year in the name of Jesus.
32. By the mighty hand of God, my enemies shall die in my place in the name of Jesus.
33. By the mighty hand of God, I take divine insurance over my life and my family, in the name of Jesus.

The Battle Against Wasting Serpents

Vol. 6. No. 27

Numbers 14:28-33: *"Say unto them, As truly as I live, saith the Lord, as ye have spoken in mine ears, so will I do to you: Your carcases shall fall in this wilderness; and all that were numbered of you, according to your whole number, from twenty years old and upward, which have murmured against me, Doubtless ye shall not come into the land concerning which I sware to make you dwell therein, save Caleb the son of Jephunneh, and Joshua the son of Nun. But your little ones, which ye said should be a prey, them will I bring in, and they shall know the land which ye have despised. But as for you, your carcases, they shall fall in this wilderness. And your children shall wander in the wilderness forty years, and bear your whoredoms, until your carcases be wasted in the wilderness."*

These are the end times and there is a lot of wastage going on. There is a terrible rage of the wasters now and many things and people are being wasted. There are different categories of wastage that are taking place and many people do not understand what is going on in their lives, Many do not understand that what is happening is a gradual wastage, It is a tragedy to discover after life here on earth, that you have wasted your life.

If you look through the Bible, you will find many people whose lives were wasted. Adam was in the garden but he and his wife Eve, were wasted; Lot was wasted, Reuben was cursed by his father and he was wasted. Dathan, Korah and Abiram were equally wasted. Achan was wasted with the members of his family. Samson, the great man was eventually wasted; Eli and his sons, Saul the king, Solomon etc, were all wasted.

The children of Israel still remain an important case study in the area of the operations of wasters. The wasters not only prolonged their journey to the Canaan land, but also wasted their lives. They were at the edge of the promised land but could not enter. For about 38 years, they were going about a place called Cadesh Barnea. About three million people were going in circles for almost thirty-eight years because the wasters came in. They were wasted because they listened to powers that divert destinies.

In the text above, a whole generation of people was wasted, it is a tragedy, when the wasting serpents are against a person and he or she does not realise it. It is possible to waste life, career, marriage, brain, time, money, salvation, etc. One day, an 80-year-old man was celebrating his birthday and he had only ten candles ten on the birthday cake. When asked why he said he had spent 70 years of his life in the world, without knowing the Lord Jesus Christ. He got born-again at the age of 70. Which means that those years were wasted. He said the ten years that he had spent in the Lord, were the meaningful years of his life. Technically, he was ten years old. This means that he understood what it meant to be wasted.

There is a kind of wastage going on right now, especially of the youth. All over our campuses of higher learning, the devil has unleashed a most dangerous spirit disguised as cultism. What you hear all over the place is massacre here and there. Human life has ceased to have any meaning to the youth. By the time you read the report findings of the security agents on what supposedly caused the fracases, you wonder where the souls of these human beasts came from. Whoredom of the highest cadre is the order of the day in our institutions. Morals that we grew up with is at an all time low ebb. Nakedness is the latest fashion in town. When you drive through the campuses, you wonder whether you are on a popular prostitutes streets. You will have a hard time of convincing yourself that you are actually in school compounds and not brothels. The cankerworm of the 'oldest trade' as they call it, has eaten deep into the fabric of our modern world. I use to think it was a trade for the illiterate and the ill-fated but not so anymore. Sophisticated ladies are now ever so proud to display their wares openly. It is only God that can have mercy on this generation.

SYMPTOMS OF THE PRESENCE OF WASTING SERPENTS IN A LIFE:

1. **Lack Of Knowledge Of One's Purpose In Life** Not knowing why one is in the world. Pilate looked at Jesus with the intention of making fun of Him, and said Jesus called Himself a king. Jesus told him that was the very reason for His being born and coming to the world. He knew the reason for His existence. Do you know your purpose in life? If you do not know your purpose in life, it means that the serpents are already at work in your life.

2. **When A Person Is Experimenting With His Or Her life.**
Trying all sorts of things, not knowing that life is too short to experiment with. If it will take you one month to know the direction that God wants your life to take, then, you should pray fervently in order to know it and flow into it. Immediately you locate where God wants you to be, your destiny will begin to explode. Many people are in the wrong place. There is an adage in Yoruba that says; "there is no way a monkey could receive blessings inside a river." It is because it is in the wrong place.

Are you experimenting with your life? You really do not know what to do? Then, the serpents of wastage is working against your life. No one is getting younger. By 12 noon, the day is almost gone; you cannot go back to the hours that have passed by. It is impossible to go back to 7:00a.m. at 12 noon. It is gone forever, you cannot go back to it. This means that there is actually no time to waste. Life is too short to experiment with.

3. **Pursuing The Wrong Profession, Career, Business, Ministry, etc.**
A woman was in a financial mess. Although she was the principal of a school, she could not make ends meet. Before the end of the month, she would have borrowed money from her subordinates. One day, she attended one of our meetings and it became clear to her that her life was not supposed to be the way it was. When she got home, she started to pray fervently, that the Lord should show her the secret of her life. She asked the Lord to show her, her destiny secrets. Suddenly, she heard the Holy Spirit ask her if she really wanted to prosper and she said yes. The voice then asked her what was behind her house and she said it was a marshy piece of land. The voice said she should go there to plant vegetables and sell. She revolted and bound the voice, thinking it was the enemy that was trying to down-grade her, despite all her degrees and certificates.

The Lord ministered to her, that it was He that was speaking. Later, she obeyed. She started to plant the vegetables and it was as if the whole town was waiting for her vegetables. She made good sales; anytime she took her vegetables to the market, no other person could make good sales. Within one year, this teacher had built a house. This happened because she did what God wanted her to do.

4. **Operating In The Wrong Position.**
If you are operating in the wrong place, you cannot prosper. If God wants you to he a pilot and you are a tailor, your prayers for prosperity will not be answered because heaven will say that you were not sent to the place you are. A man prayed fervently for God to show him what to do.

Later, he saw a pair of scissors in a dream. He did not bother to ask what it meant; he just assumed that God wanted him to be a barber, who cuts people's hair with scissors. He started and he ran into serious problems. He should have found out what God wanted him to do with the pair of scissors. It could have been for tailoring.

Today, you have to pray seriously so that, if you have been wrongly located and your life has been plugged into the wrong socket by the enemy, God will unplug it from there and plug it where He wants it to be.

5. **Operating Below God's Level.**
You might be rejoicing that you have made it in your

business, career or ministry; but as far as heaven is concerned, you are operating at God's minimum for your life.

6. **Losing Unrepeatable Opportunities.**
Some people for unexplainable reasons, get the opportunity of advancing in life, but they lose it.
The opportunity comes back in another form, but they still lose it.

7. **Allowing Heaven To Transfer One's Assignment.**
If God expects you to do one thing or the other and you are not doing it, you will be replaced because, God does not permit any vacuum in what he has planned. All the Israelites that left Egypt, were all wasted in the wilderness. Do not allow the wasting serpents to waste your life in the wilderness of life.

WHAT TO DO, TO KILL THE WASTING SERPENTS:

1. Surrender Your Life To Jesus

2. Pray To Know The Secret Of Your Destiny.

3. The Mysteries To Be Exposed To You.

4. Pray For Spiritual Empowerment Which Will Allow You To Flow Into The Place That Gods Wants You To Be.

Are you gathering and the enemy is squandering what you have gathered? The enemy is causing you to lose things or is destroying what you are doing or making what you do to become profitless hard work? Today beloved, you have to do some serious praying, right there where you are. So that, the Lord God will kill all the wasting serpents - that have been assigned against you.

God did not create you to have a wasted life. God has a glorious and marvelous plan and purpose for your life. You are not on the surface of the earth by mere chance or mistake. There is a divine purpose you need to fulfil. He has promised in Isaiah 49:24-26 and it is a promise you can believe and hold on to: *"Shalt the prey be taken from the mighty, or the lawful captive delivered? But thus saith the Lord, Even the captives of the mighty shall he taken away, and the prey of the terrible shall be delivered: for I will contend with him that contendeth with thee, and I will save thy children. And I will feed them that oppress thee with their own flesh; and they shall he drunken with their own blood, as with sweet wine: and all flesh shall know that I the Lord am thy Saviour and thy Redeemer, the mighty One of Jacob."*

As this provision has been made, however, it is open only to those who have the right to appropriate it. The Book of Isaiah 5:13-14 says; *"Therefore my people are gone into captivity, because they have no knowledge: and their honourable men are famished, and their multitude dried up with thirst. Therefore hell hath enlarged herself, and opened her mouth without measure: and their glory, and their multitude, and their pomp, and he that rejoiceth, shall descend into it."*

What qualifies you to claim the promise in Isaiah 49: 24-26? In case you are not yet born-again, you have not yet surrendered your life to the Lord Jesus Christ, I would advise that you do so at once. There is no way that you can destroy the wasting serpents, when you have not yet surrendered your life to the, Lord Jesus. You have a very good opportunity today, Jesus is waiting for you.

All you need do is to acknowledge the fact that you are a sinner and that you cannot approach God in your sinful state. The Bible says that the eyes of God cannot behold sin. Right there where you are, repent of your sins; confess them to God and ask Him to forgive you. Name them one by one and renounce them. Ask God to cleanse you with the Blood of Jesus that was shed on the Cross at Calvary. Claim the redemptive power in the Blood and believe that you are cleansed.

If you have taken this decision, I congratulate you. It is the most important decision in life. I pray that it shall he permanent in your life, in the name of Jesus. I pray that the Lord will uphold, you and keep you from falling, in the name of Jesus. I pray that God will lay His mighty hand of power upon your life and. will do great and mighty things in it. I pray that He will keep you standing. I pray that He will write your name in the Book of Life, and nothing shall by any, means, rub it off in the name of Jesus.

Take some time off to meditate and focus on the areas that you know that you would like to direct your prayers. Perhaps you have noticed that some areas are blocked against you; it is as if all roads are closed. You have laid your hands on one business or the other but nothing is moving. There are certain things which seem to be working against you and you do not know what they are. It could be the wasting serpents that are working against you.

Beloved, the prayers that I am suggesting below, are acidic prayers. Remember that this bulletin is called: "Sound the Battle Cry", it is important that you pray violently and with acidic concentration. Do not allow your mind to wander here or there; after all, you have been worrying about your problems for a long time and that has not solved them. I want you to pray with faith in your heart, believing that the God of the suddenlies is right there where you are. Know that there is no situation that is beyond His power. There is no problem that you are going through now, that God has not solved for someone before. Therefore, pray these prayers with fervency and holy anger. You must be expectant because God is going to open doors in areas that you do not expect.

1. Every strongman assigned to waste my life, die! in the name of Jesus.
2. The power base of witchcraft in my place of birth, die! in the name of Jesus.
3. Every word spoken with annoyance against my destiny, die! in the name of Jesus.
4. Thunder of God, arise and destroy, every hank of darkness that is holding my wealth, in the name of Jesus.
5. Anything in my life, that does not glorify God, die! in the name of Jesus.
6. Padlock of darkness, assigned against my progress, catch fire! in the name of Jesus.
7. Every power of my father's house, that wants to waste my life, be wasted! In the name of Jesus.
8. Every power of my mother's house that wants to waste my life, be wasted! In the name of Jesus.
9. Every power that wants to divert my destiny, release me and die! in the name of Jesus.
10. Every swallowing grave of my father's house, that is speaking against me, I silence you by fire! in the name of Jesus.
11. Every swallowing grave of my mother's house, that is speaking against me, I silence you by fire! in the name of Jesus.
12. Every power assigned to waste my destiny die!, in the name of Jesus.
13. Any power that wants me to die like this, die, in the name of Jesus.
14. Every power preparing failure for my destiny, die in disgrace in the name of Jesus.
15. Thou power masquerading in order to destroy my life what are you waiting for, die, in the name of Jesus.
16. *Confess this out loud*: I refuse to operate below God's standard for me, in the name of Jesus.
17. Lord by your mercy, let all my wasted years be restored by fire, in the name of Jesus.
18. You powers from the grave, my life is not for sale, in the name of Jesus.
19. Every internal decay, receive the resurrection power of the Holy Spirit now, in the name of Jesus.
20. Every power delegated to stagnate my life and destiny scatter by thunder, in the name of Jesus.
21. I shall reach my goal in life, whether the devil likes it or not in the name of Jesus.
22. Thou power from the grave, release my virtues, in the name of Jesus.
23. My life, if you are on the wrong track, be straightened by fire! in the name of Jesus.
24. Lord, show me the secret of my destiny, in

25. Power to ask and receive answers, fall upon my life! in the name of Jesus.
26. Every opportunity that has passed me by. I regain you by fire, in the name of Jesus.
27. Arrows of the wasters, come out of my life, and locate your sender! in the name of Jesus.
28. O God arise and manifest yourself in my situation today, in the name of Jesus.
29. Problem expanders of the last days, my life is not your candidate.
30. Any rock of offence in my path, clear away! in the name of Jesus.
31. Shout this out loud: Father Lord, do not replace me with stone, in the name of Jesus.

Begin to thank God for the testimonies that will follow this prayer session

Problem That Are Not From The Enemy

Prayer Points: 1. Any power that say I will not enjoy my life, O God arise destroy them in the name of Jesus

2. O God of Elijah, challenge with your fire every stubborn spirit troubling my life in the name of Jesus.

A careful study of the word of God would make you to understand that there are five causes of suffering for the Christians.

1. It could be due to satanic activity. In Job 2:7; *So went Satan forth from the presence of the LORD, and smote Job with sore boils from the sole of his foot unto his crown.*
2. From ungodly men in 2 Timothy 4:14; *Alexander the coppersmith did me much evil:*
3. The Lord rewards him according to his works.
4. From the world system in 2 Peter 2:8; For that righteous man dwelling among them, in seeing and hearing, vexed his righteous soul from day to day with their unlawful deeds.
5. It can come from man's falling nature in Rom. 7:14, *For we know that the law is spiritual, but I am carnal, sold under sin. For that which I do I allow not: for what I would, that do I not; but what I hate, that do I.*
6. From carnal Christians Phil. 1:15-16; *Some indeed preach Christ even of envy and strife; and some also of Good will. The one preach Christ of contention, not sincerely, supposing to add affliction to my bonds.*

2 Timothy 4:10; *for Demas hath forsaken me, having loved this present world, and is departed unto Thessalonica; Crescens to Galatia, Titus unto Dalmatia.* There is that man in the book of Matthew who planted wheat and the enemy came and planted another thing. When they say we planted wheat and were seeing another thing, where did it come from? The master said the enemy has done this. So you could easily identify that one. In the book of Jonah, the Lord himself created problem for Jonah. Many people always blame things that happen to the devil. Most things that happen, they say are from the devil. The question is why did you turn your back to the devil? God gave us defensive material in the Bible. God does not expect us at any time to turn your back to the devil. He does not expect you to turn your back to the enemy and run, so even if the devil come to you, why did you supply your back to him.

Long time ago in England, there was cartoon in one of the major news papers. They do a big picture of a church, they bring the picture of the devil and the devil was standing outside the church and crying bitterly. Then somebody came to the devil and say why are you crying? The devil said, the reason am crying is that anything that goes wrong in this place they blame it on me. There was a Christian naming ceremony, the devil send one housefly there to cause cholera. One brother came there, everybody suppose to have one plate of rice the brother selected three plates of rice. He was eating one and hid the other two under the chair. Then the devil went to plate number three and planted something there. If the brother have eaten just his one plate and left the place there would have been no problem. But he ate plate number one up to plate number three which happen to be the one in which the cholera devil brought was put now the brother develop cholera. You cannot blame the devil. The problem in our lives is not only demonic in many instances. And no matter how we paint ourselves of being innocent, the blunt truth is that most times, we are not innocent. Many of man problems would disappear if we just remove selfishness from inside our lives, And the idea of engaging in doing something without even thinking about it. The selfishness of a man or a woman can run the whole family into trouble. A lot of problem can disappear if you can just remove selfishness from your life. And because of that many people shut themselves of blessings.

Many people concern about their comfort not for the others. Then you shut yourself out of the door of blessing. Most of the people that are blessed in the Bible are those who went on their way to be a blessing to others, while they go out to bless others, God bless them. If Jesus was selfish he would not have come to die for us. The Bible says he came to die for us. It is because he came to die for us, that is why me and you are here today.

I had a friend a long time ago. He heard that a man had an accident and he rushed the man to the hospital and the nurses on duty were suppose to close by eight o'clock but normally by quarter to eight, they start packing up. So this woman was already dressing up, painting her lips to go. The nurse said, the person that is supposed to take over is resuming by eight o clock and me am going home. This man who brought an accident patient begged her to treat the man she said no I have to go home. She went home only to discover that her husband was not at home by the time she ran around, she found out that she has failed to treat her husband's relation, and the man died hereafter. Now, is that the devil?

Many Christians may not want to face this fact because a lot of believers are very selfish. And majority of the prayers that most people prayed are for themselves. All form of anger that most people engage in are motivated by selfishness. Most people are angry because somebody has violated their rights. So when you are bitter against somebody, it is because you have done something to high your pride. And the heart of rebellion is always inspired by selfishness, although this would be difficult for most people to agree. Many problems are from our selfish techniques. And a lot of people are specialized on what we called blame system. A lot of people can never agree that am wrong they would look for somebody to blame.

They would be apportioning blame on this or that. We blame ourselves about the words or deed, and many speak words carelessly this day. Those words can be irrevocable. The principle of the Bible in Galatians 6:7, can never be defeated. Those who sow a seed of family destruction take another man's wife, kill the man. Those who did not know will reap the sword of destruction after him. If you must throw mud on others, you must first of all clean your own hands. Any activities done, either good or evil must be inherited. God himself can be the source of our problem. Not all problems are bad problems. God can design problems that would make you come closer to him, something that would make you more prayerful.

When the kingdom of Israel was divided into two, they were going into battles to fight each other but the prophet came and say don't worry yourself, don't cry for blood, this things is from me saith the Lord, I started it. So if God want you to learn a lesson from your problem, until you have learnt the lessons there is no solution. Until Naaman learnt that a proud person cannot get close to God, he didn't get close. The flesh is another cause of problem, is the old carnal nature. And all these things that we call demons and evil spirits they are the vultures that eat our flesh which is the carnal nature. If somebody is having problem and the problem is from evil spirit you can solve it by expelling the evil spirit. But if the problem is from the flesh, there is only one solution to crucify the flesh.

I remember a story of that brother who entered a bus and somebody gave him a dirty slap and the people in the bus said are you a fool? Slap him back. The brother said I cannot slap him back because my hands have been nailed to the cross. This is your hand, there is no nail. The brother said no, it has been crucified, I cannot slap. How many of us can do that? Some of you will reply the slap immediately without looking back. The person has not crucified the flesh. Most of all those church workers and leader you are dealing with when you come to church, most of all the countenance you are playing about is still the flesh. Satan always send demons in an already bad situation. Sometimes for solution to come what you have to do is just to avoid certain things. Every bit of anger you throw could be your problem activator. Every exercise of worry you engage in may be you problem activator. Sometimes you memorize the scripture that speak to a certain life problem. You keep confessing one problem and you do your normal praying many problems will disappear. But the flesh is still keeping away from confessing scriptures.

Many people that come to church, all they need is regular confessing of scriptures and regular bombarding of prayer but the flesh is still keeping away from doing those things. By the time people come to church and they would be able to deal with the spirit of worry, anxiety, discouragement, lust, impatience, not able to repent, not able to resist temptation. Then the whole problem would have been over. Sometimes some people have some problems, to cast out demon is not a solution, for example if the enemy have removed part of somebody's body you don't need deliverance, you need a creative miracle. So it is a great prayer point for you to ask for creative miracle where it is necessary in your life. Deliverance cannot restore any part of the body that is lost or replace it.

There is a sister that has a breast operation when we are at Old Yaba Road, and she has been having problem in that breast to the extent that she feel like cutting it off. But one day as we were praying she notice that something is coming out from that breast. It was a needle that they forgot on the day of the surgery. Now deliverance could not solve that one. God has to intervene and bring out the pin. All the mistaken surgery etc. a creative miracle is required in those cases.

Most Christian need to check what they eat and find out the things recommended by the bible we are not expensive. But the problem is this, what most people want is not what they need. Mark 12:3; *and thou shalt love the Lord thy God with all thy heart, and with all thy soul, and with all thy mind, and with all thy strength: this is the first commandment. And the second is like, namely this, Thou shalt love thy neighbor as thyself. There is none other commandment greater than these.*

There are three groups of people for you to love. You must love God, your neighbor and yourself. A lot of people need to increase interest on themselves God made us body, soul and spirit. God is interested in every department of your life. You are the temple of God. Although there are some people who are the temple of Satan. If you now try to defile the temple of God which is your body, the bible says God will destroy such people. So if you destroy the temple of God which is your body or you are misusing it, you will have problem with God for destruction and you think it is witches and wizards. God is interested in what you do with that body either physically or spiritually. And a lot of Christians can eat poison every day. You can over eat, you can eat sugar, oil, butter and when you over eat, it will touch your digestive organs. Your body cannot process the food fast now.

When the children or Israel were in the wilderness, God told them not to eat certain things, because there was no doctor in the wilderness to look after them and a lot of people specialize in eating such things. A lot of Christians kill themselves daily because of what they eat. Some people have become tea addict, coffee addict, sugar addict, soft drink addict, can food addict, chocolate, all those kind of things. And it result in problems and problems. If they injure themselves then they resort in going for deliverance. Some hate fasting of any form, not knowing that is another way of purifying their system. This is why sometimes God call people fools because of what they meant to know, they don't know. A lot of people add intense effect on themselves. As you are sitting down there, do you know that you can be your own enemy? You could actively be against yourself. But one thing is certain any failure in anybody's health is not God's fault, it is the person's fault.

As I was saying, sometimes ago, a lot of people have turned themselves to masquerades. They are the ones pursuing themselves. How long can you run away from yourself? You need to stand and tell the truth about yourself the first step is spiritual maturity. For how long would you repeat the mistake of Adam? As far as you don't want to tell the truth about yourself, you give the enemy a hiding place in your life. The person would enroll in the school of self deception. Then you would be fighting against yourself. You don't blame yourself for your mistakes, rather you lay the blame on other people. You will not be able to succeed when you are working like that. If there is any failure or defeat, blame yourself first. Because God does not fail and his word does not fail. The most thing people need to learn to do is to point accusing finger at themselves a person cannot succeed in Christian life when you are so lazy, you are a spiritual slumber and you cannot pray or read the Bible. Then the lazy Christians will come and say am not encouraged. A lazy Christian would watch television for four hours, listen to radio for three hours. Then pray only for twenty minutes. A lazy Christian would come to the house of God not to really do God's work. So a lot of people are battling against themselves while they think they are battling against the enemy.

If you change from all these things, we have been saying here, there is no demon that can stand against you. The problem is that many people have refused to change. Apart from the devil, another terrible enemy is sex. When sex is at work, God's work will cease, man's work will begin. And the devil who is the enemy knows that these things you are doing is not from God is from yourself. And there are so many lives which God's work have seized and is only man's work that is going on. All that you do for God, may be you have been coming to church for a long time or you just started coming. Everything that you have ever done for God, if it is yourself that you are using to do it is of the little value to God. Any anything you are doing for God not energized by the spirit is of no value. So the subject with the highest mark in God's school is deliverance from self. A lot of people are in bondage to themselves. They are spoiling themselves and pampering their own lives. The subject with the highest mark in devil school is self exaltation. Every postponement of repentance means you are wrestling against God and it is sad. All the senior prefects in the school of self exaltation, they would rather die than to ask for forgiveness or to apologize. Those people are fighting actively against themselves. Failure to carry self analysis, you refuse to come to terms with yourself. Know that you are fighting against yourself. The Bible says examine yourself whether you be in the faith or not. You need to ask yourself am I not proud? do I not exaggerate? do I not tell lies? do I really like fasting and prayer or am I doing it because others are doing it? Do I not love Jesus because of the bread and butter He is supplying? Am I really ready to die for Jesus? If I say I want to send people to go and do evangelism in the village that's demonic now, how many people would like to go? Am I serious with God when I have money? Is not when am broke that am serious in praying? Am I not lazy in prayer? Do I not keep malice? Do I have love? Do I always tell the truth about myself? Or do I avoid those who always tell me the truth about my life? Do I enjoy being criticized? Or do I hate criticism in any form? Do I have faith? Am I really obedient to God? Am I the kind of person who likes to be noticed? Do I really have baptism of the Holy Spirit or do I still rely on the dream I had long time ago? Do I tell lies to obey God? Do I think or meditate on immorality? Do you think when you are alone on your bed how you live as a bachelor? Do I not commit secret sin? Check the truth beloved, may be you are fighting yourself and the person won't get far. Check the faith beloved. Tell yourself the truth beloved. And when you start praying against the forces of darkness you make a mistake.

Is like that guy who was preaching putting on the whole armor of God, and in order to make people to understand the message he brought physical helmet, shoe, clothes etc. and he was wearing them one by one until he was well covered. Then he asks the congregation. Do you have where the devil will come in now? Then one old man of God who was sitting there said young man from the inside? You are wearing armor of God but the devil has already entered you. You are just using the armor to cover it inside. The inside, what have you done about that one, that is our biggest problem.

If the Bible says touch not my anointed and you're being touched, carrying out such analysis the enemy would use your wickedness and unconfessed sin in your life to attack you. So those who fail to carry out analysis of themselves, they are fighting themselves. And God like sincere people. Whether you are a believer and you are living an unfruitful Christian life. God did not create hell fire for Christians but one thing that will drag a Christian to hell fire is unfruitfulness and useless Christian life. How can God invest much in a person and the person is not bringing any fruit? Or have you forgotten that tree in the garden and is not bringing any fruit and the owner of the garden came and said cut it down.

God is turning his back against many people. I fill you with Holy Ghost, I bring you to the house of God and you're not yielding any fruit. God will say cut him down. Many Christians will get into trouble without their family. The bible say pour your anger on the family that did not call on the name of the Lord. Many people would wake up in the morning, no prayer, they just prepare, eat and go out.

When they come back in the evening, no prayer, no Bible reading, they just eat, watch television and sleep. God have mercy on us, unfruitful life. So what fruit are you producing unto God? All your intelligence, your academic success, your financial position, your influential personality, your capacity to communicate, your God given ability, what steps are you taken to use it to propagate the kingdom of God?. Unfruitful Christian is fighting against himself. You cannot blackmail God. Those people in the Bible who refuse to use their talents, God said cast them unto utter darkness because they refuse to use their talent. By hiding your talent you've given your enemy opportunity to destroy you. Those who engage in family strife If you hate your wife, your husband, your children, you're fighting yourself. if you're keeping demonic material in your house, you're harming yourself. You're just inviting demonic invitations. You cannot fight the devil successfully when you have their material in your body or in your house, all the amulet, the headband the enemy would be using it against you. If you just experience partial deliverance and you are attacking the enemy, you are sting your time because part of the enemy is still in you. All those engaging in sexual immorality, you may still be enjoying yourself mow, but you're actually waging serious war against your own life. All the children that is disobedient to parents. Those children are fighting themselves. Those who engage in worldly pleasure, they are killing themselves. They are strengthening the enemy. Why should you be fighting against yourself?

Most of the problems we are casting out and binding, we caused it by ourselves. Ask yourself a question. A lot of people are masquerading to themselves. They don't know themselves and they are attacking the enemy. It will back fire on you.

Prayer Point

1. O Lord reveal to me who I am in the name of Jesus.
2. O Lord I repent on everything I have done to and my enemy in the name of Jesus.
3. O Lord, deliver me from every evil accusation of the evil one against, in the name of Jesus.

The Final Separation - 1

Matthew 25:31-34: *"When the Son of man shall come in His glory, and all the holy angels with Him, then shall He sit upon the throne of His glory. And before Him shall be gathered all nations; and He shall separate them one from another, as a shepherd divideth his sheep from the goats. And He shall set the sheep on the right hand and the goats on the left. Then shall the King say on to them on his right hand: "Come, ye blessed of my Father; inherit the Kingdom prepared for you from the foundations of the world."*

Matthew 25:46:
"And these shall go away into everlasting punishment: but the righteous into life eternal."

The theme of this message centres on a very serious matter. It is very clear that you did not pick this bulletin by chance. Many people have testified to the fact that they had never heard of the Mountain of Fire and Miracles Ministries before, but one way or the other, the Lord ministered to them, through dreams or visions, and they got in touch with the church. For such a thing like that to happen to a person, it means that God has an agenda for such a person.

It is clear that there are many people; men and women that the Lord is grooming for serious spiritual assignments that will affect the nations. It is also clear that many of these people are working behind the schedule of God for their lives and that is why the Lord is allowing the enemy to raise warfares all around them. God allows such to happen so that this kind of people will not relax at all, but will pick up their baton and run, and if they have dropped their baton, it will make them to pick it up and continue running.

You are not reading this message by chance; God has a purpose for it and that is why you have to take it seriously and pray the prayers vigorously. This, if understood well, will make a difference between where you are now, and where you should be. The texts above show that no matter what you call yourself you shall as a matter of necessity, appear before the throne of God.

Verse 34:
"Then shall the King say on to them on his right hand: "Come, ye blessed of my Father; inherit the Kingdom prepared for you from the foundations of the world."

No matter how long you live on earth, no matter how fervent you are or become in the Christian faith, if when you close your eyes in death, you do not hear this voice, then you are finished.

Verse 46:
"And these shall go into everlasting punishment: but the righteous into life eternal,"

The ones on the left side, shall go into eternal condemnation. One sober, solemn truth that all pastors face, is the fact that some people that they have preached to are heading for hell-fire. They will see that the meeting place for many of those that they have preached to is in hell and not in the gathering of the saints. It is a very sober thought, a solemn thought that is worth shedding tears for. Beloved, when the Bible says that there shall be weeping in heaven, the major part of the weeping shall be in two-folds:

i. Weeping because a person did not do what God expected him or her to do.
ii. Weeping because those that you expect to be there with you in heaven are not there.

What benefit is it, when mummy is saved and daddy is gone to hell-fire? Or vice versa? What benefit is it, when the parents are saved and the children are in the bottom of the pit of hell? A day is coming beloved, a day of fear and wrath, a day of destruction of the ungodly, a testing day for all Mankind, a day which shall burn as oven. It is the day that God shall blow His final whistle. By that time, He would have been fed up with everything that Man is doing here on earth.

There is a big city, where there was a volcanic eruption. Whenever the volcano started, hot liquid called lava comes out of it and anything that touches it dies. Because of this, people ran for their dear lives and abandoned the city. One day, it happened and a woman could not escape from it. Later, her skeleton was discovered in the solid lava and she had a clenched fist. When the fist was opened, a pair of gold earrings was found in it. Apparently, she must have gone back to look for those earrings, instead of running out of the house, because she never made it; she was caught up in the hot lava!

Very soon, many people, who are gathering the things that will be destroyed by fire, will discover that it is all a waste of time. Many people will know, that those things that they are getting excited about, and are thinking that they are the most important things in life, are actually vanity. God will blow His final whistle.
His final subject on his timetable is about to finish. Very soon, it will not matter what name you call yourself: "General Overseer. Superintendent, Pastor, Reverend, etc" because it will no longer be relevant.

You could be a church-goer that chooses which sermons to listen to, you could be the most senior of the senior pastors, or the chairman of house fellowships, or anything, you could be painted in any colour but by the time the whistle blows, you might discover that you are not up to the level of a cleaner or houseboy.

Revelation 6:17:
"For the great day of the wrath is come; and who shall be able to stand?

If you do not hear the sound: 'Come, ye blessed of my Father; inherit the Kingdom prepared for you from the foundations of the world," you would have wasted precious time.

There will be gathered before Him, all manners of men and women from all nations. There are many big men and women politicians, who do not have time for church services. Many, who go to church, arrive late; including workers and members of the choir.

On that day, you must arrive in time, at the judgement seat, whether you like it or not. That is when the Scriptures will become clear to you that; "At the name of Jesus, every knee must bow..." either willingly now, or unwillingly at that time. All those Jews, to whom the Law of God was given, will be there. The Gentiles and all the nations that have been resisting the word of God will be there. The nations that have just heard the Gospel will be there. All the extinct nations that we no longer hear of, the Roman Empire, etc will be there. All those who perished during the flood of Noah will be there. All those Egyptians, who perished in the Red Sea will there. All those who died in unknown lands, are not lost, they will come out. Even all those who were sacrificed to idols and were cut into pieces, will be joined together and they will come out.

The land we are treading upon, which is becoming more and more a great grave-yard, shall answer the roll call on that day of the Lord, and yield up all the dead people in it. Everyone born of a woman shall come forth, out of the prolific womb of the sepulcher, the cemetery and the earth. The sea too shall become like a solid pavement and yield up the dead people in it. All those who sank in the sea, will come out. Multitudes shall be gathered in the valley of decision. All of them shall gather for one purpose; to appear before The Judge. What a gathering, that would be! No imagination can capture it; our Lord shall sit on that throne. The Shepherd and The Judge shall then go in, for the final separation. The Shepherd knows His sheep so; He will separate them from the goats. It is easy for any shepherd to separate goats from sheep; without any mistake.

There are many goats in the house of God though in sheep's clothing. That explains why some people are not broken and why some are living in sin. But on that day, the clothing will be removed and it will be clear that they are goats inside. This goat situation explains why many cry to God for His anointing to fall on them, and it does not and why some spirits refuse to leave, despite fervent prayers.

Herein is the great thought and question. When that separation will take place, my brother, my sister, on which side will you be? You might automatically say you belong to the sheep side, but the question is: Are you sure? Has iniquity left your heart? Many people criticise others, that there is no love amongst the brethren, but they themselves, do not let love radiate from them. Has rebellion left your heart? Have you stopped telling lies? The way some Christians tell lies these days, makes one to wonder if they have heaven in mind at all. The fear of God is not in the heart of many people; many, it seems do not want to make heaven at all. It appears as if they are here to play.

It is one thing to pray fire prayer points, it is another thing to prepare for heaven. No matter what breakthroughs you obtain through fire prayers, they will amount to nothing, if on that day, you do not hear: "Come, blessed of my Father ...." For example, if one dies, those entire breakthroughs would end at the gate of the cemetery, where it will be pronounced that: "Dust to dust, ashes to ashes." In other words, you cannot take cars or houses with you when you die. Most of the houses that we see around now were built by people who died years ago, and who could not take these houses with them.

Some sisters clamour for dresses and shoes, forgetting that they can only wear one at a time, and that they will be buried with only one and that that one, will rot in the grave, at the end of the day; it will be vitamin for termites.

I would like to ask you these questions: What are you rushing after? Why are you abandoning God's cry? Christian, have you stopped telling lies? Have you really met the Lord'? You could have met the General Overseer of your church, or your pastor, you might have met fire prayers and deliverance, but have you met the Lord? It was Job that said: "I have heard of thee, by the hearing of the ear, but now, my eyes seeth thee." Have you met the Lord?

One great problem of the church of God today, is the fact that, many people are trying to run the affairs of the God that they have not met. A person, who has never seen the shadow of Christ is singing: "Since Jesus passed by ..."

Beloved, are you part of the problem of Christendom or are you part of its solution? Are you really a Christian broken by God? Have you allowed yourself to be passed through His furnace, tried seven times and purified to reflect His image? Are lust and hatred, not dwelling in the laboratory of your heart? Are lust and terrible affection not in your heart? God is getting fed up with the hypocrisy and the unrighteousness of Christians.

One day, some Christian students were to have a meeting on campus, in the room of a brother. The first person to arrive, was the most beautiful sister in the fellowship and for about one hour, no other person came in. The host was with the sister and they were chatting. One way or the other, the thoughts of fornication filled their hearts and they could not resist the temptation. They began to commit fornication and as they went far, the other brethren arrived and could not gain access into the room. The brother and the sister realising that they had wasted precious time looked for a way out; they cleverly devised an idea; and started singing praises. The people outside suddenly heard voices singing: "I've just come to praise the Lord ..." The brethren thought they were praying and decided to wait. Suddenly, one of them thought they should join them, since they came for a meeting. They forced the door open, and found the brother and sister naked. Suddenly something like thunder, struck them and they died on the spot. The brethren did not know what to do and one of them ran to their pastor, so that it would not become a scandal in the campus. God warned the pastor not to go with them, but he felt he was the one that could help cover the scandal. They managed to carry out the corpses and later, the pastor conducted a burial for them. As he was returning from the burial, his car got involved in an accident and he lost his legs. Today, he cannot walk.

In the face of God right now,

there is no smile; the people who are supposed to be running are crawling. The Bible says the sheep and the goats, shall be separated; the Lord will ask the sheep to enter into everlasting joy, then He will tell the goats to go away and they will go into eternal damnation. There will be no third group; there is no neutrality in the things of God. You are either for God, or for Satan. Jesus Christ says: "He, who is not for us, is against us." Your name is either in the Lamb's Book of Life, or is not there. Some people say that there is a place called purgatory, where you will go, to be cleansed before going to heaven. There is nothing like that. Purgatory is an invention of the brain of Man. The Bible says: It is appointed unto Man once to die and after that, the judgement."

As you are reading this message, you must know that there are only two groups of people at the end of the day; the sheep and the goats. The ones who are dead in sin or the ones who are alive in God. There is no middle camp; you are either spiritually alive or spiritually dead. Do not be deceived beloved; as you are there, where you are, you are either on your way to heaven or to hell; there is no middle camp. Your character will speak for heaven or hell fire. The human flock will he divided into two parts. That is why you will need to cry out to the Lord today. The goatish spirit of pride in you must depart because God has no respect for a proud person. If you allow the goatish pride to stay in you, it will eventually become a waste of destiny. For example if you command a goat to stay in a place, it will not. If you chase it from a place and you give it some strokes of the cane, it will leave, but will soon be back.
John 3:36:
"**He** *that helieveth on the Son hath everlasting life: and he that believeth not the Son shall not see life; but the wrath of God abideth on him."*

On that day beloved, the eyes of God, will reach everywhere with His fire. The pastor's eyes might not be able to reach everywhere you go, or see everything you do, but you must know, that no hypocrite will get to heaven. They will have nowhere to hide on that day. There is no bribing of the judge; you cannot say that he is from your village. You cannot avoid the tribunal of the Almighty. Some people were summoned by the "Oputa Panel" in Nigeria, for prosecution but they did not go. The summoning that I am talking about is a compulsory one. As a matter of necessity, you must be there. Are you ready for this eye that will look and see you inside out? If it finds any spot, you will be disqualified. The separation will be final. Right from that meeting you will no longer see some people.

When people tell me that they lost one relative or the other, the question I ask is, whether the person is born-again or not: If a person is born again, there is an opportunity for him or her to see other brethren in heaven. The sinner that dies in his or her sin goes to hell. The herbalist, etc will be there. I always tell those who cry and mourn for the sinner, that died, to cry very well, because they will never meet again, except the person too, decides to become a sinner and go to hell. There is no linking bridge, no crossing over, no hope of restoration, that lost sinner is separated from Jesus forever. That separation can not be changed.

If you say you are a witch or wizard, or that you have familiar spirits and you do not want to repent. I feel sorry for you. Since you have been in those associations, what good did it do to you? What do you gain from killing the person, who will help you? What will you gain, if you kill the children that should bury you when you die? it is a foolish thing really; the enemy is just manipulating the lives of people. These are very serious matters and they are very heavy; so heavy that right now, I feel like sitting and weeping. It is difficult not to feel sorry for a person that is heading for hell and does not want to change. It is clear that one will never see such a person again, because there is going to be a final separation.

If hitherto, you have not surrendered your life to Lord Jesus Christ, you are likely to be amongst the goats. Do not wait for that day, when He will send you into eternal damnation. I would advise that you surrender your life to the Lord Jesus Christ; make a sincere commitment to follow

Him all the way. All you need to do is to acknowledge the fact that you are sinner and that you cannot reach out to God in your sinful state. Confess your sins to Him. Name them one by one; ask Him to forgive you and to cleanse you from all unrighteousness, forsake those sins and say bye-bye to the world and the devil. Invite the Lord Jesus Christ into your life. Ask Him to come into your life and become your personal Lord and Saviour. Enthrone Him over your life. Hand over the affairs of your life to Him and ask Him to take absolute control of your life. Surrender your totality to Him, and it shall be well with you.

I congratulate you for taking this decision, that is the most important decision that you could ever take in life. I pray that it shall be permanent in your life in the name of Jesus. I pray that the Lord will uphold you with His right hand of righteousness, and will not let you fall. I pray that He will write your name in the Book of Life and nothing shall by any means, rub it off in the name of Jesus. It shall be well with you in the name of Jesus. Amen.

Take these prayer points with holy aggression and with all seriousness even if they do not make sense to you:

1. I pull down the stronghold of evil strangers in every area of my life, in the name of Jesus.
2. Any negative transaction currently affecting my life negatively, be cancelled, in the name of Jesus.
3. I command all the dark works done against me in secret to be exposed and nullified, in the name of Jesus.
4. I loose myself from any dark spirit, in the name of Jesus.
5. Every prayer failure, I command you to cease in the name of Jesus.
6. I pull down every stronghold erected against my progress in the name of Jesus.
7. Lord arise, and use me for Your glory in the mighty name of Jesus.
8. Anything in my life contradicting the plan of God for my destiny be wasted in the name of Jesus.
9. Lord, purge me afresh with Your fire, in the mighty name of Jesus
10. Holy Spirit, promote divine possibilities in My life, in the name of Jesus.
11. Lord, I choose to believe Your report, I will not believe the report of the enemy in the name of Jesus
12. Lord Jesus, in Your power I crush all my enemies in the name of Jesus.
13. I trample upon every satanic wisdom fashioned against my life in the name of Jesus.
14. I prophesy signs and wonders on my prayers in the name of Jesus.
15. Lord let Your rain of blessing be permanent in my life in the name of Jesus.
16. Let all weapons and devices of the oppressors and tormentors be rendered impotent, in the name of Jesus.
17. Let the fire of God destroy every power operating any spiritual vehicle working against me, in the name of Jesus.

The Final Separation -2

Matthew 25:31-34; *"When the Son of man shall come in His glory, and all the holy angels with Him, then shall He sit upon the throne of His glory. And before Him shall be gathered all nations; and He shall separate them one from another, as a shepherd divideth his sheep from the goats. And He shall set the sheep on the right hand and the goats on the left. Then shall the King say on to them on his right hand: "Come, ye blessed of my Father; inherit the Kingdom prepared for you from the foundations of the world."*

Verse 46 continues: *"And these shall go into everlasting punishment: hut the righteous into life eternal."*

In the last bulletin, we started this important topic. We mentioned the fact that at the end of the day, God will separate the goats from the sheep. We saw the fact that those who abide in the will of God are the sheep and will be rewarded. We saw who the goats are and where they will end their lives. This week, we shall continue in the same light. I pray that at the end of this message, you will know where you will be on the last day. I pray that you will take the decision that will make you worthy of being at the right hand of God.

Matthew 3:10 says; *"And now also the axe is laid unto the root of the trees: therefore every tree which bringeth not forth good fruit is hewn down, and cast into the fire."*

It is unfortunate to note that, the ancient marks of salvation are no longer present in the lives of Christians. Spiritual death is now rampant; some people dabble into sin without remorse and they dare to go to church. It is as if the enemy has turned the heart of such people into a concrete.

As a young Christian. I knew a 70 year old man, who gave his life to Christ. He was very zealous for the Lord; his prayers were always with fervency, his singing and clapping were always joyous and loud. One day, he came to church and was not happy; he was not singing aloud and not clapping his hands; he was cold. After the service, I approached him and asked what was wrong with him. He said he committed a sin, I asked what he did and he said he told a lie. He said someone came to look for him and because he did not want to see the person, he changed his voice feigning to be a child and answered from inside the room saying: Baba is gone out. Immediately, he lost his peace and was not free. He felt so sorry because he knows that God does not tolerate lies and it would land anyone in hell. The Bible says that "All liars are of their father, the devil and will go to hell." That old man's experience is real Bible salvation. We prayed together and asked God for forgiveness and restoration, and he regained his peace.

Many Christians today, commit sin and still have the boldness to go to church. Some pastors do abominable things and still pick a microphone to speak in the church. When the conscience is as dead as this, it means that something terrible is about to happen to the person. If you begin to commit sin and something does not convict you and break you down, it means that your spiritual sensitivity is gone: therefore, you are spiritually dead. The day that you are able to look at someone straight in the eyes and tell him or her lies, it means you are finished. You will need to go back to the foundation of faith and build yourself up again.

During a crusade, there was an altar call and many people came out. One of them was crying bitterly. Later, she came to ask the preacher to allow her to talk to the congregation. She confessed that as the treasurer to the church, she had been stealing money every service day throughout all the five years that she held the post. She wept her eyes out and asked for forgiveness. That is

Bible repentance unto salvation.

You must note that, you cannot sin successfully. That Bible says; *"Surely, your sin shall find you out."*

Someone defined sin as: Success - In - Nothing.

Your sin is a detective and will eventually find you out. You might think no one sees you, but God is just watching you and putting you in slippery places. Very soon, He will remove you and replace you with someone else. One of the major tasks that God has conferred on His ministers is compassion. That is why a pastor can forgive and bring back an erring child to the Lord.

A man brought his wife one day for prayers. He said the sickness started suddenly and the whole of her thigh was covered with sores. It was as if something ate up the skin into the flesh, including her private part. As I was about to pray, the Lord told me not to waste my time, that she had not told the truth about what happened. I asked the husband to excuse us and I asked her what she had done. She said they went to a burial ceremony in their village and as the party was going on, she spotted her former boyfriend. They got attracted to each other again and made signals to meet at their old meeting place. She took a bottle of spring water and asked her husband to excuse her for a while. She went to the mechanic workshop where they used to meet in those days. It was a deserted and dark place. They could not resist each other and they use a stall to have sexual intercourse.

When they finished, the old boyfriend left and she bent down to clean herself up with the spring water that she had brought. She did not know that there was another bottle around. She grabbed it and poured the content on herself to wash her private part. She did not know that it was acid left in the workshop by the mechanic. Immediately, the thing started to devour her and she cried out. She got to the place of the ceremony in pains and people ran here and there to get help, they poured water, oil, sand, all they could think of, to ease the pain and stop the corrosion. The husband brought her back to Lagos and no one could tell what kind of disease it was. Therefore, they drew the conclusion that it was a spiritual attack. That was why the husband brought her for prayers. Her sins finally found her out.

Your sins shall find you out, no matter how fast you run. It is a detective, it will pursue and find you out. Your pastor might not know and might not even bother to probe into your activities, but the way your sin will find you out, it will be a terrible thing. The enemy deceives people into thinking that they can sin and go scot-free; that there is nothing to it. You must note that there is no harmless sin. Every sin will attract a consequence. Although life is a mystery as there are many things about life that are not clear to human beings; but one thing is certain, your sin will find you out. The pay-day will come one day and your sin will find you out. One day, those who listen to the devil will discover with a bleeding heart that, the price of sin is extremely high. The thing that will make you a goat is the one that makes you to harbour sin and befriend the things that God hates. Your sin will eventually find you out.

I once read a story in a foreign newspaper. Two people were friends but suddenly, one of them disappeared after a quarrel. The other friend denied all interrogations and affirmed that he did not know anything about it. He was set free and he moved to another town and started life afresh. Twenty-three years later, the small pond in his former compound in the former town, dried up. At the bottom, the new inhabitants found a skeleton and a chain which had the initials of the man that was living there before. The police started to search for him. By the time they found him, he was already aged and was dying of tuberculosis. In that state, he was brought to court and tried. His sin eventually found him out.

Ecclesiastes 8:11:
"Because sentence against an evil work is not executed speedily; therefore the heart of the sons of men is fully set in them to do evil."

Beloved, the issue of heaven is a serious matter. It could appear as if a sinner has escaped now, but there will be a payday. Sin will always take a person farther than he or she is ready to go. It will cost more than a person is willing to pay. It will keep him or her longer than he or she would want to stay. A little sin will strengthen the enemy and add to the person's trouble. If a person is ruled by sin, he or she will be ruined by sin. As soon as a person begins to sow the seed of sin, the harvest comes in almost immediately. It is unfortunate to find out that these days, Satan is succeeding in convincing people and giving excuses in support of their going into sin. People say they do one thing or the other because of one situation or the other. It is because of the spirit of the goal that is in them.

If you have heard or read a message like this and you also claim to be a Christian, it will do you good to take action at once. It will be a tragedy, to have read this kind of message and still go to hell. It should not be allowed to happen. If at the end of the day, God looks at you and says; "Go away", it will be a tragedy. It means He has grouped you with goats. A goat would hear the word of God, but will not do it. Goats will not heed warnings that they should be broken. They are the ones that fight at the bus-stop or car-park. They are the ones that will refuse to queue up and be orderly. They do all kinds of terrible things.

In 1998, a 'pastor' committed fornication and was disciplined. He got furious and left the church. Later, he got into a strange relationship with a lady and got married. Soon afterwards, things turned sour between them and she left. Meanwhile, he could not do the work that God called him to. All this started from condoning sin. He is now in jail. Some people do not take the teachings of the Bible serious; although they attend church services, they still harbour malice, they quarrel and backbite.

They want God to talk to them; they want to overcome the battles of life but do not know that without discipline, it is not possible. You cannot continue to live in sin and ask for grace to abound -Romans 6:1. The eyes of God cannot behold sin! When a person does not want to live a disciplined life, he or she will have the tendency of being subject to fake prophets and soothsayers - who will see evil visions and prophesies. Such people need to hear the truth about their lives and decide to change. Many people have gone to places where their problems have been compounded and they run back to church, to ask for prayers.

I would like you to understand the fact that, if you are a goat, the voice that you will hear on that day is; "Go away." There are goat ushers, goat pastors and goat members; they have to repent before it is too late and cry to heaven. Pray this prayer point:
* **O Lord! I do not want my name to he written amongst the damned; I want my name to be written in the Book of Life.**
Are you living an empty life? No vision, no revelation, you do not hear anything from God verbally, or through His words in the Bible? Do you attend fellowship, do you attend Bible Study sessions? Are you one of those who say they want breakthroughs and testimonies, but are living empty lives? Such people will go with the goats. Are you living a dirty life? Repent because God cannot use someone with a dirty life.

A sister was praying seriously that God should use her, and God kept telling her that her life was filthy. She did not understand until one day, when she saw a vision. In it, she was pressed and wanted to go to the toilet. There were four toilets in a row; she opened the first one and found out that the closet was full; she shouted and went to the second toilet. That one was filled to the brim and was overflowing to the floor. She opened the third toilet and there were maggots all over the place. She could not open the fourth one because faeces had overtaken the whole floor and was blocking the door. She sighed in disgust and left the place. As she was trying to control the pressure of her need to go to toilet, she heard the voice of the Lord asking why she did not use any of the toilets. She said they were full and smelly and disgusting. The Lord asked if it was not dirt that she herself wanted to pass out. She said it was. The Lord then told her that as she could not pass out her faeces in a filthy place, so also could He not use her in her filthy state.
If you are living a floating life; that is, you are pretending to be

what you are not, living above your spiritual experience, saying that the Lord said this or that, or you saw this or that when you did not see anything, it means you are floating. You are wasting your time. You had better fall at the feet of God and tell Him who and what you are and ask Him to change you.

Some-Christians cannot buy a N300 Christian book that will enhance their spiritual life, but they can buy N6,000 shoes on credit and then, when the time comes to pay up they keep dodging the creditors, Do you know that God is not worried about your shoes or bags being old? What He is worried about is your spiritual life. Do not be a floating Christian!, Stop pretending! Do not be a goat!

Are you living a loose life? Are you very loose with the opposite sex? As a sister, are you always in the midst of brothers and are uncomfortable with sisters? Are you a brother and you are very loose with sisters? You are always jesting and playing with sisters? Are you a pastor and all your counselees are women? You do not have time for male counselees? If you are loose with the opposite sex, you are writing an application to failure. Are you living a lazy life? Too lazy to pray, to intercede for sinners and brethren? Are you too lazy to tarry for one hour? Jesus asked His disciples why they could not tarry with Him for just one hour. Some people are too lazy to pray, so, they just summarize their requests and they are done.

Do you have dirty hands? Are you into a dirty business? Are you a '419" person? Do you play worldly games? Are you a thief? Are your hands bloody? Do you have an angry spirit? Are you quick to being provoked? Are you a person that shouts at people and scream to the extent that people are afraid of you? Are you one that even your husband hesitates, when he has something to say, because he does not know what you will throw at him in anger? If any of these apply to you, it means you are a goat and it means that you have to repent; otherwise, you are heading for hell-fire.

Do you have a doubting spirit'? Do you have familiar spirits? Do you have a hypocritical spirit? ; are you a hypocrite, who cannot pray for himself to get healed and is swallowing analgesic tablets and drinking concoctions, yet is laying hands on people to receive their healing? Are you a fornicator; daring to lay hands on a person that needs deliverance? If any of these also applies to you, it means you are a goat.

One day, a strange boy entered a bus and someone stepped on him and he said the person's leg should become paralysed and it happened instantly. A woman shouted in awe and her mouth began to widen. The passengers became afraid and asked the driver to stop the vehicle and they all rushed out. There were two Christian brothers in the bus; they challenged the strange boy and asked him to come with them to their church, so that they would conduct deliverance on him. To their amazement, he agreed to go with them. When they got to their church, they met deliverance ministers, praying for people. When it was his turn to be prayed for, he challenged one of them, calling him a fornicator that he slept with a satanic agent, a few days earlier, the brother could not deny it. He challenged another one, of being a drinker of alcohol. Out of eighteen ministers, only two had no charges against them. That was how the head of the deliverance team eliminated the accused and only one person prayed for him and he was delivered. This means that, two out of eighteen ministers, were not hypocrites. The others were goats in sheep's clothing. Are you like the goats?

I do not know if you go to church, only to keep the bench warm. I do not know if you have the intention of going to heaven. Are you ready to make heaven at all cost? Those who are ready to make heaven at all cost, do not mind being ridiculed or being laughed at. They do not mind being called all sorts of names. Even though people make different kinds of proposals to them, they do not yield. They do not succumb to the pressure of the world, even if people tell them to leave Jesus and come and serve idols, they do not yield; they are ready to make it. They have made up their minds, like Meshach, Shedrach and Abednego, that they would rather burn than bow. These Hebrew boys confronted King

Nebuchadnezzar and told him that they would not bow to his idol. They said that God would deliver them from the fiery furnace. They went on to add that, even if God decided not to deliver them, they would rather burn than bow to his idol. When you have one leg in, one leg out of the house of God; criticising the principles of the Bible, it means you are not serious.

Right there where you are, I would like you to examine yourself. Is there anything in your life, that will convert you into a goat, on that division day; on the day of the final separation? Tell the Lord to forgive you and take it out of your life. Why would you allow yourself to be destroyed? Why should God look at His Book and rub your name off? Why should you become a bad example unto others? Why should it be said of you, that you served or sang in this world, but will not sing in the world to come? Why should it be said of you that you should have entered heaven, but your fornication and sin in your heart, will not allow you, they are blocking you from entering?

All the cleverly concealed sins will be exposed. Do you think that God cannot see you and your fiance(e) committing fornication? Do you think that He does not know about the aborted pregnancy that people do not know of? If you think so, you are only deceiving yourself; because as an abortionist, many voices are crying against you already at the throne of God; they are accusing you of being a killer.

If heaven is your goal, I want you to cry to the Lord like this:
* **Save me, O Lord, and I shall be saved in the name of Jesus.**

You will discover that in present times, fewer and fewer people, are seeing the picture of the Rapture. Even fewer still are seeing the picture of heaven. Many have never seen anything about heaven, either in dreams, visions or revelation. What kind of terrible state is this? You would need to cry out to the Lord again like this:
* **Lord, purge me with Your fire in the name of Jesus.**

* **Lord, drain luke-warmness away from my life in the name of Jesus.**

Ananias and Saphira sold their land and brought the money to church. They meant well; but the good thing they thought they were doing, brought death to them. God can still kill. Anyone who is doing the work of God deceitfully, is applying for the wrath of God.

Know that if you want to kill a witch, the witch in you must die first. What is the witch in you? Rebellion. If God says you should not say anything and you talk, it is rebellion. If God says you should go on a three-day fast and you do not do it you are rebelling against Him. I wish God would open your eyes, to see your heavenly record. If you could see just one page of your record, you will sit up. If God comes and shows you how much longer you have got to live, you will have no other choice than to change. There is a song which says: "Change my heart O God make it ever new. Change my heart O God, may I be like You."

At this stage, if you are not yet born again, it is clear that you are a goat. You cannot therefore even think of finding your name in the Book of life. However, you have the opportunity of changing the situation today. All you need do is acknowledge the fact that you are a sinner and that you cannot approach God in your sinful state. Repent of your sins; confess them to the Lord and ask Him to forgive you and cleanse you from all unrighteousness. Claim the redemptive power in the Blood of Jesus, that was shed on the Cross of Calvary, for the remission of your sins. Invite the Lord Jesus Christ into your life, ask Him to come into your life and become your personal Lord and Saviour. Hand over your life to Him and let Him take pre-eminence in all that concerns you. Surrender your totality to Him; say bye to the world of sin and the devil, and as you do so. God is ready to accept you as His own.

I congratulate you for this decision that you have just taken, it is the most important decision in life, and I pray that it shall be permanent in the name of Jesus. I pray that the Lord will uphold you with His right hand of righteousness and will not let you fall, in the name of Jesus. I pray that God will write your name in the Book of Life and nothing shall by any means rub it off in the name of Jesus. Go and sin no more!

Now, take these prayer points with all the seriousness that you can gather:

1. O thou that troubleth my Israel, my God shall trouble you today in the name of Jesus.
2. God arise and kill the goat in me in the name of Jesus.
3. Every voice calling me to hell-fire, be silenced forever, in the mighty name of Jesus.
4. Everything causing distraction against God's ways in my life, be terminated, in the name of Jesus.
5. I shall hear the trumpet sound when my Master shall call, in the name of Jesus.
6. Every power that does not want me to be raptured, release me now and die, in the mighty name of Jesus.
7. Every spirit in me offending God disappear by fire, in the mighty name of Jesus.
8. Everything in my life posing as a threat to the goodness of God be destroyed by fire, in the mighty name of Jesus.
9. I refuse to be a problem. I am a solution in the hands of God, and in my generation, in the mighty name of Jesus.
10. Lord, save me and I shall be saved, heal me and I shall be healed, deliver me and I shall be delivered, in the mighty name of Jesus.
11. Let the wickedness in me die in the mighty name of Jesus Christ.
12. Every wickedness against my salvation, die in the name of Jesus.
13. Let the witch in me die in the name of Jesus.
14. Lord, let my obedience to You be perfect in the name of Jesus.
15. Every goat in my being, be terminated in the name of Jesus.
16. Let the sword of deliverance touch my spirit, in the name of Jesus.
17. Anything God has not planted in my life, be uprooted by fire in the name of Jesus.
18. Enemies of God in my life, be disgraced, in the mighty name of Jesus.
19. Every power that wants me to miss heaven, release me and die in the mighty name of Jesus.
20. Let my spirit, soul and body receive the baptism of fire, in the mighty name of Jesus.
21. Heavenly surgeons, remove contrary things from my life, in the name of Jesus.
22. Let the fire of the Holy Ghost begin to burn in every department of my life, in the name of Jesus.
23. Every enemy of God in me, die by fire in the mighty name of Jesus.
24. I key in to God's Divine agenda for his people this year in the mighty name of Jesus Christ.

Thank the Lord for answered prayers.

The Goat And The Sheep

Psalm 100:3; *"Know ye that the Lord, He is God: it is He that hath made us and not we ourselves; we are His people and the sheep of His pasture."*

Mathew 25:31-34; *"When the Son of Man shall come in His glory, and all the holy angels with Him, then shall He sit upon the throne of His glory? And before Him shall be gathered all nations and He shall separate them on from another, as a shepherd divideth his sheep from the goats. And He shall set the sheep on the right hand and the goats on the left. Then shall the King say unto them on His right hand: "Come, ye blessed of my Father; inherit the Kingdom prepared for you from the foundations of the world."*

From the verses above, it is clear that the world is divided into two, before God. One part consists of the sheep and the other part; the goats. The sheep belong to the shepherd and obey his voice but the goats are out of place in the flock; the sheep are gentle but the goats are heady and stubborn.

Many people will be surprised when they arrive at the gate of heaven and find out that money, position, certificates, etc. cannot enter into the Kingdom of God; it all ends here. All those that are on part-time with God will be surprised to know that they are direct prey for the devil. God does not manage people, it is the devil that manages people; no matter how useless they are he will manage to give them something to do, he will keep hammering them together temporarily, although they are fast out of place. Instead of him to dismantle such and remold, he cannot and does not do this because he is never God. For example, if a person is into witchcraft, and he or she is still at the amateur stage, the devil will still use the person in carrying out the small errands that he wants to carry out.

Jesus is coming soon and His reward is in His hand to give to everyone, according to the works of his or her hands.

It is a pity that many church goers including pastors and priests, need deliverance. They do things that they are not expected to do; they take things for granted and take God's laws into their hands. Obviously, there are some powers behind the actions of such people which must be chased out through prayers. Many people think that it is only those who have familiar spirits or are witches and wizards that need deliverance. That is why we have a book titled: How to obtain Personal Deliverance; so that people can pray on their own, if they cannot go to the deliverance ground.

I have a friend who used to be a priest. He said whenever he was serving communion, he would be winking at girls and he would hear a voice saying he was going to hell. It persisted until the voice became loud and clear. When he no longer had peace, he had to resign and properly surrendered his life to the Lord Christ. Today, he is born-again and living a life of holiness. There are strangers in the lives of some people; some people are aware of these strangers while some are not. If there is any stranger in your life, you have to chase it away. They must fade and run out of their hiding place because it is not the will of God for you to continue living with strangers in your camp. Today, there are many Christians who keep malice and bear grudges against fellow Christians. There are some who have unforgiving spirit and keep record of those who offend them.

Many Christians have unclean spirits, Jezebel spirits, etc. that make them dress half naked and paint their faces, while many have lustful eyes. Is it not true that some people who have the spirit of infirmity and all kinds of spirits, claim to be born-again and sanctified? Is it not true that some of them would like to be free? Is it not true that some of them have tried to get out of these webs and have failed? Many have tried to fight these strangers and have failed. Many are hiding under the cloak of religion; many call themselves Christians but have boy or girl-friends and they commit fornication, saying that they are engaged and that their parents already know them. Some are carrying out abortions, thinking it is the only way out. Some people have sicknesses that have been resisting medicine, while many have incurable diseases. Many people are sad without reason; many are secretly committing sin. Some pretend not to take alcohol but drink Dubonnet or Guinness, saying that it is a wine or tonic or that they are taking it for the sake of their stomach. Some people drink alcohol or smoke cigarettes in secret and then lick peppermint, or other minted sweet to cover up the odour.

All these explain why many people are powerless and are constantly bombarded by satanic forces, when they are supposed to be doing exploits for the Lord. That is why some sisters go to pastors for counseling but end up having sex with them. You might wonder how that could be possible. Do not forget that the gift and calling of God are without repentance; God does not withdraw His gifts from His children just like that. That is why a pastor could have backslidden, but miracles could still happen when he prays; these gifts will stand against him on the Day of Judgment. Spiritual gifts are not a ticket to heaven; it is holiness that is required, after accepting the Lord Jesus Christ into one's life. There are some pastors who fall prey to some ladies who come under the guise of having problems, but end up seducing them. Sometimes, they are able to control the situation but sometimes, they fall a prey, especially after seeing signs of unseriousness in the ladies. Such people have to repent and seek deliverance today.

Many people are poor today because they find it difficult to part with their money or to give towards the work of God. As Christians, our hearts should be like that of the sheep; broken, humble, corrigible. When the Lord decides to use us, we should see ourselves as nothing, but servants of the Lord, and submit our totality to Him. No matter what your educational level is, no matter how rich you are, no matter which post you occupy in the household of God or anywhere else; you should see yourself as nothing before the Lord. The Bible says that we should not let our actions make our brethren to stumble. Some people have backslidden today because: they were disappointed in the actions of their spiritual leaders. The Bible says that the blood of such people will be required of those leaders; even the Bible also says that nobody has an excuse for falling.

One day, we had a prayer meeting scheduled for 5pm. I got there at 5.35 pm. As I was alighting from my car, a neatly dressed man in a three-piece suit, looking sternly, approached me and said: "Dr. you are late; this meeting was scheduled for 5p.m, that is not good enough." I said: "I am sorry sir, it will not repeat itself." The man said: "That's better." And walked away. Later I was surprised to hear him testify to the fact that he was encouraged by my reply, that I did not ask if he knew that I was the PASTOR-IN-CHARGE, OR GENERAL OVERSEER. This means he would have been disappointed, if I had answered him in an unfriendly or haughty manner. We should surrender every area of our lives to the Lord.

Take this prayer point as we proceed:
* *I shall not cause my brother to stumble in the name of Jesus. Amen.*

Some people have problems, but feel too proud to share it with other brethren. They do not want to look for help where they know it can be found. Sometimes, when I tell some people to go for deliverance, they feel insulted. They remind me of their religious background. They say: "God forbid..." Therefore instead of commanding the strangers in their lives to come out of their hiding places and fade away, they leave them there. They do not know or cannot understand that when Jesus saw that people were buying and selling in the Temple, He chased them out. He made them to understand that His Father's house is not meant for buying and selling. Today you must do likewise; you must chase out the traders in your own life and you must be violent about it. Beloved, this is because there is no nice way of cleaning a toilet; you have to scrub hard on the dirt and use powerful a detergent to make it clean.

Man is a spirit that lives in a body and has a soul. All these parts that make up Man, if not yielded totally to God, will harbour strangers. The love of money is a stranger. The rich people want to accumulate more wealth; the poor thinks that as soon as they have money, their problems will be over. The rich and the poor are running after money. They refuse to yield that aspect of their lives to God. Today you must really declare that certain things should run out of your life and not follow you about again. Through the prayers I am proposing below, I want you to attack the foreigners and strangers inhabiting the parts of your life. Pray these prayers to scare the enemies and to chase them out of their hiding places. You must pray till you know that something has happened to you.

Psalm 18:44-45 says,
"As soon as they hear of me, they shall obey me: the strangers shall submit themselves unto me. The strangers shall fade away, and be afraid out of their close places."

The spirit of the goat opens doors to the enemy and prevents people from entering the Kingdom of God. Do you know that ordinary headache sometimes, could be a stranger? At that point, all you need to do is speak to it, and it will flee. Sometimes, it could behave as if it is dumb; you have to be violent with such things and address them the way they should be addressed.

Zacchariah 10:3 says this;
"Mine anger was kindled against the shepherds, and I punished the goats: for the Lord of hosts hath visited his flock the house of Judah, and hath made them as his goodly horse in the battle."

Beloved, for how long do you want to allow the goatish spirit to rule your life? For how long do you want to run the ship of your life by yourself? You know that you have been doing it your own way and it has not helped you in any way. The Lord is calling you today and wants to get you out of your confusion. Come out of your sinful ways and be cleansed by the Blood of the Lamb. I want to assure you that you have not picked this bulletin in vain; the Lord has a purpose for your life. It is only the power in the Blood of Jesus that can set you free from the goatish spirit and make you a sheep. The Lord is ready to break chains, demolish cages and to touch your life in a new way. Do not feed the strangers in your life.

Many people go to church, read the Bible, read Christian literature by different pastors, read books on brokenness, on how to be on fire for God, etc. but unfortunately, they still fall back into sin. It means something went wrong somewhere. There are many people who speak in tongues but there is no power. It is a pity to find out that many Christians who are supposed to be prevailers and should be able to move God to do things, are not who people think they are. They who are supposed to pursue the enemy are being suppressed by the enemy. If you will get angry in your spirit today and decide that something good must happen, then it will happen. How can a person be speaking in tongues and still be a liar or fornicator or thief? The tongues will be powerless. That is not the Holy Spirit; such people have to reorganise their thinking.

It is frightening to note that, most people who say that they have received the baptism in the Holy Spirit do not receive the genuine one. Drinking half a cup of water is different from drinking a full one. When a person is thirsty and you give him a teaspoonful of water, you have just encouraged him to salivate and the thirst cannot be quenched that way. If you give another person who is thirsty three bottles of water, he will drink to his satisfaction and the thirst will disappear. Water touched the tongues of both people but the thirst of only one is quenched. The baptism of many people can be likened to a teaspoon of water in the throat of a thirsty person. If you will cry unto the Lord today to fill you with His power, He will do it, right there where you are. He will fill you to the brim. The Bible says, *"Ask and ye shall receive."* It means that if you do not ask, you are not likely to receive. When people are not genuinely "baptised in the Holy Spirit, they go into terrible things and many things that are not supposed to walk about in the garden of their lives, will be there. The fire that is supposed to destroy every evil power around your life will not be there if you are not genuinely baptised in the Holy Ghost; the energy that some people are supposed to use in getting the power of the Holy Ghost is what they spend on complaints. They go from place to place, seeking help instead of sitting down and receiving the power of God personally, and the enemy knows that they are only wasting their time. John the Baptist said:

Matthew 3:11;
"I indeed baptize you with water unto repentance: but he that cometh after me is mightier than I, whose shoes I am not worthy to bear: He shall baptize you with the Holy Ghost and with fire."

Beloved, you cannot see the Lord, if you are still a goat; you have to surrender your totality to Him. This means that you have to decide to be born-again. All you need do is repent of your sins, confess them to the Lord, ask Him to forgive you. Name those sins one by one renounce them and ask God to cleanse you of all unrighteousness. Claim the redemptive power in the Blood of Jesus that was shed on the Cross at Calvary, for the remission of your sins and say goodbye to the world of sin and the devil. Open your heart and ask the Lord Jesus Christ to come into your life. Ask Him to become your personal Lord and Saviour. Enthrone Him over your life and hand over all that concerns you to Him, and let Him take over all that concerns you.

If you have just taken this decision, I congratulate you. It is the most important decision in life. I pray that it shall be permanent in your life in the name of Jesus. I pray that the Lord will write your name in the Book of life and you will not by any means, rub it off in the name of Jesus. I also pray that the Lord will keep your feet from falling in the name of Jesus.

CONFESSION:
I would urge you to declare these words aloud, with determination in your heart:
The Lord will bless and keep me, He will make His face to shine upon me and give me peace, and be gracious unto me. Blessed shall I be in the city, blessed shall I be in the land; blessed shall be the fruit of my body and the fruit of my land and of my cattle and of my sheep. Blessed am I when I go out and when 1 come in.

Beloved, I counsel you to take the under listed prayer points with determination in your spirit and with aggression against the kingdom of the devil:

1. All unprofitable strangers in my life, I command you to flee away! in the name of Jesus.
2. Heavenly surgeons, remove contrary things from my life, in the name of Jesus.
3. Every lust in my flesh, be roasted by the Holy Ghost fire! in the mighty name of Jesus.
4. Every pride of life over my spiritual life, die by fire! in the name of Jesus.
5. Satan shall not harvest me in hell-fire, in the mighty name of Jesus.
6. Anointing of the Holy Spirit, always fall upon me, in the name of Jesus.
7. Everything God has not planted in my life, be uprooted by fire! in the name of Jesus.
8. The sweetness of sin in my life, dry up and die! in the name of Jesus.
9. Let the Spirit of the living God, overhaul my spirit, soul and body, in the name of Jesus.
10. Let God arise, and scatter every power that is planting unprofitable strangers into my life, in the name of Jesus.
11. Whatsoever wants to stop me from being a source of blessing, be roasted! in the name of Jesus.
12. Let the fire of the Holy Ghost begin to burn in every department of my life, in the name of Jesus.
13. Let every spirit of Egypt, fall after the order of Pharaoh! in the name of Jesus.
14. Let every spirit of Herod, be disgraced! in the name of Jesus.
15. Let every spirit of

Goliath, receive the stones of fire! in the name of Jesus.
16. Let every spirit of Pharaoh, fall into the Red Sea of its own making, in the name of Jesus.
17. Every spirit of rebellion in my life, jump out and die! in the name of Jesus.
18. My life, receive the touch of fire and explode for God, in the name of Jesus.
19. Angel of the living God, as you touched the lips of Elijah, touch my lips today so that my mouth can carry power, in Jesus' name.
20. Let all satanic manipulations, aimed at changing my destiny, be frustrated! in the name of Jesus.
21. Holy Ghost fire, burn, from my heart unto my tongue in the name of Jesus.
22. Anything in my life dragging me to hell fire little by little, catch fire by fire, in the name of Jesus.
23. I receive the spirit that is always interested in the things of heaven, in the name of Jesus.

Thank God for answering your prayers in the name of Jesus.

The Power Of The Sheep

Vol. 6. No. 32

Matthew 10:16: *"Behold, I send you forth as sheep in the midst of wolves: be ye therefore wise as serpents, and harmless as doves."*

Verse 28:
"And fear not them which kill the body, but are not able to kill the soul: but rather fear him which is able to destroy both soul and body in hell

God wants us to be His sheep. As sheep, we are supposed to operate in the midst of fierce, aggressive, senseless animals like wolves. A wolf is a carnivorous animal, which means that, it can eat up the sheep; the sheep has to go into the midst of many of them and operate there. For the sheep to be able to do that, there has to be something in it that will either shield it, or scare away the wolves. In the text above, Jesus says we should not entertain fear at all. We should not entertain fear for anything or happenings around us. The only one that we should fear is God Himself; He is the One who is able to cast the body and the soul of a person, into hell fire. Those who fear death, sickness, poverty, do not know the God they are serving.

THE SHEEP
It is a simple, dumb, stupid, unintelligent animal. It goes where the shepherd directs it. It recognises the voice of the shepherd and does not listen to strange voices. A sheep cohabits with other sheep without fighting. A true sheep does not jump over the fence. It is more difficult to deal with one goat than to deal with twenty sheep. The energy that you will spend trying to put one goat under control can be spent on 100 sheep without any problem. If you see a sheep jumping over a fence, look closely; it is likely to be a goat in sheep's clothing.

A sheep does not feed on just anything; it eats good food, unlike the goat, dog or pig that can eat just anything; even rotten human food. God does not want those who are clever in their own eyes and are independent of Him.

The enemy takes advantage of those who think they are clever and wise in their own eyes. Some people even claim to be kinder than Jesus and know the Bible more than Him. In the church today, there are many who look pious, go about like gentlemen and women, but are rotten internally. Many Christian devour anything; they read anything that comes their way, they claim to want to widen their knowledge in order to evangelise. This is wrong; what you need for evangelism is the word of God and the demonstration of His power. It is by the spirit of God, that sinners are convicted, when they hear the word of God.

Matthew 11:25;
"At that time Jesus answered and said, I thank thee, O Father, Lord of heaven and earth, because thou hast hid these things from the wise and prudent, and hast revealed them unto babes."

ICorinthians 1:26-29;
"For ye see your calling, brethren, how that not many wise men after the flesh, not many mighty, not many noble, are called: but God hath chosen the foolish things of the world to confound the wise; and God hath chosen the weak things of the world to confound the things which are mighty; and base things of the world and things which are despised, hath God chosen, yea, and things which are not, to bring to nought things that are; that no flesh should glory in his presence"

The above text shows us that, God is the One Who calls people, no matter what their status is. He does not pick people by their might or intelligence or knowledge. If you are educated and you come to Him, all is well and good. The disciples were unlettered men but they turned the whole city upside down for Jesus. They were accused of turning Jerusalem upside down and filling the whole place with their teachings. Even when they were brought before the Sanhedrin, the highest ruling body at that time, which was made up of learned men who could quote the Scriptures off heart, the disciples were not afraid of them. God is not waiting for lettered men, but if you are and you come to Him, He will use you. He wants us to be like babies, who will depend on Him. trust Him and obey Him. God wants us to be like sheep that do not know anything, which is obedient and simple. The Gospel is simple: it is human beings that have made it to look complicated. They have turned it into a religion of robes, caps. candles, incenses and decorated altars.

Isaiah 5:21 says;
"Woe unto them that are wise in their own eyes, and prudent in their own sight!" While the Psalmist cried out in Psalm 131:1 saying:
"Lord, my heart is not haughty, nor mine eyes lofty: neither do I exercise myself in great matters or in things too high for me."

Simple people do not have high tastes. They are like the Lord Jesus Christ-that was moving about amongst simple people, the sick, and was accused by His critics of being friends with sinners. It is difficult to understand why a person who earns N5,000 should buy a pair of shoes that costs N2,500 and would pay over two months. Why does he not buy a pair that is cheaper'? Why should a person buy clothes on credit, when he or she has clothes at home, that he or she could wash, iron and wear? Certainly, God does not want us to wear dirty clothes or rags, but He does not want us to owe people money either. Some people are looking for 'class'; they forget that it all ends as soon as they die. It does not matter where a person is buried, who attended the funeral, who conducted the service, the soul is gone and is already facing judgment. Some people see us as not being 'fashionable', they forget that it all ends in this world. Many Christians these days, cannot live peaceably with fellow Christians. They devour each other, which means, either one of them or both parties are not sheep. Since you cannot bite yourself, you should not get offended by the actions of other people. Many Christians gossip and backbite, thereby becoming a mouthpiece for the devil; if a person comes to recount stories about another person and you listen and entertain the ideas, you too have become a collection depot for the enemy's letters. A sheep will always heed a call to service. A 'Sheep for Jesus' will always heed the call to go out for evangelism and would always go for prayer meetings. The sheep will always take to correction and will not think that the preacher is talking about him or her in order to spite him or her.

I was invited to preach in a church and as the service ended. I saw some ushers struggling to hold a woman back from addressing me she had removed her head-gear and tied it round her waist. She said I preached about her, that someone had gone to talk to me about her. As I approached her, I said 'Madam, please do not beat me up, then she started to cry.

In MFM, we lay emphasis on 'brokenness.' Many members are managing directors of reputable companies but they obey simple instructions from ushers in the church, who themselves could be managing directors in their own companies too. Christians should understand the fact that their wealth, certificates, medals, fame, all end here on earth. If we are what the Lord wants us to be, our lives will be better off. The language and vocabulary of God is different from ours; when Man says something is hopeless, God says there is hope. Man talks about time, night, years and so on. The Bible says that a thousand years in the eyes of Man, is like one day before God. That is why on the judgment day, some people will be wondering when the proceedings will end; they will just find out that it never gets dark because there is no night there. Jesus Himself is the light and I know that I will be with Him on that glorious day. It is on, earth that we talk about time and season. It is here that we talk about transport and transportation.

LANGUAGES:
The Bible shows us the different kinds of languages that exist:
1. **THE LANGUAGE OF GOD:**
It is filled with absolute power and authority, glory, might, faith and love.

2. **THE LANGUAGE OF ANGELS:**
It is filled with delegated power from God. They say what God asks them to say; they do not waste words. They are always specific and direct. Their language is filled with absolute obedience and commitment to God. Once an angel does not want to tell you his name, it means it is not part of the assignment given him by God. The angels of God could be mean. When the Israelites were going to possess their land, there was an angel that accompanied them and God told them that they should make sure that they did not offend him, because if they did, he would not pardon them.

3. **THE LANGUAGE OF THE NATURAL MAN:**
It is filled with negative things, fear, doubt, poverty, confusion, hatred, envy, hopelessness, sin and death.

4. **THE LANGUAGE OF THE DEVIL:**
It is filled with lies, deception, woes, destruction, death. His diction is carefully selected from the pit of hell.

5. **THE LANGUAGE OF THE WOLF:**
It is that of defeat, debt and impossibility.

6. **THE LANGUAGE OF THE SHEEP:**
It is filled with godliness, faith, power, authority, love and holiness.

Beloved, which language do you speak? Are you one of those who say: "What will be, will be; that there is nothing anyone can do about it"? Is your language that of the God Who created you? Or is it that of the devil or of the natural Man where there is failure and death? When Jesus was informed about a child's death, He told them that the child was sleeping. The people around laughed at Him, they must have thought He was mad or that something was wrong with Him. No wonder He drove them out as He was about to pray for the child and of course, the child woke up.

Exercising the power of the Sheep:
1. **Re-Adjusting Your Vocabulary.**
The language of the natural Man that you were speaking before you came to the saving knowledge of the Lord Jesus Christ must be dropped. Put into practice, the word of God. See your situation from God's angle.

Matthew 17:20:
"And Jesus said unto them, Because of your unbelief: for verily I say unto you: "If ye have faith as a grain of mustard seed, ye shall say unto this mountain: "Remove hence to yonder place and it sit all remove; and nothing shall be impossible unto you."

Right there where you are, I want you to say to yourself that: "Nothing shall be impossible unto me"
(Say it ten times). This verse is showing us that, no matter how a situation looks, no matter how terrible it might have been described. God is the One that has the final say on it; and with Him, nothing shall be impossible. If you as a sheep, use the language of defeat, then, you are the one spoiling things by cooperating with the enemy. You should not join those who say they do not know where this country is heading to. Do not use your anointed mouth to worsen the situation of the country by making negative pronouncements on the leadership, or the way things are going on. What you should do is to nullify the negative things that unbelievers are saying. You have only one country and you should not run it down with your mouth. When the sheep goes amongst the wolves, its language is that of optimism; that of faith that, "although I am in the midst of danger, I am indestructible." "Although I look small and feeble, GREATER IS HE - that is in me, than he that is in the world." "Although I walk through the valley of the shadow of death. I will fear no evil, for **THE LORD IS WITH ME.**"

Matthew 19:26:
"But Jesus beheld them, and said unto them: "With men this is impossible; but with God all things are possible."
Luke 1:37; *"For with God nothing shall be impossible."*
Luke 18:27;
"And He said: "The things which are impossible with men are possible with God."

The problem with many people is the fact that, they see things with their physical eyes. What you should do as a Christian, is to close your physical eyes and open the spiritual ones and you will behold the goodness of the Lord and everything will be possible unto you.

John 14:14;
"If ye shall ask anything in My name, I will do it."

The language of the sheep is absolute. There is no limit. Today you must operate like a sheep; you must command blindness into the eyes of your doubts. Pray that your eyes of faith will start to see and you will see the solution, not the problem so that you can see the possibilities, not the difficulties; so that you can see the way out and not the prison walls; so that you can see the limitless power of God and not the narrow vision of men. You have to retire from the school of limiting God and have to believe that God does not lie. The Bible says in Numbers 23:19 *God is not a man, that he should lie; neither the son of man, that he should repent: hath he said, and shall he not do it? or hath he spoken and shall he not make it good?"*

Matthew 10:16;
"Behold, I send you forth as sheep in the midst of wolves: be ye therefore wise as serpents, and harmless as doves."

This means that, in the house you are living in or in your place of work or in the church, you are likely to be in the midst of wolves. You have to be as wise as a serpent and as gentle as a dove. What is the wisdom of the serpent? It is to bite and hide whereas the gentility of the dove is that, it runs away instead of fighting back.

Take these prayer points with determination in your heart:
* Lord, magnify Yourself in my life, in the name of Jesus.
* Lord, advertise Your power in my life, in the name of Jesus.
* I will decrease and God will increase in my life, in the name of Jesus.

Compare the following situations.
Mark 9:22;
"And oftentimes it hath cast him into the fire, and into the waters, to destroy him: but if Thou canst do any thing, have compassion on us, and help us."

Mark 9:23:
"Jesus said unto him: "If thou canst believe, all things are possible to him that believeth."

If you examine the words of the man talking in the first text, you will note that he was negating his purpose of coming to the Lord for help. That was why Jesus said if he could believe, it would be possible. This means that, unbelief on his part would have hindered his son's miracle. Thank God he cried out in the next verse, that he believed.

Mark 9:24;
"And straightway the father of the child cried out, and said with tears: "Lord, I believe; help Thou mine unbelief."

The defeat of the sheep comes from his mouth. After praying hot prayers, some people negate them with their mouth.
John 11:21-26;
"Then said Martha unto Jesus "Lord, if Thou hadst been here, my brother had not died. But I know, that even now, whatsoever Thou wilt ask of God, God will give it Thee. Jesus saith unto her "Thy brother shall rise again". Martha saith unto Him: "I know that he shall rise again in the resurrection at the last day". Jesus said unto her: "I am the resurrection, and the life, he that believeth in me, though he were dead, yet shall he live: And whosoever liveth and believeth in me shall never die. Believest thou this?"

Verses 39-40:
Jesus said: *"Take ye away the stone." Martha, the sister of him that was dead, saith unto Him: "Lord, by this time he stinketh; for he hath been dead four days." Jesus saith unto her: "Said I not unto thee, that, if thou wouldest believe, thou shouldest see the glory of God?*

In the first text. Martha affirmed that God could raise her brother from death, Jesus asked. In the second text, she was negating it by asking Jesus not to bother, because Lazarus had been dead for four days.
Luke 8:49-50:
"While he yet spake, there cometh one from the ruler of the synagogue's house, saying to him: "Thy daughter is dead; trouble not the Master." But when Jesus heard it, He answered him, saying: "Fear not believe only, and she shall be made

whole."

A neighbour was going to negate the initial belief or the ruler, that Jesus would heal his daughter. Jesus Himself countered the negative statement by reassuring the man that his daughter would be made whole.

John 5:5-8;
"And a certain man was there, which had an infirmity thirty and eight years. When Jesus saw him lie, and knew that he had been now a long time in that case, He saith unto him: "Wilt thou be made whole?" The impotent man answered Him: "Sir, I have no man, when the water is troubled, to put me into the pool: but while I am coming, another steppeth down before me." Jesus saith unto him: "Rise, take up thy bed, and walk.

This man was face to face with the Great Physician and he was still telling stories about getting into the pool. He would have missed out on his miracle, if he had continued that way.

Beloved I hope you have learnt something from these situations in the Bible. I hope you can see the differences in the language of the different people concerning their situations. It is the devil that puts a lid on the mind of Man. How could a person believe that what the doctors are saying is truer than what the creator Himself has said? Do you know that there are thousands of things that medical experts do not understand concerning the human body? How could you insult the creator of heaven and earth, by saying that certain things are impossible, difficult, and hopeless? You must retire from the school of impossibility and of limiting God. God will work in the life of the sheep. One of the awesome powers that He has given us is the power of agreement; it can move mountains.

Matthew 18:19;
"Again I say unto you, that if two of you shall agree on earth as touching anything that they shall ask, it shall be done for them of my Father which is in heaven."

The power of agreement can change any situation. God has delegated His power to the body of Christ and when they come together, they are immovable. United prayers are very powerful, but it is unfortunate to note that sometimes, there are doubters and sinners in the midst. However, when two people who are sheep, live a holy life and they confirm that a thing is the will of God, they have faith and they come in agreement to pray about that thing, the Bible says it shall be done. If a person is watching a bird, with the aim of killing or catching it, there is a possibility of it escaping. However, if 100 people watch and aim at the same bird, it has to be extra-smart and clever, to be able to escape. That is the power of agreement. The Bible says: *"One will chase one thousand and two will chase ten thousand, therefore, two is better than one."*

Here are some prayers that I would suggest that you pray in agreement with at least, one person. They are prayers that can bind, loose, lock up, claim, destroy, bruise and paralyse the works of the enemy. 1 Timothy 6:12 advises us thus; **"Fight the good fight of faith, lay hold on eternal life, whereunto thou art also called, and hast professed a good profession before many witnesses."**

Take these prayer points in agreement, according to the word of God which says: **"If two of you shall agree concerning a thing, it shall be done unto you."**

1. Let God arise and let my enemies scatter! in the name of Jesus.
2. You (name of prayer partner) receive the desires of your heart, in the name of Jesus.
3. You household wickedness, lose your hold upon my life and that of my partner! in the name of Jesus.
4. Every internal warfare in my life, be quenched! in the name of Jesus.
5. Every internal thief, be exposed! in the name of Jesus.
6. Anything planted in my life by my enemies, come out with all your roots! in the name of Jesus.
7. Every inherited battle in my life, die! in the name of Jesus.
8. Let every evil imagination against me, wither away from

the root! in the name of Jesus.
9. Lord, begin to clean away from my life, all that does not reflect You, in the name of Jesus.
10. You the spirit of deceit, hiding in my life, come out and die! in the name of Jesus.
11. The power to be obedient. even unto death, fall upon my life! in the name of Jesus.
12. Holy Spirit fire, ignite me to the glory of God, in the name of Jesus.
13. My Father, deliver me from myself, in the name of Jesus.
14. Lord, do not let the cares of this world, make me loose the mark, in the name of Jesus.
15. The spirit to be heavenly minded, fall upon my life! in the name of Jesus.
16. Every 'goatish' spirit, warring with the spirit of God for my life, release me and die in the name of Jesus.
17. God of deliverance, deliver me from hellfire, in the name of Jesus.
18. Every power that wants me to loose my heavenly candidature, die in the name of Jesus.
19. Any portion that I have in hellfire blood of Jesus, buy me back in Jesus name.
20. Let the seal of the Blood of Jesus, fall upon these prayers, in the name of Jesus.

Thank God for the miracles he has done in your life during this prayer session.

The Dead Garden

Vol. 6. No. 33

In Ezekiel 33:31-32 God made this bitter statement about the rebellious house of Israel:

"And they come unto thee as the people cometh, and they sit before thee as my people, and they hear thy words, but they will not do them: for with their mouth they shew much love, but their heart goeth after their covetousness. And, lo, thou art unto them as a very lovely song of one that hath a pleasant voice, and can play well on an instrument: for they hear thy words, but they do them not."

Matthew 13:20-21;

"But he that received the seed into stony places, the same is he that heareth the word, and anon with joy receiveth it. Yet hath he not root in himself, but edureth for a while; for when tribulation or persecution ariseth because of the word, by and by he is offended."

Naturally, if you throw a seed inside the soil, it should grow. However, if the enemy has already mixed cement with the soil, the seed will not grow because it will become concrete when it comes in contact with water. These two passages tells, us the characteristics of a dead garden. The life of Man is like a garden, in which God wants to plant the seeds of blessing. There is nothing wrong with God's seeds, but some gardens are dead and they cannot grow what God wants them to grow.

When we talk about divine blessings, there are always four groups of people:
1. **Those who will not see the blessings.**
2. **Those who see the blessings but will not have any.**
3. **Those who have the blessing but cannot hold it; i.e it slips off their hand and they lose it.**
4. **Those who see it, have it and hold it.**

This is where the seriousness of the matter comes in. Beloved, I had better sound this note of warning before you go on; if you are not interested in aggressive praying, you had better not read this message. Most Nigerians fall into the third category (those with holes in their pockets).

People in this country are very intelligent; they have a lot of fantastic ideas and are very smart. By the time a law is drafted, the Nigerian would have found a way of going around it. The main problem here therefore, is not the problem of not starting a good thing, but that of starting and maintaining it. The anti-maintenance spirit is a curse and it has to be broken. Many people find it difficult or impossible to maintain a good thing for a long time. Some people find it easier to manage failure than success. If some people tell you the amount of money that has passed through their hands, you will be shocked. Today, they have nothing; the anti-maintenance spirit came in and so, they could not maintain their wealth. What I am trying to put across goes across everything; physical or spiritual.

Many years ago, a man came to see me for counsel. His face looked very familiar and when he mentioned his name, I was shocked. He was a very rich man and a musician sang his praises. In the primary school then, although we did not know him, we knew his name and the song. There he was before me. shabbily dressed; he had bathroom slippers on and had no money for food or transport back home. Here was someone who was 'swimming' in money in those days. This is a big problem and it is rampant here amongst the black people. The average Black Man does not know how to plan things. It is because of the anti-maintenance spirits; that keep many people away from greatness.

There was a mad man, who could play the mouth organ very well and could even blow it with his nostrils. He was also good in mathematics, if you asked any question, he would answer correctly. He could even give equations and logarithms and anti-logs of those things offhand. This was an intelligent man, but the enemy had turned him into a mad man and he was living in the streets. He was not useful to himself or to the society and not to God. That is the work of anti-maintenance spirits. These are the spirits that I would like you to identify today and I would like you to pray seriously about them.

Many ladies got married but are now without husband because they could not maintain the marriage. Some people received the baptism in the Holy Spirit, but today, the power is no longer in them. Many people come across money, but these spirits that energises the dead garden, have taken over.

John 3:27;
"John answered and said, A man can receive nothing, except it be given him from heaven."

This is an amazing verse and I would like you to pay attention to it, so that you would know what to do. This verse is telling us that there are two sources of receiving things; from heaven or from earth, from above or from below. The one that will last is the one you receive from heaven. The one you got on earth is for you, you have it, but you did not receive it from God and it will not last. That is why some people become poor after giving their lives to Christ and become serious with Him. God drains them of the ill-gotten wealth which is fake blessing, so that He could give them genuine blessings.

There are some group of spirits which are enemies of Man and they are:
1. Distributors of Counterfeit Blessings.
They give gifts to people in order to destroy them. They are blessings that will not last because they are mixed with impurity. There are many blessings like that in the lives of many people. This is why you should pray aggressively before you inherit anything from anyone or take charge of it. Questions must be asked on the source of the money used in purchasing or constructing the inheritance; where it came from, what it was used for etc. A single polluted thing that you inherit could spoil or hinder several others in your hands.

A man of God inherited several houses from his mother and let them out on rent. He then found out that immediately he started to collect rent on these houses, his finances went down the drain. He then started to ask God questions and God told him that the houses were built with polluted money and he was joining it to the money that God gave him. You cannot bless whom God has cursed. If the source of your money or inheritance is unclean, I pray that God will have mercy on you because such blessings will not be permanent and could even kill. If the money came through bribes or robbery or stealing, prostitution, cheating deception, oppression of the poor etc, it will bring trouble. The blessing that comes from such money will be as slippery as an electric fish.

God will have mercy upon children that were trained with such money because, they will become unprofitable unless God have mercy on them. Investigate the source of the blessings that you have. If it is unclean, make restitution so that the distributors of counterfeit things will not catch up with you.

Right there where you are, pray like this:
* **I refuse to accept counterfeit blessings, in the name of Jesus.**

Beloved, how did you get your husband or wife? How did you conceive your children? Where did you get the money with which you constructed your house or bought your car? What about your certificate, did you really study hard to obtain it or you cheated? That wealth, is it from God? Do not think you can bribe God with tithes and offerings. If your wealth is polluted, it is not acceptable before God. Perhaps the foundation of your blessing needs purging by the fire of God: allow it to burn, so that you can get God's blessing. If you obtained your husband through the use of charms when the competition was keen, do not be surprised that he is now gone with another woman. If you constructed your house with bloody money, do not be surprised that strange things are happening there now. You have to call on God to purge the foundation of these things, with His fire.

2. The Evil Mixers.
Proverbs 10:22 says this;
"The blessing of the Lord, it maketh rich, and He addeth no sorrow with it."

The evil mixers add sorrow and grief to blessings, making it difficult to maintain. Evil powers give things to people and it brings trouble. They make people sign in for trouble. A man thought he had spent too much time being poor; so he went to money-makers. He was asked to bring a cock and that the number of grains that the cock ate, would be the number of years that the man would spend being rich and then die. The cock ate three grains and stopped; the man could not do anything to make it eat more. He actually became rich but he got sorrow with it.

If a person like that goes to a hungry prophet to pray for him before the expiration of the timing he had signed for, nothing will happen. He will then conclude that there is no power in the church. Whereas, nobody forced him to make the covenant, neither did anyone hinder his cock from swallowing more grains.

Pray like this:
* **Let sorrow depart from my blessings, in the name of Jesus.**

The aim of this message is to let you know that, the wealth of the Gentiles that God talked about, is due for possession by the children of God, that is the rightful owners. It is time to put an end to the subjection of the children of God to evil people because they are poor. It is a shame to pay your house rent to a herbalist; you ought to have your own house. It is time for a change. These are the powers that are hindering many people. It is not that you were not made to be great, but there are some factors that have to be cut off and you will be surprised at the result.

3. The Spirit Of The Tail.
Deuteronomy 28:13 promises that;
"And the Lord shall make thee the head, and not the tail; and thou shall be above only, and thou shalt not be beneath; if that thou hearken unto the commandments of the Lord thy God, which I command thee this day, to observe and to do them."

The tail is close to the anus, which is the passage for defecation. It has no defence, no teeth like the mouth. It can be cut off from an animal, without any serious consequence. If the head of an animal is cut off, it will die. That is why some people just leave their place of work and nobody feel their absence. The way God has made Christians is such that, if anyone dare remove you from your place of work unrighteously, your absence there should create restlessness in the place. **If you are given the sack and nobody feel your absence, it means something is wrong with you; you are not where God wants you to be and that is the spirit of the tail.**

If a person, who has the spirit of the tail is exalted, the person will be brought down because the spirit and nature of the tail is in his life. It could be that the day meant for the promotion of that person, is when someone will lay allegations against him or her and that will hinder the promotion. One day, during a wedding ceremony, the priest got to the point where the question is asked that, if anyone had any reason for which the man and woman should not be joined in holy wedlock according to the ordinances of God, the person should come out and say it or be silent forever. Usually, the address is a formality and no one expected anyone to have anything against it. However, on that day, a woman raised her hand and came out with a baby strapped on her back. She asked the congregation to look at the face of her baby and that of the man and see the resemblance. The man said he did not intend to marry her, that she just got impregnated by him. The woman said if she was good enough for the bed, she was good enough for the altar. Meanwhile, the bride had fainted and her mother was already fuming and getting ready for a fight. The priest had to terminate the ceremony. There was confusion and the guests left in sorrow. Everything that was prepared for the reception, wasted.

You might think that it is was wickedness or coincidence, but it was actually the spirit of the tail that was working against the bride; that she would never get married. She had a Masters Degree in

English Language from a reputable university, but the spirit still caught up with her at the dire minute. If there had been no complaint on that day, she would have been married.

Think about it beloved, so that you will know how to cry to the Lord today. The spirit of the tail is not our lot; that is what the Bible says in Deuteronomy 28:13. If you find out that you are always below and when you sit for an examination, you always get low marks, you should know that the spirit of the tail is against you and that is not your lot.

4. Household Enemies.
They carry out their mission in different ways; they have limited the progress of many people in life. They cause sicknesses that takes away money, cause dismissal for a person where he or she has the chance of advancement. They put the mark of hatred and rejection on a person or remove the memory of a person and cause confusion in his or her life. There is a Chinese adage that says: **"God, save me from my friends, and I will take care of my enemies."** The believer must be careful about these things and must know how to pray. The more unbelievers in a family, the more trouble they create; no matter how nice they are.

5 Wrong Placement.
Operating in the wrong position. When a person is in the wrong job, he or she will not be open to God's blessings. No fish can get blessings outside water. You cannot harvest maize from a mango tree. You cannot prosper in the thing that the Lord does not want you to do. When you get to the right place and you begin to pray, abundance will be your lot. Many traders are working in offices. Many gospel musicians are doing typing and shorthand. Many pilots are driving cars. Find out what God wants you to do and you will see His blessings, flow. Whatever spirit keeps you away from finding the right place, is something that you should not play with at all, because it knows that if you leave the pattern God wants for you, you will be in trouble as God will not bless what He does not support.

6. Unprofitable Friends.
If you are a student and you move about with people who fail, you too will fail. If your friends are at the bottom, you too will be there. If they are not filled with the Spirit of God, you too will not be filled. If you move about with discouraged people, you will be discouraged. Once these things are there, you have unfriendly, unprofitable friends, friends that you are afraid to tell the truth, friends who will do things that are anti-God and you just smile, then you are planting in a dead garden. If you pick an enemy of God and go into business with him or her and you are praying for breakthroughs, you are planting in a dead garden. If that friend is under God's curse, you cannot bless him and you cannot be blessed, until you do what God wants you to do. If you have no other business partner than an unbeliever, it is better to be a lone-ranger. No matter how much you pray in a business venture like that, it will not work because, you have an unfriendly friend, an unprofitable collaborator.

7. Powers of The Emptiers.
Nahum 2:2;
"For the LORD hath turned away the excellency of Jacob, as the excellency of Israel: for the emptiers have emptied them out, and marred their vine branches."

These are some of the most powerful anti-progress forces. They do not disturb people from working hard and amassing things, they will wait until the cup is full, then they will empty it. They are the ones who change the heads of people.

Many years ago, we prayed for a boy who was a dullard at school. We prayed for a long time and one day, his younger sister confessed to witchcraft and said she and her mates in her witchcraft group had exchanged the brain of the boy with that of a goat. She said his real brain was in their bank in the third heavens. When asked to release it, she said she did not have that kind of power. The emptiers can only empty, they cannot refill. The boy was only delivered by the matchless power of the Lord Jesus Christ. These powers change the virtues of people and transfer their goodness.

If you have ever gone to a herbalist or fake prophet and

he or she asked you to have a special bath at the riverside or in a forest, what you have done is a transfer of your virtues. People transfer their virtues through the use of hair attachments and that is why we do not allow it on our deliverance grounds. The goodness of some girls have been transferred to 'sugar daddies' with whom they had sexual intercourse. Some poor men through sex, have captured the virtues of women that had good business potentials and the men became rich. They survey people and lure them into sexual relationships. There are people who really have business potentials, that is why it is possible for two people to display the same kind of goods, but one will sell more and faster than the other. In fact, the other one might not get anything sold until hers is finished. The virtues of some people have been captured through the use of demonic rings, perfumes, pomade or water that so called prophets 'prayed' on.

8. Curses.

They are supernatural negative words uttered against a person. They are the opposite of blessings. No curse should be taken lightly, no matter how jovially it was uttered. Anytime a negative word is uttered against you, you must reject and nullify it immediately. The person could be a Balaam lured to curse you. There are some evil utterances that have become cliches in a place like Lagos, where people would say: "God go punish you". "Your head is not correct" etc. Do not accept such utterances, nullify them immediately. The issue of curses is so serious that you might need to consecrate a day to the breaking of every evil utterances, issued against you since the time that you were in your mother's womb.

Prayerless and ignorant people go from pole to pole. For you to be completely cleansed from curses, you must repent of all form of disobedience. Many parents talk to their children in curses, they call them names like: "Good for nothing" and those words eventually work in the lives of the children, if not nullified. Many are doing really badly because of the curses issued against them by their parents, either consciously or unconsciously.

9. Comparison.

If you compare yourself with other people, you are working with their vision and that will create problems for you. Some parents have professions in mind that they want their children to pursue; because those professions are considered prestigious. This way, many have misled their children into doing what God did not ordain them for. Hardly would you find a parent that would wish that his or her child grow up to become an evangelist or pastor. Some even force their children into doing the course that the child does not want and is probably incompetent in, thereby making him or her a failure in life. They forget that God has a specific plan for each person in life. There is an example of someone in the Bible, who worked with someone else's clock but quickly repented, so as not to have problems. You must pursue God's plan for your life and not anyone's else.

10. Laziness.

It keeps a person permanently in the tail position, both spiritually and physically. A believer that has the spirit of slumber will never move to the top. A believer who is dependent on the alarm clock is in trouble. Those who are slack in God's work are also known to be slack in their own physical activities. Progress is far from lazy people. I would like you to think about these things. They are the factors that result in 'Dead Gardens.' Things land there, stay for a while, could even start sprouting, but after a while, stops growing and then dies.

Are you expecting a breakthrough in one thing or the other? Then pray the prayers that I am suggesting below with aggression. You will experience an overflowing of God's power in your life today. There is *a* difference between a bucket that is filled to the brim and overflowing with water, and the one that contains three drops of water. Would it not be wonderful for you to ask God for a Volkswagen beetle and He gives you a Rolls Royce? That is what we call overflowing. Would it not be wonderful to ask God for the gift of prophesy and He shower all the live gifts of the Holy Spirit upon you? That is an overflow of God's blessing and that is what you are going to ask Him for today.

A sister was looking unto God for a husband and I gave her some prayer points. After a few days, she took ill and it was so serious that she landed in the hospital and had an intravenous transfusion. She knew that it was an attack as a result of her prayers and so, she took the prayer points with her to the hospital and when she could, she prayed. A few months later, she had another problem; three men came to propose marriage to her. She had to start praying that God should help her make the right choice. Thank God for her stubbornness. It was a holy one like that of Jacob, who refused to let go on the angel of his blessing.

A brother needed a job and we prayed some breakthrough prayers. After a while, he got six letters of invitation to interviews from different companies. That was a better problem, which is, the one to choose from.

I would like you to get this fact straight. The enemy will only let go of what you forcefully recover from him. He will only yield as much ground as you are ready to take from him. Are you ready to revive your garden? If you are, you must get really aggressive as you reclaim your land from the enemy today. I would like you to ginger up yourself, so that you will pray the prayers below with all the aggression that you can gather. They are prayers that have fire in them. You have to battle these things, so that you will bring in testimonies of breakthroughs in many areas.

However, if you have not yet surrendered your life to the Lord Jesus Christ, you might not be able to make a meaning out of this message and the prayers. The starting point is the recognition of the fact that you are a sinner and that you cannot approach God in your sinful state. All you need to do is acknowledge the fact that you are a sinner and confess your sins to God. Name them one by one and ask Him to forgive you and cleanse you from all unrighteousness. Claim the redemptive power in the Blood of Jesus that was shed on the Cross at Calvary, for the remission of your sins. Renounce the world and the devil; say good-bye to them and make sure you do not go back to your sinful ways again. Invite the Lord Jesus into your life; ask Him to come in and become your personal Lord and Saviour. Surrender your totality to Him and ask Him to take absolute control of all that concerns you.

If you have taken this decision, I congratulate you. It is the most important decision in life and I pray that it shall be permanent in your life in the name of Jesus. I pray that the Lord will uphold you with His right hand of righteousness and will keep you from falling. I pray that He will write your name in the Book of Life and you will not by any means, rub it off in the name of Jesus

Take this prayer points with aggression in your spirit:
1. I break every placental bondage, in the name of Jesus.
2. I release myself from every serpentine spirit, in the name of Jesus.
3. Every evil family tree in my life, be uprooted! in the name of Jesus.
4. Every bondage of inherited sickness, be uprooted! in the name of Jesus.
5. You that strongman, delegated by the devil against me, die! in the name of Jesus.
6. Every triangle of darkness. operating in my father's house, die! in the Name of Jesus.
7. Every triangle of darkness, operating in my mother's house, die! in the Name of Jesus.
8. Anointing to go out completely for the Lord, fall upon me now! in the Name of Jesus.
9. Every idol of my father's house, your time is up, therefore, die! in the name of Jesus.
10. Every idol of my mother's house, your time is up, therefore, die! in the name of Jesus.
11. Every power delegated to waste my life, die! in the name of Jesus.
12. Anointing to go out completely for the Lord, fall upon me now in the name of Jesus.
13. You the garden of my life, receive fire, now! in the name of Jesus.
14. Every evil plantation in the garden of my life, be uprooted! in the name of Jesus.

The Old Pathway (1)

Proverbs 22:28; *"Remove not the ancient landmark, which thy fathers have set.*

The foundation of the Pentecostal Church can be traced back to the Acts of the Apostles. However, if you take a close look at the present day church and compare it with what you read in the Acts of the Apostles, you will find out that we are still joking and need to be more serious. There are some people who complain that Mountain of Fire and Miracles Ministries is too strict. Whereas, we have not yet attained the level of the Apostles and have not yet started to experience what they experienced. We shall experience the touch of power that was upon their lives. We shall experience a situation where ushers like Philip, Stephen, etc worked signs and wonders. In our days, they would have been general overseers and pastors but they were ushers. It means that if we had 20 ushers like them, or 100 choristers like them, the pressure on the pastors will be less. As soon as any case approaches the church they would deal with it and the person will be liberated. But now, it gets clearer that the church has strayed so far away from that pathway.

This message is for those who want to be spiritual eagles; not for those who are just seeking signs and miracles, who do not want to change and who do not want to soar high like an eagle. If the desire of your heart is to be numbered among the champions like the Apostles, if you do not want to depart from this world without leaving your foot-prints on the sand of time, without having anything to show for your existence, if you don't want to mark time in the army of the devil, I want you to take this message serious.

The Apostles set ancient landmarks which can be removed but the Bible advises us not to remove them. One of the reasons for not finding power in the Church again is that, we are removing the old landmarks and are setting ours with our brains. No man can satisfy God using his brain or intelligence. It is even an insult to God, to want to satisfy Him with your brain which He Himself created.

Jeremiah 6:16;
"Thus saith the Lord: "Stand ye in the ways and see and ask for the old paths, where is the good way and walk therein and ye shall find rest for your soul." But they said: "We will not walk therein."

The Israelites did not walk in the old paths that the Lord suggested, and they really suffered exceedingly for it. The Lord said: "Stand ye in the ways" that is, suspend everything you are doing now, open your eyes and see, then ask questions for the old path, where the good way is, walk therein and you shall find rest for your soul. This means, until you locate it and begin to move therein, there will be no peace. Whatever peace you say you have will just be a short holiday; peace on a tight rope. Gideon was trying to do manual agricultural labour in hiding. He had to hide from the Midianites so that they would not take everything from him. While he was doing it, an angel of the Lord came to him and said; "Peace be unto you; thou great man of valour." He answered back, wondering what the angel meant by "Peace." He said there is no peace; otherwise, he would not be in hiding. He now asked where all those signs and miracles that their fathers performed in Exodus were. He asked why they were no longer happening in their days; what went wrong? It was then that the angel knew that Gideon had located himself and so, he offered a solution. Many Christians today, need to locate themselves and stop running after prophets and pastors. Find the old pathway, move in it and you will see what will happen.

Isaiah 35:8;
"And an highway shall be there, and a way, and it shall be called The way of holiness; the unclean shall not pass

over it; but it shall be for those: the wayfaring men, though fools, shall not err therein."

The passage above explains that although the people of the world refer to you as a fool, you will not make mistakes if you tread on this path. As they are calling you names, if you continue, you will make progress. There are many people who go to places where everything has become a routine and religion. They spend time singing, dancing, contributing money, but are not growing spiritually. They dream of preaching, doing deliverance but are not doing anything physically. Note that God is taking a record of everything and is recording all the time you are wasting, joking with the enemy and warming yourself in his fire.

Many people go to church only to pray fire prayers, so that witches will not destroy their lives but the assignment that God is asking them to do, they are not doing it. They are roaming around, not wanting to work in the old pathway and are scared of what they should do. They come to us with excuses; saying that Christianity is not a religion of "dos and don'ts;" they are making a mistake because Christianity actually has "dos and don'ts."

When God says; "Thou shall not" He means "Don't." When He says: "Thou shalt" He means "Do." He tells us the consequences of doing some things which will land in perdition and some which lead to salvation. These are serious matters. The Church these days can be likened to Noah's Ark. If it was not for the death that was outside, it would have been difficult to stay inside the Ark because of the stench. All kinds of animals were put in one place, snakes, elephants, rats, birds; some could be defecating or vomiting, whilst some were eating. It would have been a stinking atmosphere but it was safer than being outside, at the mercy of the floods.

In many places, what Christians say and preach do not match what they do. Beloved, what you need now is not pampering but surgery. The need for now is a surgeon who will diagnose a state and say: "It is cancer" and he uproots it. That is what John the Baptist was doing: he saw the Scribes, Pharisees, Sadducees etc, and gave them their portion of the Gospel. He told them that the axe is laid at the root of the tree, any tree that does not bear good fruit, will be cut off and cast into the fire. Christians are referred to as the salt of the earth but it seems we are not strong enough to hinder the corruption in our society. In fact, many people who claim to be born-again are part of the corruption.

If there is Sharia today in Nigeria, it is the making of the Christians. **Many people preach what they do not practice, pray what they do not mean, pretend to be what they are not, pretend to do what they can't.** They hold all kind of programs; symposia, deliverance, convention, retreat, etc. but there is still no change in the lives of many who go to church day and night. This thing is bothering the heart of God.

A church would have failed in her duties to humanity, if she brings people together, who are not serious. **Many people use the deliverance ministry as a fire-brigade; they go out and get themselves into trouble, run back for deliverance, go out again to get polluted or attacked and then run back again.** They get delivered from the oppression of the enemy but run out and mess themselves up again and the power that gave them temporary relief, comes back in full force.

Matthew-12:43-45 says; *"When the unclean spirit is gone out of a man, he walketh through dry places, seeking rest, and findeth none. Then he saith, I will return into my house from whence I came out; and when he is come, he findeth it empty, swept, and garnished. Then goeth he, and taketh with himself seven other spirits more wicked than himself, and they enter in and dwell there: and the last state of that man is worse than the first. Even so shall it be also unto this wicked generation."*

A Christian, who understands spiritual warfare as we preach in the Mountain of Fire and Miracles Ministries, should be a power generator; not a spiritual bat, a lilipute, or a spiritual football that is kicked here and there by the enemy or by the falsehood of doctrines. I pray that the Lord will reschedule you if you have been wrongly placed, in the name of Jesus. There are some who distribute biscuits and minerals, I pray that the Lord will open their eyes and they will know that life is more than eating and drinking everyday in the church, in the name of Jesus. Many people who have been wrongly programmed need change. But unfortunately, many people hate things that will change any part of them. Whereas, it is change that brings progress. I used to be in a place and God told me that he had not committed the salvation of that place into my hands. I felt reluctant to leave but one day, the Lord showed me a vision where I saw myself on a pulpit and there, I was having a bath. The Lord said if I did not get out of there, I would be disgraced like that. When you are wrongly programmed and the Lord wants to reprogram you, you will not find it easy but you have to comply with what the Lord is asking you to do. Many people have the spirit of religion. Beloved, the best time to collect rainwater is whilst it is still raining. A time will come when the rain will cease and men and women will run around, looking for the true Lord of God but will not find it. All the 'strange', 'unusual' preachers would have gone at the sound of the trumpet. The ones that would be left are these hypocrite pastors, the 'Gehazis', the temperamental pastors, ushers, fornicating choir members; they will be there, preaching and singing during the Great Tribulation. The Anti-Christ will deal with them mercilessly. I pray that you will not be here at that time in the name of Jesus.

Many people go to church and still belong to one club or the other; they still drink alcohol etc. If you are playing church and you do all these things, the arrows of the enemy will easily get you. Can you imagine a gathering where the preacher has seven women as wives and others as concubines, and people still go there claiming that God is 'using' him mightily?

One day on television, a man said he had just added three to the seven wives that he had before and the 'power' was increasing. The question is; which power is he talking about, the power of God or that of witchcraft? A sister's husband was snatched from her in a church and she kept going there, claiming that she was the Chairperson of the Ladies' Society. It was when she became blind that she ran to M.F.M for deliverance. You do not stay in a place simply because you were born there. If your parenthood was sincerely wrong then, you are in serious problem. If you find out that you are stagnant spiritually, if your church cannot change you, then, change your church. The same people you are trying to satisfy in a dead gathering, are the ones that will make fun of you soon. They are attached to religion.

God does not want the Pentecostal or Catholic or Muslim. All He want is your heart and a personal relationship with Him.

He is not looking for those who will carry placards and sing: "All we are saying, devil leave us."

Several years ago, a brother and I were conducting deliverance on a sister. We were inexperienced and so, the sister wasted much of our time. At a point, she said there was a calabash in her stomach and we started praying against evil calabash. After more than one hour, she told us to stop, that it was only the queen of heaven that could remove the calabash. Inexperienced that we were. we asked how to get her. She asked us to get a bucket of water. We did and she began to speak one demonic tongue. I got interested because I had never seen the queen of heaven at that time, so I wanted her to appear. After a long time, she said the queen could not appear in the water because there was an angel at the door. Then the brother started to sing: "Come down Jesus, O Lord."

Many who are talking about heaven are doing so because they are broke. They have no food to eat, their husbands are beating them, or their wives have eloped with other men. Our fathers in the faith went through a lot; they were stripped of their possessions, driven away from their homes, they sealed their salvation with their blood, were falsely accused of dreadful crimes. Any time there was calamity, they accused them of being the cause - famine, earthquake, etc. They were seen as pests in the society. It is these days that you would see pastors and men of God being appointed as chairpersons at public gatherings. At that time, if anyone dared it, they would throw him into the den of lions. Right from the beginning of the world, God has always worked with the minority - 600 thousand men left Egypt but only two got to the Promised Land. About 20 million people perished in the flood during the time of Noah; only eight were saved. Gideon's 32,000 men were reduced to 300. Jesus had so many disciples and followers, but only twelve were chosen as the Apostles.

In the early days of Christianity, great numbers of Christians were thrown into the lion's dens, many were burnt live in amphitheatres, they were used as human torch lights and some were crucified sideways or upside down, others were caught and made to wear animal skins and put in the arena of dogs and were torn into pieces. These were the people that started Christianity; where are we today? If a man like Stephen, who wrought signs and wonders was an usher, it means the standard then was high. Today, if a person lays hands on another and commands the demon in him to come out, he would be hailed and reverenced; whereas, in the time of the Apostles, he would have been one of those who went on errands for the Apostles.

During the persecution of Christians, their children were killed one after the other; if they refused to deny Jesus. They were turned into public shows. They were haunted down by beasts; thousands were imprisoned and slain. They plucked out their beards but they did not give up. They placed their gaze on the Lord Jesus. There was one who witnessed the killing of his children and when they were about to kill his wife, he almost said he would renounce but his wife said he shouldn't, that she would rather die. They killed her and eventually killed him too. Thousands were killed this way. Vast multitudes witnessed the deaths of Christians this way and greeted it with applause.

During the time of the Apostles and the Prophets of old, they would command fire to fall and it would. They commanded demons to come out of people and healed the sick without hustles. Paul commanded Bar Jesus to go blind for a season and it happened. When you imagine what they went through, all they did and are in heaven, you would wonder if you are on your way to that same heaven. **Many people are influenced by friends who are pushing them out of the way of the anointing of God. They forget that the farthest these friends can go with them, is the graveyard and they are soon forgotten.** Think about it beloved; the world is moving dangerously to a close and many strange things that the Lord Jesus said, that men's heart shall fail them for fear, are already happening.

There was a woman in MFM Jos who was being prayed for and she went into labour and delivered a live fish. Another one in Port Harcourt vomited a black stone which had hairs on it, that looked like the hairs of a rat. It had been inside her for years and she was even a praise worship leader in her church. Beloved, we need to re-order our steps.

Jeremiah 6:16 is resounding this message;
"Thus saith the Lord: "Stand ye in the ways and see and ask for the old paths, where is the good way and walk therein and ye shall find rest for your soul." But they said: "We will not walk therein."

What kind of Christians will cope these days? Is it the unmarried that are committing fornication? Is it pastors that rape their counselees? Is it the hypocrite who has never been to the airport and is pretending to be an American? Is it the Christians that are dressing weirdly like demons? Those who pretend and dress piously at church but dress otherwise outside? Is it those who are breaking the laws of God without an atom of sorrow? Is it those who get angry and are unforgiving? Is it the pastor that is worldly and is concerned only with rich members of the congregation? Is it the people who want the God of miracles but do not want to totally obey him? Whereas the Bible says: *"And having in a readiness to revenge all disobedience, when your obedience is fulfilled"* **(II Corinthians 10:6).**

Is it the miracle performers who do not have God the miracle worker in their hearts? Is it those who are scared of hell but reject salvation? Those who want healing but reject the healer? Those who want spiritual gifts without maturity? Those who want protection but do not want to follow the path of holiness? Those who want power without purity? Those who want the presence of God but don't allow Him to penetrate their hearts? Those who keep malice? Husbands and wives who want popularity but reject the depths of the Holy Spirit; they have anointing but lack character; they have itchy ears but lack obedience. Is it those who are being entertained by their pastors and are applauding them as they head for hell? Is it those who have dullness of heart?

Is it those who cannot boldly tell the rich Lodge member and occultist man that his money will perish with him if he does not give his life to the Lord Jesus Christ?

A man came to our church one day and looked at the premises and said he would give me N2 million to build it up, but that I should pray for him so that he could sleep. He had not been sleeping well for the past two years. I told him that we would not take money but that he could be prayed for and he should give his life to the Lord Jesus Christ. Some believers blow powerless tongues but when they sleep, they are pressed down on their beds.

Beloved, a time is coming, when you will not be able to hold in your hand, the money that you are running after today. You will be lifeless and if the money is put in your palm it will drop. If those women who are making you not to concentrate on God today, come before you at that time, even though naked, you will not be able to react. A time is coming when all your designer wears will be useless, now that you are refusing the Holy Ghost to re-design your life. The time is coming when you will know that what the world is referring to as enjoyment is not so. **Real enjoyment is to be in God's favour now and in eternity. Drinking alcohol, womanizing and keeping late nights, are not enjoyment - they are elements of bondage.**

One day, you will smoke the last hidden cigarette, take your last drink, put on your last dress or chain, read your last book, sing your last song, etc. You do not know when that last day will be. You will know that all is vanity, like the preacher says. When a person is not on the old pathway of God, he will commit sin and cleverly conceal it. The Bible says; *"He that covereth his sin shall not prosper."* (Proverbs 28:13a)

There are examples of those who sinned and covered it, but the Lord saw it. Adam and Eve sinned and when they heard the voice of God in the garden, they hid themselves but God called them out. The reason why many people cannot face the powers of darkness is because, they have cleverly conceal sins in their lives stealing, lying etc.

Jeremiah 23:23;
"Am I a God at hand, saith the Lord and not a God afar off? Can any hide himself in secret places that I shall not see him? Saith the Lord. Do not I fill heaven and earth? Saith the Lord."

Psalm 139:7-10;
"Whither shall I go from Thy Spirit? Or whither shall I flee from Thy presence? If I ascend up into heaven, Thou art there: if I take the wings of the morning, and dwell in the uttermost parts of the sea, even there shall Thy hand lead me, and Thy right hand shall hold me."

Jonah tried to escape from the Lord; but he soon learnt that there is no escape from the Lord. Those who are far from the old pathway are men and women, who are always trying to cover up. How futile it is to try to run away from God. All things will eventually be brought to judgement; whether it is good or bad. You may think and say nobody sees you but He does: the all-seeing eyes of the Lord, sees you.

The Bible says people like darkness more than light, but even that darkness cannot conceal nor hide you from God. A man was on his way home from church one day and he just mentioned the fact that his son was sick. A man who also was coming from the same church service, offered to take him somewhere. They went to a remote part of the city and entered the house of a herbalist. He took them into a dark room where there were witchcraft birds flying about. The herbalist did the consultations and prescribed some concoctions. Here are people who went from a church service to the house of a herbalist. It means that they went to the house of God with their hidden agenda. Some people try to cover their sins by telling lies. They forget that God is all-knowing and all-seeing.

At this juncture, I would like to pause and we shall continue in the next bulletin, if the Lord tarries in coming back. Meanwhile, I would like you to examine your ways. Are you on the right path that leads to God? Are you born-again? If you are not yet born-again, you have the opportunity of taking that decision today. All you need to do, is to acknowledge the fact that you are a sinner and that you cannot get to heaven in your sinful state. Repent of your sins; confess them to the Lord; name them one by one and ask Him to forgive you and cleanse you from all unrighteousness. Renounce the world and the devil and make sure that you do not go back to them anymore.

Invite the Lord Jesus Christ into your life; ask Him to come into your life and become your personal Lord and Saviour. Enthrone Him over your life and hand over all that concerns you to Him. Submit your totality to Him and ask Him to take an absolute control of your life.

I congratulate you on this decision that you have just taken. It is the most important decision in life and I pray that it shall be permanent in your life in the name of Jesus. I pray that the Lord will write your name in the Book of Life and you will not by any means, rub it off in the name of Jesus.

Take these prayer points with all the aggression that you can gather:

1. Every environmental power, harassing my destiny, die! in the name of Jesus.
2. I destroy the habitation of witchcraft in my life, in the name of Jesus.
3. Blood of Jesus, deliver my life from bewitchment, in the name of Jesus.
4. Forces of frustration and failure tormenting my life, die! in the name of Jesus.
5. Forces of demotion and shame tormenting my destiny, die! in the name of Jesus.
6. Lord! deliver me from the evil of this generation, in the name of Jesus.
7. Thou right hand of the Most High God, do valiantly in my life today, in the name of Jesus.
8. Blood of Jesus, speak destruction to the works of the devil in my life, in the name of Jesus.
9. My Father, make me Your object of divine love for ever, in the name of Jesus.
10. Any power that wants to derail my life, receive destruction, in the name of Jesus.
11. Every spirit of diversion, release my life! in the name of Jesus.
12. Unbelief, release my heart! In the name of Jesus.
13. Sin! as the Lord liveth, you shall not have dominion over me, in the name of Jesus.
14. Father Lord, by Your mercy, separate me from every evil influence, in the name of Jesus.
15. Light of heaven, dispel every darkness lurking inside of me. in the name of Jesus.
16. The glory of the Lord will never depart from my life and my family, in the name of Jesus.
17. The Spirit of God will never depart from my life and family, in the name of Jesus.
18. Father Lord, make me a man / woman of Your right hand, in the name of Jesus.
19. Power like as of old, fall upon my life in the name of Jesus.
20. Power to be heavenly conscious every moment of my life, possess me by fire! in the name of Jesus Christ.

The Old Pathway (2)

Proverbs 22:28 commands us; *"Remove not the ancient landmark, which thy fathers have set."*

Jeremiah 23:23 says; *"Am I a God at hand, saith the Lord and not a God afar off? Can any hide himself in secret places that I shall not see him? Saith the Lord. Do not I fill heaven and earth? Saith the Lord."*

In the last bulletin, we started this important topic, which is meant to open our eyes to what is happening to the Christian folk today. We talked about the Apostles of old and the kind of experience that we had in our country at the beginning of the Pentecostal awakening. We went on to say that there is nothing hidden from God, no matter how small or far away. In this edition by the grace of God, we shall continue. I pray that the Lord will open the eyes of your understanding and will help you to see what He wants you to see, that will prepare you for a glorious tomorrow and the great beyond. God bless you as you read on.

The brothers of Joseph told their father a lie about Joseph. For many years, the lie seemed to be successful but eventually, their father knew what happened. Of course, God knew all the way, that it was a lie.

Can you imagine a person coming before a man of God and telling lies; recounting false stories? In such situations, I just look on with my hand under my chin; when they finish, they go. Such people do not know that the angels of the living God, the Holy Spirit and the anointing of God will fight for His children. In fact, such people are looking for trouble. It is better not to say anything, than to come and tell lies. The Bible says; *"Neither is there any creature that is not manifest before Him. But all things are naked and open before the Lord."*

Some people try to hide their sins by hiding the evidence, If you have been collecting money from a person that you are not supposed to collect money from, and you think nobody is seeing you, you are deceiving yourself. Can you imagine a man who has just committed adultery having a bath, sprays perfume on himself, throws away his condoms, thinking his sin is covered and then buys bread to take to his wife at home; gets home and says; "Hello darling, how are you?" as if he really loved her. Whereas, he had just come back from his arena of destruction. Some people smoke and lick mint-sweets to freshen their breath; they are trying to cover up the evidence of their sins. Moses buried the Egyptian thinking nobody knew that he had killed someone, but everybody including Pharaoh, soon knew. Achan buried the stolen treasures from Jericho under his tent, eventually, it was exposed and he was put to death. Some people try to cover their sins by hypocrisy or by pretension; like Judas who exposed his Master by giving Him a kiss. No wonder Jesus said; *"Woe unto you scribes and Pharisees, you are hypocrites; you are like white sepulchres which appear white outside but within, are full of dead men's bones and uncleanness."* The fact that people call someone a man of God, Pastor or Apostle, does not mean he is in good terms with God. If he is living in carefully concealed sin, he amounts to nothing before the Lord and God will spew him out.

If as children of God, we want to tread the old pathway, we have work to do from the top to the bottom. Many people come to church but do not heed simple warnings and instructions. When the marriage feast was set, the invited guests gave excuses. One thing about God is that, He excuses people who want to be excused. All the excuse makers were excused and He went and invited people who were on the streets; the blind, the lame, etc. to come and replace them. Ask yourself this question: "What place does the Kingdom of God have in my daily life; is it the first or the last place? Jesus says: *"Seek ye first the Kingdom of God and His righteousness, and all other things shall be added unto you."* If you ask yourself that question and you are sincere with yourself, you will be able to detect if you are on the old pathway or you are travelling on your own way; where there are robbers attacking you.

Are you a person that does things for personal desires and put the things of God to occupy the last position? Do you allow your family, friends, position in the society, your possessions and other things to take first place in your life instead of the kingdom of God? Are you guilty of putting off what you should do to advance the Kingdom of God? Does God have the first place in your life? Do the health and the well-being, of the church mean more to you than any other institution on earth? Are you serious with the work of God? Are you doing anything that will make it move forward? What part of yourself are you giving to God and His church? Are you sacrificing yourself for the Lord? Do you sometimes inconvenience yourself to serve the Lord? Are you so busy that you do not have time for God? Do not forget that if you should fall and die today, someone else will replace you at that job which is keeping you so busy.

What is your attitude towards the Gospel? The Gospel is God's power to save the lost. Are you ashamed of the Gospel? If you are not ashamed, why are you not telling people about the good news? Why is it that many people are so indifferent to evangelism and soul winning? Some Christians are not bothered at all that so many people are heading for hell. Are you constant in prayer or do you only pray when you are in the church? Do you deny yourself in order to serve the Lord? These are the questions you need to ask yourself, to know whether you are in the old pathway or not. Do you find nights for entertainment or social activities but you do not have time to attend to, and fellowship with the saints? Do you find money for other luxuries of life but none for the church of God?

One day, a boy caught a fish and brought it to his pastor. He said it was the tithe of his catch for the day. The pastor took if from him and asked where the other nine were. He said they were still in the river; that he was going back to catch them. That was faith and giving, in action. That meant he was paying his tithe first and was going back to catch his own. Do you find money for the luxuries of life, yet when it comes to giving to the church, you have none? You need to think about it. God cannot be modernised. He is still the same old-fashioned God.

We now have branches of the Mountain of Fire and Miracles Ministries everywhere, meaning there are many people joining us day and night. These people alongside being members should know where they are and why they are joining us. M.F.M does not mind closing down any branch that does not follow the statutes of the Bible and the laid-down principles of the church. We do not mind closing down any branch that is becoming worldly and that is about to bend the standards that the Lord has given to us.

Daniel 7:9 describes purity of God;
"I beheld till the thrones were cast down and the Ancient of Days did sit, whose garment was white as snow, and the hair of His head, like pure wool; His throne was like the fiery flame and his wheels as burning fire."

Malachi 3:6 says;
"For I am the Lord, I change not; therefore ye sons of Jacob are not consumed."

Hebrews 1:10-12;
"And Thou, Lord, in the beginning hast laid the foundation of the earth, and the heavens are the works of thine hands; they shall perish; but thou remainest and they all shall wax old as doth a garment; and a vesture shalt thou fold up and they shall be changed: but Thou art the same and Thy years shall not fail."

Hebrews 13:8;
"Jesus Christ the same yesterday and today and forever."

In the Old Pentecostal pathway, when women went to church, they did not go there to display their hairstyles. They covered their heads because of the angels. These days, some put on a particular hat or scarf, so that their hairstyle could be seen. They are able to do this because their head is not covered with rashes and is not smelly. In those days, women were not putting on trousers. Trouser wearing actually started after the World War II in Europe and America, when women started going out to work. In those days, men did not use to put on chains. Some put it on and leave their shirts unbuttoned, so that the chain and pendant could be seen.

If we want the Pentecostal Power of old, we have to go back to those things that we have abandoned. It is unfortunate that many churches are not helping the situation. They call people to come as they are, to come and receive miracles. These people too come with their mini skirts, painted hair and faces, rings on the nose, etc. Actually, there is no problem coming that way; that is, as you are to God. The problem lies in remaining the way you are.

Whereas Romans 12:1-2 advices us that:
"I beseech you therefore, brethren, by the mercies of God, that ye present your bodies a living sacrifice, holy, acceptable unto God, which is your reasonable service. And be not conformed to this world: but be ye transformed by the renewing of your mind, that ye may prove what is that good, and acceptable, and perfect, will of God."

It is unfortunate that such people are not corrected. Rather, they are assured that God will answer their prayers. God cannot deny Himself; the name of Jesus is too powerful to be denied. His sacrificial offer on the Cross at Calvary is painful and His love too precious to trample upon. If you call Him, He will answer but then read Hebrews 1, and you will find many people there who were giants of faith but who ended up in hellfire. In those days, there was humility written on the faces of Christians, singing was done from the heart; their songs may not have been kind but they were sung from the depths of their hearts. At that time, spiritual gifts flowed all over the place through the service. Prophesy would always flow and one could feel the heat of the anointing when one arrived at the service. The Christians then, were experiencing joy on a regular basis and there was joy on their faces, radiating from their hearts.

For us to go back to the Old pathway therefore, we must practise what they practised. If you want to practise liberal and compromising Christianity, M.F.M is not the right place. The present-day believers are yet to discover the roots that we find in the Acts of the Apostles; even the roots that we got in Nigeria in the 1930s, let alone walking therein. We have not discovered it! Many people, who call themselves born-again, are not ready to part with their worldly past. They do not want to look different from the world; they find it difficult to discard their makeup, jewellery and Jezebelian attachments. They try to correct God's creation by colouring their lips and fingernails. Some try to copy the texture and the hair of the White people. Some wear unholy shirts, skin-tight and sexy dresses to church. There are also many who are not prepared to sweat in prayers; they have only come to church for fancy.

In many churches, the women do not pray fervently on Sundays because they have carefully constructed their headgears and want to be careful, so that their headgears will not fall off. Sometimes, when they are sitting in front of you, you cannot see the preacher. They are not prepared to do spiritual warfare. Many Christians today, go about with no spiritual gift; some have a lame spirit of prophesy. These days, Christians tell lies to cover up their mistakes. They are more worldly-minded than heavenly minded. The mountain of power that our fathers climbed, are not appealing to many Christians today, therefore, they are powerless and spineless. Many are really part-time Christians.

We need to sit down and really look at all these things and reorganise ourselves. When you get out of Egypt, the whole of Egypt must know and see it. When the Israelites left Egypt, the Egyptians saw, and felt their departure and lost many things to them. There must be something in us to show the world that we do not belong to the same boat any more. Egypt for Christians is the world. You cannot mix Egypt with the Promised Land. These days, many people came out of Egypt but Egypt is still in them. Some came out of Egypt but their business is still in there. Some still have their dressing; outward appearance, etc, in Egypt. We have to become serious, if we want to experience the power that the Apostles experienced.

We have many unbroken people coming to church today; that is why we have personality clashes, gossip, misunderstanding, spiritual and physical pride, personal ambition, personal frustration, critical spirit, immaturity, lack of love, living above one's experience, proud hearts, proud looks, selfishness, self-centeredness, etc, filling the whole place. We have many Christians with the spirit of reacting when not loved or appreciated. Hypocritical Christians who avoid people who tell them the truth about themselves. They neither want to listen, nor be corrected. These are also very revengeful and pull down those who correct them. That is what you find in today's 'Church.'

There was a woman who used to be a prostitute. One day, she gave her life to Christ and as she was being led through the sinner's prayer, she started to shout: "Please sir I don't want to go there." She was becoming so hysterical and people had to come around and help. When she calmed down, she said she saw hell-fire. She said she saw a woman tied to the stakes with her lips; another with her breasts, some men were tied to the third floor with their penis (all these things were their weapons of sin). There was fire burning under them, they were screaming, and she saw worms and live fire, coming out of their nostrils and ears. She said she screamed that she did not want to go there and her screaming came out in the physical. I pray that the Lord will open your understanding

If you are reading this bulletin and you have been able to look through your life, you must have seen where you are. Many people are spiritually stagnant; they read the Bible as if they were reading novels. Nothing jumps alive from it at them. Many find it easy to memorise fuji music than to memorise the Scriptures. Many are busy beating up their wives instead of the devil, while some are so used to being pampered. They cannot come out to help the course of God because they have not been pampered yet.

Look at yourself now, and face reality. **Who are you on the inside?** Forget about the title and name you are being called. The title could be G.O, Superintendent, Pastor, etc. Forget about those things and find out what you really are. Face reality! You will not get to the gates of heaven and introduce yourself as Reverend, Pastor, Most Revered Reverend, Arch-Bishop Elijah. You will be told that all those titles are vanity and they mean nothing to them in heaven. What they want to know, is what is going on in the inside of you, whether you are fulfilling your destiny in God or you are minding the agenda of the enemy. It is either you are allowing the devil to use you, or you are using yourself as you like, or you are allowing the world to use you. Something definitely must use you, as there is no vacuum in nature.

If you have examined your life and you can see where you are heading to, you will be able to reach your goal.

Ask yourself questions like these. "If I had the kind of power that Stephen had, will household witchcraft pursue me? If I had the kind of power that Elijah had, would anyone threaten me with death? Would I not say: "Let fire fall," as Elijah did? Even if it is not physical fire, would they not feel the heat of the touch of God upon my life? Have you asked yourself when last God talked to you in a two-way communication? The Bible always say; "And God said...." God called people by their names and they heard and had answers.

God called Moses, Samuel, Saul, they replied and God talked to them again. Does that happen in your life? It is time we stopped having ceremonial choirs, or workers, but those who are ready to work for God at all times.

It is time we had ushers or technical crew members, who will lay hands on the benches and pray and the benches will become so hot, that if a witch sits on it, he or she will somersault and start confessing her evil deeds. For us to get to that stage, we need to do what the Bible says; **stand, open our eyes wide, meditate, think and find out about this Old pathway, wherein our forefathers walked.** The Bible says: *"A highway shall be there and a way; it shall be called the way of holiness; no unclean thing shall move therein; but wayfarers, though fools, shall not err therein.*

In those days, we used to sing a song that says: *"Give me that old-time religion. It was good for Paul and Silas. It will do when the world is on fire. It is good enough for me."*

Beloved, bring genuine repentance before the Lord, for the powerlessness of your life. For the areas where you have failed God, for when He called you and you did not hear; for when His words did not enter into your ears. For where He told you to act and you refused to act. For where He asked you to move and you refused to move. He is talking to you and you do not understand; Ask Him to forgive you. There is a song that says: *"I suffered much for you, but what have you done for me?*

All those small assignments that God gave you and you have abandoned or you are no longer serious about, you have to repent before Him.

When He says: "Come," you don't come; when He says: "Go' you don't; time is going and you are not getting any younger. By 12:01 a.m now, another day would have gone and you would have become older and the timetable of God is ending. He is recording His champions. You have looked at your life and you see that you are not a champion yet, you are far from it and you are still failing Him everyday. God has been trying to talk to you in your dreams and visions but you do not understand. He spoke to you in parables, but it is not clear to you. Your eyes are dark in the spirit; what you should see, you are not seeing. Do you want this trend to continue? Some people are planning to marry their enemies; they do not know it because their eyes are closed. Make the decision to change and tread the path that the Lord wants you to tread, TODAY!

Beloved, if hitherto, you are not born again, you have not officially surrendered your life to the Lord Jesus Christ, then, you have not yet started to prepare to tread the Old pathway. If you are ready to surrender your life to the Lord Jesus Christ and accept Him as your personal Lord and Saviour; you can do so right now, right there where you are. All you need do is acknowledge the fact that you are a sinner and that you cannot approach God in your sinful state. The eyes of God cannot behold sin and He has already made a provision for setting Man free from his sins. Confess your sins to Him, name them one by one and ask Him to forgive you and cleanse you from all unrighteousness. Claim the redemptive power in the Blood of Jesus that was shed for your sins, on the cross at Calvary. Ask the Lord to cleanse you with His Blood, and write your name in the Book of Life.

Invite the Lord Jesus Christ into your life and enthrone Him over your life and everything that concerns you. Promise Him that you will stop gambling with your life and you will decide to tread the Old pathway, although it could make you look like a fool, you will not make any mistake in treading it, because it is the way that leads to eternal life.

Beloved, the Lord Jesus Christ is passing your way and wants to help you out. Call upon Him while He is near; seek Him while He may be found. Forsake your wicked ways and your unrighteous thoughts; return to the Lord your God and He will pardon you abundantly.

Now, take these prayer points

with all the determination that you can gather:

1. Lord, deliver me from the spirit of blindness, in the name of Jesus.
2. Lord, if I am already travelling on the wrong road, correct me, in the name of Jesus.
3. Lord, make Your way plain before me, in the name of Jesus.
4. Lord, set my spirit on fire, by the Holy Ghost, in the name of Jesus.
5. Every destructive family pattern in my life, break! in the name of Jesus.
6. Lord, shake every lukewarmness out of my life, in the name of Jesus.
7. Any power working against my walk with God, depart from my life! in the name of Jesus.
8. I refuse to strengthen the hands of my enemies, in the name of Jesus.
9. Lord, I will no longer disobey You, I will do what You ask me to do, in the name of Jesus.
10. Spirits that waste good things operating in my life, die by fire, in the name of Jesus.
11. Anointing of "old for nothing", my life is not your candidate, dry up and die, in the name of Jesus.
12. Every pattern of hell fire targeted against me, break in the name of Jesus.
13. God arise and do anything that needs to be done for me to make heaven, in the name of Jesus.
14. I receive abundant mercy in the name of Jesus.

Thank God for answered prayers.

Spiritual Patching

Jeremiah 6:14: *"They have healed the hurt of my daughter slightly and they are saying peace, peace, when there is no peace."*

Man is fighting with clever spirits that have been in the world before him; these spirits have over 6,000 years' experience.

The devil can groom somebody up for years, so that he will use the person at a later date. By the same token, he can cause a fatal accident, just because he wants to capture one person.

Also, the enemy of our soul knows how to arrange and re-arrange problems. It is unfortunate to find out that people go to the devil's agents for help. They offer no solution, but a rearrangement of problems and destruction. The only place where problems cannot be re-arranged is in heaven. That is why the Bible says; *"Thy will be done on earth, as it is in heaven."* This means that His will is not automatically done on earth; at least, not completely.

As long as a person continues to make friends with the devil, he or she will remain a toy in the hands of the enemy. But this is never God's plan; instead, He wants you to become a container, where Christ will reign continually within and without. Many people because of one life's problem or the other run to the devil for assistance; but the truth about life is that, only Christ has solutions to all problems. What some people see as solution to their problems is actually a re-arrangement, a cleverly coated trade by barter of the devil. Let us see some life-changing facts; these facts are the keys to receiving permanent solutions to problems, so that the enemy will not re-arrange them.

They are as follows:

1. **Always give thanks to God.**
The devil wants you to worry and cry over your problems and not see what God has done. In other words, the devil wants people to count their woes and failures, instead of seeing the goodness of God in their lives and families.

2. **Walk by faith and not by sight.**
If you want to go far with God, you must get to a stage, where you see things the way God sees them; a stage where you are able to fix your internal eyes unto God, and see what is ahead.

3. **Learn to listen and hear from God.**
Every human being is a descendant of Adam, and as such, is deaf to God. Adam rendered himself deaf when he exhibited disobedience to the instruction of God in Eden, this he passed on to all mortals. For you therefore to listen and hear from God, you have to learn how. If Christians would listen and hear from God, they will not need to go to anyone for counselling. If you can learn to listen to God, you will move ahead.

4. **Be sure that you have carried out God's last instruction, before asking for a fresh one.**
If you do not, God may speak but it may not sound loud to you and it will look to you. as if God is not speaking.

5. **Stop doubt at the door of your mind.**
Do not allow it to enter, neither give it the time to develop. Of course, we know that there are many things throwing doubts about but as a child of God, you must stop doubt at the door; don't give it a fraction of chance to enter. It can be done and is being done, until Jesus comes.

6. **Be holy.**
The Bible says; **"Without-holiness, no man can see the Lord."** Many evil things come into an unclean life to pollute it and render such an enemy of God.

7. **Train yourself for spiritual warfare.**
The Bible says that we are not

wrestling against flesh and blood, but against principalities and powers, against the rulers of the darkness of this world. Therefore, the weapons of our warfare should not be carnal, in pulling down the strongholds of the devil in prayer.

Beloved, know that a failure in any of these seven areas will make a re-arrangement of the prison of the prisoner; making it very difficult for the prisoner to be let out from every satanic cage.

There was a great revival crusade somewhere and people got healed of diverse sicknesses and diseases. They were asked to come back for regular Bible study and prayers, in order to put a seal on their testimonies. A blind man received his sight after 13 years but shunned the Bible study. It was at this time he started to remember that there was a palm-wine bar along the road. He also remembered how to play draft and started talking to beautiful women. Then one day, while he was drinking palm-wine in the bar, he felt something in his eyes and he became blind again. He could not leave the bar, then he started to cry out that those fanatic healers were fake. It was an Alhaji who was standing by that rebuked him and reminded him of the fact that he did not go back to the church for prayers, since he got healed.

A prisoner, who is content with his bondage, is the one that would not comply with these great keys, thus allowing the enemy to re-arrange his problems. We have got to realise the fact that we are living in a time of terrible spiritual conflict. There is a serious war going on around, underneath, ahead and about us. Although there are many churches around, there is also a proliferation of satanic synagogues. Although this is a period of an outpouring of the Holy Spirit it is also a time of intense demonic activities. Although this is a time for abundant life and prosperity, it is also the time for abundant death and poverty, if one is not careful. Poverty has nothing to do with the amount of money that a person has in his or her bank account. If a person has a lot of money and is suffering from cancer, the person is like a pauper who has nothing in his pocket. As far as the person has no power to heal the cancer, he or she is a pauper. The cancer could also drain the bank account of a person and make him a pauper.

This is the time for abundant search for God. Many people are beginning to see that other kinds of powers are beggarly powers. But still, this time exhibits a time of great hatred for God; therefore, Christians should really know, what they are doing.

In our opening text, we discover that the enemy patches-up hurts slightly. What people see as solution, is what some people put under the canopy of the word: 'deliverance;' they think it is for witches and familiar spirits only. They do not know that there are more terrible things that people need to get delivered from. These terrible things camouflage under suits and "dresses of people; so that many do not know. Many do not know that deliverance is necessary, for one to possess his possessions; especially those priceless greatness that have been held down for a long time.

For there to be true deliverance, and not just a patch-up therefore, the following things are required:
1. **Removal of wicked spirits.**
A man had a tyre shop and was doing very well. After sometime, he noticed that sales dropped, even his regular customers were bye-passing him to go to other shops. He found out that in two weeks, he sold only three tyres, sometimes one. One day, he saw one of his customers going to another shop. He called him and asked if he had offended him in any way. The customer said he didn't offend him but he just had an impression that he should not buy from him. Further effort on the part of this trader to encourage the customer, angered him and made the customer to leave. At that juncture, the man knew that there was trouble. He came to M.F.M and we prayed. It was later discovered, that a co-shop owner, packed sand from the front of the shop of this troubled man and did some charms with it; there was actually a demon assigned to chase customers away. Of course from there, the brother

knew the next step.

When there is true deliverance, such a demon goes back to its sender and carries out that mission. Sometimes, the problems of some people need just a removal of the demon assigned against them but unfortunately, they go to a herbalist, who just re-arranges the problems for them. He replaces a weak demon with a more powerful one. Such people would thank the herbalist for having solved their problem but would not know that they have been caught in an evil web.

I hope you do not consult herbalists and white garment people. If you have ever done it, you have to repent and go through deliverance. No one goes to a herbalist without coming back with a load of demons. Sometimes, people go to white garment herbalists, who see visions for them and prescribe all sorts of things. There is always a demon dispatched against such a person and the demon, would first befriend the person and then strike at an unguarded time. These people do not also know that they have traded their souls for a temporary relief; the person is sold to Satan, who gives fringe benefits and advances to the person. I hope you do not consult such. If some powers from home are pursuing a person, and he or she decides to go to a white garment herbalist, the person has only succeeded in constructing his or her coffin, because they will destroy the person.

A man married a fair complexioned woman but later discovered that she was from the waters. In real life at noon, she would scratch her body and salt would come out. One day, her husband decided to take her to a white garment herbalist. She quickly went in the spirit, to warn the herbalist not to do anything to help, but to make sure that the husband pays dearly for it. True to her word, the herbalist charged her husband a huge sum of money that he could not pay so he took her back home. Somehow, the man got to know M.F.M and brought her for deliverance. Later, the lady confessed that she had a crocodile bodyguard that could not enter into the church premises because of the fire of God. As she was being prayed for she was shouting and calling the crocodile to come to her aid. Eventually, the Lord delivered her from the water kingdom. As she was testifying to what God did for her, a man we invited listened to the testimony in amazement and was stunned at what she said. He later told me that that woman, because of her beauty and physical nature was the kind of girl that he gets attracted to and makes sure he befriends; not knowing that they could be from the waters.

Many people become members of Lodge fraternities, occult groups and clubs, thinking they would find solution to their problems. They thus enter into covenants in exchange for what they desire.

A boy used to have epilepsy and his parents took him to a herbalist, who gave him an amulet. Later, the boy found his way to M.F.M. As we were about to pray for him, we saw the amulet and asked him to remove it. He thought he would die if he removed it but we persuaded him and he removed it. When it was broken, we saw that there was an inscription in his local dialect inside it saying that the bearer had been dedicated to the devil.

Some people go to those who press sand, not knowing that all they do is transfer the problem to someone close to the client. They could also send the power behind the problem, on casual leave, to come back later. Meanwhile the person would feel a relief. To worsen the case, some churches are begging the demon, instead of solving the problems. They occupy people with activities and induce them to slumber, with spiritual 'valium.' They make a lot of noise with music and empty excitement. The powers oppressing people will only wait for them and, reinforce the attacks when they get home When the person realises what is going on, he or she would know that all those so-called activities are only a waste of time. Beggarly powers rearrange problems; they shift one from the back to the middle or front. This makes people concentrate on the non-essentials. These wicked spirits must be removed; there are powers that can patch up the existence of these powers. One would think they have left, but they are hiding.

2. Restoration of normal functions

The aim of deliverance is not just to overcome the enemy; but it is to restore the person or thing, to a normal life and function. That is why, after going through deliverance, the eyes that were blind, open, and those whose lives were once in shambles, now begin to live a normal life.

Sometimes, the enemy tries to blindfold people. He patches up so many places in the lives of individuals. He removes a physical sickness, but leaves a demon inside. Such a demon tries to re-arrange the problem, so that it would seem as if the initial problem had gone. That is why when one problem leaves, another enters the life of a person, and that is why some problems find their way back into the lives of people. Sometimes, it is the herbalist or fake prophet that sends them on errand, so that the person would come and seek counsel and would give them money. The money that some people do not want to pay as tithe or offering to God will be wasted like this while the herbalist or prophet gets fatter.

3. Re-direction of life in a Godly fashion.

This is the ability of a person to be able to order his or her life according to the dictates of God. Such a person will no longer follow the directives of the former life, but will choose a new course of life and service; and thus do the good things that he or she was unable to do before. When a person is under the influence of satanic problem re-arrangement, he or she could be nice and everybody would appreciate him or her; the person may look holy but internally, such could be something else.

I would like to advise you today beloved, to get out of cosmetic Christianity. Be frank with yourself; for how long do you want to offer protection to your enemies? For how long do you want to pretend to be what you are not? For how long do you want to live above your Christian experience? For how long will you remain under satanic propaganda and control? You have to unmask the masquerade in your life. It is then, that things will begin to happen.

There was a blind man that was healed by Jesus and the Pharisees challenged Him. When the man was asked who Jesus was, he said he did not know but that he knew that he was once blind and could now see. Later, Jesus met him in the temple and warned him not to go back to sin. Jesus then asked him if he believed in the Son of God. The man was ready to know and believe Him. He was a honest man: God is looking for such men, that would 'call a spade a spade' and not 'an agricultural equipment.'

Two men went into the temple to pray. The Pharisee protected his demon and also re-arranged his problem; he patched his problems up by telling God how good he was, but the tax collector threw the mask away from the face of his enemy and left his demons in the cold. If you would remove the mask and stop masquerading, you will discover that many things that are hiding in your life will fly out of their hiding places.

Many years ago, in the town called Akure, masquerades were going about and taking delight in whipping people. One of them ran after someone who ran into a house and whipped him mercilessly. A man got angry and challenged the masquerade. Before anybody could intervene, the man had carried and thrown the masquerade down; he unmasked him and we found out that the masquerade was actually a slim, lazy boy, whom everyone knew could not even fight. Likewise, many problems are wearing masks and bragging. You must take off the mask; to know what exactly you are facing. You must take the mask off your spiritual face, if you do not want to continue in the life of spiritual patching. Get a permanent solution. Take off the mask and see the reality of who you really are.

Some Indians saw that their people were dying. They blamed the gods, the rivers, themselves, White men, their neighbours, everybody. One day, someone unmasked the problem; he noticed that they had a blanket with which they covered anyone that died. The same blanket was used in covering anyone that took ill. The man pointed their attention to it and they realised that they were the ones transmitting the killer disease, from one person to the other, through the blanket.

We know that the devil is the active force behind every evil, but you must know that the devil cannot be everywhere at the same time; he has his agents. The real enemy of many people is yet to be unmasked. A person could try everything possible; prayer, fasting, spiritual exercise, etc. and the problem could still continue. In such an instance, there could be a need to unmask the real enemy.

When a person wears a mask, which is the face of a lion or snake or some fierce-looking creature or even the face of a child, the purpose is to conceal the true identity of the wearer of the mask, who is pretending to be someone or something else. When the mask is removed, the real identity is known. A problem might look big but the key to it could be a small thing. This is why we need to pray for divine revelation and wisdom. Balaam was a prophet; he was harassed by an angel, he paid many useless visits; visits he shouldn't have paid ordinarily, he was to be paid to carry out some duties; thus inviting God's anger. If you look closely at his problems, the major one was covetousness.

A lady noticed that whenever she got a man that wanted to marry her, something would happen after a few months and the man would leave. She tried some prayers but there was no change. She tried 'head washing", it did not work. She tried dressing more attractively; she tried painting her face more colourfully, etc, but that didn't also work either. She tried attending parties, organised by unbelievers and she would serve rice to men that she did not know, etc, she started checking her horoscope but nothing worked. One day, she discovered that her problem was anger; the masquerade was unmasked and she identified her problem. Meanwhile, she had blamed many people for her predicament; her step-mother, the witches in her village, her former classmates, stolen clothes, etc. None of them was the problem. My prayer today, is that God will help you to unmask your problems in the name of Jesus. When a problem is unmasked, you offer no protection to the enemy.

4. **Loss of strange powers**. Supernatural powers or ability disappear when the wicked powers are expelled. There are some people, who were speaking in tongues before they got born again; such tongues are not from the Holy Spirit. If a white-garment herbalist prayed for you, and you started to speak in a strange tongue, you need deliverance. If you go through deliverance, such tongues should disappear and then you will ask God to fill you with His Spirit, so that you can speak real tongues.

Some people just wish in their mind, that something bad should happen, and it would. When they get delivered, such things should disappear.

Some people, who used to enter strange vehicles in their dreams, should no longer see the vehicles, when they get born again.

The Bible recounts the story of the girl in Acts 16. She used familiar spirits to prophesy to people. When Paul and Silas came to town, she shouted, saying they were the servants of the Most High God Paul allowed her to go on for two days and then rebuked the foul spirit in her. The Bible records that immediately Paul rebuked the spirit in her, all the satanic abilities in her disappeared.

Many people would not have been in problem today if they had not gone here and there to consult satanic agents. Even those that parade as white-garment prophets, you do not know the kind of spirit by which they are operating.

One night, during a vigil in church, a lady in white garment, walked in. I checked the time; it was 1:00 am. I thought it was a spirit, but as I drew closer, I found out that she was a human being. I told her that it was an unusual hour for a person to walk about. She asked if it was a sin to come and participate in the prayers. I said it is not a sin. Then she said she was a prophet. I asked how she prophesies and she said she 'enters into the spirit.' I asked if she could demonstrate it and she sat on the floor, crossed both legs and hands and closed her eyes. I prayed a short prayer to arrest every foul spirit in the vicinity. A few seconds later, she opened her eyes and I asked what happened. She said something slapped her and her spirit came back. I told her to try again and she tried several times but she could not go into the spirit. She got up in anger and left. Beloved, this is a person that people called 'prophetess' and she would lay hands on them and see visions for them, not knowing that the spirit in her would only re-arrange problems for them and they would not know

Your head is the most important part of your body. When you allow just anybody to lay hands on you, in the name of prophesying or seeing visions, you are giving them access to your glory. Satanic agents transfer the virtues of people, that way, while their own children prosper at the expense of the ignorance of the people who come to them.

When I was young, we had a strange pastor in the church I was attending. He used to say strange things and he had thick beards. One day, as the service was going on. he ran to the back, towards the entrance and shouted at a woman. He commanded her to turn and stand upright. He challenged her for daring to come into the house of God with her legs up and her head down. She said she was sorry and would not do it again. Those of us that were watching only saw a woman standing normally and who had a baby strapped on her back. We would have thought it was the pastor that was strange but the woman apologised. This was actually coming to church, but she still had strange powers. Normally, when a person gets born again and goes through deliverance, such powers should disappear from his or her life.

5. **Remarkable freedom for spiritual growth.**

We had a three day prayer meeting somewhere. On the first day, the message was; 'Back to Sender', the second day. It was; 'Overcoming Fear" the third day was a ministration on the fire of the Holy Ghost, Many people came out and the Lord baptised them. I noticed that there was a woman struggling and was almost crying that she did not receive the baptism. She must have been in her 50's and was well dressed and she lamented that she wanted a touch from the Lord. I drew back from her and prayed a short prayer, to ask God what her problem was. The Lord told me to look at her fingers. I drew close to her and found out that she had a ring on one finger and asked her to remove the ring. She said it was the only thing that she inherited from her grandmother. The ring had the inscription of a half-moon on it. Then she obliged. Immediately she removed it, she burst out in tongues. This means that the ring had something to do with her inability to receive the touch of God's power. Beloved, a simple-looking ring like that or any other possessed object could be heavily dozed with demonic power, it could look simple but could still be able to stop the spiritual growth of a person.

People look at us in M.F.M and say we are looking dull. I think it is better to do away with things that will make you look bright physically, but will keep you in spiritual bondage. Anyone who knows M.F.M and decides to be a perpetual deliverance candidate is free to remain that way. Any true man of God that knows about spiritual warfare, demon possession and deliverance would agree with me that, most of the things that people use to embellish themselves, could be demon possessed. How could you argue in favour of such ephemeral things, when you cannot even discern the kind of spirit that is in your house help? Your inability to pray and detect a witch around you will strengthen the enemy against you and he will use your ignorance to continue molesting you, and your spiritual life will be stagnant.

One evening, we were praying for a man, who took the prayers seriously. He prayed along and was sweating profusely and he asked for water to drink. When we rounded up and said he should go home he said he would continue praying since we were not coming the following day, The Lord told me that he had some strange objects at home and he confessed that he used to be an occultist, and had different kinds of powers and things, with which he could destroy people or make himself disappear, or even bind death. He also had something that could make him rich. I asked if his house was not far and he went to bring the things and we destroyed them. Today, the man *is a mi*nister of the Gospel. If he had not renounced and destroyed those powers, they would have caused a hindrance to his spiritual growth.

When a person gets delivered, all the hindrances to his or her spiritual growth disappears, the joy of salvation expands, praying becomes easier, fear and confusion depart, and all the demonic voices and calls will seize. The person will have greater respect for Christ and a greater awareness and hatred for evil. Nightmares will come to an end and the person will have peace and joy. All the weakness and sleep during prayers will disappear.

6. Establishment of a true identity.

Wicked spirits can cover a person and hinder him or her from knowing him or herself. They can confuse thoughts and emotions. They can substitute one person with another. The behaviour of some people indicate the presence of another personality in them. It is only when they get delivered, that their real self will come up. Their real identity has been clouded by wicked spirits and when these spirits get cleared out other people discover that they are really nice people; the marital situation of some, then improves. This is to say that what your husband or wife is doing now, could be because of the presence ot those spirits. Fighting him or her is not going to yield any result; it is the spirit behind his actions that you should bind.

7. The return of some problems.

After true deliverance, problems that were formerly removed or recycled by the devil will return. It is better to be free from the wicked, than to continue harbouring their favour in exchange for your soul. The reappearance of a problem which you solved demonically in the past is a good sign of deliverance. It means you can now pray, the correct prayer to God and He will remove the thing.

What I am saying in essence is that, you must refuse to settle for a re-arrangement of problems. You should not drop one sickness and pick another. Do not drop one problem for another. That is why, the Bible says: "They have healed the hurt of my daughter slightly and they are saying peace, peace, when there is no peace." It is better to pray for wholeness than patching up.

Psalm 46:1:
"God is our refuge and strength; a very present help in trouble,"

You must receive total victory today, do not accept half-wholeness or soundness. Do not accept half miracle. You should not hold allegiance to any power, for solving one problem or the other. You should not receive spiritual patching; it is better to be whole; and this is not a decision.

Beloved, if hitherto, you are not born-again, I would advise that you decide to surrender your life to Christ today. All you need to do is acknowledge the fact that you are a sinner and that you cannot approach in your sinful state. His eyes cannot behold sin; therefore repent of your sins. Confess them to the Lord and ask Him to forgive you and cleanse you from all unrighteousness. Name those sins one by one, renounce them and decide that you will never go back to them again. Say bye-bye to the world and the devil. Make a turn to the Lord and remain with Him.

Invite the Lord Jesus into your life; ask Him to come into your life and become your personal Lord and Saviour. Surrender your totality to Him and ask Him to take control of all that concerns you.

I congratulate you for this decision that you have just taken. It is the most important decision in life; I pray that it shall be permanent in your life in the name of Jesus. I pray that the Lord will uphold you with His right hand of righteousness and will keep you from falling, in the name of Jesus. I pray that He will write your name in the Book of Life and you will not by any means, rub it off in the name of Jesus. Go and sin no more.

The prayers that I am suggesting below are prayers that are meant to be prayed with aggression. I would advise that you pray them with all seriousness, and the determination that something good must happen to you today and that the enemy must cease to re-arrange problems in your life.

1. I break every evil promise that was made on my behalf in the name of Jesus.
2. You enemy of perfection in my life, be bound in the name of Jesus.
3. Every power exchanging my glory for ashes, die in the name of Jesus.
4. God arise and let my enemies be scattered in the mighty name of Jesus.
5. Every power managing problems in my life, die in the name of Jesus.
6. Enemies of my full-scale laughter be exposed and be disgraced in the mighty name of Jesus.
7. You my full-time enemies, scatter unto desolation, in the name of Jesus.
8. Everything in my life making me an enemy of God, come out and die, in the name of Jesus.
9. Anything in my life that is offending God, catch fire now in the name of Jesus.
10. You my life, refuse to be a refuse-bin of the devil, in the name of Jesus.
11. Anointing that destroys all yokes, fall upon me now, in the name of Jesus.
12. God arise and turn my pains to gains in the name of Jesus.
13. I shall reach my Promise land whether the devil likes it or not in the mighty name of Jesus.
14. Any evil padlock fashioned against me, be roasted in the name of Jesus.
15. Let all my benefits be removed from the hands of household enemies in the name of Jesus.
16. Every enemy of my breakthroughs be roasted in the name of Jesus.
17. Every stigma of the devil upon my life be rubbed off by the blood of Jesus.
18. Every evil attachment to my life be detached in the name of Jesus.
19. Thou power of God, deliver me from satanic prison in the name of Jesus.
20. Thou creative power of God, work in my life today, in the name of Jesus.
21. I refuse to be patched up; I receive soundness and wholeness in Jesus name.

The School Of Stagnancy

Vol. 6. No. 37

Deuteronomy 1:6-7; The LORD our God spake unto us in Horeb, saying: "Ye have dwelt long enough in this mount: turn you, and take your journey, and go to the mount of the Amorites, and unto all the places nigh thereunto, in the plain, in the hills, and in the vale, and in the south, and by the sea side, to the land of the Canaahites, and unto Lebanon, unto the great river, the river Euphrates."

The School of Stagnancy is a school that has a large number of students with many of them becoming Senior Prefects in it. Today, the same word in verse 6 is coming out to you that you have dwelt too long in your present spiritual state.

II King 7:3-8;
"And there were four leprous men at the entering in of the gate: and they said one to another: "Why sit we here until we die? If we say, we will enter into the city, then the famine is in the city, and we shall die there: and if we sit still here, we die also. Now therefore come, and let us fall unto the host of the Syrians: if they save us alive, we shall live; and if they kill us, we shall but die". And they rose up in the twilight, to go unto the camp of the Syrians: and when they were come to the uttermost part of the camp of Syria, behold, there was no man there. For the LORD had made the host of the Syrians to hear a noise of chariots, and a noise of horses, even the noise of a great host: and they said one to another: "Lo, the king of Israel hath hired against us the kings of the Hittites, and the kings of the Egyptians, to come upon us". Wherefore they arose and fled in the twilight, and left their tents, and their horses, and their asses, even the camp as it was, and fled for their life. And when these lepers came to the uttermost part of the camp, they went into one tent, and did eat and drink, and carried thence silver, and gold, and raiment, and went and hid it; and came again, and entered into another tent, and carried thence also, and went and hid it."

The men in this passage are lepers who were ostracised. They took the decision to leave their present state and go into the camp of the enemies, of whom they were afraid. They did not know that God had already taken care of the enemies. God had ordained terrifying noises in their camp and they had fled, thinking it was a host of enemies that were coming to attack them. (This explains the prayer point that goes thus; **O Lord, ordain terrifying noises in the camp of my enemies in the name of Jesus.**)

Though these men were lepers, they attacked their lack; they were bold to move forward. They were lepers, yet they went into the camp of the enemy, with violent faith. They said if the Syrian Forces spared their lives, it would be good and if they decided not to save them, it would be fine with them. They knew that the option of remaining where they were was not a good one.

Whether you know it or not, whether you like it or not, you are committed to something. God has deposited in our individual lives, certain talents, abilities, knowledge, strength, energy, time, etc. and everyone has committed this gift, to a selected end. That is, whatever God has deposited into your life, you have whether thoughtfully or thoughtlessly, righteously or unrighteously, legitimately or illegitimately committed it to something. The way we spend our time, money, etc is an eloquent testimony of what we are already committed to.

A woman prayed fervently one night, asking God to show her, her position. She saw herself in a vision, climbing a fleet of stairs. There were 17 steps in all and she was on the 3rd. She also saw 1964 written on the first step. She was well read and very active in the church. This was in the year 1994. She also saw her score, it was 22%. It means that all she had done since 1964 when she gave her life to Christ earned her only 22% and by 1994. she was supposed to have been on the 17th step, but was on the 3rd. She screamed. There was also an angel of the Lord by her side who told her that as far as God is concerned, 99% is failure that only 100% is accepted.

When people are stagnant, all kinds of things meet them there. All the periodical godliness is the same thing as perpetual hypocrisy. A sinner in an expensive, beautiful dress, is just like the sinner in rags. The sinner living in a luxurious part of town is the same as the sinner living in a remote area. They are both the same, in need of the same message; **REPENTANCE**. There is no modernisation or pampering of it.

I would like to ask you a serious question: Why should a person experience hell on earth, and still end up in hell when he or she dies?

The dead, weak prayer life, failure at holiness, is an evidence of the fact that a person has the enemy of God living inside him or her and that enemy must die otherwise, the person will remain in the school of stagnancy.

A white man said if you remember you are going to heaven and the devil is at your heels pursuing you, you will not sleep or play on the way. I would counsel you to know that you and your sins must part ways, otherwise, you cannot be God's friend. The Bible is straight forward; there is no middle camp; it says: "He that committeth sin, is of the devil." The school of stagnancy has a lot of academic religious, intellectual sinners in it. It has a lot of pen-robbers, academic-prostitutes. Many people speak in tongues, quote the Bible, yet they have thoughts of fornication, adultery, malice, etc, overshadowing their heart. They therefore remain at one level; exactly where the enemy wants them to be, they are exactly where household wicked powers want them to be, so that they could be boxed to a corner and fired and people would pity them, saying that; he or she was once strong and has fallen. The question is: Did the person ever walk? Did he or she ever have the strength of God? The truth of the matter beloved is that, you must leave where you are and move to where God wants you to be.

Take this prayer point with holy madness:
* *God arise and ordain terrifying noises against the forces of Egypt delegated against my life in the name of Jesus.*

Many people are very selfish and they are wasting away. Many are missing out on what God has ordained for them, because they do not want to do away with some habits or way of life. Therefore, they sit tight in a place where they are 'playing church.' They want to dress like the people of the world, contrary to what the Bible says, that a woman should not wear that which belongs to a man and vice versa. The Bible says those that do such things, are an abomination to God. As far as God is concerned, He does not know that they exist.

Many people hate changes. It is unfortunate that it is only a change that brings progress. When I came back from England with a PhD, I was called Doctor, by everybody. They were going to make me the District Choir Master. They just bought an organ, and I was happy. In that church, a few of us were born again and during Bible Study, our questions and contributions sounded strange. Sometimes, we were not allowed to say anything. One day, I saw a vision, where all the 'S.Us' were fighting a tall black strange man. We knew that he was the one responsible for all the problems in our church. But the more we beat him, the stronger he became. One of us thought the whip we were using, was not effective but when we tried it on one of us, he cried out and his body started to bleed, and this man made fun of us. Suddenly, I heard a voice saying; "Son, I did not commit the salvation of this place into your hands so, get out immediately." That vision made me know that I had to leave the place. When I left, many people begged me to stay but I thank God that I heeded His call. If I had stayed on, there would probably have been no M.F.M today.

Some people think they can change others, when they themselves have not changed. Many people criticise others, as if the salvation of those people, was in their hands. Except God instructs you to do the revival of a place and change and reorganise it, you cannot, no matter how long you stay there; then the Lord will query you for being stagnant. Even if your father was the founder, that does not mean you should remain there. This is a serious point for those who have the call of God upon their lives, but are joking with it. Some people will go to hell-fire because of their love for positions and recognition. They like to be revered; they want to see their names on posters and be given special seats at harvests and other functions. Some like titles so much, even in the church; they call themselves names like: 'Apostle', Most Senior Apostle' and they have special regalia that they put on.

God's message for you today is that, your Bible Study and prayer life must change. Some people are giving testimonies of mini-elevation from the valley, when they are supposed to be on the mountain top. They are many years behind God's schedule for their lives. The testimonies are good, but God wants you to change from where you are now, to where He wants you to be; not where you or your friends or enemies want you to be. Your friends might want you to be in hell-fire, while you yourself might want to be a political Christian; you have to leave that place. There are some brothers who go from a sister to another, proposing marriage. There are also many who go about canvassing for positions and posts in the church. This is how the devil cleverly pushes some people to hell fire where they will know that all those names are nothing; they are vanity, as far as the Bible is concerned. In fact, the Bible says some of these things are lighter than vanity. Your witnessing to other people must change; your consecration to the work of God must change. If you decide not to change, God will abandon the temple of your life as He did to Jerusalem.

A woman went on a pilgrimage to Jerusalem and brought oil, which she poured on another woman that was dying and nothing happened. She cried her eyes out. She did not know that the oil carries no power, until the anointing of God has been commanded upon it. Jerusalem is a city of rebellion that Jesus spoke to, that she has been left desolate, and Jesus wept because of the city.

Matthew 23:37-39:
"O Jerusalem, Jerusalem, thou that killest the prophets, and stonest them which are sent unto thee, how often would I have gathered thy children together, even as a hen gathereth her chickens under her wings, and ye would not! Behold, your house is left unto you desolate. For I say unto you: "Ye shall not see me henceforth, till ye shall say: "Blessed is he that cometh in the name of the Lord".

Jesus had already said that if a city rejected the Gospel, the disciples should shake off the dust of their feet at it; that it shall be terrible for that city on the day of judgement. Imagine what it then means, for Jesus to have wept on that city and someone brings oil from there, without praying on it. If you refuse to be purged, your house will be left unto you desolate; that is abandonment from the Lord.

Do you want God to abandon you? If you do not want that to happen, then quit the school of stagnancy. Otherwise, you will graduate into the school of backwardness and decay.

That is what happens when a person is not moving forward or growing. If a person remains in the school of stagnancy, he or she will collect evil spiritual deposits. It means when witches and wizards are coming back from their evil meeting, the bad things that dropped from them, will get into the life or body of such a person. If yellow fever drops from the witch and the stagnant person is around, he or she will collect it. When the devil is looking for people to receive his arrows, it is those in the school of stagnancy that will collect them. If you are stagnant, you will lose your freshness in God. That is why some people's prayers are no longer effective. The devil knows exactly what they are going to say.

If a person remains in the school of stagnancy, he or she will be spiritually redundant and irrelevant and God will replace the person with a stone. That is, God could raise a herbalist or Muslim scholar that surrenders his or her life to Christ. This new convert will become fervent and enthusiastic and will do exploits for the Lord. So much so, that the old ones will go to him or her for counselling. If you have been born again for ten years and you have never read through the Bible, you are in that school. If you have been born again for five years, and you cannot count five people that have become born again through your witnessing, you are in that school. If you have been born again for one year and nobody has ever told you that there is a change in your life, it means you are in that school. If you have been born again for six months, and you are still quarreling with neighbours and people have to intervene, then you are in that school.

If a person remains in that school, he or she will lose his or her usefulness and will eventually be demoted and that becomes a very serious matter. If you cannot do without evil thoughts or alcohol and you say it is ordinary wine, or you cannot do without taking bribe, then you are in that school. If you cannot do without seducing or being seduced by the opposite sex, you are in that school.

When we tell a married man not to commit adultery, or an unmarried boy or girl not to commit fornication, we are just helping them because every fornication or adultery, is a salary-advance, that the person has to pay back. In fact, the devil will charge the person interest which could be in any form; an incurable disease like AIDS, herpes, etc. Do not form the habit of falling into sin and asking for forgiveness and falling again. It means you are on your way to hell-fire, without any bus stop. If you say you cannot do without telling lies, even 'business lies', or that you cannot do without worldly fashion, you are in the school of stagnancy.

Many sisters have lost the power that God bestowed on them, because of fashion; they want to be like the people of the world, they want to 'dress to kill.' Some get into wrong relationships because they think they are getting too old to be unmarried. Some people cannot do without watching immoral films. In fact, some of them go to cinema houses. Some Christians watch magic shows on television or cultural dances in films where incantations are chanted. Whereas, they cannot go to physical magic shows or stand where a person is chanting incantations physically. When asked why they watch these things, some of them say that they are learning from them; whereas, they have a Bible, which God has given them to learn from, but they do not read it. Some people go to church and still impersonate others during examinations. Some cheat in examinations in order to acquire certificates. That is stagnancy. Some cannot do without cracking dirty jokes, and they would fight anyone who tries to correct them. There are so many also who are proud and boastful.

I asked a sister to go through deliverance and she said:"I beg your pardon, I have a Master's Degree in English." I asked if the certificate could solve the spiritual problems that she had. These days, many professors carry sacrifices in order to get promoted. Some Christians cannot do without attending parties, going from one prophet to the other for visions and prophesies. They do not know that the more they do that, the less power of God they have. Some mechanics who go to church, still feign car problems and steal spare parts. Many people drive recklessly, and they see it as nothing.

One day, a man drove recklessly and the other person shouted at him and he got down to 'straighten' things out. He found out that the person was a member of his church and he was ashamed of himself. Many sisters dress modestly and appear holy but they are chronic fornicators, while you find some among them carrying out abortions.

Christians do things they are not supposed to do, and insist that they have to defend their rights. God is not looking for protestants but soldiers. You cannot carry placards and sing that the devil should leave you alone. Christians are not supposed to cause confusion, or complain about other people. The lives of many people, discourage others from being fervent with the Lord, they are becoming a stumbling block to others.

As a small boy, I wanted to help an elderly man run an errand. I did not know what he had in the plastic bag in his hand, but I wanted to help him carry it. He refused and even got angry that I insisted on helping him. Suddenly, the bag fell and the content broke; it was a bottle of beer. This man was a chorus leader in his church.

Many people live on debts and some borrow from others, some beg others, whilst they have money tucked away in the bank. Many are afraid of spending their money; it means it has become an idol. It is stagnancy. Many people praise and give glory to themselves. The Bible says; "Comparing themselves with themselves they are not wise." Many judge, criticise and condemn others. Many seek the success of their businesses at the expense of others. Many read immoral, sex-novels and magazines. If you still have such things in your possession or you read them, I can assure you that you are putting yourself in bondage; you are on your way to hellfire. Overeating encourages stagnancy. If you still gamble and bet, you are practising witchcraft because it means two teams are having a competition and you now decide their fate on paper, saying that one should win and the other should lose. That is witchcraft. You cannot grow that way and it can take you to hell-fire. If you read the horoscope, it means your life will remain as the stars decide. Getting angry and a refusal to forgive, hatred, malice, misappropriation of funds, false humility and pretence, etc all give room to stagnancy.

Some people hang calendars of nude girls in their rooms or go to church in search of girlfriends and deceive them with marriage proposal. They do not know that they are only toying with hell. Some do not mind committing fornication and terminating any pregnancy that comes out of it. Many deceive their parents to get money. Many exaggerate, even couples; by the time a wife recounts her story, you would think her husband is a terror from the pit. If the husband is the one that comes, you would think the woman is a witch from the bottom of hell; they would say she always does this or that, whereas, the person only did it once. Many do not accept their mistakes. Many use abusive and worldly cliches in their conversations. They call God's creation: 'Bush Meat,' this is stagnancy.

Many will seek to revenge whatever evil is done to them, many curse and insult. Many are tribalistic, they sectionalise the church, forgetting that the Bible says as born again Christians, we do not have a continuing city here on earth. Some parents hinder their children from marrying the will of God for them, because of their tribal sentiments. Some people are unhappy when others are promoted above them. Many are hot-tempered; and many imagine evil in their heart.

All these things I have mentioned above, are the reasons why many people are still marking time on one spot. There is no change in their prayer lives, Bible reading and witnessing. They are actually going down because the mystery of iniquity has gripped their hearts.

2 Thessalonians 2:7:
"For the mystery of iniquity doth already work: only he who now letteth will let, until he be taken out of the way".

Matthew 24:12:
"And because iniquity shall abound, the love of many shall wax cold".

My prayer is that, all the children of God that are in the bondage of iniquity, shall be set free and the bondage shall be broken today in the name of Jesus.

A father beat his child mercilessly because the boy lit a mat strand and inhaled the smoke. Whereas, the father himself is a chain-smoker of cigarettes. That is the mystery of iniquity. Once the person starts, he or she will not be able to stop. Such will be glued down to iniquity and will be weighed down by it. Such people follow the Lord from afar off. Sinners are wounding God in the heart. Their master, the devil, was looking for the Lord's head but was only able to bruise His feet. The person that is wounding the heart of God, is doing more than the devil.

Today, I would like you to be serious about yourself. It is not the time to gauge the life of another person by what you are reading, but yours. If you do not kill that thing which is inside, then things will not improve. There is no other name that you can call iniquity. It is not God's will for you, it will drag you back.

I do not have anything else to say to you, than to encourage you to make a move to change. If you love yourself and you love heaven and love light and you do not want that voice to sound on that day saying; "Depart from me, ye workers of iniquity," you have to change. The activities you engage in, in the church, cannot stand for you; your singing, teaching Sunday school, giving, etc cannot replace the relationship that God is asking from you.

What I am talking about today has nothing to do with your age. You could have been a Christian for the past fifty years and God would have 20 steps for your life but you are only on step 3 that is, the primary department of faith. This is why the devil is having a filled time; he is doing what he likes; because people are not at the level where the powers of darkness cannot touch them. They are marking time at the level where the devil can do them anything and anyhow.

I am suggesting some prayers below, which I would like you to pray with all seriousness. If you have backslidden, you had better slide back to the Lord now.
If you are not born again, you have never surrendered your life to the Lord Jesus; I would advise that you take that decision today, right there where you are. Do not deceive yourself. You might be going regularly to church, you might be baptised and confirmed but not have a personal relationship with the Lord Jesus Christ.

All you need do, is acknowledge the fact that you are a sinner and that you cannot approach Him in your sinful state. Repent of your sins; confess them to the Lord and ask Him to forgive you and cleanse you from all unrighteousness. Claim the redemptive power in the blood of Jesus that was shed on the Cross at Calvary, for the remission of your sins. Invite the Lord Jesus Christ into your life, ask Him to come into your life and be your personal Lord and Saviour. Enthrone Him over your life and ask Him to take control of all that concerns you. Renounce the world of sin and the devil and make sure you do not go back to them anymore.

I congratulate you for this decision that you have just taken. It is the most important decision in life. I pray that it shall be permanent in your life in the name of Jesus. I pray that the Lord will uphold you with His hand of righteousness and will not let you fall.

Beloved, know for sure that if God is calling you a corpse, witches and wizards will overpower you;
Revelation 3:1b;
"I know thy works, that thou hast a name that thou livest, *and art dead".*

If you know in your heart that you are not at the level that God wants you to be, mirror yourself in the light of God's word and don't just walk away but adjust yourself. God called unto Adam and asked where he was. It is not that God could not locate where Adam was; but he was not where God wanted him to be. The same question goes out to you Brother, Sister, where are you? What is the definition of your spiritual location? If God should weigh you today spiritually, what would be your weight?

Take these prayer points with holy aggression:
1. Lord, remove me from the school of stagnancy in the name of Jesus.
2. I pull down, every evil kingdom working against me in the name of Jesus.
3. My heart will not be a stony ground for the word of God in the name of Jesus.
4. Let the power of resurrection fall upon my life now, in the name of Jesus.
5. God arise, and let stagnancy die, in the name of Jesus.
6. Let God arise and let every school of stagnancy around me die, in the mighty name of Jesus.
7. I refuse to be a student in the school of stagnancy in the name of Jesus.
8. God promote me from the valley to the mountaintop, in the

name of Jesus.
9. My life, move forward by fire, in the mighty name of Jesus.
10. Let God arise and His enemies be scattered in the name of Jesus.
11. Anything in my life, contradicting the power of God, die, in the name of Jesus.
12. Every emptiness in my life, be filled by the blood of Jesus.
13. Every weakness in me turn to strength by the fire of the Holy Ghost, in the name of Jesus.
14. I shall reach my goal whether the devil likes it or not, in the name of Jesus.
15. Every power, pushing weakness into my life, die, in the name of Jesus.
16. All the spiritual amputators, amputate yourselves in the name of Jesus.
17. Enough is enough, of poverty, sickness, lack, in my life in the name of Jesus.
18. I refuse to be harassed by household wickedness in the name of Jesus.
19. Every multiple cage around my life, be roasted by the fire of the Holy Ghost in the name of Jesus.
20. I destroy the strength of every stubborn problem in the name of Jesus.

Students In The School Of Confusion (1)

Isaiah 24:10; *"The city of confusion is broken down: every house is shut up, that no man may come in."*

More than at any time in the history of the world, there are many more confused people. Most of those who see visions these days, see confusing visions, and many people are becoming senior prefects in the school of confusion. But the Bible says our lot as Christians, ought not to be so.

Many years ago, when we were at the university, each department used to interview final-year students, just before their final examination. These students were asked questions on their course of study, the problems they encountered and their prospects for the future. When it got to the turn of a particular boy, he did not know the answers to the three questions he was asked. When the examiners saw that he was confused, they asked him his name and he still could not answer correctly; this is what confusion can do. The largest pathway to confusion is the lack of knowledge.

Confusion is one of the most powerful spirits operating these days. The reason why many people get confused however, is because they lack knowledge. There are many questions that we ask ourselves everyday, there are many questions emanating from our personal lives or that our personal lives will ask us, there are also many questions that the people and things around will ask us, and except a person has knowledge, he or she will get confused.

1 Corinthians 14:33;
"For God is not the author of confusion, but of peace, as in all churches of the saints".

God is never the author of confusion and His children are not supposed to get confused. God does not design confusion. That verse in Isaiah 24:10 says a confused city shall fall to the enemy; it shall be broken down. Likewise, a confused life cannot make progress because the school of confusion is filled with uncertainty whereas Paul says; "I fight, not as one who beats the air; I run, not with uncertainty." Beloved, there are many Christians, who are now beating the air, there are also many of them, who fight with uncertainty. They are not sure where it will end. They just want to play along with others, and see what happens.

Leviticus 18:23;
"Neither shalt thou lie with any beast to defile thyself therewith: neither shall any woman stand before a beast to lie down thereto: it is confusion ".

Do you know that these days, there are women who have turned dogs into husbands, and men who have turned dogs into wives? The Bible says it is confusion; it is a perversion of God's order of doing things.

Let's see Leviticus 20:12;
"And if a man lie with his daughter in law, both of them shall surely be put to death: they have wrought confusion; their blood shall be upon them".

Also, Isaiah 41:29;
"Behold, they are all vanity; their works are nothing: their molten images are wind and confusion ".

And Isaiah 45:16;
"They shall be ashamed, and also confounded, all of them: they shall go to confusion together that are makers of idols".

All the above are abomination and confusion. Incest etc, the worship of false gods and idols, are all confusion. Know also that there are different kinds of modern-day idol worship and worshippers these days.

James 3:15-16;
"This wisdom descendeth not from above, but is earthly, sensual, and devilish. For where envying and strife is, there is confusion and every evil work".

All the wisdom of Man is confusion. Many people do

not know what they are doing. Some think they know, but actually, they do not know what they are doing; their lives are like the sound of the trumpet which no one can decipher. The Bible says; "If the trumpet gives an uncertain sound, who shall get ready for battle? When people look at you from the outside and see you as a liar and that your life does not show any sign of being born again, neither does it show any sign that you are a Christian, or that the power of God is in your life, it means you are not worthy of being called a Christian. Some people make an empty boasts that witches or wizards cannot touch them; whereas, they have no power; that person will only end up becoming a bush-meat for the devil and that is not what God wants for His children. This happens when people are confused.

There was a blind man at Bethsaida; a cursed city; he met Jesus, Who took him out of the city and then touched his eyes. When Jesus asked him if he could see, he said he could see, but that he could see men like trees. Jesus touched him again and he saw clearly. Many people are like that; they do not see clearly; because they are living in a world, filled with all kinds of things, which they see or know nothing of. They have become subject to prophets and priests. Such people need a second touch today.

When the early Pentecostal fathers started in this country, practically everybody in the church was a prophet. They could see; they did not need to go to the pastor to see visions for them; they could all see. Anyone who cannot see, will get confused; he or she would not know where and when to go; they would not know when anybody is saying the right or wrong thing. Sometimes, when people come for counselling and they recount how they had gone to satanic agents for help, I would ask them why did they go there and they would say that their problems put them in a confused state that anywhere they were asked to go, they were ready to go; they would say they were ready to do anything just to get a solution to their problems. That is confusion. Many people are confused in the church today; even to the extent that these people are living with witches and wizards, without knowing it.

A pastor friend came to see me one day. He wanted me to help a lady, who had problems. She was the one who used to go and buy his lunch everyday at the office and he praised her that she was very nice. When he brought her to my office, the Lord told me that she was a principality. I asked the pastor to excuse us and I confronted her with what she was and she accepted my word; she agreed to it. She confessed many of her activities in the spirit realm. Later, I called in the pastor and told him what she was. He cried out! This was a man, who had been to Bible College and even had PhD in Theology, but could not see spiritual things. What I am trying to say is that, academic knowledge and theology, are nothing when we consider the plan and organisation of the powers of darkness. The powers of darkness are well organised and they work strategically. Many people do not realise this and they are confused.

Elisha's servant saw fear, he saw the enemies but he did not see the host of heaven that were with him and his master. He was confused until his master asked God to open his spiritual eyes. The physical eyes are useless, as far as spiritual matters are concerned. The physical eyes could even land one into trouble.

A man was invited to a party somewhere outside Lagos. He got to the party and found out that everybody else was served food, except him. He had to draw the attention of the waiters that he came all the way from Lagos. Eventually, he was served last and as he was eating, a snake crawled from the backyard of the place they were, without anyone seeing it and crawled up the man's legs to his neck, licked his face and crawled back into the bush. He was petrified and he got up from the food and went back to Lagos. After a while, trouble started in every part of his life. What happened? He lacked spiritual sight hence confusion set in unnoticed.

Many people are like that; they follow the crowd and dance to the tune of the world. They eat anything, anywhere; use anything they get from anybody. Some people sing that their blood is bitter, that witches cannot suck it, but these same people are not careful.

Many people are looking for power or even double portion anointing but the secret of double portion is servanthood. If you are not ready to be a servant of God, you cannot receive any portion of His anointing. Elisha was first the servant of Elijah, before he could get a double portion of his anointing. Many people are so confused, that they do not want to serve the Lord, but they want double portion anointing. They feel too big to carry benches or clean the church. They see it as the job of other people; Joshua served Moses and eventually, God allowed him to lead the Israelites to the Promised Land.

Many people come to the church and expect to be worshipped. They would like to become spiritual giants, but they do not like to serve. God's concern is different from ours. His major concern now is that, the harvest is plenteous, but the labourers are few. Many want to be bosses; only a few are ready to be labourers. Anyone who has received the Holy Ghost has received Him, in order to work for God. If you have received the Holy Spirit, you have an urgent task to do for God, otherwise, on the Last Day, that gift will stand against you.

God does not just distribute the Holy Spirit anyhow. He has a purpose for bestowing Him upon each of us and if anyone's life does not fulfil that purpose, he or she will be heading for the judgement seat of Christ, where such will be judged. God gave you the Holy Ghost, in order to deliver others. If you feel that the Holy Ghost is there to protect you and make you feel good, it means you are confused.

If you are a soldier in the army, your gun is supposed to be used against the enemy. It would be foolish, to say that because you were not made the captain, so, you will not shoot the enemy. Many people want to be captain, to give orders, but cannot take orders from anyone. Some have drawn the conclusion that God cannot use them. Others are saying they are too old or too young; this is confusion. If you wasted time in the wilderness of life, not knowing God, your zeal now, should be that the Lord should use you, during the years that remain. Invest the rest of your life in the work of God, so that you will stop getting confused.

All the nine gifts of the Holy Spirit that the Bible mentioned in 1 Corinthians 12, are not for pastors and evangelists alone. They are for everyone and you can receive them. Anyone who tells you that the gifts are for a selected few is telling you a lie. All the members of the church at Corinth had at least one of these gifts. The Bible says that God has given each of us, a measure of faith. What will you do with your own measure of faith?

Do you just want to go and come out of church services and remain the same way you are? Do you just go for fellowship to warm the benches? If after six months that the Lord has poured His Spirit upon you and invested salvation on you, you cannot point at one person that got born again because of your own testimony, or as a result of your witnessing, then you have not yet reached the level God wants you to be. Not everybody will be a preacher but everybody can witness; everybody can tell the sinner what Jesus has done, and what He can do.

Are you insensitive to the fact that sinners will perish, if they do not repent? Do you not feel sorry for them? Do you find it degrading, to preach in the bus or on the streets? If you are not careful, you will get to a stage where you will beg that you should be allowed to preach but it will be too late then. When the Bible talks about people shedding tears in heaven, it is referring to those who will be regretting not having done enough work for the Lord. The converts that they won; are doing better in glory than them.

If you claim to be born again and your life does not show that something has actually happened to you, and your husband or wife is not getting converted because of you, then there is confusion. If you, as the husband is born again and the members of your family do not know that you now have the Fire of God in you or whilst others are praying, you, the head of the family that is supposed to be the priest of the house is sleeping, or you are the one even complaining about having bad dreams, it means you are in the school of confusion.

Christians are members of the body of Christ and the body is a living organism. If the eyes are blind, the ears are deaf, the hands and legs are maim, then, that body is of no use. So also, if the body of Christ lacks the fruit of the spirit, it means she has no spiritual sight and cannot hear from God nor do exploits for Him, then, there is confusion.

God does not want us to go to church, for the sake of attendance. He wants us to minister to Him. There are hundreds of ways, whereby you can minister to God. Many people will be surprised, at the kind of allegations that God will levy against them. He would tell them what He expected them to do, which they did not do or failed in. I pray that you will not fail God in the name of Jesus if you are a student in the school of confusion, it is possible for you to be in a place and not know why God took you there.

We used to have an old lecturer, who always asked us where we stopped at the last meeting. We would tell him and the lecture would start. One day, we decided not to tell him, so that we would know what the problem was. When he came in, he asked us where we stopped at the last lecture. Nobody answered. He then went to a boy sitting at the front row and looked at his notebook. The boy did not come to school the previous week so, his notes stopped at the lecture we had two weeks earlier. The old man then proceeded from there; we gave a loud shout that we had gone past that lesson. He rebuked us and one boy asked why he never knew where we stopped, each time he came. The old man said we were lucky to have him, that the lecturer he had in that course in the United States, did not have much time to explain anything to them; that he would say he was a lecturer and not a teacher. He explained that they could hardly hear that lecturer because he always faced the blackboard to write and talk at the same time. Most of the time, those at the back would not hear what he was saying. The fact of the matter is that, even though the lecturer was educated, he was confused. It means that education is not a way out of confusion.

Sometimes, those who are not educated are more orderly than the educated ones, especially when the Spirit of God is in them.

The Psalmist says:
"I am wiser than the ancients for the Spirit of God is upon me."

You must be something for the Lord; you cannot just attend church services without doing anything. You could pray with sinners, invite people to meetings, witness to people at work or at school, or on the streets or even in the bus. I have seen someone preach in an aircraft; this man was comfortable, and was not ashamed of preaching. You could send tracts to people, you could prophesy, teach, exhort others, give things to the needy, give to the Lord etc. You do not have to be rich, before you give to the Lord. Everyone must have spiritual gifts.

1 Corinthians 12:7;
"But the manifestation of the Spirit is given to every man to profit withal."

You do not have to be complacent, regarding other brethren as super spiritual, as if they dropped from the moon. They are not from the moon and if you could develop yourself, you would find out that you could be better. The problem with many people is the fact that they are confused. Many are also fearful. They are like a cow that is being taken to the abbatoir; as soon as it perceives the odour of blood, it would know that it is being led to be slaughtered, like the other cows that went before it. Such people want to continue in their worldly ways, attending parties and dressing like the people of the world. These people are smelling blood on that altar, where self is crucified and they do not want to part with it, so they choose the way of destruction. No pastor or minister can do everything alone by himself in the church. That is why there are many departments in the church. It is worthwhile for you to prayerfully select the group, where God wants you to function, and work there, with the whole of your heart.

If everyone is busy working for the Lord, there will be no time for gossip. A working church is a powerful force. In the early church in the book of Acts of the Apostles, everybody worked. Even the deacons were preaching on the streets. Stephen, Philip, were deacons and the Bible recounts their exploits. Today, many Christians prefer watching television than attending fellowship and when they do come, they arrive late. We should all go to the church charged; that is, each person should have prayed concerning the programme so that as the preacher is preaching, sinners will get on their knees and repent of their sins, the sick will receive healing and everyone will receive a miracle. If the Lord wants you to work for Him and you are dodging, things will stop going on well physically and spiritually. God wants you to serve Him first and then He will add other things to you. If you pack aside what He wants you to do, and you are looking for the additions, things will not go well with you.

This is an important message, which I would not want to rush over. I would like to pause here; we shall continue in the next chapter. Meanwhile, I will advise that you pray the prayer points with all the seriousness that you can gather. However, if you have not surrendered your life to the Lord Jesus Christ, it means you are a student in the School of Confusion. I would advise that you take the decision to become born again today. All you need do is recognise the fact that you are a sinner and that you cannot approach God in your sinful state; the Bible says that the eyes of God cannot behold sin. Repent of your sins; confess them to the Lord, name them one by one, renounce them and ask the Lord to forgive you and cleanse you from all unrighteousness. Claim the redemptive power in the Blood of Jesus that was shed on the Cross at Calvary, for the remission of your sins. Say bye-bye to the world of sin and the devil.

Invite the Lord Jesus into your life; ask Him to become your personal Lord and Saviour. Enthrone Him over your life; ask Him to take control of all that concerns you and surrender your totality to Him.

If you just took this decision, I congratulate you. It is the most important decision in life. I pray that it shall be permanent in your life in the name of Jesus. I pray that the Lord will uphold you with His right hand of righteousness and keep you standing till the end in the name of Jesus. I pray that He will write your name in the Book of Life and you will not by any means rub it off in the name of Jesus. Go and sin no more!

Take these prayer points with all the aggression that you can gather:

1. Any power stealing the milk and honey of my life, die, in the name of Jesus.
2. Father Lord, grant me Your miraculous visitation today, in the name of Jesus
3. My Father make me a candidate of Your great deliverance today, in the name of Jesus.
4. My Father let every resistance to my breakthroughs crumble, in the name of Jesus.
5. Every slow progress in my life, receive the resurrection power of the Lord Jesus Christ, in the name of Jesus.
6. My Father, make Your grace sufficient for me this year, in the name of Jesus.
7. Let all weapons and devices of the oppressors and tormentors be rendered impotent, in the name of Jesus.
8. Every power attacking my glory, die by fire in the name of Jesus.
9. Every arrow organised against my prayer life, backfire in the name of Jesus.
10. Every power that wants me to miss the fullness of my destiny, be terminated by fire in the mighty name of Jesus.
11. Let God arise and let his enemies be destroyed, in Jesus' name.
12. Every power organised against my calling and my ministry, die in the name of Jesus.
13. I shall reach my goal, whether the devil likes it or not, in the name of Jesus.
14. Let the fire of God destroy every power operating any spiritual

vehicle working against me, in the name of Jesus.
15. Let all evil advice given against my favour crash and disintegrate, in the name of Jesus.
16. Let the wind, the sun and the moon run contrary to every demonic presence in my environment, in the name of Jesus.
17. You devourers, vanish from my labour, in the name of Jesus.
18. Let every tree planted by fear in my life dry up from the roots, in the name of Jesus.
19. I cancel all the enchantments, curses and spells that are against me, in the name of Jesus.
20. Let all iron-like curses upon my life, break, in the name of Jesus.
21. I bind every spirit of confusion in my life, in the name of Jesus.
22. Every power sponsoring confusion in my life, die in the name of Jesus.

Students In The School Of Confusion (2)

Isaiah 24:10; *"The city of confusion is broken down: every house is shut up, that no man may come in."*

1 Corinthians 14:33;
"For God is not the author of confusion, but of peace, as in all churches of the saints."

James 3:15-16;
"This wisdom descendeth not from above, but is earthly, sensual, devilish. For where envying and strife is, there is confusion and every evil work."

In the last bulletin, we started this important message; we mentioned the fact that, all the wisdom of Man is confusion, and that many people do not know what they are doing; unfortunately, many people think they know, but actually do not know what they are doing. Their lives are like the sound of the trumpet which no one can decipher. The fact that many people are confused makes progress slow or non-existent. It also leads to disunity in the body of Christ and is giving the enemy a free hand, to operate against God.

We shall continue and conclude this topic. Also, the prayer points at the end of this message are to be prayed with all seriousness, and not just to be read like statements.

Many people are busy selling one thing or the other, whereas, God wants them to be doing some other thing somewhere or working for Him. If what God wants for you in His agenda is to be busy for Him and then, get your prosperity, but you shift it aside to do what you want, you cannot blame God for whatever happens to you. With whatever you have that you use for God, God will set blessing in motion for you. Jesus says: *"Go into the world and preach the Gospel, and make disciples..."* If we use all the information that we have to serve the Lord, we will be better off. If we put our lives on fire for God, catch the zeal for His kingdom. He can't leave us comfortless. If you have a Primary School Leavers Certificate, use it for the Lord. If you have a West African School Certificate or a University degree, set it in motion for the Lord. Whatever you have, whatever God blesses you with, set it in motion for Him.

If each member of the church decides to talk to at least twenty people in a week, about their souls, our lives will become better. For example, if you go around your area, preaching and telling people not to commit fornication, that it will lead them to hell, you would have overpowered the temptation to commit fornication yourself, notwithstanding the temptation to commit fornication on the people you have preached to; that is the power of confession; when you preach about something, it keeps you away from that sin. If you preach in the office, that it is not good to steal, you will find out that you would have overcome stealing. If you preach love at home, you will be able to act it, you will not be able to go back on your words. If there are ten thieves in your street and you preach to nine of them and they get converted; your life is safer. If you do not preach to them, or you just manage to preach to one of them, the situation will be critical because they can attack at any time and take away the property of people on the street, including Christians or including yours. Or as a child of God, you might be able to recover your property but you would have suffered first. It would have been the fault of the Christians in that area, for not preaching to them.

We must therefore reach out to lost sinners; we should not sit and wait for them to come and meet us where we are. The Bible says; "The Son of Man has come to seek and to save that which was lost, (the lost)" Many people do not know the joy that is in talking to people about Christ; it is the greatest service that you can do for God because that is why the Lord Jesus came to the world. If you just go to church and leave the way you came in; you are not bothered about the souls that are perishing beside you, if your life is not a testimony, then you are playing an uncertain trumpet sound. It will not earn you any credit before God. This is the spirit of confusion and it must get out of you.

If you are converted and filled with the Holy Ghost, you must work for God, otherwise, He will pull out that thing that you love so much and is occupying your heart, until you learn. Some people have parents that pray for them, so they relax; they do not get serious with God until one or both parents die. Some women are not serious with God, until their husband starts having girlfriends outside or even get a second wife. I pray that the Lord will help you to understand this message in the name of Jesus.

All the gifts in the Bible are for us. I pray that the Holy Spirit will open our eyes to them in Jesus name. When a person gets spiritually confused, it leads to physical confusion. That is why some people are on their own; they do not belong to any fellowship of Christians, they do not witness to people, they go to church late, they have no fire in their spirit for prayers, they dose off during sermons and cannot recount what they learnt from any message, or lack concentration during prayers. Many people are addicted to worldly dressing; it is confusion. God is not the author of confusion. If you belong to Him, there are certain things that are not expected of you. All the fits of anger, verbal attacks at people, are signs of confusion. Many people are not sure of their salvation; if Jesus should come now, they are not sure of going with Him. Many cannot explain what redemption is; if a person has been going to church for one year, and does not know what redemption is, then the person is in the school of confusion. If you have no interest in your spiritual development, if you cannot define your role in the house of God, you are in the school of confusion and must get out of it.

If you talk to your husband anyhow, you address him as a servant, and still want him to play the role of the head, it will not work. If you treat your wife as a glorified slave, and you still want her to play the role of a wife, it will not work. If as a believer, you still go to the so called 'prophets', for them to see visions for you and prophesy into your life, you are in the school of confusion. Many people have gone to such prophets and have collected witchcraft prophesies which they believed and the things are now happening to them. If you mix up your faith with beggarly powers, you are in the school of confusion. Lack of respect for elders, is a mark of confusion. The Bible says you should respect your father and mother, so that your days on earth will be long. Also, some people spend many years in churches where they are not growing spiritually; they stick to doctrines that are not in the Bible.

Smith Wigglesworth was dying of appendicitis and brethren from his church came to sympathise with him. Some of them wept, lamenting that their brother was about to die. One day, a woman came with her six-year-old son, to pay him a visit. She wept and as she got up to leave, her six-year-old son jumped on the bed and laid his hand on Smith's tummy and commanded the devil to release him, in the name of Jesus. Smith was made whole immediately and he got up. When his doctor came in, he was surprised to see him cleaning his apartment; he thought he was coming to certify him dead on that day. The mother of that boy was confused but the boy wasn't. God has no respect for human achievement or a person's position in the society. Everyone is a child before Him.

But the question is "What have you done for Him so far?" I am not asking how much you have spent but what spiritual significance you are putting into the house of God? God does not want you to just go to and fro the church warming benches, or doing evil in secret; anything you do in secret, that you cannot do openly, is a mark of confusion. Some sisters want to be prayed for, in order to get pregnant. When asked who or where the husband is, they say that they are not married, but the man gave the condition of getting pregnant before going to the altar. That is confusion.

The most confused people in the house of God today, are

those who claim to be born again, but whose lives do not bear the testimony. They claim to be sanctified, but still abuse people, beat up their wife or fight their husband. Many claim to be filled with the Holy Ghost, but speak powerless tongues.

When we tell some people to go through some spiritual rigour, they threaten to leave the church, as if they were there by themselves or for the sake of one person or the other. Anyone that goes to church does so for his or her own benefit. In M.F.M, we do not have special seats for people; everyone is the same before the Lord. Whatever you are, when you get to the house of God, put it in your pocket and humble yourself before Him. If what you have or are, could deliver you from the hands of the oppressors, you would not have had to go to church to pray; you could have used your money to beg the devil, but that cannot work.

There are many people, who have made others to stumble; the blood of such people is on their necks. Some people say they drink beer, but do not get drunk. How about those people who saw them drinking beer and decided to start drinking too; those who stumbled because of Christians who drink beer? Such people will account for the blood of those people. Some people wear clothes that expose their body, and say they dress to please themselves; they will account for the blood of the people that fall, through looking at them. Even without tight or open skirts, some brothers are having problems resisting the devil's temptation to sin. When they now see such obscene dressing, they fall flat. If you are one of those that 'dress to kill,' you are aiding the devil to do his work and you will account for the lives of those that fall through you.

My prayer day and night, is that the Lord should send to us, people who are ready to hear the word of God and change. M.F.M is not a commercial organisation and will not by any means, aid anyone, who is heading for hell-fire. We would rather pull them back. If you are a New Testament reader, you would have found out that God wants every believer to be a servant, a priest and a king. You would have noticed in the Old Testament, that a king cannot combine his office, with that of a priest. Today, our own priesthood is after the order of Melchesedec, who was both a king and priest. The function of the priest, is to offer sacrifices and his greatest mistake, would be to offer the wrong sacrifice. Many people come to the house of God with the wrong sacrifice, even though it could be a good one; like that of Cain. God wants you to present yourself as a living sacrifice. He needs you first and in your totality. It is then, that He can use your money or anything you want to offer Him. All must be given out with a freewill heart. Even the songs of praise that we sing to Him, must be voluntary and from the heart. Any offering that you give out of duress or pressure or intimidation, will not get you anywhere. It is also necessary to pray that God should stop all the commercial prophets that are going about deceiving people and confusing Christians.

One day, a preacher, asked the people in his congregation to rise to their feet, with their car keys. He then started to recount how a man gave his car to his pastor and he got ten others within one week. Many of the people standing got carried away and stepped forward to donate their cars, by dropping the keys. One of them had a sensible wife, who drew his attention to the fact that he was acting under duress and not from the heart. She reminded him of the fact that they had only one car so he should go back and collect the key. The man went back to the pastor who made fun of him and asked if it was his wife that was controlling him, or the other way round. That was a commercial preacher.

If you donate ten cars to the church and you are not born again, both you and the preacher taking them from you will likely find yourselves in hellfire. It does not bother God, because the money that will be used for His work, has been prepared and He knows how it will come out. Your first priority here on earth, is to make yourself a candidate of heaven and every other thing will follow. If people say that there is power in the body of Christ, get that power, let people and evil powers, recognise you as a power generator; become a vessel of honour, be close to Jesus.

You might wonder how close a person could be to Jesus. The simple answer is that you can be as close to Jesus, as you want to be. If you claim to be a Christian and you do not hear directly from God and are not following in the Holy Spirit, you are wasting time. God could tolerate you but not bless you because of your unseriousness. God wants power and purity in your life. Any power you ask for, to come on top of uncleanness will lead to confusion.

The life of a Christian is in a threefold progression:
1. **Egypt:** When you were in the world before giving your life to Jesus Christ.
2. **Wilderness:** This signifies dryness, temptation, hardship, the flesh. Here the devil and his demons are waging war against you. It is unfortunate that many people die in the wilderness, even after having succeeded in leaving Egypt behind.
3. **Canaan:** This is where the flesh no longer controls your life. It is where God wants you to be. It is the Promised Land.

Beloved, where are you? Do you still have one leg in 'Egypt' and the other in the wilderness? Since you became born again, are you still battling with the flesh? Or has it even overcome you? This three-fold progression, can be likened to the tabernacle of Moses, which had the outer court, inner court and the holy of holies. Some people are 'outer-court' Christians; they are looking at the power of God from afar and are not getting it. Some are in the inner-court, not far from God, but are not really where He wants them to be; these still have time to be upset or angry; they are not yet in the holy of holies. While some people are in the holy of holies; here the enemy cannot attain them. Beloved, if you live a holy life, no weapon of the enemy can prosper against you.

There are also 30-fold believers, who get just 30% of what is taught in the church. The Bible recounts the Parable of the Sower; some seeds fell on the stony ground, some by the road side, and some on the good ground. The ones that fell on good ground, were the ones that thrived and yielded good fruit. They are the 100-fold believers; the word of God enters into their hearts and yields good results.

Just take the Levites as a case study. There was a tribe in Israel called Levi; priests were from that tribe. They were called Levites. Not all Levites were priests but all priests were Levites. A priest could become a high priest. It means not all Christians have the holy of holies life, though God wants them to be.

Where are you beloved? You might stay in the spiritual wilderness throughout your life, if you are not careful. You might stay in the outer-court, if you are not careful. Find out the higher ground that the Lord wants you to occupy; then take possession of it. Today, you will pray about spiritual powers and gifts, so that you too can live in the gift of the Holy Spirit.

Maybe your business is not working out well right now. Maybe you have employed members of the secret cults, or witches, or agents from the water, or people with familiar spirits and you do not know. That kind of business cannot thrive because you the owner is in darkness. If you close your eyes and walk, you will stumble on many things and eventually fall. How long do you want to continue in darkness? A blind person can fall, even during the day, because he cannot see, so also a spiritually blind Christian will make mistakes. You have to determine within yourself that that must stop today in the name of Jesus.

I am suggesting some prayer points below and I would want you to pray them the way that you have never done before. The Bible says: "The gift of the Spirit is given to every man, to profit withal." You too, are a candidate for claiming the Holy Spirit; do not settle for less; even if anyone is telling you something contrary, do not believe the person. You must see, hear and be able to discern. You should not see men as trees; know them for what they are.

There is no point calling yourself a Christian, if you cannot see spiritually. The Bible says that God is not the author of confusion. You are not supposed to get confused. Maybe you even think that God has forgotten you, or that He is too late. That is confusion. If God should open your eyes, you will be able to ask Him questions and you will rest content in your soul.

Elisha could rest in the midst of the enemies, because he could see. He knew that they would never defeat him. He was sure of that. How wonderful it is, to start from the position of victory, knowing that you will never lose and rest assured on it. It does not just come like that; your eyes and ears have to be open!

Concentrate on the Lord Jesus Christ. Do not give your heart, the time to wander. Pray with decision and determination, believing God, that your life will never be the same again.

This is a prayer that I am praying for you, right there where you are. I pray that the Shekinah glory of God will envelope you right there where you are in the name of Jesus. Read this prayer aloud, as a confession: "Our Lord and our God, Your promise to us, is that we shall receive power, after the Holy Ghost has come upon us. You also said that the gifts of God are given to every Man, to profit withal. Lord, I pray that today, the manifestation of the Holy Ghost will completely envelope my life, so that my eyes will begin to see, my tongue will being to speak out. All spirits of confusion will be chased out of my life in the name of Jesus. Wonderful God, let your Shekinah glory envelope my life completely in Jesus' name.

I counsel you to take the following prayer point with a full concentration and to continue praying until you receive a touch from the Lord. Do not bother about time; remain on this prayer point, for as long as it will take you to feel the touch of the Lord. Do not worry about what is going on around you.

* **Father Lord, incubate me with the fire of the Holy Ghost in the name of Jesus.**

However, you are likely to remain a student in the school of confusion, if you are not born again. The first step out of confusion is a total surrender to the Lord Jesus Christ. All you need do is acknowledge the fact that you are a sinner and that your sins are constituting a hindrance to your spiritual growth. Repent of your sins and confess them to the Lord; name them one by one and ask Him to forgive you and cleanse you from all unrighteousness. Claim the redemptive power in the blood of Jesus that was shed on the Cross at Calvary, for the remission of your sins.

Invite the Lord Jesus into your life; ask Him to come in and become your personal Lord and Saviour. Ask Him to take absolute control of your life and all that concerns you. Surrender your totality to Him. Say bye-bye to the world and the devil. Take up the New Life that is in the saving knowledge of the Lord Jesus Christ. Go and sin no more!

Congratulations! The decision that you have taken, is the most important decision in life. I pray that it shall be permanent in your life, in the name of Jesus. I pray - that the Lord will uphold you with His hand of righteousness and will not let you fall, in the name of Jesus. I pray that the Lord will write your name in the Book of Life and you will not by any means, rub it off in the name of Jesus.

Now, take the following prayer points with aggression and with the determination to get liberated from every form of confusion.

1. Lord, shake away all the shakeables in my life, in the name of Jesus.
2. Lord, open my eyes, that I may see all that You want me to see, in the name of Jesus.
3. Lord, open my ears that I may hear from You in the name of Jesus.
4. I bind the spirit of confusion in my life in the name of Jesus.
5. Let the fire of the Holy Ghost burn away every handiwork of the spirit of confusion in my life in the name of Jesus.
6. Let the anointing of the Holy Ghost, saturate my life right now, in the name of Jesus.
7. I withdraw my progress from every satanic regulation and domination, in the name of Jesus.
8. Every garment of darkness be roasted by fire, in the name of Jesus.
9. Spiritual deafness in my life, die, in Jesus' name.
10. Spiritual blindness in my life, clear away by fire, in Jesus name.
11. Every gate of hell-fire in

my life, be destroyed by fire in Jesus' name.
12. Every seed of hell-fire in me, catch fire in the name of Jesus.
13. Anointing of success, overshadow me by fire in Jesus' name.
14. Thou spirit of confusion, my life is not your landing space, release me and die in Jesus' name.
15. I delete my name from the school of confusion, in the name of Jesus.
16. Every register of confusion containing my name and profile, catch fire in Jesus name.
17. God arise and give me a new name, in the mighty name of Jesus.
18. Environmental powers introducing confusion into my life, die now, in Jesus name.
19. Every foundational power of confusion, die by fire, in Jesus' name.
20. Every power of my father's house introducing multiple battles into my life, release me and die, in the mighty name of Jesus.
21. I refuse to live a floating life, in the name of Jesus.
22. Every deeply entrenched problem, dry to the roots, in the name of Jesus.
23. I destroy the weapons of satanic night raiders, in the name of Jesus.
24. Every stronghold of failure in my life be broken, in the name of Jesus.
25. Every internal warfare in my life be quenched, in the name of Jesus.

The Last Warning

Vol. 6. No. 40

Hebrews 12:25-26; "See that ye refuse not him that speaketh. For if they escaped not who refused him that spake on earth, much more shall not we escape, if we turn away from him that speaketh from heaven: Whose voice then shook the earth: but now He hath promised, saying: "Yet once more I shake not the earth only, but also heaven."

Ezekiel 21:27-28;
"I will overturn, overturn, overturn it: and it shall be no more, until he come whose right it is; and I will give it him. And thou, son of Man, prophesy and say: "Thus saith the Lord God concerning the Ammonites, and concerning their reproach; even say thou, the sword, the sword is drawn: for the slaughter it is furbished, to consume because of the glittering."

I would like you to take every word of this message, serious. In these two passages, God is asking us to heed the warning of listening to Him, so that we will not enter into trouble. Things are being shaken; strange things are happening in the world today and it will continue until Jesus comes; the world and all the things that are in it, will be over-turned, as God warns. Therefore, the act of not heeding God's warning is a disaster. God warns you because He knows you better than you know yourself. He knows the future and everything. He understands you and your situation, better than you do.

When He gives His warning, He would have looked back and forth and seen the things that you cannot see. He then issues a warning, in His position as Divine Excellence. When He warns and you do not heed therefore, it is disastrous.

Before God sent the floods, He warned Noah and asked him to build an ark. Noah obeyed and built it, amidst the mockery of all and sundry, and it was a good thing he obeyed. Before God destroyed Sodom and Gomorrah, He warned Abraham and Lot and their obedience made them escape the destruction. If you also go through the Scriptures; from Genesis to Revelation, you will discover that God always warn the Israelites and any time they did not heed His warning, He promptly handed them over to their enemies. I pray that the Lord will not hand you over to your enemies in the name of Jesus.

At a time, the children of Israel were taken captive and they wept. They wept when they remembered Zion; they said those who held them captive, required of them, a song and they were wondering how they could sing the Lord's song in a strange land. The problem though should not really be singing but the question they should have posed to one another was; how did we get to this strange land? If they had heeded God's warning they would not have landed in bondage.

Before anything happens, God sounds a note of warning. Beloved, even now there is a great trouble that is approaching; it is the Great Tribulation. It is going to be a time of great suffering in the world. Everything that is happening now, is pointing at it. Note that God will judge everyone, according to the privilege he or she has been given, according to what each person knows or has heard. Therefore, you and I will have no excuse; we will not say that we do not know what God has been telling us. God has started to shake the earth; there is no good news anymore.

An American got fed up of hearing bad news every day on the radio, television and in the newspapers. He said all they recount, are stories of woe; marriages that are broken down, adultery, bomb attacks, hijackers, armed robbery, etc. He set up a news agency, which was publishing only good news. Within two weeks, he closed down because there was nothing to publish. This is what I am talking about. The shaking has started and it seems as if people are sitting on God's time-bomb, which will soon explode. God has numbered all the kingdoms of the earth and has finished His arithmetic. His voice that once shook the earth, will shake it again. Many people do not understand but that is not surprising. Let us see a prophecy in the Book of Daniel;

Daniel 12:10;
"Many shall be purified, and made white, and tried; but the wicked shall do wickedly: and none of the wicked shall understand; but the wise shall understand."

I know I am one of those who will be purified in the name of Jesus. Sometimes, when you talk about things, some people just do not understand. Some others however claim to know everything; but God says that the wicked and the ungodly shall not understand.

There is a pathetic story of a sister who travelled home for christmas with her only sister, they both died in a car accident; the vehicle caught fire and they roasted. The most painful aspect of it however is that they had lost their brothers and sisters in bizarre conditions. This sister surprisingly happened to be introduced to M.F.M a few weeks before the end of the year. We had a three-day fasting and praying programme and the Lord warned that nobody-should travel but if it was highly inevitable, the person should come to us for serious prayers. When a friend of this sister heard that this sister wanted to travel, she reminded her of the warning. (Apparently, she was a sister who ran to the M.F.M because her brothers and sisters were just dying one after the other and she was seeking God's protection.) She did not listen to the sister but took off for the village with the only sister left also in their family. And this was a lady, who had just found a man who wanted to marry her. She died and that accident also ended the whole family.

When God warns, it is because He sees and knows everything. Naturally, the flesh would complain but you have to do what God says. That thing that the flesh hates most times, is exactly what will favour you. God means what He says and He says what He means. The good news is that Jesus is coming soon.

Unfortunately, many people do not know it; some who know, do not care.

The devil is very wicked; he keeps people's mind blinded to these facts. They will engage in every other ceremony but will fail to recognise that when every other thing will come to an end, God will jingle the bell, that: "It is enough, the end has come." Even if you are no longer alive at the time Jesus comes, the Bible says the dead in Christ will rise first. Death is a leveller and it does not sound any warning. The devil is wicked, he is the one who puts the spirit of witchcraft in a person and when he has finished using the person and wants to get rid of him or her, the person goes to the market place and confess to witchcraft. The same devil will now rouse a mob that will stone the person to death and he or she will go straight to hell. The same devil will also go before God and accuse those who killed the person, of murder.

Ask yourself these questions:

* Am I troubled by the events of the future?
* Am I getting worried about what I am reading in this message?
* Does the thought of death trouble me?
* Am I confident that if I die today, I will go to heaven?

During a church service somewhere a long time ago, a man slumped on his seat and died. The ushers quickly carried him to the back of the church and prayed that he should come back to life. In faith, they took him back to his seat and placed him normally, as if he was sitting by himself. After about two hours, the man opened his eyes and asked what he was doing here on earth; he said he was in a better place, that he went to heaven and even saw a couple that got married a week before that time. Some doctors were summoned and they said he had a brain lapse, as a result of his slumping into a coma; they said that was the explanation of the incoherence in his speech. The following morning, news got to the church that the couple that got married the previous week, died in an accident, as they were coming back from their honeymoon. It was then, that they took the man's word serious; they realised that he actually died and went to heaven.

Are you aware of the fact that the devil hates you with serious hatred? Do you know that the devil would like to kill all Christians and send them to hell-fire? Do you know that if you are in a gathering that does not believe in the second coming of our Lord Jesus that it means you are in a wrong church?

Man is sitting on a bomb that will soon explode. All the temporal things, that people are cleaving to will eventually perish. A woman died and when people were taking stock of her belongings, she had 2,500 clothes, 500 pairs of shoes. What was she doing with them? Those things were eventually auctioned. Unfortunately, when she was going to be buried, her corpse was dressed in only one dress and one pair of shoes. The Bible says we should lay up our treasures in heaven.

Going to church and not being sure of one's salvation is the most dangerous activity that a person can engage in. If you are just blank, or you are living in sin, or you are doing things that are contrary to the will of God, then you are God's enemy. We thank God for the miracles that we receive from Him in our physical lives, but the final and most important one, is finding oneself in heaven, where the devil does not want us to go. Jesus is still calling right now. When the Bible talks about anything, it shall be so; whether you believe it or not. Some people say that heaven and hell are here on earth. The Bible says: *"And death and hell were cast into the lake of fire. This is the second death"* (Revelation 20:4)

The prophecies of the Bible about the second coming of Jesus Christ cannot be shifted aside; whether you believe them or not. Whether you are expecting Him or not, Jesus will come. The question is; in which position will He meet you? There is a song that says:

When Jesus comes to reward His people,
Whether it is night or day;
Will He find you still watching?
Waiting, for the Lord shall come.
Can we say we are faithful to what He has given to us?
Will He find you waiting?
Waiting for the Lord to come?

All kinds of things are being given pre-eminence in the church now; dancing, singing, quarrels, contentions, prayerlessness, positions, committees, leadership, etc. The most important things are being kept aside and are forgotten.

A man discovered the remains of Noah's Ark on Mount Arafat, where the Bible says it is. He filmed it, on video, so that those who do not believe the Bible as being the Word of God will know that it is not a story book; what the Bible says is true, and it can never change. Every prophesy in the Word of God will happen; so much so, that even a blind man will know that something is happening.

God wants you to revise your life, knowing fully well, that as His coming is close, more and more things will begin to happen. Many false 'christs' shall arise, many false prophets shall arise and the love of many shall wax cold. Those that were hot for the Lord, will find out that they cannot pray any more; they are doing things that they are not supposed to do and some are becoming stronger students in the school of disobedience. The question is this: Where will you be, when the Lord shall call His people home?

Where will you be, when the saints go marching home? Will you be in that number? Where will you be when all the saints have been removed? Will you be with them? I know that I shall be there.

1 Corinthians 15:51-54:
Behold, I shew you a mystery; we shall not all sleep, but we shall all be changed, in a moment, in the twinkling of an eye, at the last trump: for the trumpet shall sound, and the dead shall be raised incorruptible, and we shall be changed. For this corruptible must put on incorruption, and this mortal must put on immortality. So when this corruptible shall have put on incorruption, and this mortal shall have put on immortality, then shall he brought to pass the saying that is written: "Death is swallowed up in

victory."

When the trumpet sounds, it will take the twinkling of an eye and every child of God will be taken up. When scientists calculated the time for an eye to twinkle, they found out that it is $^{11}/1,000$ of a second. In the twinkling of an eye, the saints will be gone. The question is: Will you go? A frog cannot pretend to be a bird even if it attaches feathers to its body, so that it can fly, it cannot fly; it is still a frog.

When false 'christs' begin to arise and there are wars and rumours of war, violence, famine and pestilence all over the place, hatred is filling the earth, false religions, cults on the increase, iniquity abounding, men do not seem to care whether there will be an end or not, when the hearts of men are filled with evil communication and imaginations, and many strange things begin to happen, the Bible calls it perilous times, that men shall be lovers of themselves, lovers of money, boasters, blasphemers, disobedient to parents, that when there shall be increased satanic activities all over the place and doctrines of the devils, being preached all over the place, know that the end is coming. Jesus told His disciples about three times, after He had talked to them about the end, that: "Behold I have told you Watch and pray, so that, you will not fall into temptation." This means; "Behold I have warned you." He also told them this; "In my Father's house there are many mansions; I go to prepare a place for you and I will come again to take you there." *That is what is called The Rapture, in the twinkling of an eye, whether you believe it or not, when it happens, you will see it. My prayer is that God will enable you to go. Anybody who does not go is like someone who took a pen, and wrote out his or her obituary and signed it.*

When God's children begin to dress like the people of the world, when men relax their hair, put on heavy chains and rings, when it becomes difficult to differentiate between those going to the House of God and those going to night clubs, (the only difference is that one group is carrying the Bible and the other group is not.) When pastors dress like people of the world, and men of faith, who are supposed to lead people in the way of God are now joining them, for fear of being laughed at, then the end is coming.

When Christians commit sin and they cannot find the fear of God again, it is a very serious matter; their heart is so strong, that they just tell God in passing, that they are sorry, and then proceed to asking Him for blessings, it is a serious case, when a person does not feel bad, that he or she has offended God, then the end is getting close, when some people go to fellowship and they hear that God wants a man to be the husband of only one wife, they grumble that the message is in favour of women, some people amuse themselves by calling the prostitutes that they commit adultery and fornication with, 'bush meat.' They forget that they themselves are the 'bush meat.'

When a believer tells a lie to cover up the track of his or her actions, then the end is really close, when you cannot hear the truth from a Christian, on an issue, you should know that the end is close. Some people prefer keeping quiet instead of speaking out.

They do not know that silence means consent and that could be a lie. When men of God abort pregnancies for their wife or daughter, it means the end is really close and many bad things are happening.

I would like to expose a blank truth to you. Many Christians will have to really work hard, to make the Rapture. If you are nurturing the hope of going to heaven, you really have to work hard. You have to do more submission to God, than you are doing now. The fire of God has to burn in you, more than now. Your prayer life has to be better than what it is now. Your 'Wedding Garment' has to be clean and spotless. *The whole armour of God has to be on you.* You would need a double portion of God's power; you need to be filled with the Holy Ghost, if you hope to make the Rapture.

We should not deceive ourselves; by thinking that everyone that goes to church is interested in making heaven. The basic purpose, for which some people go to church, is for fear of being overpowered by their enemies or witches.

God could help a person to overcome enemies in order to make him or her serve God better. But many people go back to the things they left behind once they get a brief relief from the grip of the thing(s) that held them captive. They go back to their worldly way of life and relent in their fervency in the things of God. When the enemy sees that they have got to that stage, he would dispatch a clever demon to them that would disguise and trouble them.

The point is, if only ten people want to go to heaven, they should make up their minds, and they will get there. If the whole world wants to make heaven, there is enough room for everybody. You have to make up your mind that come what may, you will not allow the devil to push you to hellfire. Decide not to allow yourself to be destroyed, then you will get there. If you allow room for complacency; taking things soft and easy, you may be far from the truth, because the Bible says; 'The kingdom of God suffereth violence and the violent, take it by force.'"

WHAT TO DO:
We brought nothing into this world and the Bible says it is certain that we shall take nothing out of it. It is not wrong to own good things, the best place to lay up treasures, is heaven where nothing can spoil them.

During my youth service, I saved up a lot of money. One day, when I got there to withdraw, the cashier laughed and said I could not get up to that amount because they were short of funds. That is the bank of the world. It can run short of funds but the bank in heaven cannot.

Think about it beloved, the day will come when we will be taken up, our bodies will be changed and we shall be caught up in heaven with Him. The Bible says; **"Behold, He cometh in the clouds; all eyes shall see Him, those that even laughed Him to scorn, will wail..."**

Those who mocked Him will behold Him and regret it. He is no longer the Jesus that walked on their streets, who rode on a donkey into Jerusalem. He would be a changed Jesus on that day. He came as a lawyer before but will now come as a judge. He was slain on the cross before but now, He is holding a sword. Many people will wake up on that morning and find out that their friends and family are gone. Ambulance sirens will blast without end, vehicles will run into ditches, aeroplanes will crash because the pilots and drivers have been raptured. Anyone who dies in such a crash and is not born again will go straight to hell. A wife and husband could be on their bed and one is taken because he or she is born again.

A man of God saw a vision where he saw many people, waiting to go to heaven. It was as if heaven was on the other side of the river and they had to go in a canoe. Each man with his wife. For lack of space, the men were asked to swallow their wife and they did. But there was a man who had ten wives and he did not know which one to swallow and could not also swallow all of them. That was how he lost the chance of boarding the canoe, to cross over to heaven.

Smith Wigglesworth was at a crusade one day and a woman who has cancer was brought in. He asked the ushers to bring her to the stage and they did. He asked them to make her stand on her feet and leave her. As soon as they left her, she fell; he asked them to do it a second time and she fell. A man in the congregation shouted and called Smith names, saying that he wanted to kill the woman. It did not discourage Smith and he asked the usher to stand her on her feet again. This time, the woman did not fall. She was made whole and she leapt for joy.

You cannot argue against the words of the Scriptures. The truth is that many people do not know what they are arguing about. When God opens your understanding, you will know what He is saying in His word.

Many years ago in England, a boy and his mother were riding a horse. It was getting dark and they did not know the area. When they got to a riverbank, the horse stopped. They did not see that it was a river so, they were wondering why it stopped. They beat it and forced it to moved, it did and it stumbled and fell into the river. The boy caught the branch of a tree but the mother was struggling to get out. The boy let out one hand

and asked his mother to catch it. She thought he was too small to be able to pull her. She kept struggling but could not swim and eventually, she drowned. The boy wept and kept saying; "'Mother, I tried to save you, but you wouldn't let me." He kept repeating it utill he became abnormal. He lost his senses and all he could say, was that sentence.

I pray that you will never hear the Saviour say to you; "I tried to save you but you wouldn't let me." How pathetic would it be; after being a member of a living church here on earth, and then hear God say; "I know you not, depart from Me!" Talk to the Lord about your life, to patch up any area that is leaking in it.

Beloved, you have read this message and I hope you now know that there will be a time, when it will be too late to do any thing. Are you born again? Have you ever made a declaration of accepting the Lord Jesus Christ into your life? If you have not yet done so, I would advise that you take that decision today right there where you are.

All you need do, is acknowledge the fact that you are a sinner and that you cannot approach God in your sinful state. Therefore, repent of your sins; confess them to the Lord, name them one by one and ask Him to forgive you and cleanse you from all unrighteousness. Claim the redemptive power in the Blood of Jesus, that was shed on the cross at Calvary, for the remission of your sins.

Invite the Lord Jesus Christ into your life; open your heart, ask Him to come into your life and become your personal Lord and Saviour. Enthrone Him over your life, ask Him to take a total control of your life and all that concerns you. say bye-bye to the world and the devil. Make sure you do not go back to them again.

This is a very important decision, infact, it is the most important decision in life. If you have just taken it, I congratulate you. I pray that it shall be permanent in your life. I pray that the Lord will uphold you with His hand of righteousness and will keep you from falling in off in the name of Jesus. Go and sin no more.

Take the prayer points below with all the aggression that you can gather.
* **Blood of Jesus, wash away every sinful nature from my life in the name of Jesus.**
* **Everywhere my spiritual life is leaking, O Lord, seal it up in the name of Jesus.**

Peter followed Jesus from afar off; so he went to warm himself with the fire of the enemy and there, he denied Christ. Many say that they are following the Lord but their hearts are far away. Focus your attention on the Lord Jesus Christ make a review of your life and rededicate your life to the Lord.

* **My heart, come home to the Lord in the name of Jesus.**

The Lord is stretching forth His hand to you and is calling you to come. For how long do you want to remain where you are and be captured by sin? Do you not know that the trumpet might sound anytime and if it finds you in this rising and falling position, you will not go with the Lord, God did not ordain your body for fornication, He did not ordain your life to be kicked about by the enemy. Why then, do you want to sing the Lord's song in a strange land? Why have you become a student in the school of procrastination? Why are you Miss Almost there? Why are you Mr. Almost there? If a thing is almost there, it is not there. He almost quenched the fire, does not mean that the fire is quenched. He almost locked the door does not mean the door is locked. He almost came late does not mean he came late. Almost got to heaven does not mean that a person is in heaven.

1. Lord, break me and remould me in the name of Jesus.
2. Heal me Lord, and I shall be healed, save me Lord and I shall be saved, deliver me and I shall be delivered in the name of Jesus
3. Every chain of collective captivity of my father's house holding me from the plan of God, break and release me, in the name of Jesus
4. My Father, I cannot bear the pains in hell-fire, help me; I cannot help myself, in the name of Jesus.

5. Every seed of hell-fire in my life, die by fire, in Jesus' name.
6. Every tree my heavenly Father has not planted, that is growing in my life, be uprooted now, by fire in the name of Jesus.
7. Where is the Lord God of Elijah, arise and contend with every opposition to your Word in my life, in the name of Jesus.
8. Anointing to please God, fall upon my life, in the mighty name of Jesus.
9. Power to please God, fall upon my life afresh, in Jesus' name.
10. Wherever I have missed my way, oh Lord help me to retrace my steps in the name of Jesus.
11. Lord, open the eyes of my understanding in the name of Jesus.
12. Every spiritual cataract in my eyes, clear off by the fire of God, in the name of Jesus.
13. Spiritual deafness! What are you doing in my life, die now in the name of Jesus.
14. I shall reach my goal, whether the devil likes it or not, in the mighty name of Jesus.
15. You devil, you will not harvest my soul in hell-fire, in the name of Jesus.
16. Every strange voice calling me into hell-fire, shut up and die, in the name of Jesus.
17. Every register of hell-fire opened unto my life, catch fire now in the name of Jesus.
18. Every seed of stubbornness in my life, catch fire and die, in Jesus' name.
19. Every evil attachment in my destiny, catch fire in Jesus' name.
20. Every power that has vowed that I will not make it, be disappointed now by fire in Jesus name.
21. Lord, give me the grace, strength and provision to work for You, in Jesus name.
22. Every occupation that is in direct opposite to what God wants me to be that I am occupied with, be consumed by the Fire of God, in the name of Jesus.
23. Lord, hold me by your right hand in the name of Jesus.

Your Time Of Visitation

Luke 19:41-44; *"And when he was come near, he beheld the city, and wept over it, saying: "If thou hadst known, even thou, at least in this thy day, the things which belong unto thy peace! But now they are hid from thine eyes. For the days shall come upon thee, that thine enemies shall cast a trench about thee, and compass thee round, and keep thee in on every side, and shall lay thee even with the ground, and thy children within thee; and they shall not leave in thee one stone upon another; because thou knewest not the time of thy visitation.*

Bible readers would have found out that the Lord Jesus Christ wept on three occasions:

* At the tomb of Lazarus
* In the Garden of Gethsemane, and
* Over Jerusalem (as in the above text)

Why did Jesus weep over Jerusalem? Was it because of the suffering that He encountered or because of anything concerning Him? No! It was because the people did not know their time of visitation; Jesus wept because of their ignorance. If ignorance could make Jesus weep, then it must be a serious matter. That is why God Himself takes the issue of ignorance serious. The Bible says: "My people are destroyed for lack of knowledge"

One of the complaints that God has about His people, is their ignorance. Jesus Himself complained bitterly about the Jews being ignorant of the Scriptures and about their not knowing the power of God and their time of visitation

The Bible says that Jesus came to His own, but they did not receive Him. Why? It is beause they lacked knowledge. If you read through the Epistles of Paul, you would find Him say; "I will not have you ignorant ..."

There are many people however who do not know their day of visitation. There are surprisingly many people who do not bring out their buckets while it is raining. It is when the rain has stopped, that they will realise that they could have stored water in their bucket free of charge; by just putting it under the rain. In order words, these people are just busy practising religion, whilst time is flying! They are yet to know that it is a tragedy for a person not to know his time of visitation and to also miss it.

Why do people not know their time of visitation? It is because an evil surgical operation has been carried out on them. The enemy has their eyes, ears and their minds.

Acts 28:27;
"For the heart of this people is waxed gross, and their ears are dull of hearing, and their eyes have they closed; lest they should see with their eyes, and hear with their ears, and understand with their heart, and should be converted, and I should heal them."

So many people cannot see what God is doing though they call themselves Spirit-filled Christians. The enemy makes them confused, deaf and spiritually blind. He also tries to puncture the faith of God's people by making them go weary especially when there is an expected blessing but which is delayed; for some people, the enemy wears them out with worry when victory is delayed. Many people are still battling with some forces that are hindering their breakthroughs, but with that, one of the principles of God is this; He has an appointed place and time for everything.

The disciples asked Jesus if it was at that time that Jesus would restore Israel. Jesus answered and said it was not necessary for them to know the time or season that the Father had appointed by His authority. He said they would know when it happens.

Zechariah did not know that the Lord was visiting him; he did not believe that it was his own time now; that it was time for him to have a child; he was considering the age of his wife and himself, so the angel who came to deliver the message made him to go dumb until the child was born. Also, when King Herod sought to kill Jesus at birth, God asked Joseph to take the mother and child to Egypt. When it was time, God told him to go back with the baby because those who were seeking the life of the child had died. I pray that every power that is seeking your life shall die in the name of Jesus. I also pray for you to understand the times and seasons, in Jesus' name.

There is a time to take over, and there is a time to take cover. Every deliverance prayer point that you utter, weakens the structure of the enemies. It causes them internal cancer, so if you now give up on the day that you should have given the last blow, you will become the greatest and a painful loser.

Psalm 37:10;
"For yet a little while, and the wicked shall not be: yea, thou shalt diligently consider his place, and it shall not be."
Perhaps you have been expecting some blessings from the Lord; I am telling you today that you do not need to despair; do not lose heart, do not backslide; do not give in to the enemy. The enemy operates a primitive "'Trade by Barter" i.e. if he gives you anything, he will take something (greater and costlier) in return. But the truth is that, the devil has no gift at all. I pray that you will not miss your divine visitation in the name of Jesus. Beloved, I want you to know that anything you collect from the camp of your enemies will dismantle your structure. It is unfortunate that many people go to rivers, forests, idols, etc to ask for things and at the end, those things they get, turn around to harm or kill them.

Know that this is a special message beloved. God has His TIME and I want you to believe Him for a visitation. Something might have been harassing a child of God for a long time, but the day God arises, that thing will scatter unto desolation. It means that if God is for you, it does not matter who is against you, no matter who is for you, and if God is against you are doomed

Some people around you would prefer to die rather than see you prosper. However, if God says: **"It is Time"** then, it is Time; at that particular time, it does not matter if you believe it or not.

God has a purpose for your reading this bulletin. It is because He has an appointment with you. So, since it is time for the Lord to bless you, I would like you to be serious with the reading of this message and take the prayer points with determination in your heart. The Lord has an appointed time for everything He wants to do in your life and once that time comes, it is dangerous to backslide, or not to be aware.

You might wonder why this message is coming your way; it is because the Lord says it is time for the breakthroughs of many people, that it is time for the prosperity and healing of many. Just like Jesus' declaration; "Father, the hour has come..." I am asked to tell you that the time for your breakthrough has come. When the Lord says that this is the hour of your visitation, it is the wrong time to start crying or worrying. It is the wrong time to reduce your fire for the Lord or to be discouraged.

Immediately the Lord says that your season has come, every other thing will cooperate with you and then, anyone that stands against you, will just be removed from your way. I pray that you will not miss your time of visitation in the name of Jesus.

There was a time when the Lord gave some land to Judah. When the enemies came against Judah, Judah(as a people) was only able to conquer just a part of the enemies. Others could not be overcome because they had chariots of iron. If you go through this story, you would wonder why He allowed Judah only to overcome a part and not all the enemies. Later on, God allowed the enemies to enlarge in number and the king who wanted to fight with him had 900 chariots of iron. The

Lord then stepped in, to defend His people. Sisera wanted to fight but when his chariots got to Kishon, they could not move because the water in the river was muddy. When Sisera saw that his chariots could not move; he jumped down and started to run away. It was a woman that eventually killed him. I pray that your enemies shall be disgraced today, in the name of Jesus.

The Bible says; "Some trust in chariots some trust in horses, but we will remember the name of our Lord." When God says it is time to bless you, even you, will have no choice, because it will surely come to pass. It is like someone sitting outside and when the rain starts, he refuses to get up, saying that he got there before the rain. Anything can happen to such a person in that place.

Our God has an appointment with you today. I wish to prophetically declare unto you, that today is your day of visitation! Maybe you have been going to church and you have been asking Him to allow you to experience His power and His visitation I would like you to know that this is that day that the Lord has purposed to visit you. One thing you must do, right there where you are, is ask Him to remove whatever will cause a hindrance to that visitation; whether in you or around you. No matter how much you love that thing, you should decide to let it go. Do not deceive yourself; you know it, it could be anger, adultery, malice, unforgiving spirit, deception, etc. All these things will hinder you from getting His visitation, and I do not want you to be hindered at all. You have been suffering for so long, you too, look at it, you have been tossed and turned by various waves, challenging your God. I declare that this is your day of visitation, in Jesus' name.

Many people are crying in their closets, but I have a good news for them; the Drier of Tears is right there by you. Take the bold step of humbling yourself before Him, look unto Jesus, the Author and Finisher of our faith. He has allowed you to read this bulletin for a purpose. His aim is to save, heal and deliver. He is waiting for you to come to Him.

The Bible says; "Right from the time of John the Baptist, the Kingdom of God suffereth violence and the violent taketh it by force." I would like you to pray the following prayers with violence and with determination in your heart. Cry unto the Lord, after the order of blind Barthemeus. I want you to cry to the Lord, the way the children of Israel did in Egypt and were delivered.

However, if you are not yet born again, please do so very quickly, right there where you are; so that you can experience the salvation of the Lord, become a candidate for heaven and enjoy the joy of salvation. Why not do it now; tomorrow might be too late.

All you need to do beloved, is recognise the fact that you are a sinner and that you cannot approach God in your sinful state. The Bible says the eyes of God cannot behold sin. Repent and confess your sins to Him and ask Him to forgive you. Name them one by one and decide to forsake them. Ask Him to cleanse you with the precious Blood of Jesus that was shed on the cross at Calvary, for the remission of your sins.

Ask the Lord Jesus to come into your life and become your personal Lord and Saviour. Promise Him that you will never go back to the world anymore. Say bye-bye to the devil and the world of sin and death and enter into the kingdom of Light

I congratulate you for this decision, that you have just taken. I pray that it shall be permanent in your life in the name of Jesus. My prayer is that the Lord will uphold you with His right hand of righteousness and will keep you till the end and your name will be written in the Book of Life.

Now, before you take the prayers, I would like you to examine your life and bring quality repentance before the Lord. I do not want you to have read this message, and still have a threatening Goliath; bragging and boasting of his ability to destroy you. Ask the Lord to forgive you every sin that could cause a hindrance to your prayers. I want you to experience the mighty power of God as you pray these prayer points that I am suggesting below. You have to do away with anything that will hinder your visitation; that thing could be anger, worry, lying, or anything that is not of God.

Now, pray these prayers violently.

1. God, arise and let all my enemies scatter in the name of Jesus.
2. Every spirit behind my problem, be arrested now, in the name of Jesus.
3. Any evil power pursuing my parents, or that pursued them in their lifetime, you will not pursue me; therefore, I cut you off in the name of Jesus.
4. Every following power of my father's house, die, in the mighty name of Jesus.
5. Let God arise, and let His enemies be scattered, in the name of Jesus.
6. Every power challenging my God, die in the name of Jesus.
7. Every power supervising tears in my life, release me and die, in Jesus' name.
8. Every chain of collective captivity in my environment, attacking my life, break and release me now, in the mighty name of Jesus.
9. Lord arise, and visit me today by force, in the name of Jesus.
10. Every power mocking God in my life, shut up and die, in Jesus' name.
11. My Father, arise today and change the story of my life by fire in Jesus' name.
12. Every power turning my Prince to a servant, you are a liar, die in the name of Jesus.
13. Every contention against my glory scatter, in the name of Jesus.
14. Every contention against my star, what are you waiting for? Scatter in the mighty name of Jesus.
15. Power to reach my life goals, fall upon me now, in the name of Jesus.
16. Lord, today, You must, visit me and change the story of my life, in the mighty name of Jesus.
17. Ancient of days, speak to every troubled part of my life, and let it receive peace, by fire, in the mighty name of Jesus.
18. Every transmission from the graveyard, die in the name of Jesus.
19. Every evil power pursuing me from my community, die in the name of Jesus.
20. Every cage of witchcraft break in the name of Jesus.
21. Every evil dream fashioned against my life, die in the name of Jesus.
22. All you bondage repairers lose your hold in the name of Jesus.
23. I cancel every evil interference in the affairs of my life in the name of Jesus.
24. Let every power keeping me longer in the waiting room of God, die, by fire, in the name of Jesus.
25. Thou power hindering the manifestation of the glory of God in my life, what are you waiting for, fall down and die, in the name of Jesus.
26. God of new beginning, begin new things in my life today, in the name of Jesus.
27. God arise and manifest yourself in the presence of those powers laughing my destiny to scorn, in the name of Jesus.
28. God of suddenly, show yourself in my situation now by fire, in the name of Jesus.
29. I shall arise and shine by fire, in the name of Jesus.
30. You my enemies do not rejoice over me, for my God shall arise and you shall be scattered by fire, in the name of Jesus.
31. God arise and lift up my head in the presence of those demoting my life, in the name of Jesus.
32. I command all stubborn yokes affecting my breakthroughs to break in the name of Jesus.
33. I bind all stubborn pursuers militating against my home, in the name of Jesus.
34. Let all the imaginations of the enemies against my life, begin to fail in the name of Jesus.
35. You spirit of defeat and failure in my life, lose your hold in the name of Jesus.

Provoking The Finger Of God

Exodus 8:19; *"Then the magicians said unto Pharaoh, This is the finger of God: and Pharaoh's heart was hardened, and he hearkened not unto them; as the Lord had said."*

There is something known as the "Finger of God". A situation could travel a long route, but the day the Finger of God goes out and points at that situation, there is an absolute change. Things will change instantly. I pray that you will experience the Finger of God today, in the name of Jesus.

The powers of darkness have their own agenda. In Exodus 7 and 8, we read about a contest between the powers of light and the powers of darkness; the powers of God and the powers of the enemy. These two chapters, show that the enemy can travel some miles, but immediately the Finger of God gets into operation, an end comes to the joy of the enemy. The magicians finally recognised this to be God and not the result of the witchcraft that they practiced.

Today, heavens are declaring that the enemy has gone too far in your life and that the process of the enemy must stop today, because of the Finger of God. Moses stood in the court of Pharaoh, saying that God sent him. Pharaoh asked him to prove it, so Moses threw down his rod and it became a serpent. The magicians of Pharaoh did the same thing too. Moses turned water into blood, they too did it. The score became 2-2 draw. Moses commanded frogs into being, and it happened. The magicians did theirs, too. Moses commanded lice to come upon beasts and human beings and it happened. The magicians tried hard, BUT, they could not make it happen. They had to succumb and say: "This, is the 'Finger of God.

Luke 11:20;
"But if I with the finger of God cast out devils, no doubt the kingdom of God is come upon you."

If you want to experience the Finger of God in operation, you are reading the right message, In the text above, Jesus Himself is throwing more light on what is known as the "Finger of God".

The Finger of God has power over the devil, demons and the powers of darkness, and over any situation that anyone could be going through.

THE FINGER OF GOD:
1. It is the miracle-working power of God.
2. It is the operation of God that brings excitement.
3. It is the operations that are above the powers and operations of nature.
4. It is the manifestations that cannot be explained by the human brain.
5. It is an event that is beyond the ordinary.

The Bible says; "With man, this is impossible; but with God, all things are possible." When God stretches out His Finger, it is for a purpose and things begin to Happen.

WHY GOD POINTS HIS FINGER
To punish His enemies - He pointed His Finger at Sodom and Gomorrah and fire and brimstone fell on them. He pointed His Finger at the Red-Sea and it parted for the Israelites to pass through; then it closed up again and swallowed Pharaoh and his chariots. That same Finger was pointed at Bar-Jesus and he became blind. When the Finger of God is stretched out, it will destroy your enemies.

God points His Finger in order to deliver His people from their enemies - It was the Finger of God that delivered Daniel from the den of lions. Although the lions were fierce and hungry, they could not eat Daniel because he was the son of the 'Lion of the Tribe of Judah.' The Finger of God delivered Shedrach, Meshach and Abednego from the fiery furnace. The fire became an air-conditioner and the Bible says that, not one single hair of their head was burnt. Why don't you believe God and allow Him to stretch forth His Finger in your situation?

God points His Finger to fight for His people - He pointed it out at the walls of Jericho and they fell down flat. On another occasion, He pointed His Finger to fight the enemies of the Israelites; as the congregation was singing, the warriors were coming behind and the enemies began to fight each other. The Israelites did not have to fight anyone, yet, they conquered. When you leave your battle for the Lord to fight, He points His Finger at your situation and you will win.

Exodus 14:14;
"The Lord shall fight for you, and ye shall hold your peace."

He points His Finger to show His true messengers - He did it at Mount Carmel and answered Elijah by fire.

God points His Finger in order to confirm His words - Paul shook off the serpent that coiled round his hand. The people around were expecting him to fall down and die, but he did not die because the Finger of God had already been stretched out.

God points His Finger to demonstrate His awesome power - Jesus commanded Lazarus to come forth and Lazarus rose from death, after four days of being buried.

Once God's Finger is pointed out, things happen at a fast rate. **He points it out to reveal Himself as the God of providence**; He will rain 'Manna' from Heaven. He pointed His Finger and a fish became a bank for Jesus to pay the tax. The same Finger was pointed out and five loaves of bread with two fish was sufficient to feed five thousand people.

God points out His Finger in order to remove hindrances to people's blessings; to silence satanic ministers and to destroy the powers of darkness - The Finger of God, pointed out, is enough to remove any problem that you might have. The problem with many people is that, they come to God with dry faith; not really expecting anything to happen. Many people believe more, what the doctors and experts have said about their health than what the Lord is saying. Many consider what has happened to others and use it in judging their own situation.

Act 27:20-22; *"And when neither sun nor stars in many days appeared, and no small tempest lay on us, all hope that we should be saved was then taken away. But after long abstinence Paul stood forth in the midst of them, and said, Sirs, ye should have hearkened unto me, and not have loosed from Crete, and to have gained this harm and loss. And now I exhort you to be of good cheer: for there shall be no loss of any man's life among you, but of the ship."*

The situation was very dark and gloomy; terrible things had happened on the sea. Paul had cautioned the authority about the journey but they refused to listen to him, and there was serious problem. There were storms and waves and darkness for many days. It was so terrible that, the people started to throw their properties into the sea, in order to lighten the ship. They had lost hope and were expecting to die.

Are you reading this message and you have lost hope on your situation? Have you been completely written off? I decree and prophesy into your life that, the Finger of God shall arise by fire and visit your situation today in the name of Jesus. The lives of all the people in the ship were saved because of one holy man. Most of them were culprits, condemned criminals, robbers that were being taken to Rome to be tried. Paul said he believed what God showed him in the vision that he saw.

KEYS TO PROVOKING THE FINGER OF GOD:
1. **Violent Faith**.
You must have faith in God with all your heart; believing Him that whatever situation is on ground, is not beyond His power. You must have violent faith; the faith of someone who serves a BIG God. Faith that does not welcome alternatives. This means that, if you believe God, any evil situation that comes your way shall be destroyed and buried. It shall come to pass as you believe. The Bible says that whosoever shall say unto a mountain to

move and be cast into the sea and does not doubt in his or her heart, it shall be so.

2. Bold Praying.

You should pray to the extent that it will look as if it is madness to pray for the impossible to happen. The Bible says *"Open wide your mouth, and I will fill it."* If I start to share with you the testimonies that bold praying and violent faith had produced; this bulletin will become a book. Some people will even see the testimonies as being impossible, but, we serve a God who specialises in the impossible. Things that people consider as being a write-off, that cannot work, are the things that God will turn into testimonies the extremity of Man, is the beginning of divine operation. Today, I want you to believe God even as Paul declared that, "I believe that it shall be as He has told me." I would like you to pray and believe that whatever chain the enemy has used in tying you down, shall be broken off you and shall go back to the sender in the name of Jesus.

3. Praise And Worship.

When you praise God, despite what you are going through, the devil is put to shame - God Himself is elated by the praises of His people and He will arise and stretch forth His finger. The book of Psalm says, God inhabits the praise of His people. The rulers thought they had caught Paul and Silas and that would mark the end of their ministry but the Lord intervened and delivered them. Paul and Silas refused to brood over their situation, but acknowledged the fact that God was in control of the situation and so, they sang praises to His holy name. God raised His Finger and an earthquake was produced, that broke the chains and fetters that held them bound.

Acts 16:25-26;

"And at midnight, Paul and Silas prayed, and sang praises unto God; and the prisoners heard them (meaning that they were not quiet about it at all). *And suddenly there was a great earthquake."*

4. Confidence In The Lord.

You need to know the ability of our God and trust that He is able to do all things.

A woman bought a piece of land in a Porche part of Lagos. One day, some uniformed men came there to clear the land for construction, to commence work on it. Someone went to inform the woman and she went there with her anointing oil. She told them to get off her land if they want to remain alive. She then went round, anointed the place and left. One of the men asked the people around, the name of the church that the woman attends and they told him it was MFM. He then told the others that he would not like to get involved. Another one said in actual fact, they were not supposed to get involved in civil matters and the others agreed and they left. They feared the God of Elijah that could deal with them, for depriving His child of her land.

When you have confidence in the Lord and you begin to speak the words of assurance, those words will create something for you. Shedrach, Meshach and Abednego spoke confidently to the king. They told him that they could not bow to his golden calf, that he could throw them into the fiery furnace if he wanted to. They said if he threw them into the fire, God would deliver them.

They went on to add that, if God decided not to save them for whatever reason, they would still not bow. They decided to burn than bow.

When David confronted Goliath, the latter cursed David in the name of his idols. David said that he came in the name of the Lord of Hosts whom he (Goliath) had defied. Although Goliath was still standing there, David had finished him and he said he would cut off his head and feed the birds with his carcass. This is what is called: 'winning before the war.' It is using the arrows of God in your mouth to win before the war.

5. Sacrificial Giving.

Give God something that you can feel, something that you will miss; not something that you do not need. David said he would not give God something that did not cost him anything.

6. Ask for it

Ask for it; you can ask God to stretch forth His Finger at your situation and you will see Him in action. Sometimes, God wants us to call Him into our situation, before He comes in. The Bible says: *"Ask and it shall be given unto you, seek and you shall find, knock and it shall be opened unto you. Whosoever asks receives, whosoever knocks, the door will he opened unto him, whosoever seeks shall find"* Matthew 7:7-8. But, if you do not ask, and do not knock, nothing happens. There is no harm in asking.

Are you ready to pray bold prayers today and make confident pronouncements? Then, take the prayers I am suggesting below with all seriousness. You must not miss the intervention of the Finger of God today. The Lord God must arise on your behalf and point His Finger at your situation.

However, if you have not yet surrendered your life to the Lord Jesus Christ, you have no claims to Him. You must be born-again to be rightly positioned for Him. All you need to do is acknowledge the fact that you are a sinner, and that you cannot approach God in your sinful state. Confess your sins to Him name them one by one and renounce them; ask Him to forgive you each of them and cleanse you from all unrighteousness. Claim the redemptive power in Blood of Jesus that was shed on the Cross at Calvary for the remission of your sins. Renounce the world and the devil. Today is the day of salvation! Take that decision today, for tomorrow might be too late.

Invite the Lord Jesus Christ into your life; open your heart to Him and let Him come in and sup with you. Ask Him to become your personal Lord and Saviour. Enthrone Him over your life and ask Him to take absolute control of all that concerns you. Surrender your totality to Him now!

If you took this decision, I congratulate you. It is the most important decision in life and I pray that it shall be permanent in your life, in the name of Jesus. I pray that the Lord will uphold you with His right hand of righteousness and keep you from falling in the name of Jesus. I pray that your name will be written in the Book of Life and that nothing shall by any means, rub it off, in the name of Jesus. Go and sin no more!

As you pray these prayer points, the raw power of God will fall upon you and many things will begin to happen. The Lord will perform creative miracles in your life; lost organs that came with birth or through accidents or operations, will be restored in the name of Jesus. Plantations of darkness will be uprooted and destroyed. A replacement of these things will be carried out by God. Ruptured wombs will be replaced, wounds will be healed and fibroids will melt away. Sleeplessness will disappear, incurable diseases will be kicked off by the Finger of God.

Take these prayer points with boldness:
1. Finger of God, arise! and kill my problems, in the name of Jesus.
2. Finger of God, arise! and recover the keys to my breakthroughs, in the name of Jesus.
3. Finger of God, arise in your fury! and pursue my pursuers, in the name of Jesus.
4. Finger of God, arise! and kill witchcraft powers of my father's house, in the name of Jesus.
5. Finger of God, arise! and kill witchcraft powers of my mother's house, in the name of Jesus.
6. Serpents of darkness dispatched against me, die! in the mighty name of our Lord Jesus Christ.
7. God of signs and wonders, I am here, manifest Your power in my life, in the name of Jesus.
8. Fire of God, come down and fight for me now! in the name of Jesus.
9. Finger of God, arise and prosper my life! in the name of Jesus.
10. Every mountain on my way of breakthroughs, hear the Word of the Lord; SCATTER, in the name of Jesus.
11. Every strongman at the gate of the grave assigned against my life, die! in the name of Jesus.
12. My father, help my unbelief, in the name of Jesus.
13. Every raging power working against my destiny, evaporate by fire, in the name of Jesus.
14. God of possibility manifest yourself in the affairs of my life

powerfully, in the name of Jesus.
15. Thou arm of the Lord, arise and defend me in the presence of those saying there is no help for me, in the name of Jesus.
16. Finger of God arise and do me good, all the days of my life, in the mighty name of Jesus.
17. Finger of God appear in the congregation of darkness gathered to mock me, in the mighty name of Jesus.
18. My father, let your anointing that cannot be insulted, fall upon my life, in the name of Jesus.
19. Anything in my life, that will not make the Finger of God to work for me, come out and die! in the name of Jesus.
20. This year, hear the Word of the Lord: Favour my life, in the mighty name of Jesus.

Begin to thank the Lord for what He has done in your life during this prayer session.

Lessons From The School Of Tribulation (1)

The Psalmist confessed of himself in Psalms 119:67 saying; *"Before I was afflicted I went astray: but now have I kept thy word."*

What we know as metal becomes pure after it has gone through a long process in fire. For a goldsmith to operate and bring out something really nice, he has to pass the gold through fire. After that, it comes out refined. That fire, although is hot and uncomfortable; refines.

The verse above shows that the Psalmist had to go through affliction, for him to come to his senses. He was going astray before, but when he picked up some particles of affliction, they made him to come to his senses. He now said he has kept the word of God. Many people in the Bible learnt from the School of Tribulation. You must have read the story of the prodigal son, who learnt a few lessons from the School of Tribulation.

For example, **MOSES** - By the time he graduated from the School of Tribulation, he knew that he had to have a lamb-like meekness, for him to be able to lead the Israelites to the Promised Land. They were very stubborn and the Bible records a wonderful testimony about Moses. The Bible qualifies him as the meekest man on the surface of earth. If some people had ¼ of the power that Moses had, no one would have been able to talk to them. Moses also learnt that he had to have a lion-like determination. Although he was meek, at the same time he was highly determined. He also learnt that he had to be as calm as when the ocean is asleep. The Israelites did all sorts of things against him; they screamed at him, cursed him, almost stoned him, but, he knew he had to be calm. He also picked up the lesson that he had to be as firm as a rock which smiles at the storm; unafraid.

There is a Yoruba adage that says: 'The river is fearless.' It means, if a person picks a cutlass and angrily moves towards a river or lagoon, it will not move an inch; it will be as it has always been. If the person winks at it, the person will see the reflection of his or her face winking back from the river. If the person smiles, it will reflect the smile. If the person rages, it will reflect the raging face; it will not respond.

Moses also learnt that nobody can make himself great outside God. When he saw that an Egyptian was maltreating an Israelite, he killed the Egyptian in defence of the Israelite. The next time he saw two Israelites quarrelling, he tried to intervene; to let them know that they are brothers. He was shunned and asked if he wanted to kill any of them as he did the Egyptian. He had to run away because; it meant that people knew that he killed the Egyptian. That taught him the lesson that he could not become a hero without God. Nobody can make himself or herself that which God has not made him or her. If you decide to become what God has not made you, you will become a glorified non-entity. Moses also learnt how God can turn a 'nobody' into somebody. God picked him by the burning bush and off he went. The Bible records that of all prophets, there was none like Moses, who spoke to God face to face.

Personally, I picked up a few lessons from the School of Tribulation. My father was a poor Policeman. Many a time, he was warned not to preach to people across the counter in the Police Station; that his duty is to charge them to court. Several times, he suffered because he did not collect bribe from people. He was transferred to dry and tedious areas to work. When I was admitted into the University, he laughed because; he did not have money to pay my school fees. He had to go out and borrow the N60 for the first instalment that he paid. The lesson I learnt was that; I had to work hard because, the money with which I was sent to school was hard earned. God crowned my efforts with success and I got a scholarship to travel abroad for further studies. I learnt early in life that God is my source.

In those days, those who got born-again worked very hard and spent themselves to the bones for the Lord. Everyday of the week, I was in the fellowship for Bible Study, Choir Practice, Church Service, etc. After a while, I felt my workload was heavy and stopped some of those things to face my studies.

Then I began to have serious headaches. A brother came in whilst I was rolling on the floor one day and he started to pray for me, binding the spirit of headache. Nothing happened; I did not get better. It was then that I realised that, I had abandoned the work of God for my studies, as if I could help myself. The lesson I learnt is that, God should come first in everything we do. I made my way right and the Lord surprised me.

Many years ago, there was a woman who filed in a report against me; that I was raining abuses on her every night. She was living about 50 meters away from my apartment. People were surprised at the kind of words she said I was using against her, but they could not defend me. She wrote a petition to the housing authority and sent copies to the Police and to the Institute where I was working. Her last statement in the petition was: "People like Dr. Olukoya should not be allowed to live in a place like this, he should go to the suburbs."

One day, someone asked if she knew me very well and she said she had never seen me and was not interested in meeting ruffians. One day, the Police came with her and she was asked to identify me. I was in the company of a huge man and she pointed at the man. The people around told the Police that, that was not Dr. Olukoya. When she turned to me, she herself said I did not look like a troublesome person. Later, she said it was me, that in fact; I was not the only one and that there were many people in my apartment. I took the Police to my apartment and there was nobody there; I was not married then. She concluded that the others had gone to work.

The case went on for a while and I had to travel out of the country. Whilst I was away, she went to report me again that I was screaming. It was then that people realised that she had problems. That was how God delivered me. It took me time to realise that, the problem was the acidic nature of my prayers against satanic agents around. Her reaction was a way of getting me physically out of the zone. I learnt my lesson the hard way. I first thought it was a neurotic case, but, it was a spiritual rage in the physical, in other to get me out of sight so that; the evil powers could operate unhindered in the environment.

A man had five children. One night, he had a dream that a snake swallowed his son. The following day, the boy took ill and was admitted in the hospital. The wife had to stay with the son. The following night he had another dream where the snake swallowed another and that one too, took ill and was admitted in the hospital. After a few days, he had the same dream and the snake swallowed yet another child and the following day that one took ill too. It went on like that, till all the five children were admitted and their mother became resident at the hospital and the man finished all his money on medication and hospital bills. The man ran around for help and he went to a 'powerful' herbalist who gave him some things to burn inside the house, so that the smoke would drive out the evil spirits. That night, the man dreamt about the snake again and it had the head of the herbalist. The only child that had been discharged was readmitted the following day after the dream. It was then that he realised that he had to abandon all the beggarly powers and turn to God, whom he had abandoned. He went into serious praying and fasting, using Isaiah 41:11-12 as the base of his prayers.

I would like to pause and we shall continue in the next bulletin, if the Lord tarries in coming back. Meanwhile, I would like you to examine your ways. Are you on the right path that leads to God? Are you born-again? If you are not yet born-again, you have the opportunity of taking that decision today. All you need to do, is to acknowledge the fact that you are a sinner and that you cannot get to heaven in your sinful state. Repent of your sins; confess them to the Lord; name them one by one and ask Him to forgive you and cleanse you from all unrighteousness. Renounce the world and the devil and make sure that you do not go back to them anymore.

Invite the Lord Jesus Christ into your life; ask Him to come into your life and become your personal Lord and Saviour. Enthrone Him over your life and hand over all that concerns you to Him. Submit your totality to Him and ask Him to take an absolute control of your life.

I congratulate you on this decision that you have just taken. It is the most important decision in life and I pray that it shall be permanent in your life in the name of Jesus. I pray that the Lord will write your name in the Book of Life and you will not by any means, rub it off in the name of Jesus.

Take these prayer points with all the aggression that you can gather:

PRAYER POINTS

1. Let every evil effect of any strange touch be removed from my life, in the name of Jesus.
2. I command all demonic reverse gears installed to hinder my progress to be roasted, in the, name of Jesus.
3. Any evil sleep, undertaken to harm me be converted to dead sleep, in the name of Jesus
4. Let all weapons and devices of the oppressors and tormentors be rendered impotent, in the name of Jesus
5. Let the fire of God destroy every power operating any spiritual vehicle working against me, in the name of Jesus.
6. Let all evil advice given against my favour crash and disintegrate, in the name of Jesus.
7. O God arise and fight my battles for me today, in the name of Jesus.
8. My enemies shall make mistakes that will advance my course today, in the name of Jesus.

Lessons From The School Of Tribulation (2)

I would like you to read these verses out loud, right there where you are. Isaiah 41:11-12;
"Behold, all they that were incensed against thee shall be ashamed and confounded: they shall be as nothing; and they that strive with thee shall perish. Thou shalt seek them, and shall not find them, even them that contended with thee: they that war against thee shall be as nothing, and as a thing of nought."

Now, look closely at this text and appropriate the words to yourself. Do you see how powerful they are? Receive everything with faith. The man noticed that he always had a rod in his hand whenever he saw the snake, but he never did anything with it. On the third day of his fasting, he had a vision where he saw himself in a classroom; in which there was a man in a white garment with a radiant smile teaching him some things. This man was impatient and he drew the attention of the teacher to the fact that, he had to go to the hospital to see his family. The teacher told him to be patient and listen attentively. The teacher told him to write the following:

A. **His enemy was using his weakness against him, to the advantage of the enemy.**
B. **He had to identify the weakness(es) of the enemy and exploit it.** This one sounded strange to the man. He was made to believe in his church that spirits are very powerful and perfect, so he could not imagine them having any weakness. The teacher affirmed that the devil has weaknesses and so, he enumerated the things that he uses against people. They are:

(1) **Ignorance- Lack of knowledge**.
Many people think that God can only be found in a particular geographical location. So, they go to one mountain or the other to seek His face. They do not know that God has no geographic location. Some people go to the beach and stare at their Bible, thinking that is the way to communicate with God. Some go to prophets, who ask them to undress and the prophet uses an egg to rub all over their body, breaks it and the person will see needles in it and the prophet would say that God removed the needles from their body. Some prophets put a bucket of water and gaze into it and say they are seeing visions for people. Some sell olive oil and call it anointed.

(2) **The devil is not everywhere**.
The devil has agents here and there. He cannot be present everywhere at the same time. In fact, he has to walk about: Job 1:7 *"And the Lord said unto Satan, Whence comest thou? Then Satan answered the Lord, and said, From going to and fro in the earth, and from walking up and down in it."*
He does not know everything otherwise; he would not have worked people up to nail Jesus on the Cross. It was his undoing because; that marked the victory of Jesus over him.

(3) **The devil does not have all the powers.**
The Bible says that, all power in heaven and on earth, have been given unto the Lord Jesus Christ.

(4) **The devil is fighting a war that he has already lost.**
He lost the battle about 2000 years ago at Calvary. He causes trouble everywhere knowing fully well that, his defeat is already declared and that we are the ones to enforce that defeat by the power of the Holy Spirit. I hope you know that the devil is fighting a lost war.

(5) **The devil cannot pray**.
You can pray to God, so, you have an advantage over him. You can call the Supreme Excellency when you are suffering but, he has no one to pray to, when he is suffering defeat

(6) **The devil does not have the Holy Spirit but we do.**
Jesus promised when He was going, in John 14:16-18 *"And*

I will pray the Father, and He shall give you another Comforter, that he may abide with you for ever. Even the Sprit of truth; whom the world cannot receive, because it seem him not either knoweth him: but ye know him; for he dwelleth with you, and shall be in you. I will not leave you comfortless: I will come to you."

(7) **The devil hates light and loves darkness.**

(8) **Move to the light and the devil will run away.**
As long as any part of you remains in darkness, the devil will like you. Many cosmetic products are made with foetus. If you rub any of these things on your body, you are participating in the act of abortion that produced that foetus. It is darkness and if you remain there, there will be problems.

(9) **The devil hates the truth.**
Any small lie you tell gives the devil a foothold to work in your life. Tell the truth and he will flee.

(10) **The devil has no defensive armour.**
Since the Lord Jesus defeated him on the cross, He made an open show of the devil, triumphing over him.(Colossians 2:15) This also is the victory that we as children of God have, through our faith in His word.

(11) **The devil cannot praise God.**
This makes him hate people who praise God; therefore, offer praises unto the Lord. Sing songs of praise, even when things are not going on the way you expected. When the devil finds you in a depressed state, he will send his demon of frustration to you, then the demon of sickness, etc.

(12) **The devil hates joy.**
The Bible says: "Rejoice in the Lord always, and again I say rejoice" "The joy of the Lord is my strength."

(13) **The devil cannot withstand the word of God.**
He cannot stand a regular bombardment of the word of God. That is why, if you have a mouth with which you can talk, you have to say it out to him. If you utter the word of God in faith, the devil will flee. Even if you are dumb, you can mutter the word of God and he will flee.

A man was selling salt and he became very rich. He had a big store filled with bags of salt. One day there was a big storm which entered into the store and destroyed his stock of salt. When his pastor heard the news, he felt sorry and was looking for words with which to console the man. On getting to him, the Pastor was amazed to find the man unperturbed, jubilating and praising the Lord. He said the Lord allowed the stock to be destroyed, in order to build a bigger one for him.

(14) **The devil is a serpent; he can bite, spit, strangulate and swallow.**
When he bites; he poisons, when he spits; he blinds and maims, when he strangulates; he breaks bones to pieces. When he swallows; he eats the flesh. You can protect yourself from all these things by becoming fire. Psalm 104:4 says God is He; *"Who maketh his angels spirits; his ministers a flaming fire."*
When you become a flaming fire and the devil makes an attempt to bite you; he gets burnt. If he spits poison on you; the fire will dry it up. If he tries to strangulate or swallow you; he will be consumed. Do you want to become an untouchable and unquenchable fire? If you ask God, He will answer you.

Take this prayer point with thunder in your voice:
* **Lord, turn me into untouchable and unquenchable fire, in the name of Jesus.**

(15) **The devil has ways of getting his victims.**
The devil uses deception, temptation, confusion and accusation. The devil deceives people in order to confuse them and then lure them into doing evil and make them fall out of God's favour, and then goes to accuse them before the Lord.

(16) **The devil uses money, sex and power to destroy people.**
Even Christians are no exemption to these evils. These three things have done a lot of havoc in the lives of many people. They have become money and power hungry and sexually perverted.

(17) Satanic powers that have inhabited the life of a person will not go out peaceful, without a vicious fight.

The enemy will only succumb to violence. Imagine a demon living in the life of a 52 year old person since birth. If chased out, the demon will fight back because; it does not want to lose its accommodation.

Back to the narration of the man and the snake, the angel then asked the man, if he knew the meaning of Belial and the man said it is the spirit of war and death. The angel asked if he knew Beelzebub and the man said it is the spirit of flies, that controls flying objects that are causing havoc; like witches. The angel asked if he knew Jezebel and he said it is the spirit of worldliness, which is also in charge of spirit spouses. The angel asked if he knew the queen of heaven and he said it is the spirit that operates in the second heaven, where the devil operates; like the queen of the coast in the seas. Lets see these accounts in the Book of Jeremiah.

Jeremiah 44:17; *"But we will certainly do whatsoever thing goeth forth out of our own mouth, to burn incense unto the queen of heaven, and to pour out drink offerings unto her, as we have done, we, and our fathers, our kings, and our princes, in the cities of Judah, and in the streets of Jerusalem: for then had we plenty of victuals, and were well, and saw no evil,"*

Jeremiah 7:18; *"The children gather wood, and the fathers kindle the fire, and the women knead their dough, to make cakes to the queen of heaven, and to pour out drink offerings unto other gods, that they may provoke me to anger."*

These verses are cited to show the people who fry puff-puff or bean cakes in memory of the dead, that what they are doing is the offering of sacrifice to the queen of heaven. If you have ever eaten such things, it means you have partaken of the devil's table.

18. The enemy is operating with a broken head.

Genesis 3:15; *"And I will put enmity between thee and the woman, and between thy seed and her seed; it shall bruise thy head, and thou shalt bruise his heel."*

The man then understood that the enemy's head is already broken.

Bind the strongman before making an attempt to recover your goods that he stole. The angel explained the fact that the devil cannot be everywhere at the same time, so, he uses delegated demonic representatives. That demonic operations commander is called 'the strongman.' It is the ruler spirit over a system or group of spirits. It is like a commander of a unit of soldiers while the devil is the commander-in-chief. A strongman can be assigned over the life of a person, family, community, country, church, business, etc. Once the strongman is bound and overpowered, you can set his captives free, spoil his house, break his control and cancel his authority over a situation.

When this man woke up, he was dumbfounded and two things struck him:
- The enemy is operating with a broken head.
- There is a strongman over every given situation, and has to be bound and his house spoilt.

He now knew what to do. He learnt that he had been strengthening his enemies and that the enemy has been strengthened by his own weakness to the advantage of the enemy. He also learnt how to use the weakness of the enemy to his own advantage.

After a few days, the devil made the mistake of coming to this brother again. You might wonder what I mean by "making a mistake.' Yes, the devil makes mistakes. That is why we pray that the enemy should make mistakes that will advance our course. The Bible says if they had known, they would not have crucified the Lord Jesus on the Cross because; that spelt victory for us through the death of Jesus and was sealed with His resurrection.

When the devil came to this man, he shouted: "I rebuke and bind you in the name of Jesus." This man had become a new person. To his surprise, the snake stretched out as if it was electrocuted. The man commanded the snake to vomit his children and it did one after the other. The man then remembered that the head of the enemy had been bruised and that he had a rod in his hand. He smashed the head of the snake with it and the head broke into two; one part was like the face of his former girlfriend whom he had jilted and the other, took the form of the herbalist whom he had consulted. By the following day, all his children recovered from the illness and asked for food. Two weeks later, he heard that the herbalist died and the former girl-friend ran mad. It then dawned on him that the former girl-friend had consulted the same herbalist, meaning that; he had gone to his enemy to seek help, so his problems multiplied.

Beloved, victory came to this man when he learnt certain things and knew methods of breaking the backbone of the enemy. If after your spiritual bombardment the problem still continues, it means there is something that needs to be broken. No matter how strong your enemy or oppressors might be, they have their own weak points which you, as a Christian, must exploit.

I hope you have been able to learn some lessons from the examples I have enumerated. I pray that the Lord will open your eyes to see that, no matter how bad the situation that you are passing through is, the Lord is with you. If you look closely, you will find out that there is something the Lord wants to bring out from it. However, if you are the one that imposed the tribulation upon yourself, you must first retrace your steps before you can expect God to bring out a lesson from the situation. Therefore, if you have never at one point in time decided to surrender your life to the Lord Jesus Christ, you have no claim to Him. You could be an ardent churchgoer, if you have never had a personal encounter with the Lord; your church attendance is in vain. Right now, you have the opportunity of making amends today. All you need do is acknowledge the fact that you are a sinner and that you cannot approach God in your sinful state. Repent of your sins, confess them and ask the Lord to forgive you and cleanse you from all unrighteousness. Name those sins one by one, renounce them and forsake them. Say bye-bye to the world and the devil and make sure you do not go back to them anymore.

I congratulate you on this decision that you have just taken; it is the most important decision in life. I pray that it shall be permanent in your life in the name of Jesus. I pray that the Lord will uphold you with His hand of righteousness and will write your name in the Book of life. I pray that you will not by any means rub it off in the name of Jesus. Go and sin no more.

Take these prayer points with the determination that your problems will become your promotion:

PRAYER POINTS
1. Let every spirit of Egypt fall after the order of Pharaoh, in the name of Jesus.
2. Let every spirit of Herod be disgraced, in the name of Jesus.
3. Let every spirit of Goliath receive the stones of fire, in the name of Jesus.
4. Let all satanic manipulations aimed at changing my destiny be frustrated, in the name of Jesus.
5. Let all unprofitable broadcasters of my goodness be silenced, in the name of Jesus.
6. Let all leaking bags and pockets be sealed up, in the name of Jesus.
7. Let all evil monitoring eyes fashioned against me be blind, in the name of Jesus.

The God Of Daniel

Luke 21:15; *"For I will give you a mouth and wisdom, which all your adversaries shall not be able to gainsay nor resist"*

Daniel 1:8-9;
"But Daniel purposed in his heart that he would not defile himself with the portion of the king's meat, nor with the wine which he drank: therefore he requested of the prince of the eunuchs that he might not defile himself. Now God had brought Daniel into favour and tender love with the prince of the eunuchs."

There was a supernatural ability that allowed Daniel to have knowledge, skill and wisdom. Knowledge, skill and wisdom are the things that you need to help you get to the top. The kind that your friends and enemies cannot contend or compare with. I pray that, that will be your lot in the name of Jesus.

In 1998, we had a programme dedicated to teachers. It was a deliverance programme organised to address the poverty of teachers. We prayed the prayer for knowledge, skill and wisdom on that day. A teacher came with her son who is a pilot. She had seven children who still depended on her. This woman had all the problems in the world; she could not 'make ends meet' at the end of the month and had to borrow money from her subordinates, despite the fact that she was the Vice-Principal of her school. Her children were grown up and were university graduates, but they all depended on her. One of them is a pilot and was working with a local airline, but it was as if he was not working at all. During the deliverance programme, they both prayed fervently on that day.

After a while, there was an advertisement in the newspapers; that an American airline was recruiting pilots. The young man applied and he was invited to an interview. His performance impressed the airline and he was recruited immediately. When he heard the good news, he fainted. He was given a ten-year contract worth millions of dollars and was given thousands of dollars to pay off the company he was working with at the time. This job changed his life and that of the members of his family, His mother came to show me the keys to the jeep he bought for her and narrated how 'power changed hands' in their lives. He bought her a house and all she needed, and he went to the U.S.A. to assume his post as a pilot.

That is what happens when there is a supernatural knowledge and skill imparted into your life. The God of Daniel is still the same today. If you want Him to bestow upon you the anointing for skill, wisdom and knowledge, He is ready to do it. The God of Daniel is the One you will find in Daniel 1:17 who reveals the truth to His children, through dreams and revelations.

CHARACTERISTICS OF GOD OF DANIEL:

1. The God of Daniel Is The God Of Divine Revelation.
Daniel 1:17;
"As for these four children, God gave them knowledge and skill in all learning and wisdom: and Daniel had understanding in all visions and dreams."
He can reveal to you before an interview, all the questions that you will be asked and you will know all the secrets before you get there.

Since the beginning of the history of the world, there has never been a man or woman, who has the ability of divine dreams who ever failed. However, the problem is that; instead of having divine dreams these days, Christians are seeing themselves being pursued by masquerades in their dreams. They are being harassed by spirit husbands or wives and all sorts of terrible dreams. The God of Daniel is the One, Who is able to set aside all these terrible dreams and replace them with night visions and revelations.

Beloved, I want you to understand this very well. The God of Daniel is the God of revelation. I came from a very poor family; so poor that daddy would complain that the soup mummy prepared was not good enough, forgetting that, it was the amount of money he gave her that determined the ingredients she bought. It was that bad. So, when I got born-again, I began to pray and God began to show me certain things and I made up my mind that I will not be poor. You must know where you are coming from so that, you can work hard to get to where you want to be.

Many people who are supposed to be discreet in what they do are loud, thus, the enemy finds his way into their lives. Maybe nobody knows them on the street before, but the day they throw a party and lavish money on people, those who did not know them would now know that they have money to flaunt. I knew where I was coming from and so, I was able to pray and work hard. Later, I got a scholarship to travel abroad. The ticket, school fees and everything was given to me. I knew that if I made noise about it, I would probably not go. I kept quiet and prepared. It was on the day I was travelling that people saw me in my suit, with my suitcase. Sometimes, we need to be discrete, so as not to expose our secrets to the enemy.

During my stay in England, I worked hard and one day my supervisor advised that I should take a break and go to Nigeria on holiday. He persistently told me to take a break. One night during this period, I had a dream where I saw myself at the Ikeja Airport. Our flight to London was announced and I looked round, but could not find the exit to the tarmac. Eventually I found it, but by the time I got to the tarmac, the aeroplane had taken off and I was left behind. That dream made me to know that I should not go home.

So, I told my supervisor that I would not go. Some Nigerian students went and during their stay in Nigeria, there was a "Military 'Coup d'etat." All borders and airports were closed and no one could travel out. By the time they got back, some of them had missed examinations and some failed woefully. Some would not go back to England because their sponsors were killed in the "Coup d'etat' and that marked the end of their career, I could have fallen into that category too. You need divine visions to sort out your life.

2. **The God Of Daniel Is The God Of Sovereign Power.**
Daniel 2:21;
"And He changeth the times and the seasons: He removeth kings, and setteth up kings: He giveth wisdom unto the wise and knowledge to them that know understanding."

He is the God who rules nations; He has the power to remove a king, and replace him with another one. He has the power to crush the pride of earthly rulers. He does not mind giving the sack to anyone whose position is hindering the progress of His children. Today, the strongman that constitute a hindrance to your break-through shall be bound and your breakthroughs shall be released in the name of Jesus.

I met a young Nigerian in England. Anytime I preached to him, he always made fun of me. He was a First Class Material who cleared his Masters Degree with a distinction and he got ready to leave. We all bade him bye. After a few days, I received a letter which had the stamp of the maximum prison on the envelope. I read it and found out that it was that young man. He asked me to come to the prison to pay him a visit. He asked me to buy a few things and bring for him. He said he realised that what I was telling him was the truth. 1 made up my mind that 1 would not go, for fear of being arrested as an accomplice. I put the letter somewhere and the Lord talked to me expressly, that I should go to the prison to see the young man.

When I got there, he burst into tears lamenting that, if he had listened to me, he would not have been in prison. He said he got born-again there and had been preaching to the inmates about Jesus, that they only made fun of him. I prayed with him, he confessed his sins to the Lord and we asked God to intervene in his situation. When I got back to town, I informed other brethren and we started to pray. On the day he was taken to court, we were in the court room praying silently in tongues.

The judge was very aggressive and he promised to deal treacherously with him. We had to call on the God of Daniel, asking for a replacement of the judge with a more lenient person. At the next hearing, it was another judge that presided over the case. The new judge looked at the brother and asked if it was true that he bagged a First Class Honours Degree in Nigeria, and that he got a Distinction in Masters Degree in England. The brother answered in the affirmative. The judge then said for an intelligent person to steal money, he had to be mad; therefore, he would not jail him in England, but repatriate him to Nigeria We knew that the brother was not mad: that it was the God of Daniel that was at work.

3. **The God Of Daniel Is The God Of Secrets.**
Daniel 2:22;
"He revealeth the deep and secret things: He knoweth what is in the darkness and the light dwelleth with Him."
He is the God that reveals secrets. All the secrets of the universe are known to God. All the past, present and future are known to God. He can tell the destinies of nations. He can tell you what will happen in the next five or six years. If there is any conspiracy against you. God can show you the secret. God can make you to discover a witch craft meeting and you will hear their discussions so that you can counter their plans.
As you are there right now, there is a secret about your life, that you would need to know. Immediately you know it, your life will explode. Find out what it is!

Many years ago, we preached a message about destiny and prosperity. A woman was there and when she got home, she prayed fervently. She was learned, had a job, but was very poor. The Lord drew her attention to the piece of land behind her house and told her in a clear voice" to start planting vegetables there. She thought it was the devil that was making a denigrating proposal to her. She bound the voice in anger because she had a Master's Degree in Education. The Lord made her to know that He was the One speaking and she complied. She started the vegetable farm and it was as if the whole town was waiting for her. They abandoned every other vegetable and bought only hers. It got to an embarrassing stage where nobody else could sell vegetables until hers finished. Within one year, this teacher that used to be poor, had enough money to build a house with the proceeds from the vegetable farming. I pray that the Lord will reveal to you, the secrets that will move your life forward.

4. **The God Of Daniel Is The God Of Deliverance.**
Daniel 6:20-22;
"And when he came to the den, he cried with a lamentable voice unto Daniel: and the king spake and said to Daniel: "O Daniel, servant of the living God, is thy God, whom thou servest continually, able to deliver thee from the lions?" Then said Daniel unto the king: "O king, live for ever. My God hath sent his angel, and hath shut the lions' mouths, that they have not hurt me: forasmuch as before Him innocence was found in me; and also before thee, O king, have I done no hurt."

Immediately Daniel got into the Lion's den, the lions recognised him as the son of the Lion of the Tribe of Judah. Lions do not eat lions, so, they did not touch him.

One day, a friend's wife was travelling in a luxurious bus. Suddenly, one of the passengers asked the driver to stop for him to ease himself. The driver stopped and someone came to the woman to say that a man at the back wanted to see her, that he was her husband's classmate at school. The woman got up to go and see the person. A few seconds later, a trailer ran into the luxurious bus and all the people sitting at the front where the woman got up from, perished. The amazing part of the story is the fact that, the woman could not see the person who came to call her to the back. That must have been God's angel of deliverance that came to call her out of danger.

5. **The God Of Daniel Is A Faithful God.**
Daniel 6:23
"Then was the king exceeding glad for him, and commanded

that they should take Daniel up out of the den. So Daniel was taken up out of the den, and no manner of hurt was found upon him, because he believed in his God. The Bible says those that put their trust in Him shall not be put to shame.

6. The God Of Daniel Is The God Of Signs And Wonders.

Daniel 6:26-27;

"I make a decree, that in every dominion of my kingdom men tremble and fear before the God of Daniel; for he is the living God, and steadfast for ever, and His kingdom that which shall not be destroyed, and His dominion shall be even unto the end. He delivereth and rescueth, and He worketh signs and wonders in heaven and in earth, who hath delivered Daniel from the power of the lions."

A sister got married and on the wedding night, she refused the traditional 'pouring of water' on her feet. The groom's mother got angry and promised to show her 'pepper.' That night, the bride had a dream where she saw her mother-in-law, dipping her hand into her stomach and pulling out her womb. She went to the back of their house and nailed the womb to the wall. Although this sister was born-again, she did not know anything about spiritual warfare. She remembered having the dream but did not know that it could have any implication on her.

She discovered that she could not get pregnant even medical tests and scans could not detect anything wrong with her. She was childless for 16 years. The Lord brought her to MFM and she started to pray fire prayers. One night, she had a dream where she saw her mother-in-law come into the house with her womb and she collected it back. In real life, the mother-in-law died many years before then. That was how the sister got her breakthrough. She got pregnant and now has children.

I know that the God of Daniel shall visit you today in the name of Jesus. However, if you are reading this message and you have not yet surrendered your life to the Lord Jesus Christ, I would like you to take that decision, right there where you are. You must be born-again to be a partaker of the blessing of the God of Daniel. Why don't you take that decision today? Right there where you are, the Lord is with you and wants you to come to Him. All you need to do is acknowledge the fact that you are a sinner, that you cannot approach God in your sinful state. Repent of your sins right there where you are, confess your sins to Him; name them one by one and ask Him to forgive you and cleanse you from all unrighteousness. Claim the redemptive power in the Blood of Jesus. Renounce the world of sin and the devil.

Jesus is waiting for you. Let today be the day when power will change hands in your life and the miracle of God will take root in your life. God will bless you as you take that decision. Invite the Lord Jesus into your life; ask Him to come into your heart and become your personal Lord and Saviour. Enthrone Him over your life and ask Him to take control of all that concerns you. Surrender your totality to Him and decide that you will never go back to the world of sin and the devil.

I congratulate you on this decision that you have just taken. It is the most important decision in life. I pray that it shall be permanent in your life in the name of Jesus. I pray that the Lord will uphold you with His right hand of righteousness and will keep you from falling. I pray that the Lord will write your name in the Book of Life and you will not by any means rub it off in the name of Jesus. Say bye-bye to the world of darkness and enter into the Kingdom of Light.

The prayers that I am suggesting below are prayers of divine intervention by the God of Daniel. As you pray them, all the spirits that have been tormenting you will leave you in the name of Jesus. The healing power of God will go forth and heal all manner of sicknesses and diseases in your spirit, soul and body. Make sure you do not allow any distraction. Every arrow that has been fired at you will go back to the sender. The power of God will fall upon you and you will be delivered from sicknesses and even terminal diseases. The power of God will pop out like popcorn and things will begin to happen.

Take these prayer points with holy aggression:

1. God of Daniel, arise and pursue my pursuers, in the name of Jesus.
2. Every occultic power searching for my face, die! in the name of Jesus.
3. In the presence of those asking for my God, O God of Daniel, manifest Your power! in the name of Jesus.
4. Every plantation of witchcraft in my body, be uprooted! in the name of Jesus
5. I arrest every profitless hard work, in the name of Jesus.
6. I cancel every failure at the edge of breakthroughs, in the name of Jesus.
7. Every ladder of darkness, that the enemy has been using to get into my life, break and burn to ashes! in the name of Jesus.
8. Every harassment from the spirit of death and hell, cease! in the name of Jesus.
9. Let every mark of hatred upon my forehead, be rubbed off, by the Blood of Jesus.
10. God of Daniel, pass through my life with signs and wonders, in the name of Jesus,,
11. God of Daniel, anoint me for favour, in the name of Jesus.
12. Serpents and Scorpions in my body, go back to your sender! in the name of Jesus.
13. Stubborn witchcraft of my father's house, die! in the name of Jesus.
14. Stubborn witchcraft of my mother's house, die! in the name of Jesus.
15. Every child of Belial, every child of Belzebub, I cast you out of my progress, in the name of Jesus.
16. Listen to me household witchcraft, your time is up; therefore, die! in the name of Jesus.
17. Every power that has to die, for my joy to be full, die! in the name of Jesus.
18. Doors, gates of my breakthroughs, open by fire! in the name of Jesus.
19. Every personal wall of Jericho in my life, crumble! in the name of Jesus.
20. I possess my possession, in the name of Jesus.
21. I seal all my prayers with the Blood of Jesus.

When your star begins to shine, there are some boasting powers that would want to ask questions. These powers would want to impede your movement. Therefore, take these prayers with boiling anger.

Personal Pentecost

In Luke 24:49, we read the parting shot of our Lord Jesus Christ to His disciples;

"And behold, I send the promise of my Father upon you; but tarry ye in the city of Jerusalem until ye be endued with power from on high."

And in Act 2:1 **the promise was fulfilled;** *"And when the day of Pentecost was come, they were all with one accord in one place. And suddenly, there came a sound from heaven, as of a rushing, mighty wind and it filled all the house where they were sitting and there appeared unto them, cloven tongues like as of fire and it sat upon each of them and they were all filled with the Holy* **Ghost** *and began to speak with other tongues as the Spirit gave them utterance."*

When Jesus died, the disciples were very discouraged. They had expected Jesus to pull out a trick and make them governors and rulers. They had not expected Jesus to give Himself up the way He did. They were so discouraged that, someone like Peter went back to the fishing profession. Thomas did not even believe that Jesus had risen; he wanted see the holes in His hands and feet before he believed. Peter that was optimistic at the beginning denied Jesus three times and later wept bitterly. The state of the disciples was like that of a pot of vegetable soup; nicely prepared with fresh vegetables, perfect oil, plenty meat but, without salt. The lives of many Christians are like that. There is something somewhere, missing in their lives. Occasionally, some people are able to lay their hands on the problem but sometimes, they are not able to.

When you study the way God manifested Himself to the Israelites, you will see that He manifested in the form of wind, cloud, rain, etc and on the day of Pentecost, He manifested Himself as a rushing mighty wind and tongues of fire. If you have ever seen a bush burning or a great fire, you would hear a sound like human voices. The explanation is this; as the fire is burning, it is consuming oxygen and needs more oxygen to continue burning. When fire fall from heaven, great things happen. A man of God said that the sign of Christianity should be tongues of fire, instead of the crucifix that gives the impression that Jesus is still on the cross. When God touches your life with fire, people will come and watch you burning for the Lord.

One man was to preach in Russia and he could not speak the language, neither anyone interpret for him. Suddenly, the power of God fell on him and he started to speak the Russian language for thirty minutes. When he finished, he could not remember one word of the Russian language he had spoken.

Would to God that the fire would come upon us and burn in us so that, we would not need to go through deliverance or write books on deliverance or healing or bondage or curses and covenants any more! Our lives would become too hot for the enemy to touch and too hot fro the enemy to live in.

This is the problem beloved and we must tell you the truth, even if you find it hard to chew. It is when the fire in the fireplace is quenched that earthworms can go there to play. If you are still being pressed down on your bed when you are sleeping, it is because there is no fire in your life. If there is fire in your life, the earthworms and snakes will not choose your life as a play field. I wish we would have the kind of fire that Elijah had, or the kind of fire that Elisha had that even after his death, his skeleton revived a corpse. The skeleton of Elisha had more fire than many Christians who are alive today. If you want to remain a Christian in this our environment today, you must be filled with the fire of the Holy Ghost; it is compulsory! You must experience what I call a 'Personal Pentecost.' It is nice when Christians are together and the Lord is in their midst. When you get home, it is necessary to experience this Personal Pentecost as an individual.

Anything done in the house of God that is not energised by the Holy Spirit is useless and as far as the Kingdom of God is concerned, it makes no contribution to the furtherance of the Kingdom of God. The truth is this beloved; many people who claim to have received the Holy Spirit have not really received the Baptism in the Holy Ghost. It is wrong for any minister to teach people how to speak in tongues. Utterance comes from God the Father according to what is written in Romans 8:26-27

"Likewise the Spirit also helpeth our infirmities: for we know not what we should pray for as we ought: but the Spirit itself maketh intercession for us with groanings which cannot be uttered. And he that searcheth the hearts knoweth what is the mind of the Spirit, because he maketh intercession for the saints according to the will of God".

If you say that you speak in tongues and you still have strange dreams, or there is no living faith in your heart, or no fire in your spirit, or you do not have any zeal for God and you are still living in sin, it means there is a problem. What then is the use of the speaking in tongues? Some people say they are born-again and speak in tongues, yet there are serpents in their stomach eating them up each time they pray aggressive prayers. Such people will then think that they have ulcer and they spend a lot of money and time in hospitals and on medication.

The infilling of the Holy Spirit is an experience that revolutionises a person's life. How can you say that you are baptised with the power of God the Father, the Son and the Holy Spirit and not feel an evident change in your life? Why should your life remain the same, when you say you have the Godhead bodily dwelling in you? How can your life remain cold? It means something is wrong somewhere.

Some present-day believers, who claim to be filled with the Holy Spirit still put on materials that are dedicated to demons without knowing it. Some put on shoes or jewelleries that are used in initiating them into evil spiritual associations without knowing it. Some employ house-helps are serpents or fish but they do not know it. Some complicate things for themselves by laying hands on people that are possessed; whereas, they themselves need deliverance. Present-day believers cannot distinguish between friendly friends and unfriendly ones.

There was an 'Evangelist' who was not born-again. One day he made the mistake of laying hands on a demon-possessed girl. The girl rained abuses on him and the 'Evangelist' got angry and took a whip to beat the girl seriously. The girl burst out in a demonic laughter and said; "That is what I was waiting for you to do." He beats her the more until he got tired. As from that day, he was always feeling lashes on his body. He would not see the person whipping him and he would cry like a baby. People prayed for him but nothing happened until he cried to the Lord in repentance, This was a person who would preach vigorously and speak in tongues and everywhere would be vibrating. Who are you deceiving? We cannot deceive God; we can deceive ourselves and people but not God. There was another man who was not born-again, therefore, he was not filled with the Holy Spirit. He would blast strange tongues, jump here and there and lay hands on people. One day, he laid hands on a woman and behold, there was a horn on her head. It pierced through his palm and blood physically gushed out from it.

Beloved, I want you at this juncture to take this prayer point:
* **Lord, operate in my innermost being and do a surgical operation there, in the name of Jesus.**

There was another man who used to be a chorister in a choir. They used to recite: "As it was in the beginning, so is now, and forever shall be." He did not know that there was a power behind him which was reversing his confessions. In fact, he did know what the recitation meant but he was saying it. This man was practically a millionaire but he became a pauper. It got to a stage where sometimes, he would not even have up to N50 on him. One day, God decided to have compassion on him and his daughter began to confess to witchcraft. She said she had gathered all his finances and hung them on an Iroko tree. All the money that he could ever make in his life had been captured. She was brought to me and I asked her if it was true. She said" "Yes" confidently. I asked her what the solution to her father's problem was and she said there were two options; either sacrifice or prayer but she would suggest prayer. The father was astonished that it was his daughter talking. We thank God that he was delivered.

The Need For Personal Pentecost

Beloved, we all need Personal Pentecost. We need to have an encounter with the fire of the Holy Spirit; we all need to have His touch. As soon as you notice that your spiritual level is not sufficient for what you are facing, you must know that you need Personal Pentecost. When you find out that your imagination constantly engage in uncleanness, it means you need Personal Pentecost. When you find out that you have allowed something to come between you and God, you need Personal Pentecost. When you are lazy spiritually, or you are taking your ease and abandoning things that arc of God or you hate long prayer sessions or you engage in gossips and have become the devil's advertiser, you need Personal Pentecost. When you worry so much that even the smallest pimple on your face becomes an object of worry, then, you need Personal Pentecost.^ When you are distracted from the work of God; prayer and fasting becomes difficult, reading the Bible becomes hard work, then, you need Personal Pentecost. If you always have a little lie for everything and you do not seem to see anything wrong with lying, you need Personal Pentecost, If you are always depressed, easily discouraged, unhappy, you need it. If you are aggressive, abusive, rude, easily angered, you need it.

When you find out that you always plan to do one thing or the other for God and at the level of implementation, you fail to do it, then you need Personal Pentecost. If you are not known as a Christian at work and in your neighbourhood, if you are ashamed of Christ or you are a spiritual coward, you cannot tell someone that he or she needs Christ, you need Personal Pentecost. If you present a picture, different from the one you present of yourself in the church, you need Personal Pentecost. If you are so prayerless that you even forget to pray on your meals or snacks, you need Personal Pentecost. If your tongue is without control, you criticise everything and everybody or you nurse an ambition to revenge or you nourish an unforgiving spirit, you need Personal Pentecost.

There are many clever pretenders in the church; they all need Personal Pentecost. They do not have time for Bible Study or meditation, no time for prayer, no time to be alone with God; they all need Personal Pentecost. If you do not like it when your colleagues are being praised and you are left out, you need Personal Pentecost. If you are an unhappy Christian, you do not radiate the joy of the Lord, you do not tithe faithfully, you cannot look at death straight in the eyes, you are always afraid, then, you need Personal Pentecost. Jesus says: "You will receive power from on high", superior power is from on high. Many believers have been caged by sin, the world, the devil and the flesh. The fire of God is absent in their lives.

Some decades ago, Nigeria was in darkness; demons and demonic activities were all over the place. Many bad things were happening. There came a time, when some children of God who were on fire, got up and chased those demons out of the nation, straight back into hell.

Do you know that Christians are supposed to be the most dangerous spiritual powers on earth? Only those presently living on earth need power. Those in hell are already in the devil's hands; those in heaven are already out of his way. It is only those that are alive that need the in-filling of the Holy Spirit. It is not the kind of baptism that people say they receive and they only say: "Bah, bah, bah," year in year out, or they copy the tongues that their pastors speak. It is true that many believers want the power of God, but no father would give a gun to a 7-year old boy and turn him loose on the streets; WHY? It is too much power for him at his age. God cannot entrust power into the hands of some people. God is hoping, looking at them that one day, they will get to a level where He would soak them in Himself. If He expects you to move at 100 km/per hour and **you are moving like a snail, He cannot fill you with His power.**

ALTHOUGH GOD IS READY TO FILL PEOPLE WITH HIS POWER, THERE ARE SOME THAT HE WOULD NOT FILL. BECAUSE HE CANNOT TRUST THEM THEY ARE:

1. Those Who Cannot Control Their Emotions.

They hear messages but cannot control their anger. He would not give you power for you to one day get angry with your wife or husband and then command him or her to roast and it will happen and then, you start crying. God will not entrust power into the hand of those who will always shed tears for any small thing.

2. Those Who Lack Love.

Many people harbour hatred in their hearts, whereas, God commands us to love Him and love our neighbours and even go a mile further and love our enemies too. Matthew 5:43-48

"Ye have heard that it hath been said, Thou shalt love thy neighbour, and hate thine enemy. But I say unto you, Love your enemies, bless them that curse you, do good to them that hate you, and pray for them which despitefully use you, and persecute you; That ye may be the children of your Father which is in heaven: for he maketh his sun to rise on the evil and on the good, and sendeth rain on the just and on the unjust. For if ye love them which love you, what reward have ye? do not even the publicans the same? And if ye salute your brethren only, what do ye more than others? do not even the publicans so? Be ye therefore perfect, even as your Father which is in heaven is perfect".

3. The Doubters And The Fearful.

The Bible says that, a man that doubts is like the waves of the sea driven and tossed here and there and that such a person should not think that he or she can receive anything from the Lord (James 1:6-7). Peter was a fisherman; he was programmed not to fear winds and waves. So, when he asked Jesus if he could come and meet Him on the sea, Jesus told him to come. He started walking on the sea, but when he wavered, he began to sink.

Beloved, the issue of Personal Pentecost is very important and I would like you to take it serious. We shall stop here for now. I would advise that you ponder over what you have read and put it to practice. It is an individual matter but the whole body of Christ needs it so that, we can do that which the Lord has called us to. We shall continue in the next bulletin by the grace of God.

However, if you have not at one point in time, surrendered your life to the Lord Jesus Christ, you cannot expect to experience a Personal Pentecost. You cannot experience a visitation of the Holy Spirit. Therefore, I would advise that you take that bold step of faith and decide to become born-again. All you need do is acknowledge the fact that you are a sinner and that you cannot approach God in your sinful state. Right there where you are, confess your sins to Him and ask Him to forgive you and cleanse you from all unrighteousness. Name those sins one by one and renounce them. Say bye-bye to the world of sin and the devil. Decide that you will never go back to them any more. Invite the Lord Jesus Christ into your life; ask Him to become your personal Lord and Saviour. Open your heart to Him and enthrone Him over your life hand over all that concerns you to Him and ask Him to take total control.

I congratulate you on this decision that you have just taken. I pray that it shall be permanent in the name of Jesus. I pray that the Lord will uphold you and keep your feet from falling in the name of Jesus. I pray that He will write your name in the Book of Life and you will not by any means, rub it off in the name of Jesus.
Go and sin no more!

I would like you to take the following prayer points with all the aggression that you can gather. Pray until something happens.

1. Lord, deliver me from the evil of this generation, in the name of Jesus.
2. Thou right hand of the Most High God, do valiantly in my life today, in the name of Jesus.
3. Blood of Jesus, speak destruction to the works of the devil in my life, in the name of Jesus.
4. My Father, make me Your object of divine love forever, in the name of Jesus.
5. O Lord, let Your anointing fall upon my life, in the name of Jesus.
6. Holy Ghost Fire, descend upon my life today! in the name of Jesus.
7. All you strangers in my life; loose your hold! in the name of Jesus. I rededicate my life to the Lord, in the name of Jesus.
8. O Lord, let your fire of transformation, fall upon my life and transform my life to Your glory, in the mighty name of Jesus.
9. The Spirit of God will never depart from my life and family, in the name of Jesus.
10. O Lord, let Your fire go into the roots of my life, so that this wall of poverty before me, will be melted away, in the name of Jesus.
11. O Lord, let Your fire go into the roots of my life so that, this wall of sickness before me, will be melted away, in the name of Jesus.
12. O Lord, let Your fire go into the roots of my life so that, this wall of marital turbulence before me, will be melted away, in the name of Jesus.
13. Every ordination of evil upon my life will not prosper, in the name of Jesus.
14. Let the power of resurrection, enter into my life now! in the name of Jesus.
15. O Lord, open my eyes that I may be able to see, that which you want me to see, in the name of Jesus.
16. O Lord, open my ears that I may be able to hear, that which you want me to hear, in the name of Jesus.
17. Father Lord, let Your glory fall upon my life now! in the name of Jesus.
18. The glory of the Lord will never depart from my life and my family, in the name of Jesus.
19. O Lord, give me the power to fulfill my assignment for you, without failing, in the name of Jesus.
20. Father Lord, give unto me, spiritual boldness, to move out for You in power, in the name of Jesus.
21. Father Lord, ignite my spirit with the Fire of the Holy Ghost, in the name of Jesus.
22. Father Lord, remove every spiritual obstacle and hindrance from my spirit, in the name of Jesus.
23. O Lord, shower Your spiritual blessings upon me, in the name of Jesus.
24. Holy Ghost fire, my life is available for You, enter by fire in the name of Jesus.
25. By Your power, I will not be a disappointment to my God in Jesus' name.
26. O Lord Jesus, do not replace me with stone, in the name of Jesus.

The Mystery Of Terror

We are going to start this message by reading one of the declarations of God to the Israelites, concerning disobedience. Leviticus 26:16;
"I also will do this unto you; I will even appoint over you terror, consumption, and the burning ague, that shall consume the eyes, and cause sorrow of heart: and ye shall sow your seed in vain, for your enemies shall eat it."

Genesis 35:5;
"And they journeyed: and the terror of God was upon the cities that were round about them, and they did not pursue after the sons of Jacob."

There is hardly any day that passes, without the news mentioning the word 'Terror', in the newspapers and on air. Terrorism has terribly gripped the world today. One would wonder what is really happening. Why should a pregnant woman walk into a restaurant with a bomb tied around her waist, and before anyone could react, the bomb exploded and killed her along with all those in the restaurant? Why is it that people take delight in dying and killing other people with them? It is because there is a spirit called "Terror'.

Facts about Terror:
1. **It can be appointed**

2. **It can be internal and against anyone, without discrimination.**
Deuteronomy 32:25 says;
"The sword without, and terror within, shall destroy both the young man and the virgin, the suckling also with the man of gray hairs."

3. **It has no respect for anyone. It destroys everybody the same way.**

4. **There is a terror assigned to the night.**
Psalm 91:5 attests to this;
"Thou shalt not be afraid for the terror by night; nor for the arrow that flieth by day."

If you have the call of God upon your life, you must pray very well before getting married. If you are already married, you cannot unmarry. If life is getting difficult because of the marriage, all we can help you do is pray that God will intervene.

A man got married when he was an idol-worshipper. He married the girl who used to dance in front of the idol, with a pot on her head. Many years later, he gave his life to the Lord Jesus Christ and later became a pastor. One night at 1:00 am, he saw his 4 year-old daughter get up from sleep and she began to grow taller. She became a young girl instantly and some beautiful clothes appeared from nowhere and she put them on and went out. She came back at 3:00a.m. The father was not asleep but could not do anything, he could not even pray. He slept back and promised to catch her next time.

A few days later, the same thing happened. Instead of calling Jesus, the man jumped down from his bed and gave the girl a serious kick. He found out that his leg passed through the body of the girl, as a hot knife would pass through butter. His leg went and kicked his bed and the leg broke. He screamed and by the time he looked down, his 4 year-old daughter was fast asleep on her mat. The wife woke up and asked what was going on. She screamed when she saw the leg with blood gushing out. It was not a simple fracture; it broke completely and he lost a lot of blood. The wife found it difficult to understand what had happened.

The Weapons Of Terror:
1. **Seduction.**
They manipulate evil and make it look good. They magnetise people to do evil. Many men and women run immorality by seduction. Woman!, instead of checking your husband's brief-case for love letters or following him about to monitor what he is doing, you should pray because, the terror-girls are around with powerful weapons to magnetize and seduce any man who is not strong. It is true

but very unfortunate, that it is difficult to find leaders in government that are born-again. Seduction easily captures them by terror.

2. **Affliction.**
It is terrible and so horrible that, the Bible says it must not rise again. Affliction causes distress, infirmity and various kinds of discomfort.

3. **Attack.**
They use frontal attack with dreams and hardship. A woman quarrelled with a colleague and that one promised to show her that, 'prisoners have masters'. She took it lightly until one day, when she was driving along a busy road and was accosted by a gang of young boys. This fifty-two year old woman was asked to park her vehicle and was taken into a bush where she was raped one after the other. Nobody came to her rescue until she had been defiled. It was an attack arranged from the spirit realm.

4. **Depression.**
People are attacked with mental illness, anxiety, heaviness. To be quite honest with you, there is a lot of madness going on around us. Only a few display it and go naked on the streets. Majority go about depending on drugs to survive; analgesics and tranquilisers that calm pains down, but do not remove them. Many big men have to pass through such treatment before they can do anything.

If you put a bus outside and ask people to queue up to enter, you will see that someone will come from nowhere and would head for the door, not minding the people on the queue. It is madness! A man impregnated a woman and her daughter and he was rejoicing. That is madness. Someone went to a prophet because she wanted to have children. The prophet took her to a burial ground, asked her to undress and shave her pubic hair. This woman studied in England, but she obeyed because she wanted a child. The prophet took the hair from her and buried it in the cemetery and asked her to go; that she would have twins. True to it, she had twins but they were the ones that eventually killed her. That was madness.

5. **Initiation.**
People are recruited into demonic associations, consciously or unconsciously. We should teach our children not to eat just anything, anywhere and also anoint them everyday. Demonic people are using food and sweets to initiate people and even children in schools through birthdays, into demonic societies.

6. **Influence.**
They use negative influence to affect people negatively.

7. **Persuasion.**
They convince the person to do what he or she would normally not do.

8. **Oppression.**
Many people are being oppressed especially in their dreams.

9. **Possession.**
They enter into the life of a person and take possession of all that he or she is or has.

10. **Domination.**
They enthrone a person and they dominate that life

Although terror is strong and powerful, the Bible has a different opinion as to what your stand should be, as a child of God.

Isaiah 54:14;
"In righteousness shalt thou be established: thou shalt be far from oppression; for thou shalt not fear: and from terror; for it shall not come near thee."

Psalm 91:5;
"Thou shalt not be afraid for the terror by night; nor for the arrow that flieth by day."

How To Battle Against The Spirit Of Terror

1. **Surrender your life to the Lord Jesus Christ**

2. **Repent from every known sin.** Any sin in your life will open doors to terror and it will harass you.

3. **Be spiritually violent.**
The Bible says: *"From the time of John the Baptist, the Kingdom of God suffereth violence and the violent taketh it by force."*

It is unfortunate but true to note that there is no gentle way of arresting evil. There is no gentle way of harassing violence. The only language that the enemy understands is violence. God is looking for violent soldiers today; those who will drink the blood of the enemies and slay the giants, those who will refuse to be intimidated by the powers of darkness, those who will scare the enemies out of their hideouts, those who will soak themselves in prayer and in fire such that when darkness sees them, it will flee. God is not looking for those who are running away from darkness. Nor those who want to move out of their houses because of witches. God wants those who will be a terror to the enemy and he will be afraid of them.

I have a Father-in-the Lord who told me the story of one of his pastors. One day, this man of God went to the town where this pastor was working for the Lord. As he moved close to the church, he saw many people standing. They were dressed in occultist regalia; masquerades and herbalists were all there. As a man of God, he did not have any fear but he wondered what the strange people could be doing there. He drove into their midst and when he alighted from the car, they asked if he was the General Overseer of the church and he said he was. They said they were representatives of the other kingdom. They said he should remove the 'dog' who called himself pastor of the church from there. They said he should bring back the former one.

The General Overseer wondered in amazement what they meant and they went on to say that, since 'this dog' came, all the young boys had abandoned their masquerades and traditional religion and were always in the church, jumping and singing. To worsen the case, 'this dog' would walk about the streets at night, speaking a strange language till 2:00a.m. That made people uncomfortable and the environment became tense. The General Overseer pinched himself to be sure that he was awake and hearing right. He found out that it was real and not a vision or dream. It means that, that pastor had become a terror to them. The former one was not making any impact on them. I pray that today, instead of the enemy being a terror to you, you shall be a terror to the enemy in the name of Jesus.

However, if you are not yet born-again, you cannot be a terror to anything or anybody: rather, you are likely to even become a meat for the enemy. I would therefore advise that you surrender your life to the Lord Jesus Christ. All you need to do is to repent of your sins. Confess them to the Lord; name them one by one and ask Him to forgive you and cleanse you from all unrighteousness. Claim the redemptive power in the Blood of Jesus that was shed on the Cross at Calvary; for the remission of your sins. Renounce your sins, say goodbye to the world and the devil and enter into the Kingdom of the Lord.

Invite the Lord Jesus Christ into your life. Open your heart and let Him come in; ask Him to be your personal Lord and Saviour. Surrender your totality to Him and ask Him to take control of all that concerns you.

I thank God that you have taken this decision. It is the most important decision in life and I pray that it shall be permanent in your life, in the name of Jesus. I pray that the Lord will uphold you with His hand of righteousness and will keep you from falling in the name of Jesus. I pray that your name will be written in the Book of Life and you will not by any means, rub it off in the name of Jesus. The Bible says as you are now in Christ, you are a new creature; old things are passed away and all things have become new. (2 Corinthians 5:17)

Just before you take the prayer points below, I would like you to talk to the Lord, that if there is still anything in your life that He does not like, He should expose it and take it away. Anything that will not allow a divine visitation and that will hinder your prayers from being answered, must be confessed and forgiveness must be sought. Make sure you are right with God.

As you take these prayer points, the Lord will do wonders in your life and you will have testimonies. If your strength has been sapped by witchcraft powers, it shall return to your body in the name of Jesus. Any infirmity, planted by witchcraft powers or that got into your life through dreams, shall disappear in the name of Jesus. Anything planted into your life, in order to torment it, shall be uprooted in the name of Jesus. The miracle power of God will descend upon you and you will begin to do those things that you could not do before. God will enter into your situation and a change will take place, even if it seems very difficult, the Lord shall intervene in the name of Jesus.

Now, take these prayer points with all the aggression that you can gather:

1. Let the fire of God, burn to ashes, every plantation of whoredom in my life, in the name of Jesus.
2. Thou power of seduction, die! in the name of Jesus.
3. Every strange flesh, harassing my destiny, die! in Jesus' name.
4. Any power pulling me to iniquity, be destroyed! in Jesus" name.
5. My life, reject any evil attraction, in the name of Jesus.
6. My inner man, reject the hook of seduction, in Jesus name.
7. I withdraw any organ of my body, from every evil altar, in the name of Jesus.
8. I release myself from the grip of any strange man/woman, in the name of Jesus.
9. Every spirit of Delilah that is pursuing my calling, be buried alive! in the name of Jesus.
10. Every Jezebel power upon my life, loose your hold! in Jesus' name.
11. Every handwriting of affliction, I wipe you off by the power in the blood of Jesus, in the mighty name of Jesus.
12. Every power, targeted at my peace, be disgraced! in the name of Jesus.
13. I bind and cast out, every oppressive spirit, in the name of Jesus.
14. My destiny, reject the circle of affliction! in the name of Jesus.
15. I arise by the Spirit of God, to torment every tormentor and oppressor, in the name of Jesus.
16. The name of the Lord which is a strong tower, move upon my life today and let every handwriting of affliction die! in the name of Jesus.
17. Every serpent and scorpion of oppression, I trample upon you, in the name of Jesus.
18. Every yoke of the oppressor, be dashed to pieces in Jesus' name.
19. Witchcraft oppression, loose your hold! in the name of Jesus.
20. Every ladder of day and night oppression, die now! in the mighty name of Jesus.
21. Let oppressional capacity of my environment, be neutralised, in the name of Jesus.
22. I bind and paralyse, every strongman of fear in my life, in the mighty name of Jesus.
23. Let all entrances of fear in my life, be closed forever! in Jesus' name.
24. I loose myself, from all demonic fear and from all their enslaving powers, in Jesus' name.
25. Let all problems introduced by fear into my life, depart now! in the name of Jesus.
26. If I have been initiated into any dark society through the mouth gate, Holy Ghost fire, purge me now! in the name of Jesus.
27. Every disease infirmity, dry up by fire! in the name of Jesus.
28. Every power, keeping my problems alive, die! in the name of Jesus.
29. Arrows of fire from heaven, arise, and scatter the camp of my enemies! in the name of Jesus.
30. Special announcement; you road of affliction, close! in the name of Jesus.
31. Special announcement: you road of backwardness in my life, close! in the name of Jesus.
32. Every witchcraft finger, pointed at me, wither! in the name of Jesus.
33. I shall be a terror to my enemies, in the name of Jesus.
34. Arrows of death in my body, backfire! in the name of Jesus.
35. Every enchantment assigned against me, die! in the name of Jesus.

36. Every embargo on my glory, die! in the name of Jesus.
37. Every captivity of my father's house, die! in the name of Jesus. Every captivity of my mother's house, die! in the name of Jesus.
38. Every power, pronouncing poverty upon my life, die! in the name of Jesus.
39. You terror in the heavenlies, my life is not your candidate, therefore; die! in the name of Jesus.
40. You terrors of the night, my life is not your candidate, therefore;, die! in the name of Jesus.

Begin to thank the Lord for setting you free from the bondage of terror.

The Negative Dedication

Today's message is very simple and straight to the point, so I would like you to pay attention and take it very serious. Let's read something interesting in the book of Samuel.

This is the account of Hannah's vow in 1 Samuel 1:11; *"And she vowed a vow, and said: "O Lord of hosts, if thou wilt indeed look on the affliction of thine handmaid, and remember me, and not forget thine handmaid, but wilt give unto thine handmaid a man child, then I will give him unto the Lord all the days of his life, and there shall no razor come upon his head."*

Here she fulfills her promise Samuel 1:24-28;
"And when she had weaned him, she took him up with her, with three bullocks, and one ephah of flour, and a bottle of wine, and brought him unto the house of the Lord in Shiloh: and the child was young. And they slew a bullock, and brought the child to Eli. And she said: "Oh my lord, as thy soul liveth, my lord, I am the woman that stood by thee here, praying unto the Lord. For this child I prayed; and the Lord hath given me my petition which I asked of him: Therefore also I have lent him to the Lord; as long as he liveth he shall be lent to the Lord". And he worshipped the Lord there."

This message concerns everyone and today will be a day of deliverance for you, if you know what to do.

What Is Dedication?
It means to devote a thing to the worship of a spirit being. It is setting something or someone apart for a specific thing. It is to perform a ceremony or religious acceptance into something. It is an ordination. With that simple statement in verse 11 of the text above, Hannah dedicated Samuel to God. The reverse could also be true; a child could also be dedicated to the devil. Whenever something is dedicated to God, He will keep watch over it and note every detail about it.

If your name is Samuel or Isaac, there is nowhere to run to. There are some names that you should not bear, if you do not want to work for God: names like Elijah, Samuel, Isaiah, Jeremiah, Paul, Peter, etc. Means that such people have been dedicated to God for life. Once a name has been slammed on your head, you are bound by what you are dedicated to. Doing otherwise is to look for trouble. The Bible says: *"I know whom I have believed and am persuaded that He is able to keep that which is committed unto Him."*

Anything you commit into the hands of God He keeps with a jealous dedication. Once something has been dedicated to the devil, he pursues it to the last corner. Beloved, note this hard fact: "A person is a property of what he or she is dedicated to." It is like an outright sale he or she has been sold off. If it is something ungodly, the person would need to be bought back. It does not matter whether the person(s) that did the dedication is or are dead or alive, the dedication remains binding. Changing a name of dedication is also a spiritual transaction and anyone who has been dedicated is married to the power to which he or she is dedicated. The power behind the dedication sees to it that the contract is not broken. It will pursue the person to the last bus-stop.

Many years ago, a woman came for prayers because her three children, who were living in different countries abroad, suddenly arrived on the same day without knowing why. They did not plan it, neither did they tell each other that they were arriving. As prayers were going on, the Lord revealed that the day they arrived was the date that was fixed in the spirit realm, to marry them off to the same spirit-wife to which they had been dedicated.

Practically all our culture in Africa is saturated with one dedication or the other. This is clearly shown in the things that we do. The way traditional naming ceremonies are conducted, shows a dedication to evil. Some of the items used in the dedication on that day are: dead rat, kola-nut, bitter-cola, alligator pepper, palm-oil etc. Those things are given to the mother and baby and shared amongst the people that are present at the ceremony, with pronouncements which are actually incantations.

Serious and real dedications take place during coronation ceremonies, burials, circumcisions, house-warming ceremonies, etc. If you or your parents ever took part in any ceremony like that, know that you have taken part in an evil dedication. It is an evil marriage whether the person involved is conscious of this fact or not. Ignorance is not an excuse in the spirit realm. That is why we keep saying that, those who are into witchcraft could be there either by force; consciously or unconsciously or by decision or by inheritance. That there is something known as blind witchcraft, that is; the person is there without knowing it.

If a person has been dedicated to an evil thing, all sorts of strange things will happen. Therein lies the root of many stubborn problems, especially in Africa. That is why sometimes, when prayers of deliverance are going on, some powers speak out in revolt, saying that they will not get out of the person. Many years ago, in New York, a thirteen-year-old girl was brought for prayers. As we started to pray, a voice spoke out of the girl's mouth in pure Yoruba. Normally, the girl could not speak or understand Yoruba because she was born in the United States and had never been to Nigeria. The voice asked what my business was, that the family had been dedicated her to it many decades ago. It said it had the right to deal with them because they belonged to it. I said they now belong to Jesus and it said that they were not fully committed to the Lord, that they have a ring under their bed which was part of the materials of the dedication. This shows that although that family was in far away New York, the property from the dedication in Nigeria was still with them, so the power could lay claims to them and their children. This is a very serious matter and I would like you to take it serious.

One day, I was traveling to the mid-western part of the country and I saw people throwing live chickens and goats into a river. I was curious and I stopped the car and got down to see what was going on. I saw that they were performing rituals and sacrifices. There was a woman who sat by the river, with a big bowl of pounded yam and okro soup. She would cut a morsel of pounded yam, dip it in the soup and throw it into the river. I walked up to her and asked why she was wasting the food. She told me to clear out of her sight, asking if I did not know that she was feeding her husband. That woman had been dedicated to the terrible water spirit husband. I pray that if you have been dedicated to any evil thing, consciously or unconsciously, you shall be delivered today in the name of Jesus.

Herein lies the problem of Africa. Africa is very rich but is not benefiting from her natural resources. We produce all kinds of raw materials, which foreigners buy, export, manufacture in their countries and send back to us, to buy at their own price. 54% of the world gold is in Africa; but, we are not in a position to determine the price of gold in the world market. **Evil dedication brings backwardness**

Do you notice that your spiritual life is almost dead? Perhaps the day you pray most, is the day that you receive a lot of attack in your dreams? Do you notice that your life easily magnetise attacks?

Is poverty moving you from one thing to the other? Are you going through unexplainable marital attacks? There might be an evil dedication somewhere.

Many years ago, a woman ran to us for help. Her husband was a pastor and one day, he brought a strange woman into their apartment. He put the woman in their guest room and would go there to sleep with her. When the wife protested and threatened to report him to the church, he threatened to resign as pastor and continue his relationship with the strange woman fully. That was why she was introduced to MFM. As prayers were going on, it was discovered that as a young girl, she was always failing her examination and her mother consulted a herbalist who dedicated her to an evil spirit which helped her to pass the examination when she failed. Do you notice that your marital problems is as a result of your having to worship a power or you get rid of it by the blood of Jesus?

Maybe you have been obeying an evil command and you find out that there are some problems staring you in the face, it could be as a result of a dedication to evil spirits. That is why some people go abroad and do not make a headway, despite all sincere efforts. The evil spirits follow them about and so, they cannot succeed in life.

What To Do In Situations Like These:
1. **Surrender your life to the Lord Jesus Christ.**
2. **Repent of every sin that could be in your life.**
3. **Take a thorough look at your background; see if there is an evil dedication which could be speaking against you.**
4. **Destroy the altars of the evil dedication.**
5. **Rededicate your life to the Lord Jesus Christ.**

What am I trying to put across through this message? It is the fact that, some people will never move forward until evil dedications involving their lives have been destroyed. There are many people whom God purposed would be rich but are so poor, to the extent that they can hardly feed themselves. This is as a result of the dedication of their lives to evil spirits. There are many Christians who are supposed to be prophets but each time they want to move into God's agenda for their lives, there is a power that says "NO." This is a serious matter and I would like you to prepare yourself for a serious battle, but with confidence in your heart that the Bible says in; Philippians 2:9-11;
"Wherefore God also hath highly exalted Him, and given Him a name which is above every name: that the name of Jesus every knee should bow, of things in heaven, and things in earth, and things under the earth; and that every tongue should confess that Jesus Christ is Lord, to the glory of God the Father."

That Power is right there where you are now; the Power that is beyond human imagination and calculation. If you cry out today, against every dedication that is speaking against you and you command them to clear away in the name of Jesus, you will see that some things will begin to happen. You have to pray like a mad prophet and you will find out that the doors that had been closed against your breakthroughs will begin to open. That which seemed to be impossible, will receive a touch of the power of God and you will begin to move forward.

I would like you to understand that we in Africa are in a very, very special situation and here, we need serious prayers. The power of evil dedication is a serious matter that can set aside good things. A situation could arise, where God would stand aloof and be watching, without taking any action. It happened in the Bible and Jeremiah cried out and asked God why He behaved like a stranger.

Jeremiah 14:8 - 9;
"O the hope of Israel, the Saviour thereof in time of trouble, why shouldest thou be as a stranger in the land, and as a wayfaring man that turneth aside to tarry for a night? Why shouldest thou be as a man astonied, as a mighty man that cannot save? Yet thou, O Lord, art in the midst of us, and we are called by Thy name; leave us not."

A situation could arise in a person's life, when God would behave like a visitor and would not do anything. This is when a dedication is involved and the person has not broken it. One day, during Jacob's trouble, he slept in a place and he saw angels descending and ascending. He dedicated the place in totality to the Lord, built an altar there and called the place Bethel. Later, a king called Jeroboam rose up and erected an idol in Dan. When the idol was brought to Bethel, God contested it and sent a prophet there to confront the King and destroy the altar. This is because the place had already been dedicated to God. God did not contest for Dan but for Bethel.

Many people are being confronted by satanic agents today, because of the dedication that is speaking against them. Today, I would like you to pray the prayer points I am suggesting below, with all the vigour that you can gather. Pray them with fervency and you will see that you will move into your arena of breakthroughs. The power of negative dedication is a terrible thing.

However, if you have never at any one point in time in your life, surrendered your Lord Jesus Christ, you might not be able to counter the effect of any negative dedication of your life. It would mean that you are fighting the enemy whilst being part of his camp.

It is not late yet; you can still dedicate your life to the Lord Jesus Christ; right there where you are. All you need to do is to acknowledge the fact that you are a sinner and that you cannot approach God in your sinful state. Repent of your sins sincerely; confess them to the Lord; name them one by one and ask Him to forgive you and cleanse you from all unrighteousness. Renounce the world of sin and the devil; tell the Lord that you will never go back to them anymore. Open your heart and let the Lord Jesus Christ come in. Ask Him to come in and become your personal Lord and Saviour. Enthrone Him over your life and ask Him to take an absolute control of all that concerns you.

I congratulate you on this decision that you have taken; it is the most important decision in life. I pray that it shall be permanent in the name of Jesus. I pray that the Lord will uphold you by His power and lay His hand upon you. I pray that He will move you from strength to strength and from glory to glory. I pray that

the Lord will establish you by His power, in this decision that you have taken and that He will keep you standing in the name of Jesus.

Now, confess the sins of your parents and ancestors, which in one way or the other have dedicated you to one thing or the other. Seeing that the Lord is God and His power is everlasting. It is important that you do this confession, with all seriousness. I pray that the Lord will wash away by the power in the blood of Jesus, every ancestral sin caging your life. Let the blood of Jesus wash away every sin of dedication of your life to any evil power.

Please take the following prayer points seriously until things happen. As you pray them, the roads which have been closed against you shall open in the name of Jesus. If you are under pressure from any quarter, you shall be set free today. If you have a serious health problems, I want you to gather all the strength that you have and pray these prayers. The enemy might have shut down all the good things in your life-PRAY. Even if any organ is decaying inside you, it will come alive by the resurrection power of God today in the name of Jesus.

1. (Shout this loud and clear) Blood of Jesus, wash away every evil ancestral dedication speaking against my destiny by your power.
2. Every evil environmental dedication, speaking against my life, die! in the name of Jesus.
3. Every evil spiritual parent, your time is up, therefore, die! in the name of Jesus.
4. My Father, I need help; help me by Fire! in the name of Jesus.
5. Serpents of darkness assigned against me, run mad! in the name of Jesus.
6. Breakthrough keys, stolen by the enemy, I take you back, in the name of Jesus.
7. Stronghold of witchcraft in my family line, die! in the name of Jesus.
8. Any of my possessions that has been bewitched, I set you on fire, in the name of Jesus.
9. Every tongue, raining incantation against me, dry up! in the name of Jesus.
10. Every satanic hunter, hunting for my life, shoot yourself! in the name of Jesus.
11. Any organ in my body, dedicated to infirmities, receive deliverance now! in the name of Jesus.
12. Every dedication speaking against my finances, be silenced! in

the name of Jesus.
13. Every dedication speaking against my marriage, be silenced! in the name of Jesus.
14. Every dedication speaking against my family, be silenced! in the name of Jesus.
15. Every dedication speaking against my career, be silenced! in the name of Jesus.
16. Every dedication speaking against my ministry and my calling, be silenced! in the name of Jesus.
17. Every dedication speaking against my prosperity, be silenced! in the name of Jesus.
18. Every dedication speaking against my life be silenced! in the name of Jesus.
19. Earthquake of deliverance, go into the root of my life, and repair every damage there in the name of Jesus.
20. Every bitter water, flowing into my life, be sweetened by the salt of heaven, in Jesus name.
21. Father Lord, my life is in Your hands uphold me in Jesus' name

The Negative Anointing

Leviticus 10:2; *"And there went out fire from the Lord, and devoured them, and they died before the Lord."*

The title of this message is what makes the difference between one person and the other, during ministrations. That is why it can be said that one person received the touch of God and the other did not. Quite a lot of people are going about with excess luggages without being conscious of it. This is so because, the enemy of their souls knows that, if they know about the presence of the evil load, they will fight until it goes. When the enemy discovers that you are an aggressive fighter, what he does is to operate in secret. All such secrets shall fail today in the name of Jesus.

Types Of Anointing:
1. **Positive:** Divine power; it is creative, does good, is benevolent but by no means does it spare the wicked.
2. **Negative:** Power from the devil; it is dark, wicked and evil. God did not create the devil, He created Lucifer who turned himself to the devil.
3. **Human:** The power of Man; it is natural and can be directed either by the positive or the negative.

Anywhere you go, whichever man you consult, his power can only come from any of these sources. If you have ever consulted any negative power, it would have released a mark there which can only be rubbed off by the blood of Jesus, no matter how long ago. Many people have been misled by false teachings about anointing. To some, it means blowing breeze into a microphone and people will start to fall. We never read anything like that in the Bible. Some people think anointing is speaking imported tongues. Some think it is the ability to heal the sick and cast out demons only.

Anointing is supernatural equipment that will enable an ordinary human being to achieve supernatural results in whatever he does. It is a divine, supernatural electric force. It is the power of God on a person, which brings sweatless results and the divine power to produce outstanding wealth. There could be two Christians who have had the same exposure; same experience, same resource, faith, talent, facility, but, their results could be very far apart. They could have attended the same Bible College and passed out with the same grades on the same day, but their exploits for the Lord would be miles apart. It is the anointing that makes the difference.

Anointing is the expression of the Holy Spirit in the life and personality of a person. It is the divine ability to do a particular thing. God can touch your hands, your ability, your skill, strength, memory, talent, etc. It is the way to sweatless achievement. It is when you receive the baptism of the Holy Spirit and His rain falls upon you and increases the "Living Water" in your life. Then, curses and bondages will break and sicknesses can no longer stay in your life.

There were two men at a conference. The first one came in the morning and sang Psalm 23 and the congregation sang with him, with a standing ovation. In the evening, an old missionary came and sang the same song but the audience was moved to tears and they wept sore. When asked what happened, the missionary said he sang the song according to his knowledge of the writer; the Holy Spirit. That inspiration came from the fact that, he knew the writer personally. In the Bible, you will find out that God specially anointed some people to do some specific spectacular things and He still does it till today.

The crux of this message is that; for everything, the devil has a counterfeit. In fact, he has counterfeit human beings too; they are demons putting on the forms of human beings and would look extremely beautiful, just to lure people into sin. Everything that God created is good but the devil has succeeded in corrupting many things. That is why many people are entering into fresh bondage everyday.

Leviticus 10:1-2;
"And Nadab and Abihu, the sons of Aaron, took either of them his censer and put fire therein, and put in cense thereon, and offered strange fire before the Lord, which he commanded them not. And there went out fire from the Lord, and devoured them, and they died before the Lord."

In the text above, we read about two sons of a chief priest, who offered a sacrifice that the Lord had not demanded from them. He utterly destroyed them. God did not mind whether their father was a priest or not, He promptly executed them.

Beloved, the time has come when even those who claim to be filled with the Holy Spirit, need to be checked up. Many have started to light strange fires before the Lord, therefore; it is time to do serious examination of your standing with the Lord. The Bible says we should check all spirits, for the devil performs miracles too. For example; when Moses put down his rod in the palace of Pharaoh and it became a snake. The magicians too put down their rods and they became snakes, but, the snake of Moses ate up all their snakes and did not get fatter for it. Moses turned water into blood and they too did it.

They matched up with most of what Moses did step by step until they saw that they could not go further and they admitted that: *"This is the Finger of God."* All these things reveal the degree of the power of Satan and the fact that: he can imitate God. Therefore, we must be alert to deception.

Acts 7:48-49;
"Howbeit the most High dwelleth not in temples made with hands; as saith the prophet: "Heaven is my throne, and earth is my footstool: what house will ye build me? Saith the Lord: or what is the place of my rest?"
This is one of the most amazing statements in the Bible. This means that no matter how beautiful the building of a temple is, God does not live there because it was constructed with the hands of Man. Believers are regarded as the temple of God. Even Jesus Christ called His own body the temple. God lives inside Man and that temple is the heart of Man.

1 Corinthians 3:16 says;
Know ye not that ye are the temple of God, and that the Spirit of God dwelleth in you?"

1 Corinthians 6:19;
"What? Know ye not that your body is the temple of the Holy Ghost which is in you, which ye have of God, and ye are not your own?"

You and I are the temple of God. What goes on in the temple is worship. It is however unfortunate that, the devil has turned the temple of many people's lives into what is written in Revelation 2:18-20;

"And unto the angel of the church in Thyatira write; These things saith the Son of God, who hath his eyes like unto a flame of fire, and his feet are like fine brass; I know thy works, and charity, and service, and faith, and thy patience, and thy works; and the last to be more than the first. Notwithstanding, I have a few things against thee, because thou sufferest that woman Jezebel, which calleth herself a prophetess, to teach and to seduce my servants to commit fornication, and to eat things sacrificed unto idols.

Although such people could bear Christian names; they could be dedicated and baptised on the 8th day and confirmed in the church, this does not prevent the devil from making them his habitation. It is a pity that dark spirits are actually dwelling in the lives of believers, either with their knowledge or without. This is why it is very sad to see the angel of God by-passing some people in the Church and not bless them. They have ceased from being God's people because, there are bad spirits living in the temple of their lives. That is why a demon that was chased out of a person, could say that it would return to his house. Luke 11:24;
"When the unclean spirit is gone out of a man, he walketh through dry places, seeking rest; and finding none, he

saith, I will return unto my house whence I came out."

The verse we read earlier states that God's hands made all the things with which Man could construct anything, so, He cannot dwell in them. Building an altar in your house or a fantastic building with tinted or painted glass, is not the issue. The real thing is your life; that is, your body being the temple of God. Jesus said they should destroy the temple and He would rebuild it in three days. Those around thought He was referring to the temple in Jerusalem; they did not know that it was the temple of His body.

When your body becomes the Temple of God, His glory will fill it and then, you will not need to paint that body with any cosmetic before it looks beautiful. You will not need any special soap to bleach that body before it looks beautiful; this is because the glory of God is there. It is when that glory has departed, that people look for artificial panel-beating and painting. When the glory of God fills your life, no dirt can remain there. When your life is unclean, you could jump here and there and do all sort of things, the Glory of God will not be there. That is why Jesus had to chase out with a whip, all the buyers and sellers in the temple of God. He told them that God says His temple shall be a house of prayer, but they had turned it into a den of robbers. Today, the Lord Jesus shall take that same whip, and whip out all the buyers and sellers in the temple of your life, in the name of Jesus.

There were three sets of agents in the temple at Jerusalem:
1. **Jesus,**
2. **The buyers and sellers,**
3. **The temple.**

So also today, there are three agents in the Temple of Man's life;
1. The Lord Jesus,
2. The Living Word of God,
3. The temple (you).

The traders are the things that are in your temple that should not be there. Many people do not understand this phenomenon. Many men of God fall into sin and still perform miracles. Many prophesy and the next minute they start abusing people. Many pray and people get healed but they in turn become sick. Some people pray that the power of God should come upon their lives, but nothing happens. Some, in order to save their faces, feign the anointing by shaking their body. All these things happen because, there are trailers in the temple of their lives. That is why some people tell lies and exaggerate and boast in their ability and power. That is why unclean and evil thoughts take over the hearts of some people whenever they kneel down to pray. Their minds wander instead of praying. Some pray, but fear grips their hearts as soon as they finish. Some pray fervently but still require the laying on of hands from their pastors.

One of the most terrible thing that can happen to a person, is for two opposing spirits to dwell in the life of that person. Once a negative anointing descends upon a person, he or she gets under the influence of that thing. It is a fearful thing but true. There is something known as the anointing of anger; when it falls upon a person, he or she throws tantrums and the body begins to shake. Some begin to stammer and shout. They refuse to be pacified, despite all apologies. Unfortunately, the next minute, such people could start to prophesy. You would wonder why this is so; it is because the Holy Spirit has been boxed to a corner and the negative spirit is having a field day. It is a fearful thing but true. That is why the Bible says; on that day, the Lord Jesus will tell some people to depart from Him, because "they are workers of iniquity. It is because; though they prophesied in His name, healed the sick in His name, they did it with another negative spirit present in their lives which they should have chased out, but did not. If you have the anointing of anger, it shall be chased out today in the name of Jesus.

Some people have the anointing of sexual perversion; it makes them senseless. That is why a man could have sexual intercourse with his wife's house-help or even her sister. The man could be a Professor or General Manager, but would not think twice before he starts having sexual intercourse in his office, with his student or secretary. If this message is making you to feel uncomfortable, it means you need deliverance from the negative anointing. This is the blunt truth beloved. This negative anointing makes some born-again children of God, fall headlong in love with a hemp-smoker or a bully with the aim of 'converting' him or her. Some women commit abortion for the house-helps that their husbands put in the family way. They forget that it is murder; they want to protect the name of their family, whereas, they could have dealt with that negative anointing earlier on.

Many people do not see clearly until they have fallen into sin. Some people have the anointing of bad language and evil communication; they do not want to listen to counsel or advice. They want to talk to express themselves the way they feel. Many people refuse to heed the warnings of the Holy Spirit and He, being a gentleman, eventually keeps quiet and goes into a corner. Sometimes, He leaves totally. There is the anointing of depression. Some people could rejoice, praise God and the next minute, they are so sad and down-trodden, they wear the cap of worry and no message or music can lift up their spirits at that point in time. It is the presence of this negative anointing. There is the anointing of bad inspiration. Some people are taken over by this spirit and it makes them think and plan evil. The heart loses control and it does evil things.

One day, I went to the dining hall in the university and two men sat at table with me. They were speaking English language and suddenly, one of them said they should speak Yoruba, so that this one (that is me) would not understand them. Later, one of them said that Igbos sometimes understand Yoruba, so they should speak their native dialect which is a language spoken in Akure. Although I am not a native of the place, I lived in Akure for nine years as a growing youth so, I can speak the language fluently. The amazing thing is the fact that, those men were married but they were planning how each of them would approach the wife of the other and lure her into sexual intercourse. How could two friends decide to tempt their wives this way? It is the anointing of bad inspiration.

There is also the anointing of sickness. It makes people fall sick at any slight effort. God made everything perfect at the beginning, so, anything that makes a person fall sick, is a negative anointing. There is also the anointing of gluttony and drunkenness. The person cannot rest until he or she is overfed or drunk. There is the anointing of addiction, which make people chew kolanut, smoke cigarettes, drink or sniff coffee or take drugs. They could even get up in the middle of the night to take these things.

What I am trying to portray, is the fact that, a believer could have the Holy Spirit and still have demons affecting his body. That affliction is the trader in the temple. If a person who was possessed by evil spirits, surrenders his or her life to the Lord Jesus Christ, the evil spirits would leave. However, if the person falls into sin or backslides, the evil spirits will come back and will even blow the whistle to invite more wicked spirits to come with them and repossess the person. That is why you should not take the issue of strange dreams for granted. Dreams like seeing dead relatives, eating, swimming, having sexual intercourse or getting married, picking snails, suffering from strange diseases etc, are all indications that there are strangers in the temple and they cause backsliding.

Many people would have remained firm in the Lord, if there were no strangers in the temple of their lives. Although some go to Bible College, if those traders are not chased out, they will remain there and cause a hindrance to the person's calling and ministry. That is why it is possible for a Reverend or Pastor that had been burning for the Lord, to backslide. Backsliding in the Bible is not just the abandonment of one's faith. It could mean the following:
1. **Standing away from God,**
2. **Leaving one's first love for God,**
3. **Departing from the simplicity of Christianity,**
4. **Spiritual stagnancy,**
5. **Weakness in prayer and Bible study,**
6. **Hypocrisy.**

It is very sad but true beloved,

that there are many people with two spirits using them. It is therefore time for self-examination and violent prayers. You must understand these things. If you see some people who claim to be born-again behaving strangely or in an unruly manner, do not be shocked; it is because there are two spirits living inside them. The Holy Spirit has been boxed to a corner and there are other spirits trading there and are doing well in their business. An example in the Bible was King Saul.

1 Samuel 10:6;
"And the Spirit of the Lord will come upon thee, and thou shall prophesy with them, and shalt be turned into another man."

1 Samuel 10:10;
"And when they came thither to the hill, behold, a company of prophets met him; and the Spirit of God came upon him, and he prophesied among them."

Saul was not only a King; he was also a prophet. Unfortunately, Saul was a man of unstable character. He was self-willed, envious, had violent temper, impatience. Those things finished him up. The Spirit of God departed from him and an evil spirit took over.

1 Samuel 16:14;
"But the Spirit of the Lord departed from Saul, and an evil spirit from the Lord troubled him."

1 Samuel 16:23;
And it came to pass, when the evil spirit from God was upon Saul, that David took an harp, and played with his hand: so Saul was refreshed, and was well, and the evil spirit departed from him."

Whenever the evil spirit came upon Saul, David was called upon to play music and the evil spirit departed, but it was a temporary relief. He still had problems.

1 Samuel 19:9;
"And the evil spirit from the Lord was upon Saul, as he sat in his house with his javelin in his hand: and David played with his hand."

1 Samuel 19:23-24;
"And he went thither to Naioth in Ramah: and the Spirit of God was upon him also, and he went on, and prophesied, until he came to Naioth in Ramah. And he stripped off his clothes also, and prophesied before Samuel in like manner, and lay down naked all that day and all that night. Wherefore they say: "Is Saul also among the prophets?"

The Spirit of God was in the life of Saul and it made him to prophesy, but, there was an evil spirit in him too, which made him envious and he wanted to kill David. This is an example to us, to show that we have to be very careful. Spiritual inconsistency will open the door to evil spirits. That evil spirit in him, made him tear his clothes and he remained naked.

Questions:
- Is it well with the temple of your life?
- When you became born-again, did you receive the Holy Spirit?
- Is your life on fire for God or are you still your cold self?
- Are there strangers in your temple?
- Do you manifest during hot prayers?
- Are you the kind of Christian that prophesies and disobeys the prophesy?
- Do you beat your wife at home or insult your husband and then come to the church to lead choruses or pray or prophesy?
- Do you feign prophesies through information that people gave you?
- Are you one of those who are employed to give fake prophesies?
- Is anything blocking your spiritual ears and eyes?
- Do you hear sounds that indicate that God wants to speak, but you cannot hear?
- Do you hear strange, ungodly voices asking you to do strange things like jumping into a river or crossing a highway?
- Do you have difficulty in reading the Bible?
- Are you the kind of person that cannot sit and read the Bible for up to one hour? There are traders in you that do not want you to read it.
- Do you experience greater problems now that you are trying to become serious with God, than when you

were in the world? It is because there are traders in your life and they know that if you continue in the Lord, they will have no place to stay in you.
- Do you have black-outs when you do not know what is going on?
- Do you experience continuous nightmares?
- Do you lose control and regret your actions and then, break down and cry only to fall back into the same mistake?
- Are you an employee, who does not mind the boss running his hand through your body? All these strange things are traders.

A lady was going home from work one day and was accosted by two women, who told her that they were expecting her at their meeting. She did not know them, so she told them that she was not coming to any meeting that she did not know about. As from that day, her life turned upside down. The traders in her life opened the door to external, wicked powers and they called for reinforcement against her from outside. She was not conscious of the fact that she belonged to any witchcraft coven. It is the traders inside a person that will call in demons, spirit-husband or wife to come and reinforce the battle against that person. I pray that such reinforcements shall fail today in the name of Jesus. Do you find if difficult to receive the power of the Holy Spirit? Do you sometimes think of committing suicide? You need to know today that, there are some forces working against your life. How clean is the temple of your life? Think about it beloved.

If there was no dramatic change in your life, when you became born-again and got sanctified, it means there are traders in the temple of your life. Why is it that after giving your life to Christ and you left your boyfriend, your mind is still there? Why is it that you a child of God, is getting discouraged at any slight trouble? All these are due to the presence of strangers that are trading in the temple of your life. Many people have had these strangers planted into their lives right from birth. Such people are like the goat that was bought in the month of January and is being fed, to keep it alive till December when it will be slaughtered for the celebration of Christmas. It would be happy to be fed, but what interests the owner is that it stays alive, healthy and fat in order to be delicious in December.

Many lives have been converted to a boxing ring, where good things have been boxed to a corner and the enemy is just landing blows on them. The enemy does not joke when he has the opportunity to lay hold on a person, he destroys absolutely. John 10:10 "says; *"The thief cometh not, but for to steal, and to kill, and to destroy: I am come that they might have life, and that they might have it more abundantly."*

Revelation 3:2;

Be watchful, and strengthen the things which remain, that are ready to die: for I have not found thy works perfect before God,"

Perhaps this is your own trouble; good things have been boxed to a corner. The enemy has given you a technical knock out. It is time for the wind of Prophet Ezekiel to blow on the good things that are dead or dying in your life, and command them to come alive.

What I am trying to expose does not exempt anybody. I am suggesting some prayers, which I would like you to pray aggressively and be expectant. Pray them with violence and without fear. If you have decided to claim the blessings that God has for you and are determined not to allow any beggarly power to prevent you from achieving your full potentials, then, take these prayer points with all the seriousness that you can gather. However, you cannot claim the redemptive power in the name of Jesus unless you confess your sins to Him and ask Him to forgive you all your sins. Name them one by one, repent of them and promise Him that you will never go back to the world of sin and Satan. I congratulate you, for this is the best decision you can ever take and I pray that it shall be permanent in Jesus' name.

1. I reject the strategy of defeat from the enemy, in the name of Jesus
2. I renounce membership to any evil society having my name, in the

name of Jesus.

(Do not say that you are not concerned by this particular prayer point. You could belong to an evil society, without knowing it. Your mother, sister, friend or anyone, could have donated you in the spirit realm).

3. Every evil competitor for my spirit. I command you to fall! in the name of Jesus.
4. Father Lord, quench every fire of negative anointing in my life, in the name of Jesus.
5. Blood of Jesus, flush out every stranger in my body, in the name of Jesus.
6. Let every evil trend in my family, be powerless against me, in the name of Jesus.
7. You the spirit of lukewarmness, release me and die! in the name of Jesus.

If your name or surname has to do with the worship or glorification of an idol or evil spirit or witchcraft, take the following prayer point violently. Place your right hand on the centre of your head. If you know the name of the idol, place it in the blank space in the next prayer. Address it violently and then, tell the Lord to give you a new name that will glorify His name.

8. You spirit of .... release me in the name of Jesus.
9. I cancel every effect of contaminated temple, in the name of Jesus.
10. I remove my name from the book of demonic victims, in the name of Jesus.
11. Fire of revival, anoint me afresh in the name of Jesus.
12. Let the Lion of Judah chase out, every demonic animal operating against me, in the name of Jesus.

The Evil Conversion (1)

Ecclesiastes 10:7 says; *"I have seen servants upon horses, and princes walking as servants upon the earth."*

What an evil conversion! This means that a person could be re-manufactured to become what he or she is not supposed to be. In this text, the servant has taken the position of the prince and the prince has been converted to a servant and is walking barefooted. It is a terrible conversion. This means that many people are not what God made them to be. It means that someone, somewhere or something, has done some panel-beating, re-spraying, restructuring, re-manufacturing. That is what I term as 'Evil Conversion'.

THE STAND OF THE SCRIPTURE:
Psalm 105:13-15 says; *"When they went from one nation to another, from one kingdom to another people; He suffered no man to do them wrong: yea, he reproved kings for their sakes; Saying, Touch not mine anointed, and do my prophets no harm."*

What is happening in the life of a person could be the opposite of this verse, but that is the stand of the Bible. The practical reality of this verse could be absent from the life of a person, but, it is the stand of the Scripture; "Touch not my anointed and do my prophet no harm."

Some years ago, a young girl was travelling in a bus going to the interior part of the country." As she started to preach the Gospel of our Lord Jesus Christ, an. elderly man rebuked her and asked her to keep quiet. She said she would not keep quiet in the name of Jesus. The man brought out a fetish powder and blew it towards the girl. Instead of the powder getting to her, it became cloudy and the man saw flames of fire surrounding the girl. The powder then came back to the man. As soon as it touched him, he became uncomfortable and could not sit properly again. The man then asked which cult she belonged to and she said she was a Christian and that she attends M.F.M. She asked if she could help him in any way and he said no.

She continued preaching until they got to their destination. When the man got off the vehicle, he was still uncomfortable and so, he felt he should look for the church the girl belongs to. He was able to locate the M.F.M. branch in that town and he narrated his ordeal to the pastor and asked him to pray for him. The sister did not know that the man was almost a principality. She did not even know that, he had evil intentions against her. She did not know that he went to the M.F.M. branch in that town to seek help. The stand of the Scripture is straight forward: *"Touch not my anointed and do my prophets no harm."*

A strange woman tried to snatch the husband of a sister. The sister prayed fire prayers, and the strange woman was dealt with by God Himself, God should be feared because He is ready to do anything to anyone that touches His children. The amazing power of the believer is not clear to many people. The Bible says; we should not curse but bless, there fore, you should, mind what you say with your mouth.

A man used to use abusive language on his children and his wife would always caution him that, words are powerful, that he should be careful what he says to his children. He said the words could not have any negative effect on them. The man however decided to experiment with two plants. Being an agriculturist, he felt whatever worked on human beings, could work on plants. He then prepared two plants and every morning, he would water them and then, would curse one of the plants saying; it would not grow, it would not be fruitful, it would die etc. He would turn to the other one and bless it abundantly and pronounce good, positive words on it. After a while, he noticed that the plant that he was cursing, was not growing normally. It was stunted and the leaves were pale while the other one flourished and grew beautifully. It was then he agreed that as an anointed child of God, whatever he says to his children, would come to pass. That was how he stopped using abusive language.

The Bible says: "Touch not...!" This is to prevent evil transfer. Some touches are actually meant to transfer evil into the lives of people. "Touch Not...!" means to prevent spiritual contamination, evil current, harm, destruction and death. Many years ago there was an epidemic of the disappearance of sexual organs. Someone would touch another and it would disappear. A man suddenly found out, that his male organ had disappeared.

He wept sore. He was brought to our service and he wept before the Lord, promising not to sin again. The Lord restored his organ and he jumped and jubilated. We reminded him that sin would open doors to "evil touches. It is evil touches on believers that results in evil conversion.

One night, a lady dreamt that she was playing with someone she did not know, who was friendly. Suddenly, the play turned into aggression and the person jumped on her, grabbed one of her breasts and pulled her with it. It was painful and when she woke up, she felt the pain physically on her breast. That marked the beginning of breast cancer. We thank God that she was delivered after serious prayers. *"Touch not my anointed and do my prophet no harm."* It is possible to harm a person without touching him or her. That could be done through curses, spells, arrows of infirmity, evil-remote-controlled missiles, satanic breeze and bullets from spiritual guns, etc. Sometimes, they do not touch a person directly but they touch the things they own or love.

A couple had a mango tree in front of their house and it was yielding fruit every season. One day, a woman came to cut the bark of the tree. They did not object to it because the bark is medicinal and the cutting should not affect the tree in any way. They saw that her lips were moving, but could not imagine that she could be chanting incantations. After a year, they noticed that the tree was not flourishing anymore. It did not yield fruit as usual. It was then they remembered the woman and they started to pray. They anointed the tree with oil and commanded it to refuse every form of bewitchment. Shortly afterwards, there was a change; the tree became normal and it started to yield fruit again. That is the authority of the believer; the amazing power that God has given to His children. Jesus told some people that, it is written that; we are gods. It means we are small Jesus.

Take this prayer point.
* **Every evil touch affecting my life, die! in the name of Jesus.**

Tools Of Evil Conversion:
1. **Ignorance** Hosea 4:6;

"My people are destroyed for lack of knowledge: because thou hast rejected knowledge, I will also reject thee, that thou shalt be no priest to me: seeing thou hast forgotten the law of thy God, I will also forget thy children."

A sister found out that she had a monumental ignorance, when she started praying fire prayers. She had an ailment that made her unable to sleep on one side of her body. After serious deliverance prayers she was relieved. Although she had been born-again for 15years, she was ignorant of spiritual warfare and wondered why her 'monumental' (as she called it) ignorance had not killed her before then. The Bible describes ignorance as a destroyer. It is a sad thing for a prince to become a servant. It is a sad thing when a person who is supposed to be free, becomes a prisoner and it is equally a sad thing when pearls are cast before swine.

A man got fed up with life and thought his last chance was to consult a herbalist, although he was a Christian. When he gave his palm to the herbalist, the herbalist asked why he came to him, that people like him should not come to see herbalists for solution to problems. The herbalist said he had 'that thing'. The man asked what he meant and the herbalist drove him out, with the friend that brought him. The man, being a Christian, had the Spirit of God in him but he went to cast his pearls before swine. It is sad. The prince had become a servant.

Another Christian went to consult a herbalist whose demon told him that he was 'meat' for the herbalist, so he exploited him and told him that his mother-in-law was responsible for his problems. Whereas, that mother-in-law was the one interceding on his behalf before God. He went to a white-garment herbalist who said he had familiar spirits, which had to be whipped out of his body. He suffered body pains through whipping but the problem did not go. He went to someone pressing sand, who asked him to bring all the white dresses that he had. He took them to him, yet the problem did not get solved. Through these three consultations, this child of God became a servant, although he was a prince.

These things that you are reading are supposed to make feel sorry for humanity. The original picture of Man is described in Genesis 1:31^A; *"And God saw everything that He had made, and, behold, it was very good."* The devil has raped humanity and defiled the original picture of Man. Is that picture in this verse still true of you as a child of God? The devil has polluted that picture; he has converted princes into servants by planting poisonous seeds into their lives, transferring evil into their spirits and then manipulating and controlling them from afar. These evil remote-controlling powers are present in the lives of people today.

A woman said her father gave her out in marriage at the age of 16. She had to run away because the man was beating her everyday. She even lost an eye in the process. At 24 years old, she married another man and he too beats her everyday and she lost the front row of her upper teeth in the process. She ran away from him. At the age of 31, she got born, again and later got married to a born-again man. He, too beats her even whilst pregnant. When she came for counselling, it then dawned on her that, she was the one that had an evil deposit in her life that she had to shed. She could have gone through life-like that; thinking that men are to be feared; and remarrying, until one would eventually kill her. Thank God that she got delivered

The enemy plant evil into the lives of people, just to mare their image, remanufacture and convert them into something else. This is why the behaviour of some people look very abnormal, their level of education not withstanding. That is why we have some educated illiterates.

A couple had a quarrel one evening. The woman was heavily pregnant and she said her husband would not go out that day because he kept late nights. Both of them had doctorate degrees. The man got into, his car while the woman was trying to deflate the tyres. He got down, pushed her away but she sat on the bonnet of the car. One would have thought the man would have considered her state and settle the quarrel, but he drove off with her sitting on the bonnet. After a few yards, she fell off the car and he stopped, put her inside the car and took her to the hospital. She was bleeding all over. He left her in the hospital and still went where he has meant to go.

What I am trying to narrate, is the fact that, ignorance of spiritual warfare has nothing to do with university education or qualification. When the enemy is busy drinking the blood of people, they give it a scientific name, instead of dealing with it with their spiritual weapons of warfare that are not supposed to be carnal, but mighty through God. They will have one grammar to qualify everything, e.g. 'Environmental Mal-adjustment'. Acquisition of degrees does not disturb the devil from planting what he wants to plant in the life of a person.

Matthew 13:25 says;
"But while men slept, his enemy came and sowed tares among the wheat, and went his way."

This explains why a thirty year-old man would do what is not expected of a ten-year-old boy. That is why a rich man's child would go to the market and steal things, and the grammarians would call it kleptomania.

A man wanted to travel out of the country at all cost. So, he consulted a herbalist, who gave him some concoctions to swallow, so that he would become invincible and would go through airport officers unseen. He was shocked when he went past an immigration officer, who called him back. His first reaction was to ask if the officer saw him. The officer got angry that he was insinuating that he was blind. This is someone whose passport had no visa. He was thoroughly beaten and sent back home. For this man to have done a dumb thing like that, the enemy had to first plant something into his life a demon of the grave. This is why we beg people to stop waging war against themselves through sin, alcohol consumption, sexual immorality, etc. Some say they want to drink and enjoy themselves here on earth because do not know what heaven would be like. There will be no, drinking in heaven anyway.

The lives of many people is being controlled from afar. That is why sometimes, when you commit an offence against a parent or grandparent, they will know even from afar because they have remote controlling powers. Some people wanted to deal with a man of God and they could not. Therefore, they went to his hometown and made enquiry on where his placenta was buried. They located the principality that held the key to the placenta of every child born in that village. He was an eleven year-old boy physically, but had lived for generations; he was a principality. They got the placenta of this man of God, summoned his spirit, it appeared and hissed in disdain and left the place. They could not do him any harm. Why?

He had the mark of the Lord Jesus upon him the mark of "Touch Not...!" When the anointing of the Holy Spirit is moving, He moves in diverse ways: -

1. **Through the spoken word of God** "Let there be light and there was light."
2. **Through Prayer**.
3. **Through the laying on of hands**.
4. **Through anointing with oil**.
5. **Through inanimate objects** - Handkerchiefs and clothings.

Likewise, the devil has many channels through which he transfer evil deposits and bad spirits into the lives of people. It could be through the manipulation and contamination of people. It could be through the manipulation of people's clothing, food by demonic agents, sinful sexual relationships, kissing or shaking of hands with demonic agents. (Do you know that the shaking of hands originated from covenant formation and sealing?) Traditional marriage prayer by demonic relatives, wedding rites like pouring of water on the feet of the bride, allowing just anybody to plait or dress your hair or cut your finger nails, etc. All these things open doors to evil transfers and conversions.

More than ever before, our eyes have to be opened as believers because the forces that are preventing the breakthroughs of many people are inside their lives, not outside. They are the powers that hinder people from attending important prayer meetings, or services, where they are meant to be blessed. If they do not keep the person from going, they will work up an action during or after that meeting, that will get the person discouraged and would then decide not to attend such meetings again. It is because they know that their defeat is round the corner and if the person prays strategically they will be expelled from the life of that person. Sometimes, if they guess that a person is going to a place where the Fire of God is active, they will jump out of the person hide somewhere to wait him or her and then, when the person comes out, they regain access and continue their evil assignments.

These are the teachings by which the image of a person, character and being, are marred, re-manufactured, and converted. Evil things are planted into the garden of the lives of people. Evil spirits can be transferred into the lives of people, through physical blood or family blood from parents to children. If you notice that your mother never stayed with one husband, and you are seeing signs of jilting and being jilted, in you, then there is something to be renounced and cut off; before it becomes evil conversion. If you know that your father is or was poorer than a 'church rat', and you have, found out that you are always broke and in want, it means there is something you have to break.

If your parents had no direction in life, they never achieved anything and, you are seeing the traits of these things in your life, you should know that you need to pray seriously today because the seed of the vagabond, is already in your life. Some people, even without spells or curses, have the problems already in their lives.

Beloved, this is an important topic, and I would like to pause here, to continue next week by the grace of God. Meanwhile, if you have not yet surrendered your life to the Lord Jesus Christ, it means you do not belong to the camp of the Living God. The Bible says the eyes of God cannot behold sin. It means you are alienated from God: However, you have the opportunity today of turning from your sins unto the Lord. I would advise that you do so now, right there where you are: The Lord is there with you, with His arms wide open, ready to accept you into His fold. All you need do is, acknowledge the fact that you are a sinner; repent of those sins and confess them to the Lord. Name them one by one and ask the Lord to forgive you and cleanse you from all unrighteousness.

Decide that as you are forsaking those sins, you will never go back to them again. Renounce the world and the devil and do not go back to them again.

I congratulate you on this important decision that you have taken; it is the most important decision in life. I pray that it shall be permanent in your life, in the name of Jesus. I pray that the Lord will uphold you with His hand of righteousness. He will keep you from falling in the name of Jesus. He will write your name in the Book of Life and I pray that nothing by any means rub it off in the name of Jesus.

Here are some prayers that I would like you to pray with all the aggression that you can gather. Pray them, with the determination that any part of your life that has been converted by the enemy, shall be reconverted to God's original plan in the name of Jesus.

PRAYER POINTS:
1. I command every blessing, confiscated by satanic agents, to be released, in the name of Jesus.
2. I command every blessing, confiscated by principalities, to be released, in the name of Jesus.
3. I command every blessing, confiscated by evil powers, to be released, in the name of Jesus.
4. I command every blessing, confiscated by rulers of darkness, to be released, in the name of Jesus.
5. I command every blessing, confiscated by ancestral witchcraft spirits, to be released, in the name of Jesus.
6. I command every blessing, confiscated by envious enemies, to be released, in the name of Jesus.
7. Let the destructive plan of the enemies, aimed against me, blow up in their faces! in the name of Jesus.
8. Let the cause of my ridicule, be converted to a source of miracle, in the name of Jesus.
9. Lord, let virtue flow from You into my life, in the name of Jesus.
10. Any power diverting the blessings of God away from me, your time is up, die now! in the name of Jesus.
11. Heavenly constellations, cooperate with my destiny today, in the name of Jesus.

The Evil Conversion (2)

Ecclesiastes 10:7 *"I have seen servants upon horses, and princes walking as servants upon the earth."*

In the last bulletin, we started this interesting but pathetic topic. We said it is possible for a Prince to be pulled down from his horse and he will then walk barefooted, whilst the servant will take over his horse. We emphasised the fact that the devil- the enemy of our soul, is in the business of converting people into nothingness. We mentioned the fact that God's stand in the Scripture is that, the enemy should not touch His anointed, nor do him or her any harm. We said it is possible however, for the enemy to touch God's anointed and do the person real harm. We then started to enumerate the things in the life of a Christian that could open the door to the enemy that would make him convert a person to a servant.

This week, we shall continue and I pray that the Lord will minister to you as you read on. I pray that every evil conversion of any aspect of your life, shall be reconverted to God's original plan for your life in the name of Jesus. Please read on and allow the Lord to minister to you.

A prince becomes a slave, when he can be managed, controlled and dominated by the forces of darkness, even beyond his or her control or knowledge. When a person is not aware of what the enemy is doing in his or her life, he or she has become a servant. It is a terrible thing for a person to be completely unaware of the activities of the enemy in his or her life. The period of sleep is the war front of demonic attack. Some people receive attacks in their dreams, but retaliate appropriately. Others do not remember their dreams when they wake up. Your dream is your spiritual monitor; it could show you your spiritual state or could reveal what the enemy is about to do or has done. Matthew 13:25 says; *"But while men slept, his enemy came and sowed tares among the wheat, and went his way."*

Many are unaware of the fact that something has been altered in their lives. Some are aware, but they do not know what to do about it. The magnetising pull of those powers are so strong that they do not know how to get out of it The Lord will set such people free today in the name of Jesus. The enemy plant evil things in the garden of people's lives to spoil the good things that God has planted there. Sometimes, when I see or hear things like this, I feel like crying. A person who did not offend anyone or did any evil, suffering just like that; it is because something has been planted into the person's life to destroy him or her.

The enemy plant things in people's lives, to weaken or destroy them and if care is not taken, he pushes people to a point where all spiritual fire is quenched and then, he gets them. This is why one should be vigilant concerning dreams. It is bad to see oneself eating in the dream as this weakens spiritual life. The person becomes so low, that all kinds of evil things begin to happen to him or her. If you take a look at your life and you find out that you have a constant fear of death, you hear noises in your heart, things move about in your body, you are experiencing unexplainable tiredness, you have the fear of being older than you really are, all these indicate that, the evil forces are there and must be cut off and thrown out.

If you have ever consulted a herbalist or fake prophet that gave you something to insert into your private part, you need to pray seriously to expel the evil load. When a man falls into the trap of water-women, he is finished. If the proper wife at home is not prayerful, she too will be in trouble. Woe betide the man, who has three or more women competing with charms, to get him. He will be a servant, when he is supposed to be a prince. That is why the Bible is strongly against polygamy. Many young men and women have turned themselves into the play ground of the enemy. I would like you to know today that, there is an enemy lurking somewhere, wanting to destroy the image of God in you. He wants to re-manufacture and convert the prince into a servant. Technically and spiritually speaking, many believers are below the level what God wants them to be and that is making the devil happy.

The stand of the Scripture is sure: **"Touch not my anointed!"** The stand of God is very sure; the Great Jehovah will never forsake His own. The Bible says in Isaiah 49:15-16; *"Can a woman forget her sucking child, that she should not have compassion on the son of her womb?* **(and the Bible answers,)** *yea, they may forget, yet will I not forget thee. Behold, I have graven thee upon the palms of my hands; thy walls are continually before me."*

God does not want His children tossed here and there. He has promised to look after them and fight for them. Many people go about with evil powers and some dare to follow people to the Church. Many of them die; many of them receive angelic slaps and deposits of sicknesses and diseases. Whosoever (witch or wizard) touches a child of God, will suffer.

A brother was living in a house with a herbalist without knowing it. He only noticed that visitors often came to see the man. The brother was the kind of young man that would leave home very early and come back late in the evening, pray for about two hours and go to sleep. As soon as he moved into that house and started to pray, the clientele of the herbalist reduced. The herbalist noticed that people rarely came for consultation any more, so, he consulted his oracle and he learnt that his enemy was in the same house with him. He felt humiliated and so in the night, he transformed into an invisible being and went into the room of the brother. He was surprised to see a sword of fire brandishing in the air and the brother fast asleep. The herbalist stood there, stupefied and watched the sword. He could not move an inch till dawn. The brother woke up and found him there and he confessed that he wanted to harm him for disturbing his commerce. That was how the herbalist came to realise that all power belong to Jesus.

Abimelech in the Bible, made the mistake of taking the wife of Abraham. Although Abimelech did not know that Sarah was Abraham's wife, still, God punished him and his household for it. If normal pile blocks the intestines of a human being, it is very uncomfortable; can you then imagine how a person would feel if afflicted by God with pile? The household of Abimelech suffered for the act of their head wanting to acquire another man's wife. This was a crime not directly committed by they themselves, but by the father of that house. It was not until God told him to ask Abraham to pray for him that everything returned to normalcy.

God is a jealous God. Deut. 4;24 attests to this; *"For the Lord thy God is a consuming fire, even a jealous God."* He says whosoever touches His child, touches the apple of His eye. Zech. 2:8; *"For thussaith the Lord of hosts; After the glory hath he sent me unto the nations which spoiled you: for he that toucheth you toucheth the apple of His eye."* Mark 16:17-18; *"And these signs shall follow them that believe; in my name shall they cast out devils; they shall speak with new tongues; they shall take up serpents; and if they drink any deadly thing, it shall not hurt them; they shall lay hands on the sick, and they shall recover,"*

The Bible says; *"If God be for us, who can be against us?"*

Today, you have to command that some things in your life should become too hot for the enemy to handle. If a person gives his or her life to the Lord Jesus and is filled with the Holy Spirit and is living a holy life, he or she becomes untouchable to the enemy. However these days, many children of God still experience oppression and are tormented by the enemy.

Why should a woman say 'YES' to a man, who has one or more wives at home? Why should she decide to get into the problem of polygamy, where one or more of the wives are likely to be witches? Her decision to get married to such a man is a provocation of battle. She is laying a foundation of envy for the children that will be born into such a union.

WHY ARE CHRISTIANS TOUCHED BY THE ENEMY?
WHY ARE PRINCES BEING CONVERTED TO SERVANTS?

Unbelievers are already preys in the mouth of the enemy but it is also possible that a child of God be converted into a servant. Why is a born-again child of God touched and harmed even though the Bible says; "Touch not my anointed"?

1. **Inconsistency**.
Inconsistency in the Christian race has given the enemy a lot of ground. Many Christians are consistently inconsistent, so God cannot rely on them and the enemy knows it; so he takes advantage of them. Many have swinging moods due to circumstances surrounding them or a failure in their expectations. If you are consistent, you will stand firm and will be solid. Despite all odds, you will read the Bible diligently and put it into practice. If you are consistent, you will not fall when others do. If your prayer life is consistent and you have a cordial relationship with the Lord, you should become untouchable. If you are consistent and faithful, God can rely on you.

When you are consistent, you will hate absenteeism before the Lord; you will be with Him day-in, day-out, in spite of everything that will get you side-tracked. It is a mark of maturity. Today, many Christians are getting sidetracked; they are getting carried away by the things of the world. The enemy is occupying their time and heart with ephemeral things, so, their focus is no longer on the things of God. The enemy is also using fake things to make people think that they are serving the Lord.

How do you hope to serve a consistent Jesus, when you are inconsistent? The Bible says; *"Jesus Christ, the same yesterday, today and forever".* He is consistent but many Christians are not. This makes the enemy wait for their time of inconsistency to touch and harm them. Inconsistency will not earn you any good mark with God. Rather, it exposes you to the attacks of the enemy. You have a wonderful opportunity today, to pray off anything that is making you inconsistent. If in the past, you have suffered from an evil touch or the enemy is harming you, ensure that you fight back today and regain the position that God puts you.

2. **The Satanic Door You Open To The Enemy.**
Many years ago, I went on a mission to Brazil. A colleague approached me there to ask if we could stay in the same room, so that, we could save some money. It sounded like a good idea and I accepted. So, we slept on the same bed in the same room. At night, I saw that the man was struggling in his sleep. It was as if something wanted to strangulate him. After a while, he slept off. I was all the while looking at the way he was struggling. At that time, I did not know anything about spiritual warfare. I was attending a church where we danced ourselves out during the service. There was no fire.

After the man slept off, I stayed awake for fear of being the next person to be attacked. I could not sleep for two days and I began to have headaches. I had to tell the man that I could no longer stay with him. I went to another room. At about the same hour that the man was attacked, I felt a presence in my new room and heard a voice which said: "Foolish Man, who asked you to share the same bed with our prey?" You are lucky that you ran away."

Beloved, I went to the reception and asked for another room on another floor entirely. What should I have done as a child of God? I should have asked which door I opened to an evil power that came to harass me in my room. The door was compromise. I agreed to share a bed with someone who had the property of the enemy in his life.

On another occasion, I went on a journey and someone asked me to give some biscuits to someone over there. For a strange reason, I counted the biscuits and found out that there were 13 biscuits. I thought it was not normal to offer 13 things to a person, so I decided to eat one and give the person 12. If I had thrown one away, it would have been good but I ate it. As soon as I finished eating it, I fell into a deep sleep and I started to feel some strange movements in my head. It was as if there was a revival going on there. I had no fire so, the only solution was the "Holy Water" from my dancing church. Of course, it had no effect. I opened a door and the enemy came in. Although as I was eating the biscuit, I perceived the odour of perfume in it, but I still ate it.

A satanic open door, is any demonically possessed object of decoration, materials or symbol of the enemy in your possession. They are materials that invite demons into a person's life.

Many years ago, a sister was praying and all of a sudden, she started to wring her finger and tried hard to pull out a ring.

Eventually she succeeded and the ring ran under my chair. I picked it and went to ask what the ring was all about. She said it was the only thing that she inherited from her late grandmother. The sister did not know that the ring had been in her family for 600years and it was passed on from generation to generation.

Anyone who wore it, never got married because it covenants them to a family spirit husband. That is why in MFM, we advise people not to use jewelry or strange ornaments and decorations. Our early Pentecostal father who started Pentecostalism in the early 1920s, banned the use of jewelry and all those ornaments, by their members. They knew the bondage into which those things could put a person.

Any shield of immunity that allows the enemy to scale through your attacks, is the enemy's confidence in a person's life. It is the confidence of a strongman. It is a means through which covenants are removed. It is a means through which dark powers re-establish their stay in the life of a person. It is a place of refuge, where dark powers take cover. It is that which assists Satanic powers to remain in a life, even after much prayers and deliverance. It is a point of contact that opens the door to satan.

You must find out the open door that admits the enemy into your life. You must find out what the enemy is using against you and where the affliction is coming from, what is strengthening their operations and the open doors in your life.

God's Re-Conversion.
If for any reason or the other, the enemy has succeeded in converting any aspect of your life, the Lord can reconvert you today to His original plan for your life.

1 Samuel 2:7-9 says;
"The Lord maketh poor, and maketh rich: he bringeth low, and lifteth up. He raiseth up the poor out of the dust, and lifteth up the beggar from the dunghill, to set them among princes, and to make them inherit the throne of glory: for the pillars of the earth are the Lord's and He hath set the world upon them. He will keep the feet of His saints, and the wicked shall be silent in darkness; for by strength shall no man prevail."

However, if you have never at one time in your life surrendered your life to the Lord Jesus Christ, you might remain a prey to the enemy. You have the opportunity of taking the decision to become born-again today. The Lord Jesus Christ came to the world to die for our sins, so that He can reconcile us to God the Father. I would advise that you take that decision now, right there where you are. All you need do is acknowledge the fact that you are a sinner and that you cannot approach God in your sinful state. Repent of your sins; confess them to the Lord, name them one by one and ask God to forgive you and cleanse you from all unrighteousness. Claim the redemptive power in the blood of Jesus that was shed on the Cross at Calvary, for the remission of your sins.

Invite the Lord Jesus into your life. Open the door of your heart to him and ask Him to come in and become your personal Lord and Saviour. Enthrone Him over your life and ask Him to take a total control of all that concerns you. Renounce the world of sin and the devil and make sure you do not go back to them anymore.

I congratulate you for having taken this decision. It is the most important decision in life; I pray that it shall be permanent in your life in the name of Jesus. I pray that the Lord will uphold you and keep you from falling in the name of Jesus. I pray that your name will be written in the Book of Life and you will not by any means, rub it off in Jesus name. Go and sin no more!

I want you to gather enough anger that will unseat the servant that is sitting upon the horse of your life. When a prince begins to trek, it is a terrible conversion, a terrible re-manufacture. An evil conversion is the turning of a person, from the original divine quality to something else. Maybe what you have now, are crumbs of what God wants you to have. The Psalmist says; *"The day I cried...the Lord answered me"* Take these prayer points with holy anger and do not allow your heart to wander.

PRAYER POINTS:
1. I reject every evil control and manipulation, in the name of Jesus.
2. Lord! restore me to the original shape in which You created me, in the name of Jesus.
3. Lord! restore me to the original position that You created me to occupy, in the name of Jesus.
4. Any power, speaking abnormality into any area of my life, fall down and die! in the name of Jesus.
5. My life! become too hot for the enemy to handle, in the name of Jesus.
6. I unseat every servant, riding on the horse of my life, in the name of Jesus.
7. Anything opposing the perfect will of God in my life, fall down and die! in the name of Jesus.
8. I break every satanic link, between my life and my ancestors, in the name of Jesus.
9. Every power, making my heart sad, fall down and die! in the name of Jesus.
10. I uproot everything the Lord did not plant in my life, in the name of Jesus.
11. Open door of darkness in my life, clear away! in Jesus' name.
12. Every bird picking the word of God from my heart, die! in the name of Jesus.
13. Anything in my life, cooperating with my enemies, Holy Spirit expose them and destroy them in Jesus' name. (Shout this commandingly)
14. My Joseph! come out of Egypt by fire in the name of Jesus.
15. My Daniel will not die in the lion's den, in the name of Jesus.
16. My Moses will not die in Egypt, in the name of Jesus.
17. You the spirit of Esau, causing me to sell my birthright, jump out and die! in the name of Jesus.
18. Every character disorder, causing me to be inconsistent in my walk with the Lord, be expunged by fire.
19. I receive deliverance, from every ungodly character, in the name of Jesus.
20. You the spirit of the crab, jump out of my destiny! In the name of Jesus.
21. Father Lord, let me walk with You as Enoch did, in the name of Jesus.
22. Father Lord, let me walk with You as Abraham did in the name of Jesus.
23. Lord, let my hand touch the hem of Your garment today in the Name of Jesus.
24. Fresh Fire from above like the day of Pentecost, fall upon my life in the name of Jesus.
25. Divine restructuring, my life is available for you today, start now in the name of Jesus.
26. Every stronghold of sin and iniquity in my life, be pulled down by fire.
27. Every object of pollution in my possession, catch fire! in the name of Jesus.
28. Every effort of the devil to harvest and write the last chapter of my life, be frustrated in Jesus' name.
29. Every yoke of darkness in my life, be broken in Jesus name.

Fighting Using The Blood Of Jesus

If you keep pleading the Blood of Jesus, no matter how terrible an infirmity is, it will disappear by the power in the blood of Jesus.

Revelation 12:11-12;
"And they overcame him by the blood of the Liunb, and by the word of their testimony and they loved not their lives unto the death. Therefore rejoice, ye heavens, and ye that dwell in them. Woe to the inhabiters of the earth and of the sea! for the devil is come down unto you, having great wrath, because he knoweth that he hath but a short time."

I would like you to read this message with a rapt attention, so that you can key in to what God intends to do through this miracle power. It is a deep topic and this is just a scratch on it. The verse above is a very interesting part of the Bible. In it, we can see three weapons for overcoming the devil; the Blood of the Lamb, the word of our testimony, and loving not our lives unto death. It gives us weapons and it would be good if you could memorise it and appropriate it to yourself. There is a weapon that has never lost its power, but people have not learnt to use it; whereas, it is highly effective. Even the enemy is afraid, when you start to talk about it. That old serpent, that is the dragon that the Bible talks about saying; *"Woe unto the earth and the sea ..."* there is a weapon that can overcome it. There is nothing that God created that He cannot rearrange; there is no enemy that God cannot defeat.

The blood is the primary weapon for the final hour in this age.
This is the age when the devil has come down in great wrath, knowing that he has but a short time. Therefore, if it is raging so much, we must look carefully into the word of God to know the kind of weapon that will counter the rage.

They overcame him by the blood of the Lamb the Bible says. This is the number one weapon which is now the primary weapon for the final age.

A two-year old girl learnt this song and was always singing it: "There is power, there is power, there is power in the Blood of Jesus." Her mother noticed that she never took ill. One day, the mother washed the girl's clothes and hung them outside. There was a high wind which blew her small pant to the compound next to theirs and it landed in the sitting room of a neighbour, who happened to be an herbalist. Immediately the panty landed, there was pandemonium in the room; everything turned upside down. Everything he knew how to do failed; nothing could avail for him. He did his consultation and he found out that there was a strange thing in the room. He tried to pick it, but he fell.

He started to rain incantations, offered sacrifices, poured libations but he could not make a headway. He could not touch the panty and everywhere was hot. Throughout that day, no customer came for consultation and he battled throughout the night. The following day, the wind blew again and this time, the girl saw her toy flying towards the man's sitting room. She followed it and on getting there, she saw her panty.

She went straight towards it and picked it, singing her song, "There is power in the Blood of Jesus." The herbalist tried to stop her, thinking the 'strange' thing would harm her but she picked her panty casually from the centre of oil and blood poured around it. The girl picked it and left, still singing. That incidence, converted the herbalist. He surrendered his life to Christ having seen that His Power is the Absolute Power. He left his beggarly powers and came to the Lord.

What happened to that girl? She has soaked herself in the blood of Jesus by merely singing that song. The reason the blood does not work for many is because of sin. That was why the blood was shed on the cross for the remission of sin. It will then be an insult for anybody to remain in sin and still expect the same blood to avail for him or her.

There is a power that supercedes every other power. That power transforms simple things into powerful weapons. The awesomeness and mystery of the power in the blood of Jesus, is not being preached in the Church anymore. Many present day Christians do not know many things about victory in the battles of life. Learning to claim the power in the blood of Jesus is very important. It is a prayer that brings deliverance and protection.

WHAT DOES PLEADING THE BLOOD OF JESUS DO?

1. **It gives protection before adversity strikes.** It serves as prevention.

2. **Gives physical healing to the body.** No matter what name is given to any problem, it will be solved, when the blood of Jesus is brought in.

3. **Gives emotional healing.**

4. **Gives mental healing.**
5. **Helps in battling dark powers.**
6. **Helps in battling the adversary.**
7. **Gives financial healing.**
8. **Cleanses from all sins.** Jesus came to die for the sins of the world and His Blood was shed for us. You can claim the cleansing power in His Blood and God will open a new chapter in your life.

The price paid by the Son of God for our salvation was the shedding of His precious blood. God revealed this in the book of Leviticus that Jesus shed His blood. You may read the book of Leviticus chapter 16, there you will read about a ceremony called 'atonement.'. The atonement ceremony revealed to us that when Jesus comes, there is going to be a seven fold shedding of His blood. When you begin to read the story of the cruxifiction, how Jesus was killed and what happened thereafter, you will discover what I am talking about.

INSTANCES OF CHRIST'S BLOODSHED:

1. **At the garden of Gethsemane, as Jesus prayed in agony, He shed His blood.**
2. **When He was with the high priest, they struck Him across the face with a rod and blood gushed out.**
3. **The Bible told us that they plucked His beards off His lower jaw and blood came out.** The Bible said He did not hide His face from shame and did not keep Himself away from those that plucked off His beards.
4. **He was whipped by the Romans soldiers thirty and nine times and blood flowed freely.** The kind of whip they used in those days were such that have been lined with pieces of metals and bones. Once it is used on a person, it enters the skin and then it is pulled out again. While it is being pulled out, it tears the skin. So, you can almost see the thirty nine lashes because each lash would leave an indelliblemark.
5. **Now a crown of thorns was put upon His head that wounded him and drew blood** (the crown of thorns are made with thistles and some sharp objects). This crown was pressed against His head so that blood can be shed and this blood ran down His face.
6. **He was nailed hands and feet to the cross again, shedding His blood.** So, you can see now that the blood of Jesus is a serious issue.
7. **After He had died, a Roman soldier thrust a spear into His side, blood and water gushed out.**

This is the sevenfold shedding of the blood of Jesus. The book of Leviticus chapter 17 tells us that the blood is the life of man. This, made atonement for our soul. It is written that *"Without the shedding of blood there can be no remission of sin,"* the Bible says. Jesus poured out His blood as an offering for the whole of mankind. Now that the situation is like this and we have read that the devil has come down in great wrath because he knows he has a short time, we ought to be more serious.

That demon told Jesus; "Sir, what have you to do with us, You Jesus of Nazareth? Or have You come to torment us before our time?" It means that they know their time. "We know who You are. You are the Holy one, the only begotten Son of God." And Jesus looked at the man and ordered the demon to shut up and get out. Therefore, chapter 12 of the book of Revelation which we have already read, talked about our final conflict. It showed us that there can be a direct conflict between us and satan and how we can be successful. The Bible says, they love not their lives unto the death, meaning that they were totally committed.

TOTAL COMMITMENT!
In the book of first Timothy chapter 4:15 we were told to give all our service to Jesus. Do not serve God parttime, but be completely committed. Give the whole of your loyalty to what God wants you to become: your aim, joy, life, ways and every other thing that pertains to you.

There was a time a man challenged me when I was in England, I was told that the man had memorised the whole of the Quran. Whereas here are the children of the kingdom, who cannot read ten memory verses correctly from the Bible. There may even be some who sometimes attend church services without a Bible. The only Christians that frighten the devil are the ones who are totally committed. All part-time Christians are jokers in the battle field and the devil catches them very easily. He may call himself a pastor, but if he is a part-timer in his commitment, the enemy will catch him; if he is a part-timer in his services to the Lord, he will soon become a bush-meat for the enemy.

So, the only Christians that really frighten satan are those ones who are totally committed completely. The devil looks at their hands, legs, hairs and home, but find nothing to hold unto. Then when he realises that there is nothing in their lives and in everything they do, that they are totally committed to God, he gets very frightened. However, when he sees the half-hearted bread and butter Christians, he deals with them with ease.

One day, I watched an interesting film-show at Yaba bus stop. A sister packed her car by one side and there was a mad man who was quietly having his bath naked in a corner. Suddenly, as this sister got down from her car which had a Christian sticker, the mad man got startled and rushed towards her. The sister ran and she was hotly pursued by this man. Unfortunately, she was not a slim woman and the mad man almost caught up with her. Suddenly she screamed, "I plead the blood of Jesus, in the name of Jesus" and the mad man who was charging at this sister a few seconds ago suddenly became uninterested, as if he was not the one running after her.

The power in pleading the blood of Jesus is yet to be understood by Man. Some people criticise those pleading the blood of Jesus. It is because they have not passed through the valley, so they cannot know what it means. Someone who has never been tortured by a terminal disease cannot know what it means to be threatened by death, so he or she cannot understand why a cancer patient is praying fervently for healing, or why the person is jubilating after he or she has been miraculously healed. The preachers who discourage people from praying fire prayers, or pleading the blood of Jesus do so because, they have not experienced such things.

Several years back, I was in Paris, France. We closed for service one day and some people gathered around me at the door and said, "Please doctor, let us go somewhere and pray for a Nigerian sister." We left for this sister's house but as we approach the entrance, the woman that led us stopped abruptly and said," Well, I think at this stage, it will be nice if we join our hands together here and pray very well before we go in." We proceeded and entered into this beautiful home and there was a beautiful woman who looked like a ghost; the entire white of her eyes was red and had even disappeared.

The whole of the sitting room was empty and she lived on the fifteenth floor. I greeted the woman both in English and French languages, but she did not answer. Her husband was there crying. So I enquired about the matter and the husband began to explain. He said that every single item in their house had been thrown down from the fifteenth floor by this irrate wife.

Then I notice that a side of her face was swollen and on enquiry, the husband told me that he had to use blows on her when he could no longer control her outrage.

However in all these, I could see that certain spirits were there, directly transported from Nigeria to France.
I kept my mouth shut, but the woman who led us there was so excited that she opened her mouth and said, "You the spirit of 'Olumba- Olumba', get out in Jesus' name." Immediately, hell was let lose. This insane woman jumped up and almost tore her into pieces. At the end, we had to extricate her hands from the sister's neck who immediately ran out and left me there. Then, I started to pray. I said, "Whatever is harrassing this woman, depart now, in the name of Jesus." And she looked at me and forced a deceptive smile. Then I said, "Say after me, I drink the blood of Jesus." Immediately, the demon inside her answered, and said, "We do not drink the blood of Jesus, we sprinkle it." And I said," Alright, say, I sprinkle the blood of Jesus." She said, "No." Then I could see that the demon didn't like to hear about the blood, so I started talking about it until the woman calmed down and broke into tears.

What I have described to you took six hours. Victory comes by the continued application of the blood of Jesus. A person could have headache and plead the blood of Jesus against it. The headache may decide to be stubborn for half an hour, but if you too become stubborn, it will leave. However, if while you lay your hands on your head, you are thinking of panadol, then it would not work.

If you keep pleading the Blood of Jesus, no matter how terrible an infirmity is, it will disappear by the power in the blood of Jesus. If your life is pure and you lay your hands on any sickness pleading the blood of Jesus, it will vanish. You might wonder if it is really as simple as that but that is the power in the blood of Jesus.

The blood of Jesus cannot dry up; neither can it lose its power. Therefore you can plead it a million times if you want to. The more you plead the Blood of Jesus, the more the chance of totally submerging the disease, in the pool of the Blood of Jesus.

Many Christians do not understand the power in the use of the weapons that God has given us against the enemy. Unbelievers could sit throughout the night, chanting incantations or reciting things against people. If you stand in front of your shop or house and plead the blood of Jesus every day, you will find out that the powers of darkness in that environment will dissipate. If you like to seal up your house spiritually, as you know many of us receive all kinds of visitors. When a demonised visitor comes visiting and you want such demons to unite outside for their owner, or a possessed man visiting your home, shop or office, you can apply the blood of Jesus to the door post. Once they get to the door post, their demons will walk out and wait for them outside and as soon as they leave, their demons leave with them too.

Sometimes therefore, you have to be very careful when you see off unbelieving friends to their cars because, once you get away from the cover of the blood, you may get yourself into trouble. So, whenever you want to seal off your house, you say, "I apply the blood of Jesus on my door post in the name of Jesus" and once you do this, demons cannot enter. By the time you do this, you would have put a wonderful covering on that house.

The blood avails for all things. It is our protection against any evil if we can cry for it and trust it. As we are moving towards the end-time, we need to plead the blood of Jesus all the time. There is a lot of tragedy and disaster all over the place. Too many Christians are being robbed or cheated or raped or murdered. Many are being hypnotised and confused. Pleading the blood of Jesus will give you immunity against these things.

You can plead the Blood of Jesus, over any and everything; your spirit, soul and body, your house, car, work, children, spouse, business, as a form of protection or prevention against evil. You can plead the blood of Jesus over your journey, the road, the vehicle or aircraft, etc. If you are living or passing through a dangerous zone; you can draw a bloodline of protection, therefore making a boundary against any evil.

A man had a poultry where all of sudden, the chickens began to die. When he saw that he was going bankrupt with the loss, he cried unto the Lord who ministered to him about drawing a bloodline around the poultry. Thus, creating a boundary that the enemy cannot cross. He walked round and drew the bloodline around the poultry that night. The following day, he found the carcass of a wolf, about two feet into the circle that he had drawn. Alas! it was stone dead. That is to say, it had passed its bounds. Today, I pray that any wolf assigned against your life, shall die in the name of Jesus. Draw the bloodline and the enemy will keep off. These are very serious matters and we should recognise and know these secrets.

Recently, there have been disasters that have destroyed many lives in many countries. I was told of a man who saw the flood raging towards his house and he came out and pleaded the blood of Jesus. The flood obeyed him and not a single drop of water entered his house but the houses next to him were submerged. That is the power in the blood of Jesus.

The Blood of Jesus is a spiritual-weapon; through it, you can achieve the following:

1. **Cleansing**:
The blood of Jesus possesses cleansing power. If there is any form of dirt or filth in your life or environment, the blood of Jesus will cleanse them.

2. **Sanitisation**:
The blood of Jesus could serve as disinfectant. Anything that wants to pollute you, will not be able to get in. You should sanitise your life, your body, house, shop, etc. In fact, before you move into a new apartment or house, you should sanitise it and the surroundings with the blood of Jesus. The foundations of many houses were laid with sacrifices of all kinds. Houses that were built thirty or forty years ago have things buried in them by the owners and such things work negatively on the inhabitants of such houses, especially if they are not born-again.

3. **Deliverance**:
When you call the blood of Jesus into operation, it causes the enemy to flee, because it contains the life of God. It sets people free from bondage.

4. **Healing**:
It can heal all forms of infirmity. When you plead the blood of Jesus, things begin to happen.

5. **Protection**.

6. **Life-giving power**:
It gives the power to revive anyone or anything that is dead. It could be marriage, finances, business, etc.

7. **Yoke-breaking**.
Whenever you plead the blood of Jesus, people and things are set free from any kind of yoke.

8. **Overcoming power**.

9. **Door-opening power**.
The power to open every door that has been closed against good things in the life of a person.

10. **Creative and re-creative power**.
Anything that is supposed to be in the life or body of a person, or has been removed through surgery or witchcraft, can be recalled back into existence by the blood of Jesus.

11. **Renewing power**.

12. **Battle dissolving power**.
The power that makes the enemies go in disarray.

13. **Promotion power and energy**.

14. **Breakthrough power**.

15. **Miracle receiving power**.

16. **Poison destroying power**. Many have been poisoned physically or spiritually. The blood of Jesus neutralises such poisons and flushes them out of the system.

17. **Mountain-moving power**

18. **Demon-paralysing power**. The ring-tone on one of my phones is the song: **"Have you been to Jesus for the cleansing Blood, are you washed in the blood of the Lamb."** One day, I was sitting

somewhere and the phone rang; before I could answer the call, a woman had started to manifest and a strange voice spoke from her mouth, screaming: "Stop that music, stop that music!" The demon in her was affected by the song, because of the power in the blood of Jesus.

19. **Virtue-restoring power.**

20. **Burden-removing power.**

21. **Bondage-destroying power:**
When you plead the blood of Jesus into any situation, it will eventually bow. Many people do not understand the overcoming weapons that they have in the word of God. The Bible says: *"And they overcame him by the Blood of the Lamb, and by the word of their testimony."*

Today, you will watch that blood in display, if you will pray the prayers I am suggesting below from your heart. That blood was not shed in vain; it was shed for forgiveness, deliverance, protection, etc. You would be cheating yourself, if you do not use that facility. A 26 year old sister who was looking like an old woman, heard a message like this and decided to use it. She locked herself up for three days, pleading the blood of Jesus into her situation. By the time she came out, her correct body, shape, face, had been restored to her. She now looks her age.

If you want your right things to come back to you, pray with power and with fire. The power in the blood of Jesus was given to it from the beginning. Do you know that there is power and life in blood generally? If a person lacks blood, it means he or she is dying. That is why some things work for occultists, who kill goats and fowls for sacrifice. How much more, the blood of the Son of God?

There was a King in the Bible who saw that he was losing a battle; he quickly sacrificed his first son. As he was shedding that blood, Israel that was attacking them got confused. If the blood of animals and human beings can make an impact, how much more the blood of Jesus, the Son of God!

Blood is a living thing and the blood of Jesus has the power to overcome; anything that confronts you. However, there is a small condition, for you to plead the blood of Jesus and have it work for you

1. You must surrender your life to the Lord Jesus.
2. You must be completely yielded to Him.
3. You must live a pure and holy life

You have a wonderful opportunity today, to invite the overcoming power in the blood of Jesus to come into your situation. If you are not born-again. and you would like to surrender your life to Christ, you can do so right now, right there where you are. All you need do is, see yourself as a sinner and know that you cannot approach God in your sinful state. Repent of your sins; confess them to the Lord and ask Him to forgive you. Name them one by one, renounce them and decide that you will not go back to them anymore.

I congratulate you on this decision that you have just taken; it is the most important decision in life and I pray that it shall be permanent in your life, in the name of Jesus. I pray that the Lord will uphold you with His hand of righteousness and you will not fall or fail, in the name of Jesus. I pray that the Lord will write your name in the Book of Life and nothing shall by any means, rub it off in the name of Jesus. Go and sin no more!

It will be a pity if after reading this message, the blood of Jesus does not avail for you. Check yourself very well; is there anything in your life that could hinder the move or the power of God in your situation? Have you done or said something that you should not? Are you relating with people that you should not? Check yourself! Are there some things that the Holy Spirit has been telling you are bad and you do not want to listen?

Today, as you plead the blood of Jesus, His liquid raw power will come upon your life and strange and marvellous things will begin to take place in your life. God will release all sorts of blessings upon your life today; physical, spiritual, material blessings, marital and financial breakthroughs, will be released upon your life as you plead the blood of Jesus into your situation.

Some people will pray the following prayers and will never know poverty again. Many will be healed from even terminal diseases and they will have testimonies. Confess all sins, known and unknown, conscious and unconscious, parental, inherited, martial, etc. God has all the power in His Hands and is ready to move, even right there, where you are. Believe God for the move of His power in your life right now.

PRAYER POINTS:
1. Let the blood of Jesus, speak victory and prosperity into my life today, in the name of Jesus.
2. Mr. devil, see the blood of Jesus, because the One who shed that blood crushed your head and He is my Lord.
3. Let the blood of Jesus, dry up, every evil tree used against me in the name of Jesus.
4. You evil powers, be rendered impotent by the blood of Jesus.
5. Blood of Jesus, deliver me by fire! in the name Jesus.
6. I command all my blessings, confiscated by rulers of darkness, to be released, in the name of Jesus.
7. I cut myself off, from every territorial spirit, in the name of Jesus.
8. I command all demonic reverse gears, installed to hinder my progress, to be roasted, in the name of Jesus.
9. Lord Jesus, bear all my physical and spiritual burdens now! in the name of Jesus.
10. Every power stealing my virtues, die! in the name of Jesus.
11. Every power in the heavenlies, on earth and in the seas, hindering the angel of my blessing, die! in the name of Jesus.
12. I remove my life from the jaw of the lion by the power in the blood of Jesus, in the name of Jesus.
13. Any power diverting the blessings of God away from me, your time is up, die now! in the name of Jesus.
14. By the blood of Jesus, every owner of evil load, carry your load! in the name of Jesus.
15. Blood of Jesus, pursue my pursuers, in the name of Jesus.
16. Blood of Jesus, arise and fight my battles, in the name of Jesus.
17. Blood of Jesus, pursue poverty out of my life, in the name of Jesus.
18. Sicknesses, you cannot stay in my life because I am redeemed by the blood of the Lamb.
19. Let the blood of Jesus, speak destruction unto every evil growth in my body in the name of Jesus.
20. Every power assigned to follow me, to destroy me, die! in the name of Jesus.
21. God arise! and let all the rage of the enemy against me scatter, in the name of Jesus.

Books By Dr. D. K. Olukoya

1. 20 Marching Orders To Fulfill Your Destiny
2. 30 Things The Anointing Can Do For You
3. 30 Prophetic Arrows From Heaven
4. A-Z of Complete Deliverance
5. Abraham's Children in Bondage
6. Basic Prayer Patterns
7. Be Prepared
8. Bewitchment must die
9. Biblical Principles of Dream Interpretation
10. Born Great, But Tied Down
11. Breaking Bad Habits
12. Breakthrough Prayers For Business Professionals
13. Bringing Down The Power of God
14. Brokenness
15. Can God Trust You?
16. Can God?
17. Command The Morning
18. Connecting to The God of Breakthroughs
19. Consecration Commitment & Loyalty
20. Contending For The Kingdom
21. Criminals In The House Of God
22. Dancers At The Gate of Death
23. Dealing With The Evil Powers Of Your Father's House
24. Dealing With Tropical Demons
25. Dealing With Local Satanic Technology
26. Dealing With Witchcraft Barbers
27. Dealing With Unprofitable Roots
28. Dealing With Hidden Curses
29. Dealing With Destiny Vultures
30. Dealing With Satanic Exchange
31. Dealing With Destiny Thieves
32. Deliverance Of The Head
33. Deliverance: God's Medicine Bottle
34. Deliverance From Spirit Husband And Spirit Wife
35. Deliverance From The Limiting Powers
36. Deliverance From Evil Foundation
37. Deliverance of The Brain
38. Deliverance Of The Conscience
39. Deliverance By Fire
40. Destiny Clinic
41. Destroying Satanic Masks
42. Disgracing Soul Hunters
43. Divine Yellow Card
44. Divine Prescription For Your Total Immunity
45. Divine Military Training
46. Dominion Prosperity
47. Drawers Of Power From The Heavenlies
48. Evil Appetite
49. Evil Umbrella
50. Facing Both Ways
51. Failure In The School Of Prayer
52. Fire For Life's Journey
53. For We Wrestle ...
54. Freedom Indeed
55. Healing Through Prayers
56. Holiness Unto The Lord
57. Holy Fever
58. Holy Cry
59. Hour Of Decision
60. How To Obtain Personal Deliverance
61. How To Pray When Surrounded By The Enemies
62. I Am Moving Forward
63. Idols Of The Heart

Books By Dr. D. K. Olukoya

64. Igniting Your Inner Fire
65. Igniting Your Inner Fire
66. Is This What They Died For?
67. Kill Your Goliath By Fire
68. Killing The Serpent of Frustration
69. Let God Answer By Fire
70. Let Fire Fall
71. Limiting God
72. Lord, Behold Their Threatening
73. Madness Of The Heart
74. Making Your Way Through The Traffic Jam Of Life
75. Meat For Champions
76. Medicine For Winners
77. My Burden For The Church
78. Open Heavens Through Holy Disturbance
79. Overpowering Witchcraft
80. Paralysing The Riders And The Horse
81. Personal Spiritual Check-Up
82. Possessing The Tongue of Fire
83. Power To Recover Your Birthright
84. Power Against Coffin Spirits
85. Power Against Unclean Spirits
86. Power Against The Mystery of Wickedness
87. Power Against Destiny Quenchers
88. Power Against Dream Criminals
89. Power Against Local Wickedness
90. Power Against Marine Spirits
91. Power Against Spiritual Terrorists
92. Power To Recover Your Lost Glory
93. Power To Disgrace The Oppressors
94. Power Must Change Hands
95. Power To Shut Satanic Doors
96. Power Against The Mystery of Wickedness
97. Power of Brokenness
98. Pray Your Way To Breakthroughs
99. Prayer To Make You Fulfill Your Divine Destiny
100. Prayer Strategies For Spinsters And Bachelors
101. Prayer Warfare Against 70 Mad Spirits
102. Prayer Is The Battle
103. Prayer To Kill Enchantment
104. Prayer Rain
105. Prayers To Destroy Diseases And Infirmities
106. Prayers For Open Heavens
107. Prayers To Move From Minimum To Maximum
108. Praying Against Foundational Poverty
109. Praying Against The Spirit Of The Valley
110. Praying In The Storm
111. Praying To Dismantle Witchcraft
112. Praying To Destroy Satanic Roadblocks
113. Principles Of Prayer
114. Raiding The House of The Strongman
115. Release From Destructive Covenants
116. Revoking Evil Decrees
117. Safeguarding Your Home
118. Satanic Diversion of the Black Race
119. Secrets of Spiritual Growth & Maturity
120. Seventy Rules of Spiritual Warfare
121. Seventy Sermons To Preach To Your Destiny
122. Silencing The Birds Of Darkness
123. Slave Masters
124. Slaves Who Love Their Chains

Books By Dr. D. K. Olukoya

125. Smite The Enemy And He Will Flee
126. Speaking Destruction Unto The Dark Rivers
127. Spiritual Education
128. Spiritual Growth And Maturity
129. Spiritual Warfare And The Home
130. Stop Them Before They Stop You

Books By Pastor (Mrs.) Shade Olukoya

1. Daughters Of Philip
2. Power To Fulfil Your Destiny
3. Principles Of A Successful Marriage
4. The Call Of God
5. When Your Destiny Is Under Attack
6. Woman Of Wonder
7. Violence Against Negative Voices

BOOK ORDER

Is there any book written by Dr. D. K. Olukoya

(General Overseer MFM Ministries)

That you would like to have?

Have you seen his latest books?

**To place an order for this End-Time Materials
Call: 08161229775**

Battlecry Christian Ministries ... equipping the saint of God
God bless.